JOH

D1050094

"What things have we seen
Done at the Mermaid! heard words that have been
So nimble, and so full of subtle flame,
As if that every one from whence they came
Had meant to put his whole wit in a jest,
And had resolved to live a fool the rest
Of his dull life."

Master Francis Beaumont to Ben Jonson

"Souls of Poets dead and gone,
What Elysium have ye known,
Happy field or mossy cavern,
Choicer than the Mermaid Tavern?"

Keats

ADVISORY EDITOR TO DRAMABOOKS:
ERIC BENTLEY

JOHN DRYDEN

(Three Plays)

Edited, with an Introduction and Notes by
GEORGE SAINTSBURY

A MERMAID DRAMABOOK

"I lie and dream of your full Mermaid wine."—BEAUMONT

 HILL AND WANG · NEW YORK

Library of Congress Catalog Card Number: 57-7895

John Dryden was originally published in the Mermaid Series
in two volumes. This DRAMABOOK is the original Volume I.
Published by special arrangement with Ernest Benn, Ltd.

Manufactured in the United States of America
by The Colonial Press Inc.

CONTENTS

INTRODUCTION

I THINK it may be justifiable, in the comparatively limited space available for this Introduction, to depart from the usual plan of giving some considerable room to a general account of the author and of his works. Such accounts[1] are easily accessible in the case of Dryden, while the special subject of his dramatic production has, in proportion, occupied but a small part of them. Moreover, the present writer has had occasion of late years[2] to extend his knowledge of seventeenth-century drama, with the result of a conviction that something more than the usual books contain may be said—not without advantage—on its critical fortunes, and on Dryden's connection with them. A slight sketch of his life,[3] and a full dated list[4] of the

[1] Of these, besides the notices in general histories of English literature, and the matter in the standard edition by Scott (revised by the present writer, with some corrections and additions, Edinburgh, 1881-1893), the following may be mentioned: Beljame, A., Le Public et les Hommes de Lettres en Angleterre (Paris, 1886); Collins, J. Churton, an article in the Quarterly Review for 1878, reprinted in Essays and Studies (London, 1895); Garnett, R., The Age of Dryden (London, 1895); Gosse, E., Eighteenth Century Literature (London, 1889); Minto, W., article in Encyclopædia Britannica (1879); Christie, W. D., Introduction, an admirable one, to the "Globe" Dryden (London, 1870); also the present writer's "Dryden" in English Men of Letters (London, 1881), and articles on the subject—not identical with each other—in Chambers's Encyclopædia, and Cyclopædia, of English Literature. This last, published in 1901, represents the latest results of some five-and-twenty years' reading of Dryden. It should be needless to say that, for the Dramatic Works, the passages concerning them in Dr. Ward's History of English Dramatic Literature (2nd ed., London, 1899), are indispensable. Since this Introduction was written, a useful monograph by Mr. L. N. Chase has appeared on The English Heroic Play (New York, 1903).
[2] As it happens, I began my own studies of Dryden with the plays, and in the year 1876 sent an article on them to the late Sir George Grove, then editor of Macmillan's Magazine. He did not disapprove it, but thought that the public would not care for the subject. It afterwards formed the nucleus of a series of four lectures which I delivered on Dryden at the Royal Institution in the spring of 1880, as these in turn did of the Dryden which I wrote for Mr. John Morley, and which procured me the honour of re-editing Scott's edition.
[3] Dryden, born August 9, 1631, did not begin literary work (excepting the juvenile lines on Lord Hastings's death, and a few other things, of which the "Cromwell" epicede is the only one of importance) till the Restoration. But he seems, from a note of Pepys's, to have come up from Cambridge with a poetical reputation; and the new determination of interest to the reopening theatre rapidly drew him with it. After alternating between poems and plays for a few years, he settled wholly to the latter for more than a dozen (1667-1680), and derived no small profit from a regular connection with the King's House. The great polit-

dramatic works, will probably suffice instead of the usual dilation.[5]

[The exact state of the English drama at the time when Dryden began to contribute to it, and the precise nature and relations of the phenomena presented by it during the thirty years of his activity as a playwright, are questions on which there is still room for much treatment.] That there once was, and perhaps still is generally, a tendency to make rather too sharp a severance between the drama which held the stage at the closing of the theatres, and that which came to occupy it at their opening, is a thing not in the least surprising. It is convenient, and therefore tempting, to assume these rapid transformation-scenes in literature. Moreover, there is hardly any period in the whole range of literary history at which, in verse, in prose, and in drama alike, such a rare and such a rapid metamorphosis did take place as at the Restoration in England. And there is perhaps no single instance of a writer who brings out this metamorphosis in all three forms to the same extent as Dryden himself does. Compare his verse with Milton's or Chamberlayne's; his prose with Browne's;

---

ical satires arising out of the Popish Plot, and the task-work imposed on him by the economical James, drew him gradually away from playwriting. But on his disestablishment and disendowment for Nonjuring at the Restoration, he returned to it for a time, and not too fortunately. The failure of his last play, *Love Triumphant*, helped, no doubt, to send him to the more congenial work of translating Virgil, and the very much more important and valuable composition of his *Fables*. But for thirty years and more he was a playwright, and during part of them a playwright only; while his connection with the stage, in prologue and epilogue-writing, was only terminated by his death on May 1, 1700, just before which he had written a *Secular Masque* to celebrate the opening of the new century.

[4] List of Dryden's plays (dates of publication):—

The Wild Gallant, 166(3)-9.	*The State of Innocence*, 1674.
The Rival Ladies, 1664.	*Aurengzebe*, 1676.
The Indian Queen, 1665.	*All for Love*, 1678.
The Indian Emperor, 1667.	*Limberham*, 1678.
Sir Martin Mar-all, 1668.	*Œdipus* (with Lee), 1679.
Secret Love or the Maiden Queen, 1668.	*Troilus and Cressida*, 1679.
The Tempest, 1670.	*The Spanish Friar*, 1681.
Tyrannic Love, 1670.	*The Duke of Guise* (with Lee), 1683.
An Evening's Love, or The Mock Astrologer, 1671.	*Albion and Albanius*, 1685.
The Conquest of Granada, 1672.	*Don Sebastian*, 1690.
Marriage à la Mode, 1673.	*Amphitryon*, 1690.
The Assignation, 1673.	*King Arthur*, 1691.
Amboyna, 1673.	*Cleomenes*, 1692.
	Love Triumphant, 1694.

[5] Introductions to the several plays here given will be found prefixed to them, as usual in the series.

his drama with Shirley's, to take in each case characteristic survivals of the older types, and the difference is
striking enough.

Yet—for we must not make excursion beyond our present subject—it is very easy to be too much struck with it,
and still easier to assign it to wrong, or at least over-
valued, causes. Part of the old false evaluation has, especially since the publication of the Master of Peterhouse's
excellent *History*, become almost impossible to sustain,
except by mere ignorance. That Charles II saw French
tragedy and comedy during his exile, liked them (especially the comedy), and when he came home told people
to write things resembling them, used to be said, and may
perhaps have been believed, by some of the people who
said it, to be a complete account of the facts. That it is
not a complete account of them—that it is, looked at in
one way, just not all false, and, looked at in another, only
in a very small degree true, must by degrees force itself
on most careful students of the subject. But one must
undoubtedly have been familiar for a long time with the
documents, and have been accustomed accurately to compare their dates, before appreciating the questions of the
Heroic Tragedy and the new Comedy of Manners.

The Tragedy presents two sides for consideration—its
phase of sentiment and machinery *as* tragedy, and its ve-
hicle of rhymed verse. The former can only be considered
with profit when it is taken in connection with its kindred,
the Heroic Poem and Heroic Romance. This was the truth
that seasoned the old mistake (as it was in great part) of
regarding plays like *Tyrannic Love* and *The Conquest of
Granada* as direct *imitations* of the tragedy of Corneille
and Racine, and of the romance of Calprenède and Mlle.
de Scudéry. This in small degree they might be; but in a
much larger they were independent carryings out of the
same principles and ideas which had prompted the others.
The Italian criticism of the Renaissance, partly from the
difficulty of accommodating ancient critical doctrines to the
craving for romance, had excogitated the idea of a "heroic"
fiction which was not Tragedy, nor bound by the strict
rules of drama, which was not Epic, nor bound by the
strict rules of the poem, but which loosened and at the
same time adjusted both, with an eye to such work as that
of Heliodorus. The Heroic Poem, in short, and the Heroic

Romance were both, if we may put it in the language of the stable, "out of" the *Æneid* "by" the *Æthiopica*.

But it has been part of the history of the drama, in ancient and still more in modern times, to absorb and *accaparate* all forms of literature. As the *fabliau* became the farce, the Saint's Life and Scripture Miracle the modern drama of action, the allegorical poem the Morality, so did the "Heroic" narrative generate the "Heroic" play. Of "Heroic" itself many explanations have been given and many more might be devised; but the simplest, the easiest, and the most fruitful seems to be this—that the Hero, or of course heroine, takes the place of the Action, and so supplies a more flexible unity of life-interest. The "Heroic" *sentiment*, which is so important, and latterly so distinguishing, is more obscure in its origin; but I believe it to have been (at least sometimes) due to anxiety on the part of those who felt that they were relinquishing the support, at the same time as they freed themselves from the hamper, of the three older Unities. And when these were replaced, the sentimental hunger had grown by the provision of its object, and refused to be neglected.

The Heroic poem and romance had considerably anticipated the play in England itself. Of the romance, though it has never been widely known, trustworthy accounts do exist, especially that of Professor Raleigh in his *Modern Novel*. Of the poems, in the general neglect of minor mid-Caroline poetry, very little notice has been taken, though Chamberlayne's *Pharonnida*, the best of all, has always attracted the admiration of good judges who have known it, and though Davenant's *Gondibert* is better than it is the fashion to think or say. Of others it would not be proper to speak here; but they exist in some numbers, and those who choose to seek for them will not have much difficulty in finding them. Most of these minors have indeed little merit; but they show the *nisus*. It had directed itself, in their case, out of the proper line, which was not to be reached till the novel itself was discovered and practised. But it was vindicating its existence after a fashion; and the same vindication was achieved by the Heroic Play. That play, however, in English, was powerfully determined by another accidental cause which also has not always been duly recognised.

The "Heroic"—which, though the origin of the names

is different, coincides pretty exactly with the "classical"—
French play is notoriously written in rhymed Alexandrines;
and it was once taken for granted, and is still held by
some, that for this reason, and practically for this reason
only, the English Heroic Play was written in rhymed
decasyllables. This is a still less exquisite song than the
other. That the French example had no influence at all,
no reasonable person will maintain. But there is fair cu-
mulative evidence to show that if there had been no
French influence at all, the change would equally have
taken place.

For the set of English taste towards the rhymed decasyl-
lable had been more and more marked for some forty years
before "the submitted fasces of the main," escorted Charles
II to his recovered and repentant kingdom. This taste
made Waller perform that feat which appeared to the
three succeeding generations to amount to a "discovery of
the sweetness of English verses." It induced Ben Jonson
to pronounce the couplet the most perfect form of verse.
But most of all it caused couplets themselves, and couplet
passages, to crop up in English plays long before the
Restoration, in a fashion, and with an appeal, quite different from those of the rhymes, which, in Shakespeare and
his fellows, mark the close of a scene or call the attention
of the audience to some striking point.[6]

Moreover, the conquest of the couplet, as usually happens, was facilitated and almost invited by the disorgani-
zation and corruption of the existing medium of blank
verse. The rise and flourishing of this in its dramatic form
—for it was only when this latter was in its decadence that
Milton established the non-dramatic form, probably in
permanence—had been rapid and brilliant equally beyond
example. Indeed, the thirty years between the appearance
of *Tamburlaine* and the death of Shakespeare practically

---

[6] See, as an example open to everybody, the passage quoted in Mr.
Arber's edition of *The Rehearsal* from Quarles's *Virgin Widow* (1649). It
could be largely amplified from the play itself (to be found in the third
vol. of Dr. Grosart's edition of Quarles), which oscillates between prose,
blank verse, and rhyme, but with an obvious determination towards the
latter. Even more remarkable, though at first sight less decisive, are the
still earlier plays of Goffe (1631 onwards), where the staple is blank,
but the author "drops into" rhyme by a sort of irresistible impulse when
he wants to declaim. These are out-of-the-way writers, but it would be
possible, and would not be futile, to arrange an anthology from many
playwrights between 1630 and 1660, showing the set of the tide, and
the difference of the new stamp of couplet from the old.

included all its best days. The tendency towards the redundant syllable, which even Shakespeare himself latterly
displays, became more marked in Beaumont and Fletcher,
and was itself dangerous. And the system of broken lines
and of almost unlimited "equivalence" which Shakespeare
had perfected, required very unusual skill to carry it out—
skill which was probably still more heavily drawn upon by
changes of pronunciation and vocabulary. At any rate, the
chaotic state into which English dramatic versification had
fallen by and during the reign of Charles I is a fact which
admits of no dispute, and which would almost by itself
suffice to explain the alacrity with which the lightening
and supporting couplet was welcomed. Nor was it a question of mere form. Again the astonishing rapidity, force
and volume of the great Elizabethan drama had comparatively soon exhausted itself. Its glorious liberty required no small steering power of genius to guide it; and
when that was lacking, the defects of unrestrainedness, of
bombast and the like, did certainly manifest themselves.
Alike in the greater and more poetical work of Ford, and
in the lesser and less poetical work of Davenant (in his
early tragedies) and Suckling, mere blood-and-thunder,
mere horror-mongering, reappears. While, on the other
hand, in the less extravagant work of Shirley, there appears, as there had already appeared to a less extent in
that of Massinger, distinct reminiscence, whether conscious
or unconscious, of the work of earlier writers. As compared with all this the Heroic Tragedy—with its peculiar
sentimental declamation; its abundant but, so to speak,
regulated bloodshed; its machinery, which might be super-
natural, but must obey a certain etiquette; and its sword-
and-buckler play of love-casuistry or argument, abundantly
rattled with rhyme—came as fresh, as comparatively refined, and (until it too palled, which it did even more
rapidly) as a distinct improvement and reform.

The state and the history of Comedy present a spectacle
not so much of reaction as of continuous development.
Here also there has, as it seems to me, been a mistake,
though of a slightly different kind. It has been often disputed whether Etherege or Wycherley deserves the credit
of being the founder of Restoration drama, meaning
thereby comedy. I should be inclined first to bracket Shadwell with both, and, secondly, to question the right of

any of the three to anything but a fairly important carrying further of stages already some way advanced. A cause of error may perhaps be found here in the much greater familiarity of readers with Shakespeare, Jonson, and Beaumont and Fletcher than with writers like Middleton, Rowley, Shirley, and Brome. Shakespeare's own comedies are poles asunder from those of any of the three writers just mentioned, but then they are things by themselves. Jonson's, when he relies most on the "humour" system, are nearer, and in *Bartholomew Fair* very near, but still differentiated by their much greater lack of "modernity." The comedies of the Twins, though far less ethereal than Shakespeare's, are also, in a kind, romantic comedy, of the same genus as his, though of a different and inferior species. But Middleton and Rowley, old-fashioned as they are, still approach much closer to pure unadulterated comedy of manners—to the holding up of the mirror, not so much to pure nature as to society. And Brome and Shirley carry this process further yet. *The Sparagus Garden* has a great deal of it; *Hyde Park* and *The Ball* have more. Indeed, *Hyde Park* is almost startling in its modernity, with the race run almost on the stage, and the betting, and the rest of it. Now, these were all well anterior to the closing of the theatres. When they reopened, Shirley's natural force was too much abated for him to carry the matter further, and his latest plays are interesting, but out of date. The dramatists of the interval, however, as we may call that small and not very highly distinguished but far from negligible group, of whom the chief representatives were Lacy and Wilson, maintained the tradition. Lacy's *Old Troop* is almost daringly contemporary and positive; and Wilson's extremely remarkable *Cheats* and *Projectors,* while showing the influence of Jonson almost as much as does Shadwell, obey it in the *Bartholomew Fair* direction almost as much as in that of *Every Man in His Humour.*

Such was the state of the stage, and such the influences at work upon it, when Dryden began his dramatic work. For comedy, which he at first attempted, he admitted himself to have no decided genius; and the peculiar condition of it which we have just outlined was not very favourable, even to that almost superhuman craftsmanship which generally enabled him not only to take up but to better any

instruction on any pattern. He evidently saw that in the
representation of manners and society lay the future of
comedy; but manners and society themselves had changed
remarkably during the twenty years' *interlunium* of the
footlights; and it is matter of accepted biography that
Dryden himself was not much of a man of society. Neither
was the dialogue of repartee, which brought to the comedy
of manners so important a reinforcement, and which was
undoubtedly to a great extent studied after Molière, his
special forte; his guns were rather too heavy for that. It
is not therefore surprising that *The Wild Gallant,* his first
attempt, was a dead failure to begin with, and even after
revision and Barbara Palmer's support, remains no master-
piece. I still think it a little better than it has generally
been thought, perhaps not always on direct acquaintance;
but nobody could call it good.

It was probably not an accident which made Dryden
in his second play, *The Rival Ladies,* desert comedy for
tragi-comedy. The fancy for rhyme in tragedy (*v. supra*)
had already made itself evident, though it had not got
the upper hand; and Dryden was already quite conscious
of his strength in rhyme. Except as an exercise in the kind
and (partly) in the medium,[7] this play has no interest;
but it is noteworthy that some of his best comic work,
notably that in *Marriage à la Mode,* is connected with a
serious plot. If, however, these two plays only had stood
to his name in drama, we should not only have had nothing to do with him in this series, but he would have occupied no serious position at all as a dramatist. *The Indian
Emperor,* his third independent venture (his fourth if we
count that collaboration in *The Indian Queen,* which led
to it) is a very different matter. Here he partly took up
and partly invented, in the fashion so frequent with him, a
new and for a time a very popular though, perhaps, only
a second-rate kind.

The Indian Emperor, Tyrannic Love, and the two *Conquests of Granada* form—for *Aureng-Zebe,* though strictly
speaking a "Heroic" play, is apart from and above the
kind—the main body of Dryden's contributions to that
kind itself. Now that I have, as I had not yet done twenty

---

[7] In the discussions about priority in using rhyme it has sometimes
been forgotten how early *The Rival Ladies* is. It was probably acted late
in 1663, certainly early in 1664.

years ago, read most, if not all, of their companions, I am
more convinced than ever that they are almost the only
heroic plays worth reading, except by the historical student
of literature. And they are very well worth reading. I wish
I could give the whole of them here. Their faults are indeed extremely obvious. More perhaps than any other kind,
they are *artificial*, with an artifice that is at once conventional, complicated and—which even very complicated
and conventional things need not be—unnatural to the
last degree. Only a little—though certainly I think that
little—of this un-nature belongs to the rhymed form in
itself. But the rudimentariness of the argument for rhyme
which Dryden, than whom a greater master of argument
has hardly ever existed, himself uses in the *Essay of Dramatic Poesy*, gives this case completely away, and we
need say no more of it. Incidentally, however, the rhyme
does more harm than it need necessarily do, by encourag-
ing, on the one hand, the singlestick bouts of *stichomythia*
which Butler parodied so delightfully in his *Cat and Puss*,
and on the other the *tirade*. The former, beside its inevitable suggestion of the ludicrous, which even the unrhymed gravity of the Greek originals does not always
escape, has, in English at least, the further disadvantage of
drawing special attention to the anomaly of the rhyme itself. The latter, escaping this last to some extent, and even
affording scope for some admirable poetry, treacherously
invites the substitution of rhetoric for that very poetry, and
spurs the writer on to exaggerated hyperbole, bombast,
and rant. The "machinery," which even in its own day
seemed absurd to shrewd judges, seems much more so
now. And the staple of sentiment, with its burlesque of
that late chivalry of the *Amadis* type, which was itself
very nearly a burlesque of the earlier and real thing, not
only had its own dangers, but curiously and yet naturally
enough tempted authors to indulge in *plusquam*-tragic
carnage and violent action, to give foil or seasoning to
what would otherwise have been the intolerable deal of
philandering, and "Phébus," and Court-of-Love philosophy.

Never, perhaps was there a better example of what can
and what can not be done by consummate craftsmanship
in the teeth of artistic error. That Shakespeare would have
transformed the heroic play, as he transformed everything
he touched, is quite possible. Dryden could not transform

it altogether, but he did with it, in the old phrase, "what a man of mould might," and he showed, in the doing, of what a mighty mould he was. With a certain adaptability of temperament, and some little variety of experience in literature, it is easy, even with *The Indian Emperor,* easier with *Tyrannic Love,* and easiest of all with *The Conquest of Granada* to "get the atmosphere," to submit to the conditions, and to drive at full speed with the poet in his distinctly wild but still calculated career. Even when Almeria hectors her suitors, her sister, her rival, her conquerors, and everybody; even when Maximin makes a cushion of his assassin, and stabs it now and then to keep it quiet as he perorates; even when Almanzor makes Drawcansir not so much a caricature as a faded photograph— it is not impossible to gulp the sense of the ludicrous, and pursue the triumph of tempestuous petticoat-worship and roistering declamation. And there are passages where no gulp is necessary. I am not myself fond of the theatre, but I should like to see one of these plays acted. The very boards might dissolve in laughter at the first scene or two; but if this danger could be surmounted, I do not see why Valeria's modern representative—let us hope she might have a tithe of Nelly's well-attested charm—should not speak the famous epilogue (softened, of course) in a tempest and torrent of cheers.

Still the stimulant was at once too hot, too heady, and too artificial to continue its attraction for any but somewhat unrefined palates. Even if it had been otherwise, Dryden himself was too indefatigable in the quest of literary excellence to be content with one thing. Always, in creation and criticism alike, he was forsaking that which was behind, and pressing on to that which was before. Nor are there many things of the kind more interesting than the transition from *The Conquest of Granada* through *Aureng-Zebe* to *All for Love.* We are now to exhibit all these pieces here, and need therefore say the less about them; but the principal points of the exhibition may properly be picked up and set out.

Aureng-Zebe exhibits the "Heroic" scheme with its *furor poeticus* still active in the good sense, but discarding very much of the "white-satin and hair-down" convention of the earlier model. The famous passage which everybody knows, and which is one of the very apices of the second poetic range in English, gives, as it were, the key-note of the whole, a grave "criticism of life" not obliviscent of youth and its passions. The author has no need of the singlestick clatter of the couplet to excite his audience. Though he retains the couplet itself, he, as again everybody knows, proclaims his approaching relinquishment of it, and in the play itself has frequent recourse to *enjambement* or overlapping—that invaluable device which not only softens and muffles the clatter itself, but restores to some extent, while keeping rhyme, the sentence-liberty of the unrhymed verse-paragraph in regard to sense, and its varied pause and rhythm-unit in regard to sound. The *gravitas sententiæ*, as Dante has it, is once more married to the *superbia carminum*, and the total result is an exceedingly fine piece of work, still, perhaps, with a faint touch of rococo about it, but redeeming this by the mixture of piquancy and gravity which the touch gives.

In *All for Love* the divorce from the couplet is complete; and though the story of "the laughing queen that held the world's great hands" lends itself to the retention of something like the heroic tone, the influence of Shakespeare, returning to the height of flood which it had marked in the *Essay of Dramatic Poesy,* has swept away almost all the Heroic rubbish and rococo. Everyone, since the first injustices of the Romantic revolt, has noticed the extraordinary interest of the comparison with *Antony and Cleopatra* itself; but I am not sure that justice has been generally done to the imitation, far below the original as it stands, and, indeed, elects to stand. Dryden's knowledge of the limitations of his own great powers, quite as much as any mistaken critical theorisings at the moment, would always have prevented his attempting the vast chronicle-sweep of that original—the most remarkable instance perhaps of that English speciality, the Chronicle-play. Nor did those powers, great as they were, permit him to emulate the splendour and the poignancy of the passion between "Egypt" and Antony. But, with a success as great as his audacity and its due reward, he has thrown the matter, or so much of it as he chose and was able to take, into a new form almost as suitable to the subject, in its reduction of bulk and temper, as any form could possibly be. The result is no longer quite divine poetry, but it is gigantic in the manner of the good giants. And the instrument by which it is mainly effected is of all but the first interest. The only explanation—or rather in Hume's phrase, "pushing back of our ignorance a little further"—in the matter of the decay of the English serious drama, is that nobody for 250 years has been able to write really satisfactory blank verse for the purpose. How far this, in its turn, is connected with the fact that Milton set a stamp as yet uneffaced, and apparently ineffaceable, on blank verse itself, and that Milton's genius was essentially antidramatic, is a question tempting but to be resisted. Dryden, well as he knew and much as he admired Milton, was old enough to be, in a certain sense, "immune" from his influence, and he fashioned, in *All for Love*, a scheme of blank verse which strikes me as better suited for drama than any that has followed it, but which, somehow or other, nobody has been able to follow with any success.

With *All for Love* Dryden had reached, not merely as it may seem to some, the summit of his achievement in tragedy, but, as is hardly contestable, the limit of his experiments in it. His collaboration with Lee in *The Duke of Guise,* like that earlier one in *Œdipus,* produced some of his own finest work in passages, but gave no whole that can be called his; and *Troilus and Cressida,* though not, as a Shakespearian adaptation, by any means so objectionable as the again earlier *Tempest,* shows the way in which consummate work may *not* be dealt with, almost as distinctly as *All for Love* points to that in which it may. When, under *force majeure,* Dryden resumed play-writing after the Revolution, the two great tragedies (or serious dramas) of *Don Sebastian* and *Cleomenes* reach a very high level of excellence; indeed, *Don Sebastian,* which accordingly we here give, has often been, and still is sometimes, held to be his best tragedy. But there is no further progression in scheme and equipment, and the chief *reversion*—the comic scenes in *Don Sebastian*—will hardly be considered by many men an improvement. Moreover, fine as are these two, *Don Sebastian* was not popular at first, and *Cleomenes,* political causes working against it, never became popular at all. Nor can the whole blame be put upon partisanship. Dryden had maintained, on the whole, the

Cornelian tradition of relying on Admiration as a tragic passion; younger dramatists like Otway, Lee, and Southerne were partly falling back upon Aristotle, partly adapting Racine, in their reliance upon Pathos, which Dryden never succeeded in, and seldom attempted.

We must now trace the line of his comedy as we have traced that of his tragedy. A good deal of it is *tragi-comedy*; but the two strands are rarely interwoven with much art, and the comic portions have seldom secured more than lukewarm approval. In that, however, of *The Maiden Queen*, his fourth complete play, Dryden did succeed in hitting on a situation, and (according to his wont) making it something like his own, though he borrowed it originally. Shakespeare had begun, in the immortal instances of Rosalind and Orlando, Beatrice and Benedick, the representation of a pair of lovers who disguise their affection under cover of banter, if they do not actually fall in love in the mere process of skirmishing. Fletcher, as he did with so many of Shakespeare's things, took this up, treated it with a good deal less poetry, but still kept some even of that. Almost all the Restoration dramatists revived it eagerly from Fletcher; but Dryden gives to his couples a somewhat kindlier cast than most of his contemporaries trouble themselves to bestow, and with it a curious spice of individuality. Even *The Wild Gallant* shows this in Constance and Loveby; but there is no comparison between this pair and the Florimel and Celadon of *The Maiden Queen*. Florimel was played by Nell Gwyn, and if "Mrs. Ellen" gave some of her own well-attested fascination to the part, the part certainly supplied no small opportunities for its display.

The two next comedies, *Sir Martin Mar-all* and (if it is to be called comedy) *The Tempest*, are doubly unoriginal, the obligations to Molière and Shakespeare being complicated by collaboration with the Duke of Newcastle and Davenant. But *The Mock Astrologer*, though again an adaptation (from the Spanish through the French), contains a new and mainly original version of the same pair in Wildblood and Jacintha. For some years Dryden was very busy with heroic plays: but in 1672 came his best comedy, *Marriage à la Mode*, and his worst, *The Assignation*. The former is given here, and we need therefore say

the less about it. Of the latter nobody has ever been able
to say much good.[8] Another gap of some years, filled by
the eccentric but far from despicable *State of Innocence*
(the well-known if not well-read "tagged" dramatisation
of *Paradise Lost*), and the two great tragedies *Aureng-Zebe*
and *All for Love,* ushered, in the very same year with this
last, a most questionable companion to it in the shape of
Limberham, the *Lysistrata* of Dryden's theatre, and like
the *Lysistrata* (though far below it) by no means so un-
amusing as it is unblushing. In fact, Langbaine (whose
approbation, however, is discounted by the double fact
that he was nothing of a critic and very much of an enemy
of Dryden) declared it the author's best comedy. Some
fight might be made for this on the ground that its two
chief rivals, *Marriage à la Mode* and *The Spanish Friar,*
are not unmitigatedly comic, and that, some common
material of farce and *fabliau* matter excepted, it appears to
be pretty original. It is, however, not only naughty but
nasty: and its merits are rather those of situation and the
stage than of dialogue and literature.

The Spanish Friar itself followed in three years, and
partly from its own merit (which, indeed, has never
seemed to me quite so high as some put it), partly as a
"Protestant play" at the moment when Protestantism was
rampant, obtained great success, though it afterwards
brought Dryden under one of the most justly applied
lashes of Collier's cat-o'-nine-tails. The last of the comedies
—for the comic matter of the actually last play, *Love Triumphant,* is not much better than the serious—came nine
years later again in *Amphitryon,* a play of which I think
highly, and the comparison of which with Plautus and
Molière only brings out the singular independence of Dryden's craftsmanship.

Besides tragedies, tragi-comedies, and comedies, there
is a fourth division of Dryden's stage-work which, though
its interest is rather that of curiosity than of high intrinsic
merit, must be noticed. It consists of the plays or parts of
plays which he arranged more or less directly for musical
setting. Even *The State of Innocence* he himself calls an
"Opera"; the incantation scene (Act III. Sc. i.) in *Œdipus*

---

[8] The author managed, however, to go lower still in *Amboyna,* which
only deserves a note to the effect that it is a mere *pièce de circonstance,*
botched up to incite odium against the Dutch. The comic scenes are the
vulgarest, the tragic the most crudely untragic that Dryden ever wrote.

is not only fine in its way, but following as it does similar things in *The Indian Emperor* and *Tyrannic Love,* shows Dryden's partiality for the same style. His very last work was, as has been said, a "Secular Masque," and the two substantive "operas" of *Albion and Albanius* and *King Arthur* at least intend considerably.

I have thought it well to give as a specimen *Albion and Albanius,* which, though not so good as *King Arthur*[9] on the whole, is shorter and perhaps more characteristic, while it displays Dryden's faculty of lyric verse excellently. Undoubtedly, however, the curse of the musical drama is a curse never fully escaped by anybody.

Two features in Dryden's plays have always been noticed by critics and historians—the Prologues and Epilogues on the one hand, and the Songs on the other. Why Mr. Christie, giving the former in his excellent "Globe" Dryden, did not give the latter is impossible to understand, for both come from the plays, the one class of work is quite as separable as the other, and if the objection[10] of "impropriety" were entertained, it would apply equally to both, or rather more to the Prologues and Epilogues than to the Songs. As it is, the exclusion of these latter from the common editions of Dryden's Poems is, no doubt, partly responsible for the unduly low opinion often expressed of his lyrical powers. Some admirable examples will be found here in *The Conquest of Granada, Marriage à la Mode,* and *Albion and Albanius;* but hardly any play is without them.

Before saying a few words on the general character of the great mass of work which has been thus disposed for review, it may be well to say still fewer on the selection from it which is here presented to the reader. It was originally intended to give one volume only; but, when I was asked to undertake this, I urged upon the publisher that no representative selection was at all possible in such

[9] *King Arthur* did not suffer from the ill luck of some of Dryden's later plays, and, thanks to Purcell's music, held a very long lease of popularity. Indeed, Scott says it was still acted in his day. I wish space had allowed me to give it, if only to spite the shade of the spiteful (and matter-of-fact) Langbaine.

[10] I have not thought it necessary to waste space in dwelling on *this* feature of Dryden's plays. It is open, gross, palpable; the defendant confesses in more than one famous passage; and it is an acknowledged aggravation that he does it neither naturally nor with a good grace. But it was a way of the then world, and it is a long time ago; no more need be said about it.

a space, and he kindly consented to double the allowance. This gave me about eight plays. There could be very little doubt about the claims of the two *Conquests of Granada, Aureng-Zebe, All for Love, The Spanish Friar,* and *Don Sebastian.* These six are the best reputed and the most commonly quoted of Dryden's whole theatre; and the reader, at last put in possession of some representative part of that theatre, might justly resent the omission of any one of them. This left me but two, or rather (for some of the necessaries are very long), about one and a half, for free selection, and it was very desirable that the third, or "opera," division of the work should have its example. So the short *Albion and Albanius,* though not equal to the rest in merit, seemed useful for the "half." The other was almost bound to be a comedy, since the tragedies were already strongly represented: and I had to choose between *Marriage à la Mode, Limberham,* and *Amphitryon.* The first-named seemed to me for all reasons preferable. But I only wish a third volume were practicable, that I might give *Tyrannic Love* (a beautiful absurdity of the most piquant kind), the stately *Cleomenes,* and, perhaps, the bustling if not brilliant blackguardism of *Limberham.* And still I should be puzzled for the fourth between *The Indian Emperor, Amphitryon, The State of Innocence,* and *King Arthur.* For it was Dryden's fate to put good things everywhere, though in his plays he rarely made everything good: and even in those not yet mentioned in this paragraph, especially *The Maiden Queen* (*Secret Love*), and *The Mock Astrologer* (*An Evening's Love*), as well as in the collaborations, there are abundant *salvanda.*

I believe, however, that these two volumes will really give the reader as fair an opportunity as is possible in this space, of seeing what the greatest writer of English verse and prose in his own special time managed to do in that remarkable department of literature which lays both prose and verse under contribution. It is not for me to anticipate the result of the reading in others, but I may repeat with some variation what that result has been, during and at the end of a long period of familiarity, in my own case. I fear we must admit that Dryden never shows himself fully to the manner born: and though I think better of his dramatic work than some critics do, I should not be disposed to limit his disqualification—as some of these have done, and as he himself would have liked to do—to comedy. His want of lightness on the comic side does not seem to me more fatal than his want of pathos on the tragic. That he shares this, as has been said, to some extent with Corneille, is true: but this is no exoneration. A tragedy of the highest class without "the pity of it," is almost inconceivable. Dryden obtains this in *All for Love*, partly because of the inherent virtue of the story, partly because he transmits some of "Shakespeare's magic" though he could not walk in Shakespeare's circle. Elsewhere we hardly have it. Don Sebastian and Cleomenes are most respectable persons; we, as it were, leave cards of sympathy on them in the correctest manner; we admire the genius of their author. But we do not feel that "the rest is silence," that "the wheel has come full circle," that for the moment "all our" own "yesterdays have merely lighted" us "fools the way to dusty death"; that he hates us who would add anything to their tragedy. This absolute finality, which makes the reading of all the greatest tragedies, whether Greek or English, a sort of finished chapter of life, renewable it may be, but finished *pro hac vice*, never occurs with Dryden, or only in *All for Love*. As for the heroes and heroines of the Heroic plays, they are puppets—not seldom first-class puppets: but the blood in their veins is only electrified sawdust.

So also the finality and completeness of comedy, which are different but equally unmistakable, are too often lacking to his comic characters and actions. Perhaps there is most of them in *Limberham*. Woodall has actually accomplished the rascalities that he set out to accomplish, if he is less *propositi tenax* as a husband in the future. Pleasance has chosen him with her eyes open, and has only herself to thank for it. But there is something new also in the description of the curious "foursome" of Rhodophil, Palamede, Doralice, Melantha in *Marriage à la Mode:* and I seem to myself to see more character—individual genuine character—in Doralice than in any of Dryden's personages, tragic or comic. She is not *very* much better than she should be, but then the heroines of Restoration comedy are as a rule considerably worse. It is partly accident that in the actual action preserves Rhodophil from the fate which he has so richly deserved, and in fact invited: but one sees that there is not a little more than accident behind. Doralice is in fact an accomplished, but not heartless, flirt more than anything else, and it is very curious that Dryden, not merely here but elsewhere, has come nearer than any of his contemporaries, and than most of his successors before the nineteenth century, to that interesting and by no means contemptible phase of femininity.

But elsewhere he rarely attains the complete interest of character which makes action almost superfluous: and he does not give us the action itself with that smooth and round completeness which even the merest *saynète* may have, and without which, character-interest being also absent, every dramatic work, from the *saynète* itself or the marionette-show to the full five-act tragedy, lacks something.

It is partly a cause and partly a consequence of these deficiencies in character, in action, and in completeness that his wheels run heavily—that there is an absence of that currency and fluidity which are so grateful in the drama. It is most curious to compare the animation and impetus of such an apparently impossible thing as *The Hind and the Panther* with the drag of most of the plays: and certainly we shall seldom find elsewhere such companion pictures of Minerva *invita* and of the same goddess in a thorough good temper, or as Dryden's own age would have said "coming."

But it may be said, if you deny Dryden's theatre action, character, and completeness of effect, what inducement can there be for yourself to reprint, or for anybody to read him? There is a good deal: but the chief of it, according to the present writer's thinking, lies in the astonishing evidences of literary craftsmanship and of its results in good literature, which almost every play, and in some plays almost every page, contains. While the plays were commonly read and some of them commonly acted, they were constantly quoted; and though now the quotations are limited to a few things, such as "Forgiveness to the injured does belong," the *Aureng-Zebe* "Life" passage and a few more, anyone who reads them will find fillings for a bulky commonplace book in the shape of passages instinct with criticism of life itself, charged with weighty sense, pointed with keen wit and polished phrase, and driven home by the most astonishing force of intellect.

Add to this the singular stuff of which the Heroic plays are so full, and of which enough has been said above; add the interest of word-fence which is all but omnipresent; add not a few other things which reading will soon reveal; and the reason for reprinting will be obvious enough. It is true that Dryden, like other great writers, is somewhat of a touchstone. His manner to a great extent and his matter to some are out of fashion; his reputation as a classic is still so great that no one can earn the credit of cleverness by praising, and yet so vague that no one can earn this by attacking him. He cannot be made a *coterie* idol. If, especially in his plays, he is to be liked, it can only be by persons who love literature for itself, who can see and can taste good work wherever it exists, on whatever subject and in whatever fashion it presents itself. Let us hope that such persons are more numerous at the beginning of the twentieth century than some pessimists insinuate.[11]

GEORGE SAINTSBURY

[11] There is no authoritative text of Dryden's plays, there being no evidence that he revised or authorized the folio which appeared shortly after his death. Congreve's edition of 1717 (6 vols. 12 mo.) was a little altered by Scott, whose text, corrected somewhat by the present editor in collation with the first editions, is now presented after a fresh comparison with the folio. I should like to add to the authorities mentioned above, the new and very interesting treatment of Dryden's theatre in Mr. Courthope's *History of English Poetry*, vol. iv., chap. 14, which has only appeared since the text was printed.

ALMANZOR AND ALMAHIDE

or, the

CONQUEST OF GRANADA

by the

SPANIARDS

A Tragedy

THE FIRST PART

—*Major rerum mihi nascitur ordo; Majus opus moveo.*

VIRG. ÆNEID.

THE CONQUEST OF GRANADA

IN these two remarkable pieces (which are practically one gigantic drama in ten acts) Dryden took a certain amount of suggestion or canvass from Mlle. de Scudéry's two romances of *Ibrahim* (1641), and *Almahide* (1660), but treated his borrowed material in his usual manner of masterly superiority.[1] They came out as plays in the winter of 1669-1670 at the Theatre Royal, and appeared in print two years later, ushered by his usual publisher, Herringman. They are the triumph of the Heroic play in English, and their success was such that it undoubtedly intoxicated the author a little, and made him for a short time forget himself critically and otherwise, as is shown in the Epilogue of the second part, and its "Defense"—the only, or almost the only, blots on Dryden's scutcheon as a critic. The original cast was extremely strong:—Kynaston taking Boabdelin; Mohun, Abdelmelech; and Hart, Almanzor, while the women's parts were presented by Nell Gwyn (Almahide), Mrs. Marshall (Lyndaraxa), Mrs. Boutell (Benzayda), and Dryden's own special friend, Anne Reeve (Esperanza). Much of the ridicule in *The Rehearsal* was directed against the piece or pieces, and some of the hits are palpable enough. But the whole is *bravura* of astonishing talent, not seldom reaching genius, and to judge it by any other standard than its own is a critical blunder. If you do not choose to play the Heroic game at all, stand out and welcome; if you do you will hardly have a better hand than here.

[1] If any one wishes to see the common plagiarism-hunter in a perfect paroxysm, he may consult Langbaine on this play.

TO HIS ROYAL HIGHNESS THE DUKE[1]

Sir,

Heroic poesy has always been sacred to princes, and to heroes. Thus Virgil inscribed his *Æneids* to Augustus Cæsar; and of latter ages, Tasso and Ariosto dedicated their poems to the House of Este. It is indeed but justice, that the most excellent and most profitable kind of writing should be addressed by poets to such persons whose characters have, for the most part, been the guides and patterns of their imitation; and poets, while they imitate, instruct. The feigned hero inflames the true; and the dead virtue animates the living. Since, therefore, the world is governed by precept and example, and both these can only have influence from those persons who are above us; that kind of poesy, which excites to virtue the greatest men, is of the greatest use to humankind.

It is from this consideration that I have presumed to dedicate to your royal highness these faint representations of your own worth and valour in heroic poetry: Or, to speak more properly, not to dedicate, but to restore to you those ideas, which in the more perfect part of my characters I have taken from you. Heroes may lawfully be delighted with their own praises, both as they are further incitements to their virtue, and as they are the highest returns which mankind can make them for it.

And certainly, if ever nation were obliged, either by the conduct, the personal valour or the good fortune of a leader the English are acknowledging, in all of them, to your royal highness. Your whole life has been a continued series of heroic actions; which you began so early, that you were no sooner named in the world, but it was with praise and admiration. Even the first blossoms of your youth paid us all that could be expected from a ripening manhood. While you practised but the rudiments of war, you out-went all other captains; and have since found none to surpass, but yourself alone. The opening of your glory was like that of light: You shone to us from afar; and disclosed your first beams on distant nations: Yet so, that the lustre of them was spread abroad, and reflected brightly on your native country. You were then an honour to it, when it was a reproach to itself. When the fortunate usurper sent his arms to Flanders, many of the adverse party were vanquished by your fame, ere they tried your valour. The report of it drew over to your ensigns whole troops and companies of converted rebels, and made them forsake successful wickedness, to follow

[1] James, Duke of York, afterwards James II.

3

an oppressed and exiled virtue. Your reputation waged war
with the enemies of your royal family, even within their
trenches; and the more obstinate, or more guilty of them, were
forced to be spies over those whom they commanded, lest the
name of York should disband that army, in whose fate it was
to defeat the Spaniards, and force Dunkirk to surrender. Yet,
those victorious forces of the rebels were not able to sustain
your arms. Where you charged in person, you were a conqueror. It is true, they afterwards recovered courage; and
wrested that victory from others which they had lost to you;
and it was a greater action for them to rally, than it was to
overcome. Thus, by the presence of your royal highness, the
English on both sides remained victorious, and that army,
which was broken by your valour, became a terror to those for
whom they conquered. Then it was, that at the cost of other
nations you informed and cultivated that valour, which was to
defend your native country, and to vindicate its honour from
the insolence of our encroaching neighbours. When the Hol-
landers, not contented to withdraw themselves from the obedience which they owed their lawful sovereign, affronted those
by whose charity they were first protected; and, being swelled
up to a pre-eminence of trade, by a supine negligence on our
side, and a sordid parsimony on their own, dared to dispute
the sovereignty of the seas, the eyes of three nations were then
cast upon you; and by the joint suffrage of king and people,
you were chosen to revenge their common injuries; to which,
though you had an undoubted title by your birth, you had a
greater by your courage. Neither did the success deceive our
hopes and expectations: The most glorious victory which was
gained by our navy in that war, was in that first engagement[2];
wherein, even by the confession of our enemies, who ever pal-
liate their own losses, and diminish our advantages, your absolute triumph was acknowledged: You conquered at the Hague,
as entirely as at London; and the return of a shattered fleet,
without an admiral, left not the most impudent among them
the least pretence for a false bonfire, or a dissembled day of
public thanksgiving. All our achievements against them afterwards, though we sometimes conquered, and were never overcome, were but a copy of that victory, and they still fell short
of their original; somewhat of fortune was ever wanting, to fill
up the title of so absolute a defeat; or perhaps the guardian
angel of our nation was not enough concerned when you were
absent, and would not employ his utmost vigour for a less important stake than the life and honour of a royal admiral.

And if, since that memorable day, you have had leisure to
enjoy in peace the fruits of so glorious a reputation; it was

[2] The defeat of the Dutch off Harwich, 3rd June 1665.

occasion only has been wanting to your courage, for that can never be wanting to occasion. The same ardour still incites you to heroic actions, and the same concernment for all the interests of your king and brother continues to give you restless nights, and a generous emulation for your own glory. You are still meditating on new labours for yourself, and new triumphs for the nation; and when our former enemies again provoke us, you will again solicit fate to provide you another navy to overcome, and another admiral to be slain. You will then lead forth a nation eager to revenge their past injuries; and, like the Romans, inexorable to peace, till they have fully vanquished. Let our enemies make their boast of a surprise,[3] as the Samnites did of a successful stratagem; but the *Furcæ Caudinæ* will never be forgiven till they are revenged. I have always observed in your royal highness an extreme concernment for the honour of your country; it is a passion common to you with a brother, the most excellent of kings; and in your two persons are eminent the characters which Homer has given us of heroic virtue; the commanding part in Agamemnon, and the executive in Achilles. And I doubt not from both your actions, but to have abundant matter to fill the annals of a glorious reign, and to perform the part of a just historian to my royal master, without intermixing with it anything of the poet.

In the meantime, while your royal highness is preparing fresh employments for our pens, I have been examining my own forces, and making trial of myself, how I shall be able to transmit you to posterity. I have formed a hero, I confess, not absolutely perfect, but of an excessive and over-boiling courage; but Homer and Tasso are my precedents. Both the Greek and the Italian poet had well considered that a tame hero, who never transgresses the bounds of moral virtue, would shine but dimly in an epic poem; the strictness of those rules might well give precepts to the reader, but would administer little of occasion to the writer. But a character of an eccentric virtue is the more exact image of human life, because he is not wholly exempted from its frailties; such a person is Almanzor, whom I present, with all humility, to the patronage of your royal highness. I designed in him a roughness of character, impatient of injuries, and a confidence of himself, almost approaching to an arrogance. But these errors are incident only to great spirits; they are moles and dimples, which hinder not a face from being beautiful, though that beauty be not regular; they are of the number of those amiable imperfections which we see in mistresses, and which we pass over without a strict examination, when they are accompanied with greater graces. And such in Almanzor are a frank and noble openness of nature,

[3] The Dutch in the Medway.

an easiness to forgive his conquered enemies, and to protect them in distress; and, above all, an inviolable faith in his affection.

This, sir, I have briefly shadowed to your royal highness, that you may not be ashamed of that hero, whose protection you undertake. Neither would I dedicate him to so illustrious a name, if I were conscious to myself that he did or said anything which was wholly unworthy of it. However, since it is not just that your royal highness should defend or own what possibly may be my error, I bring before you this accused Almanzor in the nature of a suspected criminal. By the suffrage of the most and best he already is acquitted; and by the sentence of some, condemned. But as I have no reason to stand to the award of my enemies, so neither dare I trust the partiality of my friends: I make my last appeal to your royal highness, as to a sovereign tribunal. Heroes should only be judged by heroes; because they only are capable of measuring great and heroic actions by the rule and standard of their own. If Almanzor has failed in any point of honour, I must therein acknowledge that he deviates from your royal highness, who are the pattern of it. But if at any time he fulfils the parts of personal valour, and of conduct, of a soldier, and of a general; or, if I could yet give him a character more advantageous than what he has, of the most unshaken friend, the greatest of subjects, and the best of masters, I should then draw to all the world a true resemblance of your worth and virtues; at least, as far as they are capable of being copied by the mean abilities of,

  Sir,

    Your royal highness's
     Most humble, and
      Most obedient servant,

           J. DRYDEN

OF HEROIC PLAYS

An Essay

WHETHER heroic verse ought to be admitted into serious plays, is not now to be disputed: it is already in possession of the stage, and I dare confidently affirm that very few tragedies, in this age, shall be received without it. All the arguments which are formed against it, can amount to no more than this: that it is not so near conversation as prose, and therefore not so natural. But it is very clear to all who understand poetry, that serious plays ought not to imitate conversation too nearly. If nothing were to be raised above that level, the foundation of poetry would be destroyed. And if you once admit of a latitude, that thoughts may be exalted, and that images and actions may be raised above the life, and described in measure without rhyme, that leads you insensibly from your own principles to mine: you are already so far onward of your way, that you have forsaken the imitation of ordinary converse. You are gone beyond it; and to continue where you are is to lodge in the open fields, betwixt two inns. You have lost that which you call natural, and have not acquired the last perfection of art. But it was only custom which cozened us so long; we thought, because Shakespeare and Fletcher went no further, that there the pillars of poetry were to be erected; that, because they excellently described passion without rhyme, therefore rhyme was not capable of describing it. But time has now convinced most men of that error. It is indeed so difficult to write verse, that the adversaries of it have a good plea against many, who undertook that task, without being formed by art or nature for it. Yet, even they who have written worst in it, would have written worse without it: They have cozened many with their sound, who never took the pains to examine their sense. In fine, they have succeeded; though, it is true, they have more dishonoured rhyme by their good success, than they have done by their ill. But I am willing to let fall this argument: It is free for every man to write, or not to write, in verse, as he judges it to be, or not to be, his talent; or as he imagines the audience will receive it.

For heroic plays, in which only I have used it without the mixture of prose, the first light we had of them, on the English theatre, was from the late Sir William Davenant. It being forbidden him in the rebellious times to act tragedies and comedies, because they contained some matter of scandal to those good people, who could more easily dispossess their lawful sovereign than endure a wanton jest, he was forced to turn his

thoughts another way, and to introduce the examples of moral
virtue, writ in verse, and performed in recitative music. The
original of this music, and of the scenes which adorned his
work, he had from the Italian operas; but he heightened his
characters, as I may probably imagine, from the example of
Corneille and some French poets. In this condition did this
part of poetry remain at his Majesty's return; when, growing
bolder, as being now owned by a public authority, he reviewed
his *Siege of Rhodes* and caused it be acted as a just drama.
But as few men have the happiness to begin and finish any
new project, so neither did he live to make his design perfect:
There wanted the fulness of a plot, and the variety of characters to form it as it ought; and, perhaps, something might
have been added to the beauty of the style. All which he
would have performed with more exactness, had he pleased
to have given us another work of the same nature. For myself
and others, who come after him, we are bound, with all veneration to his memory, to acknowledge what advantage we received from that excellent groundwork which he laid: And,
since it is an easy thing to add to what already is invented,
we ought all of us, without envy to him, or partiality to ourselves, to yield him the precedence in it.

Having done him this justice, as my guide, I may do myself
so much, as to give an account of what I have performed after
him. I observed then, as I said, what was wanting to the perfection of his *Siege of Rhodes*, which was design and variety
of characters. And in the midst of this consideration, by mere
accident, I opened the next book that lay by me, which was
an Ariosto in Italian; and the very first two lines of that poem
gave me light to all I could desire:

> Le donne, i cavalier, l'arme, gli amori,
> Le cortesie, l'audaci imprese io canto, etc.

For the very next reflection which I made was this: that an
heroic play ought to be an imitation, in little, of an heroic
poem; and, consequently, that love and valour ought to be
the subject of it. Both these Sir William Davenant had begun
to shadow; but it was so, as first discoverers draw their maps,
with headlands, and promontories, and some few outlines of
somewhat taken at a distance, and which the designer saw not
clearly. The common drama obliged him to a plot well formed
and pleasant, or, as the ancients call it, one entire and great
action. But this he afforded not himself in a story, which he
neither filled with persons, nor beautified with characters, nor
varied with accidents. The laws of an heroic poem did not
dispense with those of the other, but raised them to a greater
height, and indulged him a further liberty of fancy, and of

drawing all things as far above the ordinary proportion of the stage, as that is beyond the common words and actions of human life; and, therefore, in the scanting of his images and design, he complied not enough with the greatness and majesty of an heroic poem.

I am sorry I cannot discover my opinion of this kind of writing, without dissenting much from his, whose memory I love and honour. But I will do it with the same respect to him, as if he were now alive, and overlooking my paper while I write. His judgment of an heroic poem was this: "That it ought to be dressed in a more familiar and easy shape; more fitted to the common actions and passions of human life; and, in short, more like a glass of nature, showing us ourselves in our ordinary habits, and figuring a more practicable virtue to us, than was done by the ancients or moderns." Thus he takes the image of an heroic poem from the drama, or stage poetry; and accordingly intended to divide it into five books, representing the same number of acts; and every book into several cantos, imitating the scenes which compose our acts.

But this, I think, is rather a play in narration, as I may call it, than an heroic poem,—if at least you will not prefer the opinion of a single man to the practice of the most excellent authors, both of ancient and latter ages. I am no admirer of quotations; but you shall hear, if you please, one of the ancients delivering his judgment on this question; it is Petronius Arbiter, the most elegant, and one of the most judicious authors of the Latin tongue; who, after he had given many admirable rules for the structure and beauties of an epic poem, concludes all in these following words:—

"*Non enim res gestæ versibus comprehendendæ sunt, quoa longe melius historici faciunt: sed, per ambages, deorumque ministeria, præcipitandus est liber spiritus, ut potius furentis animi vaticinatio appareat, quam religiosæ orationis, sub testibus, fides.*"

In which sentence, and his own essay of a poem, which immediately he gives you, it is thought he taxes Lucan, who followed too much the truth of history, crowded sentences together, was too full of points, and too often offered at somewhat which had more of the sting of an epigram, than of the dignity and state of an heroic poem. Lucan used not much the help of his heathen deities: There was neither the ministry of the gods, nor the precipitation of the soul, nor the fury of a prophet (of which my author speaks), in his *Pharsalia;* he treats you more like a philosopher than a poet, and instructs you in verse, with what he had been taught by his uncle Seneca in prose. In one word, he walks soberly afoot, when he might fly. Yet Lucan is not always this religious historian. The oracle of Appius, and the witchcraft of Erictho, will somewhat atone for him, who was, indeed, bound up by an ill-chosen and known argument, to follow truth with great exactness. For my part, I am of opinion that neither Homer, Virgil, Statius, Ariosto, Tasso, nor our English Spenser, could have formed their poems half so beautiful, without those gods and spirits, and those enthusiastic parts of poetry, which compose the most noble parts of all their writings. And I will ask any man who loves heroic poetry (for I will not dispute their tastes who do not), if the ghost of Polydorus in Virgil, the Enchanted Wood in Tasso, and the Bower of Bliss in Spenser (which he borrows from that admirable Italian) could have been omitted, without taking from their works some of the greatest beauties in them. And if any man object the improbabilities of a spirit appearing, or of a palace raised by magic; I boldly answer him, that an heroic poet is not tied to a bare representation of what is true, or exceeding probable; but that he may let himself loose to visionary objects, and to the representation of such things, as, depending not on sense, and therefore not to be comprehended by knowledge, may give him a freer scope for imagination. It is enough that, in all ages and religions, the greatest part of mankind have believed the power of magic, and that there are spirits or spectres which have appeared. This, I say, is foundation enough for poetry: and I dare further affirm, that the whole doctrine of separated beings, whether those spirits are incorporeal substances (which Mr. Hobbes, with some reason, thinks to imply a contradiction), or that they are a thinner or more aërial sort of bodies (as some of the fathers have conjectured), may better be explicated by poets than by philosophers or divines. For their speculations on this subject are wholly poetical; they have only their fancy for their guide; and that, being sharper in an excellent poet, than it is likely it should in a phlegmatic, heavy gownman, will see further in its own empire, and produce more satisfactory notions on those dark and doubtful problems.

Some men think they have raised a great argument against the use of spectres and magic in heroic poetry, by saying they are unnatural; but whether they or I believe there are such things, is not material; it is enough that, for aught we know, they may be in nature; and whatever is, or may be, is not properly unnatural. Neither am I much concerned at Mr. Cowley's verses before *Gondibert,* though his authority is almost sacred to me: It is true, he has resembled the epic poetry to a fantastic fairy-land; but he has contradicted himself by his own example: For he has himself made use of angels and visions in his *Davideis* as well as Tasso in his *Godfrey.*

What I have written on this subject will not be thought a digression by the reader, if he please to remember what I said in the beginning of this essay, that I have modelled my heroic plays by the rules of an heroic poem. And if that be the most noble, the most pleasant, and the most instructive way of writing in verse, and withal the highest pattern of human life, as all poets have agreed, I shall need no other argument to justify my choice in this imitation. One advantage the drama has above the other, namely, that it represents to view what the poem only does relate; and, *Segnius irritant animum demissa per aures, quam quæ sunt oculis subjecta fidelibus,* as Horace tells us.

To those who object my frequent use of drums and trumpets, and my representations of battles, I answer, I introduced them not on the English stage: Shakespeare used them frequently; and though Jonson shows no battle in his *Catiline,* yet you hear from behind the scenes the sounding of trumpets, and the shouts of fighting armies. But, I add further, that these warlike instruments, and even their presentations of fighting on the stage, are no more than necessary to produce the effects of an heroic play; that is, to raise the imagination of the audience, and to persuade them, for the time, that what they behold on the theatre is really performed. The poet is then to endeavour an absolute dominion over the minds of the spectators; for, though our fancy will contribute to its own deceit, yet a writer ought to help its operation: And that the Red Bull[1] has formerly done the same is no more an argument against our practice than it would be for a physician to forbear an approved medicine, because a mountebank has used it with success.

Thus I have given a short account of heroic plays. I might now, with the usual eagerness of an author, make a particular defence of this. But the common opinion (how unjust soever) has been so much to my advantage, that I have reason to be satisfied, and to suffer with patience all that can be urged against it.

For, otherwise, what can be more easy for me, than to defend the character of Almanzor, which is one great exception that is made against the play? 'Tis said, that Almanzor is no perfect pattern of heroic virtue, that he is a contemner of kings, and that he is made to perform impossibilities.

I must therefore avow, in the first place, from whence I took the character. The first image I had of him was from the Achilles of Homer; the next from Tasso's Rinaldo (who was a copy of the former), and the third from the Artaban of Monsieur Calprenède, who has imitated both. The original of these, Achilles, is taken by Homer for his hero; and is described by him as one, who in strength and courage surpassed the rest of the Grecian army; but withal of so fiery a temper, so impatient

---

[1] A theatre famous in mid-17th century for melodrama.

of an injury, even from his king and general, that when his mistress was to be forced from him by the command of Agamemnon, he not only disobeyed it, but returned him an answer full of contumely, and in the most opprobrious terms he could imagine; they are Homer's words which follow, and I have cited but some few amongst a multitude:

Οἰνοβαρὲς, κυνὸς ὄμματ᾽ ἔχων, κραδίην δ᾽ ἐλάφοιο.—Il. a. v. 225.
Δημοβόρος βασιλεύς, etc.—Il. a. v. 231.

Nay, he proceeded so far in his insolence, as to draw out his sword, with intention to kill him;

Ἕλκετο δ᾽ ἐκ κολεοῖο μέγα ξίφος.—Il. a. v. 194.

And, if Minerva had not appeared, and held his hand, he had executed his design; and it was all she could do to dissuade him from it. The event was, that he left the army, and would fight no more. Agamemnon gives his character thus to Nestor:

Ἀλλ᾽ ὅδ᾽ ἀνὴρ ἐθέλει περὶ πάντων ἔμμεναι ἄλλων,
Πάντων μὲν κρατέειν ἐθέλει, πάντεσσι δ᾽ ἀνάσσειν.
Il. a. v. 287, 288.

and Horace gives the same description of him in his Art of Poetry:

Honoratum si fortè reponis Achillem,
Impiger iracundus, inexorabilis, acer,
Jura neget sibi nata, nihil non arroget armis.

Tasso's chief character, Rinaldo, was a man of the same temper; for, when he had slain Gernando in his heat of passion, he not only refused to be judged by Godfrey, his general, but threatened that if he came to seize him, he would right himself by arms upon him; witness these following lines of Tasso:

Verga egli, o mandi, io terrò fermo il piede:
Giudici fian tra noi la sorte, e l'arme;
Fera tragedia vuol che s'appresenti,
Per lor diporto, alle nemiche genti.

You see how little these great authors did esteem the point of honour, so much magnified by the French, and so ridiculously aped by us. They made their heroes men of honour; but so as not to divest them quite of human passions and frailties: they contented themselves to show you, what men of great spirits would certainly do when they were provoked, not what they were obliged to do by the strict rules of moral virtue. For my own part, I declare myself for Homer and Tasso, and am more in love with Achilles and Rinaldo than with Cyrus and

Oroondates. I shall never subject my characters to the French standard, where love and honour are to be weighed by drachms and scruples: Yet, where I have designed the patterns of exact virtues, such as in this play are the parts of Almahide, of Ozmyn, and Benzayda, I may safely challenge the best of theirs.

But Almanzor is taxed with changing sides: and what tie has he on him to the contrary? He is not born their subject whom he serves, and he is injured by them to a very high degree. He threatens them, and speaks insolently of sovereign power; but so do Achilles and Rinaldo, who were subjects and soldiers to Agamemnon and Godfrey of Bulloigne. He talks extravagantly in his passion; but, if I would take the pains to quote an hundred passages of Ben Jonson's *Cethegus,* I could easily show you, that the rodomontades of Almanzor are neither so irrational as his, nor so impossible to be put in execution; for Cethegus threatens to destroy nature, and to raise a new one out of it; to kill all the senate for his part of the action; to look Cato dead; and a thousand other things as extravagant he says, but performs not one action in the play.

But none of the former calumnies will stick; and, therefore, it is at last charged upon me, that Almanzor does all things; or if you will have an absurd accusation, in their nonsense who make it, that he performs impossibilities: they say, that being a stranger, he appeases two fighting factions, when the authority of their lawful sovereign could not. This is indeed the most improbable of all his actions, but it is far from being impossible. Their king had made himself contemptible to his people, as the history of Granada tells us; and Almanzor, though a stranger, yet was already known to them by his gallantry in the Juego de toros, his engagement on the weaker side, and more especially by the character of his person and brave actions, given by Abdalla just before; and, after all, the greatness of the enterprise consisted only in the daring, for he had the king's guards to second him: But we have read both of Cæsar, and many other generals, who have not only calmed a mutiny with a word, but have presented themselves single before an army of their enemies; which upon sight of them has revolted from their own leaders and come over to their trenches. In the rest of Almanzor's actions you see him for the most part victorious; but the same fortune has constantly attended many heroes, who were not imaginary. Yet, you see it no inheritance to him; for, in the first place, he is made a prisoner; and, in the last, defeated, and not able to preserve the city from being taken. If the history of the late Duke of Guise be true, he hazarded more, and performed not less in Naples, than Almanzor is feigned to have done in Granada.

I have been too tedious in this apology; but to make some

satisfaction, I will leave the rest of my play exposed to the critics, without defence.

The concernment of it is wholly passed from me, and ought to be in them who have been favourable to it, and are somewhat obliged to defend their own opinions. That there are errors in it, I deny not;

Ast opere in tanto fas est obrepere somnum.

But I have already swept the stakes: and, with the common good fortune of prosperous gamesters, can be content to sit quietly; to hear my fortune cursed by some, and my faults arraigned by others; and to suffer both without reply.

ON MR DRYDEN'S PLAY, *THE CONQUEST OF GRANADA*

THE applause I gave among the foolish crowd
Was not distinguished, though I clapped aloud:
Or, if it had, my judgment had been hid:
I clapped for company, as others did.
Thence may be told the fortune of your play,
Its goodness must be tried another way.
Let's judge it then, and, if we've any skill,
Commend what's good, though we commend it ill.
There will be praise enough; yet not so much,
As if the world had never any such:
Ben Jonson, Beaumont, Fletcher, Shakespeare, are,
As well as you, to have a poet's share.
You, who write after, have, besides, this curse,
You must write better, or you else write worse.
To equal only what was writ before,
Seems stolen, or borrowed from the former store.
Though blind as Homer all the ancients be,
'Tis on their shoulders, like the lame, we see.
Then not to flatter th' age, nor flatter you,
(Praises, though less, are greater when they're true)
You're equal to the best, out-done by you;
Who had out-done themselves, had they lived now.

VAUGHAN [1]

[1] John, Lord Vaughan, eldest surviving son of Richard, Earl of Carbery.

PROLOGUE TO THE FIRST PART

Spoken by Mrs Ellen Gwyn, in a Broad-brimmed Hat,
and Waist-belt.

THIS jest was first of the other house's making,
And, five times tried, has never failed of taking;
For 'twere a shame a poet should be killed
Under the shelter of so broad a shield.
This is that hat, whose very sight did win ye
To laugh and clap as though the devil were in ye.
As then, for Nokes, so now I hope you'll be
So dull, to laugh once more for love of me.
I'll write a play, says one, for I have got
A broad-brimmed hat, and waist-belt, towards a plot.
Says the other, I have one more large than that.
Thus they out-write each other with a hat!
The brims still grew with every play they writ;
And grew so large, they covered all the wit.
Hat was the play; 'twas language, wit, and tale:
Like them that find meat, drink, and cloth in ale.
What dulness do these mongrel wits confess,
When all their hope is acting of a dress!
Thus, two the best comedians of the age
Must be worn out, with being blocks o' the stage;
Like a young girl, who better things has known,
Beneath their poet's impotence they groan.
See now what charity it was to save!
They thought you liked, what only you forgave;
And brought you more dull sense, dull sense much worse
Than brisk gay nonsense, and the heavier curse.
They bring old iron, and glass upon the stage,
To barter with the Indians of our age.
Still they write on, and like great authors show;
But 'tis as rollers in wet gardens grow
Heavy with dirt, and gathering as they go.
May none, who have so little understood,
To like such trash, presume to praise what's good!
And may those drudges of the stage, whose fate
Is damned dull farce more dully to translate,
Fall under that excise the state thinks fit
To set on all French wares, whose worst is wit.
French farce, worn out at home, is sent abroad;
And, patched up here, is made our English mode.
Henceforth, let poets ere allowed to write,
Be searched, like duellists before they fight,

For wheel-broad hats, dull humour, all that chaff,
Which makes you mourn, and makes the vulgar laugh:
For these, in plays, are as unlawful arms,
As, in a combat, coats of mail, and charms.

DRAMATIS PERSONÆ

MAHOMET BOABDELIN, the last King of Granada.
PRINCE ABDALLA, his brother.
ABDELMELECH, chief of the Abencerrages.
ZULEMA, chief of the Zegrys.
ABENAMAR, an old Abencerrago.
SELIN, an old Zegry.
OZMYN, a brave young Abencerrago, son to Abenamar.
HAMET, brother to Zulema, a Zegry.
GOMEL, a Zegry.
ALMANZOR.
FERDINAND, King of Spain.
DUKE OF ARCOS, his General.
DON ALONZO D'AGUILAR, a Spanish Captain.

ALMAHIDE, Queen of Granada.
LYNDARAXA, sister of ZULEMA, a Zegry lady.
BENZAYDA, daughter to SELIN.
ESPERANZA, slave to the Queen.
HALYMA, slave to LYNDARAXA.
ISABELLA, Queen of Spain.

Messengers, Guards, Attendants, Men, and Women.

SCENE—GRANADA, AND THE CHRISTIAN CAMP BESIEGING IT

ALMANZOR AND ALMAHIDE

OR, THE

CONQUEST OF GRANADA

THE FIRST PART

ACT I

SCENE I

Enter BOABDELIN, ABENAMAR, ABDELMELECH *and* Guards.

BOABDELIN. Thus, in the triumphs of soft peace, I reign;
And, from my walls, defy the powers of Spain;
With pomp and sports my love I celebrate,
While they keep distance, and attend my state.—
Parent to her, whose eyes my soul enthral,

[*To* ABENAMAR.]

Whom I, in hope, already father call,
Abenamar, thy youth these sports has known,
Of which thy age is now spectator grown;
Judge-like thou sit'st, to praise, or to arraign
The flying skirmish of the darted cane:[1]
But, when fierce bulls run loose upon the place,
And our bold Moors their loves with danger grace,
Then heat new-bends thy slacken'd nerves again,
And a short youth runs warm through every vein.

   Abenamar. I must confess the encounters of this day
Warmed me indeed, but quite another way,—
Not with the fire of youth; but generous rage,
To see the glories of my youthful age
So far out-done.

   Abdelmelech. Castile could never boast, in all its pride,
A pomp so splendid, when the lists, set wide,
Gave room to the fierce bulls, which wildly ran
In Sierra Ronda, ere the war began;

[1] The "juego de cañas" or djereed.

19

Who, with high nostrils snuffing up the wind,
Now stood the champions of the savage kind.
Just opposite, within the circled place,
Ten of our bold Abencerrages' race
(Each brandishing his bull-spear in his hand)
Did their proud jennets gracefully command.
On their steel'd heads their demi-lances wore
Small pennons, which their ladies' colours bore.
Before this troop did warlike Ozmyn go;
Each lady, as he rode, saluting low;
At the chief stands, with reverence more profound,
His well-taught courser, kneeling, touched the ground;
Thence raised, he sidelong bore his rider on,
Still facing, till he out of sight was gone.
    Boabdelin. You praise him like a friend; and I confess,
His brave deportment merited no less.
    Abdelmelech. Nine bulls were launched [2] by his vic-
       torious arm,
Whose wary jennet, shunning still the harm,
Seemed to attend the shock, and then leaped wide:
Meanwhile, his dext'rous rider, when he spied
The beast just stooping, 'twixt the neck and head
His lance, with never-erring fury, sped.
    Abenamar. My son did well, and so did Hamet too;
Yet did no more than we were wont to do;
But what the stranger did was more than man.
    Abdelmelech. He finished all those triumphs we began.
One bull, with curled black head, beyond the rest,
And dew-laps hanging from his brawny chest,
With nodding front a while did daring stand,
And with his jetty hoof spurned back the sand;
Then, leaping forth, he bellowed out aloud:
The amazed assistants back each other crowd,
While monarch-like he ranged the listed field;
Some tossed, some gored, some trampling down he killed.
The ignobler Moors from far his rage provoke
With woods of darts, which from his sides he shook.
Meantime your valiant son, who had before
Gained fame, rode round to every Mirador;[3]
Beneath each lady's stand a stop he made,

---

2 "Lanced."
3 A parapeted balcony.

And, bowing, took the applauses which they paid,
Just in that point of time, the brave unknown
Approached the lists.
   Boabdelin. I marked him, when alone
(Observed by all, himself observing none)
He entered first, and with a graceful pride
His fiery Arab dextrously did guide,
Who while his rider every stand surveyed,
Sprung loose, and flew into an escapade;[4]
Not moving forward, yet, with every bound,
Pressing, and seeming still to quit his ground.
What after passed
Was far from the Ventanna[5] where I sate,
But you were near, and can the truth relate.

                      [*To* ABDELMELECH.

   Abdelmelech. Thus while he stood, the bull, who saw
     his foe,
His easier conquests proudly did forego;
And, making at him with a furious bound,
From his bent forehead aimed a double wound.
A rising murmur ran through all the field,
And every lady's blood with fear was chilled:
Some shrieked, while others, with more helpful care,
Cried out aloud,—Beware, brave youth, beware!
At this he turned, and, as the bull drew near,
Shunned and received him on his pointed spear:
The lance broke short, the beast then bellowed loud
And his strong neck to a new onset bowed.
The undaunted youth
Then drew! and from his saddle bending low,
Just where the neck did to the shoulders grow,
With his full force discharged a deadly blow.
Not heads of poppies (when they reap the grain)
Fall with more ease before the labouring swain,
Than fell this head:
It fell so quick, it did even death prevent,
And made imperfect bellowings as it went.
Then all the trumpets victory did sound,
And yet their clangours in our shouts were drown'd.

                      [*A confused noise within.*

[4] "Fling," "kick."
[5] "Ventaña," a window.

Boabdelin. The alarm-bell rings from our Alhambra
walls,
And from the streets sounds drums and atabals.[6]
          [*Within, a bell, drums, and trumpets.*

Enter a Messenger.

How now? from whence proceed these new alarms?
  Messenger. The two fierce factions are again in arms;
And changing into blood the day's delight,
The Zegrys with the Abencerrages fight;
On each side their allies and friends appear;
The Macas here, the Alabezes there:
The Gazuls with the Bencerrages join,
And, with the Zegrys, all great Gomel's line.
  Boabdelin. Draw up behind the Vivarambla place;
Double my guards,—these factions I will face:
And try if all the fury they can bring,
Be proof against the presence of their king.
          [*Exit* BOABDELIN.
          *The factions appear: At the head of the
          Abencerrages,* OZMYN; *at the head of the
          Zegrys,* ZULEMA, HAMET, GOMEL, *and*
          SELIN: ABENAMAR *and* ABDELMELECH
          joined with the Abencerrages.
  Zulema. The faint Abercerrages quit their ground;
Press them; put home your thrusts to every wound.
  Abdelmelech. Zegry, on manly force our line relies;
Thine poorly takes the advantage of surprise:
Unarmed and much out-numbered we retreat;
You gain no fame, when basely you defeat.
If thou art brave, seek nobler victory;
Save Moorish blood; and, while our bands stand by,
Let two and two an equal combat try.
  Hamet. 'Tis not for fear the combat we refuse,
But we our gained advantage will not lose.
  Zulema. In combating, but two of you will fall;
And we resolve we will dispatch you all.
  Ozmyn. We'll double yet the exchange before we die,
And each of ours two lives of yours shall buy.

---

[6] Kettle-drums.

ALMANZOR *enters betwixt them, as they stand*
ready to engage.

Almanzor. I cannot stay to ask which cause is best;
But this is so to me, because opprest.
                              [*Goes to the Abenamar.*

To them BOABDELIN *and his guards, going betwixt them.*

Boabdelin. On your allegiance, I command you stay;
Who passes here, through me must make his way;
My life's the Isthmus; through this narrow line
You first must cut, before those seas can join.
What fury, Zegrys, has possessed your minds?
What rage the brave Abencerrages blinds?
If of your courage you new proofs would show,
Without much travel you may find a foe.
Those foes are neither so remote nor few,
That you should need each other to pursue.
Lean times and foreign wars should minds unite;
When poor, men mutter, but they seldom fight.
O holy Allah! that I live to see
Thy Granadines assist their enemy!
You fight the Christians' battles; every life
You lavish thus, in this intestine strife,
Does from our weak foundations take one prop
Which helped to hold our sinking country up.
  Ozmyn. 'Tis fit our private enmity should cease;
Though injured first, yet I will first seek peace.
  Zulema. No, murderer, no; I never will be won
To peace with him, whose hand has slain my son.
  Ozmyn. Our prophet's curse
On me, and all the Abencerrages light,
If, unprovoked, I with your son did fight.
  Abdelmelech. A band of Zegrys ran within the place,
Matched with a troop of thirty of our race.
Your son and Ozmyn the first squadrons led,
Which, ten by ten, like Parthians, charged and fled,
The ground was strowed with canes where we did meet,
Which crackled underneath our coursers' feet:
When Tarifa (I saw him ride apart)
Changed his blunt cane for a steel-pointed dart,

And, meeting Ozmyn next,—
Who wanted time for treason to provide,—
He basely threw it at him, undefied.

    Ozmyn [*showing his arms*]. Witness this blood—which
        when by treason sought,
That followed, sir, which to myself I ought.

    Zulema. His hate to thee was grounded on a grudge,
Which all our generous Zegrys just did judge:
Thy villain-blood thou openly didst place
Above the purple of our kingly race.

    Boabdelin. From equal stems their blood both houses
        draw,
They from Morocco, you from Cordova.

    Hamet. Their mongrel race is mixed with Christian
        breed;
Hence 'tis that they those dogs in prisons feed.

    Abdelmelech. Our holy prophet wills, that charity
Should even to birds and beasts extended be:
None knows what fate is for himself designed;
The thought of human chance should make us kind.

    Gomel. We waste that time we to revenge should give:
Fall on: let no Abencerrago live.

                [*Advancing before the rest of his party.*
                ALMANZOR, *advancing on the other side,*
                and describing a line with his sword.

    Almanzor. Upon thy life pass not this middle space;
Sure death stands guarding the forbidden place.

    Gomel. To dare that death, I will approach yet nigher
Thus,—wert thou compassed in with circling fire.
                          [*They fight.*

    Boabdelin. Disarm them both; if they resist you, kill.
          [ALMANZOR, *in the midst of the guards, kills*
          GOMEL, *and then is disarmed.*

    Almanzor. Now you have but the leavings of my will.

    Boabdelin. Kill him! this insolent unknown shall fall,
And be the victim to atone you all.

    Ozmyn. If he must die, not one of us will live:
That life he gave for us, for him we give.

    Boabdelin. It was a traitor's voice that spoke those
        words;
So are you all, who do not sheathe your swords.

    Zulema. Outrage unpunished, when a prince is by,

Forfeits to scorn the rights of majesty:
No subject his protection can expect,
Who what he owes himself does first neglect.

Abenamar. This stranger, sir, is he,
Who lately in the Vivarambla place
Did, with so loud applause, your triumphs grace.

Boabdelin. The word which I have given, I'll not revoke;
If he be brave, he's ready for the stroke.

Almanzor. No man has more contempt than I of breath
But whence hast thou the right to give me death?
Obeyed as sovereign by thy subjects be,
But know, that I alone am king of me.
I am as free as nature first made man,
Ere the base laws of servitude began,
When wild in woods the noble savage ran.

Boabdelin. Since, then, no power above your own you
    know,
Mankind should use you like a common foe;
You should be hunted like a beast of prey;
By your own law I take your life away.

Almanzor. My laws are made but only for my sake;
No king against himself a law can make.
If thou pretend'st to be a prince like me,
Blame not an act, which should thy pattern be.
I saw the oppressed, and thought it did belong
To a king's office to redress the wrong:
I brought that succour, which thou ought'st to bring,
And so, in nature, am thy subjects' king.

Boabdelin. I do not want your counsel to direct,
Or aid to help me punish or protect.

Almanzor. Thou want'st them both, or better thou
    wouldst know,
Than to let factions in thy kingdom grow.
Divided interests, while thou think'st to sway,
Draw, like two brooks, thy middle stream away:
For though they band and jar, yet both combine
To make their greatness by the fall of thine.
Thus, like a buckler, thou art held in sight,
While they behind thee with each other fight.

Boabdelin. Away, and execute him instantly!
                                    [*To his Guards.*

Almanzor. Stand off; I have not leisure yet to die.

To them, enter ABDALLA, *hastily.*

Abdalla. Hold, sir! for heaven's sake hold!
Defer this noble stranger's punishment,
Or your rash orders, you will soon repent.
    Boabdelin. Brother, you know not yet his insolence.
    Abdalla. Upon yourself you punish his offence:
If we treat gallant strangers in this sort,
Mankind will shun the inhospitable court;
And who, henceforth, to our defence will come,
If death must be the brave Almanzor's doom?
From Africa I drew him to your aid,
And for his succour have his life betrayed.
    Boabdelin. Is this the Almanzor whom at Fez you
        knew,
When first their swords the Xeriff [7] brothers drew?
    Abdalla. This, sir, is he, who for the elder fought.
And to the juster cause the conquest brought;
Till the proud Santo, seated on the throne,
Disdained the service he had done to own:
Then to the vanquished part his fate he led:
The vanquished triumphed, and the victor fled.
Vast is his courage, boundless is his mind,
Rough as a storm, and humorous as wind:
Honour's the only idol of his eyes;
The charms of beauty like a pest he flies;
And, raised by valour from a birth unknown,
Acknowledges no power above his own.
                    [BOABDELIN *coming to* ALMANZOR.
    Boabdelin. Impute your danger to our ignorance:
The bravest men are subject most to chance:
Granada much does to your kindness owe;
But towns, expecting sieges, cannot show
More honour, than to invite you to a foe.
    Almanzor. I do not doubt but I have been to blame:
But, to pursue the end for which I came,
Unite your subjects first; then let us go,
And pour their common rage upon the foe.
    Boabdelin [*to the Factions*]. Lay down your arms, and
        let me beg you cease
Your enmities.
    Zulema. We will not hear of peace.

[7] The royal family of Morocco.—ED.

Till we by force have first revenged our slain.

Abdelmelech. The action we have done we will maintain.

Selin. Then let the king depart, and we will try
Our cause by arms.

Zulema. For us and victory.

Boabdelin. A king entreats you.

Almanzor. What subjects will precarious kings regard?
A beggar speaks too softly to be heard:
Lay down your arms! 'tis I command you now.
Do it—or, by our prophet's soul I vow,
My hands shall right your king on him I seize.
Now let me see whose look but disobeys.

All. Long live king Mahomet Boabdelin!

Almanzor. No more; but hushed as midnight silence
    go:
He will not have your acclamations now.
Hence, you unthinking crowd!—
            [*The Common People go off on both parties.*
Empire, thou poor and despicable thing,
When such as these make or unmake a king!

Abdalla. How much of virtue lies in one great soul,
                        [*Embracing him.*
Whose single force can multitudes control!
                        [*A trumpet within.*

Enter a Messenger.

Messenger. The Duke of Arcos, sir,
Does with a trumpet from the foe appear.

Boabdelin. Attend him; he shall have his audience here.

Enter the DUKE OF ARCOS.

Duke of Arcos. The monarchs of Castile and Arragon
Have sent me to you, to demand this town,
To which their just and rightful claim is known.

Boabdelin. Tell Ferdinand, my right to it appears
By long possession of eight hundred years:
When first my ancestors from Afric sailed,
In Rodrique's death your Gothic title failed.

Duke of Arcos. The successors of Rodrique still remain,
And ever since have held some part of Spain:
Even in the midst of your victorious powers,
The Asturias, and all Portugal, were ours.

You have no right, except you force allow;
And if yours then was just, so ours is now.

   Boabdelin. 'Tis true from force the noblest title springs;
I therefore hold from that, which first made kings.

   Duke of Arcos. Since then by force you prove your title
     true,
Ours must be just, because we claim from you.
When with your father you did jointly reign,
Invading with your Moors the south of Spain,
I, who that day the Christians did command,
Then took, and brought you bound to Ferdinand.

   Boabdelin. I'll hear no more; defer what you would
     say:
In private we'll discourse some other day.

   Duke of Arcos. Sir, you shall hear, however you are
     loth,
That, like a perjured prince, you broke your oath:
To gain your freedom you a contract signed,
By which your crown you to my king resigned,
From thenceforth as his vassal holding it,
And paying tribute such as he thought fit;
Contracting, when your father came to die,
To lay aside all marks of royalty,
And at Purchena privately to live,
Which in exchange, king Ferdinand did give.

   Boabdelin. The force used on me made that contract
     void.

   Duke of Arcos. Why have you then its benefits enjoyed?
By it you had not only freedom then,
But, since, had aid of money and of men;
And, when Granada for your uncle held,
You were by us restored, and he expelled.
Since that, in peace we let you reap your grain,
Recalled our troops, that used to beat your plain,
And more——

   Almanzor. Yes, yes, you did with wondrous care,
Against his rebels prosecute the war,
While he secure in your protection slept;
For him you took, but for yourselves you kept.
Thus, as some fawning usurer does feed,
With present sums, the unwary unthrift's need,
You sold your kindness at a boundless rate,
And then o'erpaid the debt from his estate;

Which, mouldering piecemeal, in your hands did fall
Till now at last you came to swoop it all.
 Duke of Arcos. The wrong you do my king I cannot
  bear;
Whose kindness you would odiously compare.—
The estate was his; which, yet since you deny,
He's now content, in his own wrong, to buy.
 Almanzor. And he shall buy it dear what his he calls!
We will not give one stone from out these walls.
 Boabdelin. Take this for answer, then,—
Whate'er your arms have conquered of my land,
I will, for peace, resign to Ferdinand.—
To harder terms my mind I cannot bring;
But, as I still have lived, will die a king.
 Duke of Arcos. Since thus you have resolved, hence-
  forth prepare
For all the last extremities of war:
My king his hope from heaven's assistance draws.
 Almanzor. The Moors have heaven, and me, to assist
  their cause.   [*Exit* ARCOS.

Enter ESPERANZA.

 Esperanza. Fair Almahide,
(Who did with weeping eyes these discords see,
And fears the omen may unlucky be,)
Prepares a zambra to be danced this night,
In hope soft pleasures may your minds unite.
 Boabdelin. My mistress gently chides the fault I made:
But tedious business has my love delayed,—
Business, which dares the joys of kings invade.
 Almanzor. First let us sally out, and meet the foe.
 Abdalla. Led on by you, we on to triumph go.
 Boabdelin. Then with the day let war and tumult cease;
The night be sacred to our love and peace:
'Tis just some joys on weary kings should wait;
'Tis all we gain by being slaves to state.   [*Exeunt.*

ACT II

SCENE I

Enter ABDALLA, ABDELMELECH, OZMYN, ZULEMA, *and*
HAMET, *as returning from the sally.*

ABDALLA. This happy day does to Granada bring
A lasting peace, and triumphs to the king!—
The two fierce factions will no longer jar,
Since they have now been brothers in the war.
Those who, apart, in emulation fought,
The common danger to one body brought;
And, to his cost, the proud Castilian finds
Our Moorish courage in united minds.

    Abdelmelech. Since to each other's aid our lives we owe,
Lose we the name of faction, and of foe;
Which I to Zulema can bear no more,
Since Lyndaraxa's beauty I adore.

    Zulema. I am obliged to Lyndaraxa's charms,
Which gain the conquest I should lose by arms;
And wish my sister may continue fair,
That I may keep a good,
Of whose possession I should else despair.

    Ozmyn. While we indulge our common happiness,
He is forgot, by whom we all possess;
The brave Almanzor, to whose arms we owe
All that we did, and all that we shall do;
Who, like a tempest, that outrides the wind,
Made a just battle ere the bodies joined.

    Abdelmelech. His victories we scarce could keep in view,
Or polish them so fast as he rough-drew.

    Abdalla. Fate, after him, below with pain did move,
And victory could scarce keep pace above:
Death did at length so many slain forget,
And lost the tale, and took them by the great.[8]

Enter ALMANZOR *with the* DUKE OF ARCOS, *prisoner.*

    Hamet. See, here he comes,
And leads in triumph him, who did command

8 "Wholesale."

The vanquished army of king Ferdinand.

    Almanzor [*to the* DUKE]. Thus far your master's arms
      a fortune find
Below the swelled ambition of his mind;
And Allah shuts a misbeliever's reign
From out the best and goodliest part of Spain.
Let Ferdinand Calabrian conquests make,
And from the French contested Milan take;
Let him new worlds discover to the old,
And break up shining mountains, big with gold;
Yet he shall find this small domestic foe,
Still sharp and pointed, to his bosom grow.

    Duke of Arcos. Of small advantages too much you
      boast;
You beat the out-guards of my master's host;
This little loss, in our vast body, shows
So small, that half have never heard the news.
Fame's out of breath, ere she can fly so far,
To tell them all, that you have e'er made war.

    Almanzor. It pleases me your army is so great;
For now I know there's more to conquer yet.
By heaven! I'll see what troops you have behind;
I'll face this storm, that thickens in the wind;
And, with bent forehead, full against it go,
Till I have found the last and utmost foe.

    Duke of Arcos. Believe, you shall not long attend in
      vain:
To-morrow's dawn shall cover all the plain;
Bright arms shall flash upon you from afar,
A wood of lances, and a moving war.
But I, unhappy, in my bonds, must yet
Be only pleased to hear of your defeat,
And with a slave's inglorious ease remain,
Till conquering Ferdinand has broke my chain.

    Almanzor. Vain man, thy hopes of Ferdinand are weak!
I hold thy chain too fast for him to break.
But, since thou threaten'st us, I'll set thee free,
That I again may fight, and conquer thee.

    Duke of Arcos. Old as I am, I take thee at thy word,
And will to-morrow thank thee with my sword.

    Almanzor. I'll go, and instantly acquaint the king,
And sudden orders for thy freedom bring;
Thou canst not be so pleased at liberty

As I shall be to find thou darest be free.
> [*Exeunt* ALMANZOR, ARCOS, *and the rest,*
> *excepting only* ABDALLA *and* ZULEMA.

Abdalla. Of all those Christians who infest this town,
This Duke of Arcos is of most renown.

Zulema. Oft have I heard, that in your father's reign,
His bold adventurers beat the neighbouring plain;
Then under Ponce Leon's name he fought,
And from our triumphs many prizes brought;
Till in disgrace from Spain at length he went,
And since continued in long banishment.

Abdalla. But, see, your beauteous sister does appear.

Enter LYNDARAXA.

Zulema. By my desire she came to find me here.
> [ZULEMA *and* LYNDARAXA *whisper; then* ZULEMA
> *goes out, and* LYNDARAXA *is going after.*

Abdalla. Why, fairest Lyndaraxa, do you fly
> [*Staying her.*
A prince, who at your feet is proud to die?

Lyndaraxa. Sir, I should blush to own so rude a thing,
> [*Staying.*
As 'tis to shun the brother of my king.

Abdalla. In my hard fortune, I some ease should find,
Did your disdain extend to all mankind.
But give me leave to grieve, and to complain,
That you give others what I beg in vain.

Lyndaraxa. Take my esteem, if you on that can live;
For, frankly, sir, 'tis all I have to give:
If from my heart you ask or hope for more,
I grieve the place is taken up before.

Abdalla. My rival merits you.—
To Abdelmelech I will justice do;
For he wants worth, who dares not praise a foe.

Lyndaraxa. That for his virtue, sir, you make defence,
Shows in your own a noble confidence.
But him defending, and excusing me,
I know not what can your advantage be.

Abdalla. I fain would ask, ere I proceed in this,
If, as by choice, you are by promise his?

Lyndaraxa. The engagement only in my love does lie,
But that's a knot which you can ne'er untie.

Abdalla. When cities are besieged, and treat to yield,

If there appear relievers from the field,
The flag of parley may be taken down,
Till the success of those without is known.

Lyndaraxa. Though Abdelmelech has not yet possest,
Yet I have sealed the treaty in[9] my breast.

Abdalla. Your treaty has not tied you to a day;
Some chance might break it, would you but delay.
If I can judge the secrets of your heart,
Ambition in it has the greatest part;
And wisdom, then, will show some difference
Betwixt a private person and a prince.

Lyndaraxa. Princes are subjects still:—
Subject and subject can small difference bring:
The difference is 'twixt subjects and a king.
And since, sir, you are none, your hopes remove;
For less than empire I'll not change my love.

Abdalla. Had I a crown, all I should prize in it,
Should be the power to lay it at your feet.

Lyndaraxa. Had you that crown, which you but wish,
    not hope,
Then, I, perhaps, might stoop, and take it up.
But till your wishes and your hopes agree,
You shall be still a private man with me.

Abdalla. If I am king, and if my brother die,——
Lyndaraxa. Two ifs scarce make one possibility.
Abdalla. The rule of happiness by reason scan;
You may be happy with a private man.

Lyndaraxa. That happiness I may enjoy, 'tis true;
But then that private man must not be you.
Where'er I love, I'm happy in my choice;
If I make you so, you shall pay my price.

Abdalla. Why would you be so great?
Lyndaraxa. Because I've seen,
This day, what 'tis to hope to be a queen.—
Heaven, how you all watched each motion of her eye!
None could be seen while Almahide was by,
Because she is to be—Her Majesty!
Why would I be a queen? Because my face
Would wear the title with a better grace.
If I became it not, yet it would be
Part of your duty, then, to flatter me.
These are but half the charms of being great;

[9] 1st edition "for."

I would be somewhat, that I know not yet:—
Yes! I avow the ambition of my soul,
To be that one to live without control!
And that's another happiness to me,
To be so happy as but one can be.

   Abdalla. Madam,—because I would all doubts remove.—
Would you, were I a king, accept my love?

   Lyndaraxa. I would accept it; and, to show 'tis true,
From any other man as soon as you.

   Abdalla. Your sharp replies make me not love you less;
But make me seek new paths to happiness.—
What I design, by time will best be seen:
You may be mine, and yet may be a queen.
When you are so, your word your love assures.

   Lyndaraxa. Perhaps not love you,—but I will be
      yours.—   [*He offers to take her hand, and kiss it.*
Stay, sir, that grace I cannot yet allow,
Before you set the crown upon my brow.—
That favour which you seek,
Or Abdelmelech, or a king, must have;
When you are so, then you may be my slave.
          [*Exit; but looks smiling back on him.*

   Abdalla. Howe'er imperious in her words she were,
Her parting looks had nothing of severe;
A glancing smile allured me to command,
And her soft fingers gently pressed my hand:
I felt the pleasure glide through every part;
Her hand went through me to my very heart.
For such another pleasure, did he live,
I could my father of a crown deprive.—
Why did I say?
Father!—That impious thought has shocked my mind:
How bold our passions are, and yet how blind—
She's gone; and now,
Methinks, there is less glory in a crown:
My boiling passions settle, and go down.
Like amber chafed, when she is near, she acts;
When further off, inclines, but not attracts.

Enter ZULEMA.

Assist me, Zulema, if thou wouldst be
That friend thou seem'st, assist me against me

Betwixt my love and virtue I am tossed;
This must be forfeited, or that be lost.
I could do much to merit thy applause,—
Help me to fortify the better cause,
My honour is not wholly put to flight,
But would, if seconded, renew the fight.

Zulema. I met my sister, but I do not see
What difficulty in your choice can be:
She told me all; and 'tis so plain a case,
You need not ask what counsel to embrace.

Abdalla. I stand reproved, that I did doubt at all;
My waiting virtue stayed but for thy call:
'Tis plain that she, who, for a kingdom, now
Would sacrifice her love, and break her vow,
Not out of love, but interest, acts alone,
And would, even in my arms, lie thinking of a throne.

Zulema. Add to the rest, this one reflection more:
When she is married, and you still adore,
Think then,—and think what comfort it will bring,—
She had been mine,
Had I but only dared to be a king!

Abdalla. I hope you only would my honour try;
I'm loth to think you virtue's enemy.

Zulema. If, when a crown and mistress are in place,
Virtue intrudes, with her lean holy face,
Virtue's then mine, and not I virtue's foe.
Why does she come where she has nought to do?
Let her with anchorites, not with lovers, lie;
Statesmen and they keep better company.

Abdalla. Reason was given to curb our headstrong will.

Zulema. Reason but shows a weak physician's skill;
Gives nothing, while the raging fit does last,
But stays to cure it, when the worst is past.
Reason's a staff for age, when nature's gone;
But youth is strong enough to walk alone.

Abdalla. In cursed ambition I no rest should find,
But must for ever lose my peace of mind.

Zulema. Methinks that peace of mind were bravely lost.
A crown whate'er we give, is worth the cost.

Abdalla. Justice distributes to each man his right;
But what she gives not, should I take by might?

Zulema. If justice will take all, and nothing give,
Justice, methinks, is not distributive.

Abdalla. Had fate so pleased, I had been eldest born,
And then, without a crime, the crown had worn!—
　　Zulema. Would you so please, fate yet a way would
　　　find;
Man makes his fate according to his mind.
The weak low spirit fortune makes her slave;
But she's a drudge when hectored by the brave:
If fate weaves common thread, he'll change the doom,
And with new purple spread a nobler loom.
　　Abdalla. No more!—I will usurp the royal seat;
Thou, who hast made me wicked, make me great.
　　Zulema. Your way is plain; the death of Tarifa
Does on the king our Zegrys' hatred draw;
Though with our enemies in show we close,
'Tis but while we to purpose can be foes.
Selin, who heads us, would revenge his son;
But favour hinders justice to be done.
Proud Ozmyn with the king his power maintains,
And, in him, each Abencerrago reigns.
　　Abdalla. What face of any title can I bring?
　　Zulema. The right an eldest son has to be a king,
Your father was at first a private man,
And got your brother ere his reign began:
When, by his valour, he the crown had won,
Then you were born a monarch's eldest son.
　　Abdalla. To sharp-eyed reason this would seem untrue;
But reason I through love's false optics view.
　　Zulema. Love's mighty power has led me captive too;
I am in it unfortunate as you.
　　Abdalla. Our loves and fortunes shall together go;
Thou shalt be happy, when I first am so.
　　Zulema. The Zegrys at old Selin's house are met,
Where, in close council, for revenge they sit:
There we our common interests will unite;
You their revenge shall own, and they your right.
One thing I had forgot which may import:
I met Almanzor coming back from court,
But with a discomposed and speedy pace,
A fiery colour kindling all his face:
The king his prisoner's freedom has denied,
And that refusal has provoked his pride.
　　Abdalla. Would he were ours!—
I'll try to gild the injustice of his cause,

And court his valour with a vast applause.

Zulema. The bold are but the instruments o' the wise;
They undertake the dangers we advise:
And, while our fabric with their pains we raise,
We take the profit, and pay them with praise.   *[Exeunt.*

ACT III

SCENE I

Enter ALMANZOR *and* ABDALLA.

ALMANZOR. That he should dare to do me this disgrace!—
Is fool, or coward, writ upon my face?
Refuse my prisoner!—I such means will use,
He shall not have a prisoner to refuse.

Abdalla. He said, you were not by your promise tied;
That he absolved your word, when he denied.

Almanzor. He break my promise and absolve my vow!
'Tis more than Mahomet himself can do!—
The word, which I have given, shall stand like fate;
Not like the king's, that weathercock of state.
He stands so high, with so unfixed a mind,
Two factions turn him with each blast of wind:
But now, he shall not veer! my word is past;
I'll take his heart by the roots, and hold it fast.

Abdalla. You have your vengeance in your hand this
    hour;
Make me the humble creature of your power:
The Granadines will gladly me obey
(Tired with so base and impotent a sway);
And, when I show my title, you shall see,
I have a better right to reign than he.

Almanzor. It is sufficient that you make the claim;
You wrong our friendship when your right you name.
When for myself I fight, I weigh the cause,
But friendship will admit of no such laws:
That weighs by the lump; and, when the cause is light,
Puts kindness in to set the balance right.
True, I would wish my friend the juster side;
But, in the unjust, my kindness more is tried:
And all the opposition I can bring,

Is, that I fear to make you such a king.

Abdalla. The majesty of kings we should not blame,
When royal minds adorn the royal name;
The vulgar, greatness too much idolise,
But haughty subjects it too much despise.

Almanzor. I only speak of him,
Whom pomp and greatness sit so loose about,
That he wants majesty to fill them out.

Abdalla. Haste, then, and lose no time!—
The business must be enterprised this night:
We must surprise the court in its delight.

Almanzor. For you to will, for me 'tis to obey:
But I would give a crown in open day;
And, when the Spaniards their assault begin,
At once beat those without, and these within.

                         [*Exit* ALMANZOR.

Enter ABDELMELECH.

Abdelmelech. Abdalla, hold!—There's somewhat I in-
    tend
To speak, not as your rival, but your friend.

Abdalla. If as a friend, I am obliged to hear;
And what a rival says I cannot fear.

Abdelmelech. Think, brave Abdalla, what it is you do:
Your quiet, honour, and our friendship too,
All for a fickle beauty you forego.
Think, and turn back, before it be too late.
Behold in me the example of your fate:
I am your sea-mark; and, though wrecked and lost,
My ruins stand to warn you from the coast.

Abdalla. Your counsels, noble Abdelmelech, move
My reason to accept them, not my love.
Ah, why did heaven leave man so weak defence,
To trust frail reason with the rule of sense!
'Tis overpoised and kicked up in the air,
While sense weighs down the scale, and keeps it there;
Or, like a captive king, 'tis borne away,
And forced to count'nance its own rebels' sway.

Abdelmelech. No, no; our reason was not vainly lent;
Nor is a slave, but by its own consent:
If reason on his subject's triumph wait,
An easy king deserves no better fate.

Abdalla. You speak too late; my empire's lost too far:
I cannot fight.

Abdelmelech. Then make a flying war;
Dislodge betimes before you are beset.

Abdalla. Her tears, her smiles, her every look's a net.
Her voice is like a Syren's of the land;
And bloody hearts lie panting in her hand.

Abdelmelech. This do you know, and tempt the danger
still?

Abdalla. Love, like a lethargy, has seized my will.
I'm not myself, since from her sight I went;
I lean my trunk that way, and there stand bent.
As one, who, in some frightful dream, would shun
His pressing foe, labours in vain to run;
And his own slowness, in his sleep, bemoans,
With thick short sighs, weak cries, and tender groans,
So I——

Abdelmelech. Some friend, in charity, should shake,
And rouse, and call you loudly till you wake.
Too well I know her blandishments to gain,
Usurper-like, till settled in her reign;
Then proudly she insults, and gives you cares,
and jealousies, short hopes, and long despairs.
To this hard yoke you must hereafter bow,
Howe'er she shines all golden to you now.

Abdalla. Like him, who on the ice
Slides swiftly on, and sees the water near.
Yet cannot stop himself in his career,
So am I carried. This enchanted place,
Like Circe's isle, is peopled with a race
Of dogs and swine; yet, though their fate I know,
I look with pleasure, and am turning too.

[LYNDARAXA *passes over the stage.*

Abdelmelech. Fly, fly, before the allurements of her face,
Ere she return with some resistless grace,
And with new magic cover all the place.

Abdalla. I cannot, will not,—nay, I would not fly:
I'll love, be blind, be cozened till I die;
And you, who bid me wiser counsel take,
I'll hate, and, if I can, I'll kill you for her sake.

Abdelmelech. Even I, that counselled you, that choice
approve:

I'll hate you blindly, and her blindly love.
Prudence, that stemmed the stream, is out of breath;
And to go down it is the easier death.

LYNDARAXA *re-enters, and smiles on* ABDALLA.

[*Exit* ABDALLA.

Abdelmelech. That smile on Prince Abdalla seems to
say,
You are not in your killing mood to-day:
Men brand, indeed, your sex with cruelty,
But you're too good to see poor lovers die.
This godlike pity in you I extol;
And more, because, like heaven's, 'tis general.

Lyndaraxa. My smile implies not that I grant his suit:
'Twas but a bare return of his salute.

Abdelmelech. It said, you were engaged, and I in place;
But, to please both, you would divide the grace.

Lyndaraxa. You've cause to be contented with your
part,
When he has but the look, and you the heart.

Abdelmelech. In giving but that look, you give what's
mine:
I'll not one corner of a glance resign.
All's mine; and I am covetous of my store:
I have not love enough, I'll tax you more.

Lyndaraxa. I gave not love; 'twas but civility:
He is a prince; that's due to his degree.

Abdelmelech. That prince you smiled on is my rival still,
And should, if me you loved, be treated ill.

Lyndaraxa. I know not how to show so rude a spite.

Abdelmelech. That is, you know not how to love aright;
Or, if you did, you would more difference see
Betwixt our souls, than 'twixt our quality.
Mark, if his birth makes any difference,
If to his words it adds one grain of sense.
That duty, which his birth can make his due,
I'll pay, but it shall not be paid by you:
For, if a prince courts her whom I adore,
He is my rival, and a prince no more.

Lyndaraxa. And when did I my power so far resign,
That you should regulate each look of mine?

Abdelmelech. Then, when you gave your love, you gave
that power.

Lyndaraxa. 'Twas during pleasure, 'tis revoked this hour.
Now, call me false, and rail on womankind,—
'Tis all the remedy you're like to find.

Abdelmelech. Yes, there's one more;
I'll hate you, and this visit is my last.

Lyndaraxa. Do't if you can; you know I hold you fast:
Yet, for your quiet, would you could resign
Your love, as easily as I do mine.

Abdelmelech. Furies and hell, how unconcerned she
    speaks!
With what indifference all her vows she breaks!
Curse on me, but she smiles!

Lyndaraxa. That smile's a part of love, and all's your
    due:
I take it from the prince, and give it you.

Abdelmelech. Just heaven, must my poor heart your
    May-game prove,
To bandy, and make children's play in love?

　　　　　　　　　　　　　　　　　　　[*Half crying.*

Ah! how have I this cruelty deserved?
I, who so truly and so long have served!
And left so easily! oh, cruel maid!
So easily! it was too unkindly said.
That heart, which could so easily remove,
Was never fixed, nor rooted deep in love.

Lyndaraxa. You lodged it so uneasy in your breast,
I thought you had been weary of the guest.
First, I was treated like a stranger there
But, when a household friend I did appear,
You thought, it seems, I could not live elsewhere.
Then, by degrees your feigned respect withdrew;
You marked my actions, and my guardian grew.
But I am not concerned your acts to blame:
My heart to yours but upon liking came;
And, like a bird, whom prying boys molest,
Stays not to breed, where she had built her nest.

Abdelmelech. I have done ill,
And dare not ask you to be less displeased;
Be but more angry, and my pain is eased.

Lyndaraxa. If I should be so kind a fool, to take
This little satisfaction which you make,
I know you would presume some other time
Upon my goodness, and repeat your crime.

Abdelmelech. Oh never, never, upon no pretence;
My life's too short to expiate this offence.

Lyndaraxa. No, now I think on't, 'tis in vain to try;
'Tis in your nature, and past remedy,
You'll still disquiet my too loving heart:
Now we are friends, 'tis best for both to part.

> [*He takes her hand.*

Abdelmelech. By this—Will you not give me leave to
swear?

Lyndaraxa. You would be perjured if you should, I
fear:
And, when I talk with Prince Abdalla next,
I with your fond suspicion shall be vext.

Abdelmelech. I cannot say I'll conquer jealousy,
But, if you'll freely pardon me, I'll try.

Lyndaraxa. And, till you that submissive servant prove,
I never can conclude you truly love.

To them, the King, ALMAHIDE, ABENAMAR,
ESPERANZA, Guards, Attendants.

Boabdelin. Approach, my Almahide, my charming fair,
Blessing of peace, and recompence of war.
This night is yours; and may your life still be
The same in joy, though not solemnity.

THE ZAMBRA DANCE

SONG [10]

I

Beneath a myrtle shade.
Which love for none but happy lovers made,
I slept; and straight my love before me brought
Phyllis, the object of my waking thought.
Undressed she came my flames to meet,
While love strewed flowers beneath her feet;
Flowers which, so pressed by her, became more sweet.

II

From the bright vision's head
A careless veil of lawn was loosely spread:

---

[10] In the first edition this song appears next to the epilogue, with the
warning "misplaced, sung at the dance or Zambra in the third Act."

From her white temples fell her shaded hair
Like cloudy sunshine, not too brown nor fair;
Her hands, her lips, did love inspire;
Her every grace my heart did fire;
But most her eyes, which languished with desire.

III

Ah, charming fair, said I,
How long can you my bliss and yours deny?
By nature and by love, this lonely shade
Was for revenge of suffering lovers made.
Silence and shades with love agree;
Both shelter you and favour me:
You cannot blush, because I cannot see.

IV

No, let me die, she said,
Rather than lose the spotless name of maid!—
Faintly, methought, she spoke; for all the while
She bid me not believe her, with a smile.
Then die, said I: She still denied;
And is it thus, thus, thus, she cried,
You use a harmless maid?—and so she died!

V

I waked, and straight I knew,
I loved so well, it made my dream prove true:
Fancy, the kinder mistress of the two,
Fancy had done what Phyllis would not do!
Ah, cruel nymph, cease your disdain,
While I can dream you scorn in vain,—
Asleep or waking you must ease my pain.

[*After the dance, a tumultuous noise of drums and
trumpets.*

To them OZMYN; *his sword drawn.*

Ozmyn. Arm, quickly arm; yet all, I fear, too late;
The enemy's already at the gate.
Boabdelin. The Christians are dislodged; what foe is
near?
Ozmyn. The Zegrys are in arms, and almost here:
The streets with torches shine, with shoutings ring,
And Prince Abdalla is proclaimed the king.

What man could do, I have already done,
But bold Almanzor fiercely leads them on.

    Abenamar. The Alhambra yet is safe in my command;
                                   [To the King.
Retreat you thither, while their shock we stand.

    Boabdelin. I cannot meanly for my life provide;
I'll either perish in't, or stem this tide.
To guard the palace, Ozmyn, be your care:
If they o'ercome, no sword will hurt the fair.

    Ozmyn. I'll either die, or I'll make good the place.

    Abdelmelech. And I with these will bold Almanzor face.
        [Exeunt all but the Ladies. *An alarum within.*

    Almahide. What dismal planet did my triumphs light!
Discord the day, and death does rule the night:
The noise my soul does through my senses wound.

    Lyndaraxa. Methinks it is a noble, sprightly sound,
The trumpet's clangour, and the clash of arms!
This noise may chill your blood, but mine it warms.
        [Shouting and clashing of swords within.
We have already passed the Rubicon;
The dice are mine; now, fortune, for a throne!
     [A shout within, and clashing of swords afar off.
The sound goes farther off, and faintly dies;
Curse of this going back, these ebbing cries!
Ye winds, waft hither sounds more strong and quick;
Beat faster, drums, and mingle deaths more thick.
I'll to the turrets of the palace go,
And add new fire to those that fight below:
Thence, Hero-like, with torches by my side,
(Far be the omen, though) my love will guide.
No; like his better fortune I'll appear,
With open arms, loose veil, and flowing hair
Just flying forward from my rolling sphere:
My smiles shall make Abdalla more than man;
Let him look up, and perish if he can.   *[Exit.*

An alarum nearer: Then enter ALMANZOR *and* SELIN *at the
    head of the Zegrys;* OZMYN, *prisoner.*

    Almanzor. We have not fought enough; they fly too
        soon;
And I am grieved the noble sport is done.
This only man, of all whom chance did bring
                     [Pointing to OZMYN.

To meet my arms, was worth the conquering.
His brave resistance did my fortune grace;
So slow, so threat'ning forward, he gave place.
His chains be easy, and his usage fair.

Selin. I beg you would commit him to my care.

Almanzor. Next, the brave Spaniard free without delay;
And with a convoy send him safe away.   [*Exit a* Guard.

To them HAMET *and others.*

Hamet. The king by me salutes you; and, to show
That to your valour he his crown does owe,
Would from your mouth I should the word receive,
And that to these you would your orders give.

Almanzor. He much o'errates the little I have done.

> [ALMANZOR *goes to the door, and there seems to
> give out orders by sending people several
> ways.*

Selin [*to* OZMYN]. Now, to revenge the murder of my
son,
To-morrow for thy certain death prepare;
This night I only leave thee to despair.

Ozmyn. Thy idle menaces I do not fear:
My business was to die or conquer here.
Sister, for you I grieve I could no more:
My present state betrays my want of power;
But, when true courage is of force bereft,
Patience, the only fortitude, is left.   [*Exit with* SELIN.

Almahide. Ah, Esperanza, what for me remains
But death, or, worse than death, inglorious chains!

Esperanza. Madam, you must not to despair give place;
Heaven never meant misfortune to that face.
Suppose there were no justice in your cause,
Beauty's a bribe that gives her judges laws.
That you are brought to this deplored estate,
Is but the ingenious flattery of your fate;
Fate fears her succour, like an alms, to give;
And would you, God-like, from yourself should live.

Almahide. Mark but how terribly his eyes appear!
And yet there's something roughly noble there,
Which, in unfashioned nature, looks divine,
And, like a gem, does in the quarry shine.

> [ALMANZOR *returns; she falls at his feet, being
> veiled.*

Almahide. Turn, mighty conqueror, turn your face this
way,
Do not refuse to hear the wretched pray!
   Almanzor. What business can this woman have with
me?
   Almahide. That of the afflicted to the Deity.
So may your arm success in battle find;
So may the mistress of your vows be kind,
If you have any; or, if you have none,
So may your liberty be still your own.
   Almanzor. Yes, I will turn my face, but not my mind:
You bane and soft destruction of mankind,
What would you have with me?
   Almahide. I beg the grace   [*Unveiling.*
You would lay by those terrors of your face.
Till calmness to your eyes you first restore,
I am afraid, and I can beg no more.
   Almanzor [*looking fixedly on her*]. Well; my fierce
visage shall not murder you.
Speak quickly, woman; I have much to do.
   Almahide. Where should I find the heart to speak one
word?
Your voice, sir, is as killing as your sword.
As you have left the lightning of your eye,
So would you please to lay your thunder by.
   Almanzor. I'm pleased and pained, since first her eyes
I saw,
As I were stung with some tarantula.
Arms, and the dusty field, I less admire,
And soften strangely in some new desire;
Honour burns in me not so fiercely bright,
But pale as fires when mastered by the light:
Even while I speak and look, I change yet more,
And now am nothing that I was before.
I'm numbed, and fixed, and scarce my eyeballs move;
I fear it is the lethargy of love!
'Tis he; I feel him now in every part:
Like a new lord he vaunts about my heart;
Surveys, in state, each corner of my breast,
While poor fierce I, that was, am dispossessed.
I'm bound; but I will rouse my rage again;
And, though no hope of liberty remain,

I'll fright my keeper when I shake my chain.
You are——   [*Angrily.*

    Almahide. I know I am your captive, sir.

    Almanzor. You are—You shall—And I can scarce forbear——

    Almahide. Alas!

    Almanzor. 'Tis all in vain; it will not do: [*Aside.*
I cannot now a seeming anger show:
My tongue against my heart no aid affords;
For love still rises up, and chokes my words.

    Almahide. In half this time a tempest would be still.

    Almanzor. 'Tis you have raised that tempest in my will.
I wonnot love you; give me back my heart;
But give it, as you had it, fierce and brave.
It was not made to be a woman's slave:
But, lion-like, has been in deserts bred,
And, used to range, will ne'er be tamely led.
Restore its freedom to my fettered will,
And then I shall have power to use you ill.

    Almahide. My sad condition may your pity move;
But look not on me with the eyes of love:—
I must be brief, though I have much to say.

    Almanzor. No, speak; for I can hear you now all day.
Her sueing soothes me with a secret pride: [*Softly.*
A suppliant beauty cannot be denied: [*Aside.*
Even while I frown, her charms the furrows seize;
And I'm corrupted with the power to please.

    Almahide. Though in your worth no cause of fear I see,
I fear the insolence of victory;
As you are noble, sir, protect me then
From the rude outrage of insulting men.

    Almanzor. Who dares touch her I love? I'm all o'er love:
Nay, I am love; Love shot, and shot so fast,
He shot himself into my breast at last.

    Almahide. You see before you her who should be queen,
Since she is promised to Boabdelin.

    Almanzor. Are you beloved by him? O wretched fate,
First that I love at all; then, loved too late!
Yet, I must love!

    Almahide. Alas, it is in vain;
Fate for each other did not us ordain.
The chances of this day too clearly show

That heaven took care that it should not be so.

    Almanzor. Would heaven had quite forgot me this one
      day!
But fate's yet hot——
I'll make it take a bent another way.
          [*He walks swiftly and discomposedly, studying.*
I bring a claim which does his right remove;
You're his by promise, but you're mine by love.
'Tis all but ceremony which is past;
The knot's to tie which is to make you fast.
Fate gave not to Boabdelin that power;
He wooed you but as my ambassador.

    Almahide. Our souls are tied by holy vows above.

    Almanzor. He signed but his; but I will seal my love.
I love you better, with more zeal than he.

    Almahide. This day
I gave my faith to him, he his to me.

    Almanzor. Good heaven, thy book of fate before me
      lay,
But to tear out the journal of this day:
Or, if the order of the world below
Will not the gap of one whole day allow,
Give me that minute when she made her vow!
That minute, ev'n the happy from their bliss might give;
And those, who live in grief, a shorter time would live.
So small a link, if broke, the eternal chain
Would, like divided waters, join again.——
It wonnot be; the fugitive is gone,
Pressed by the crowd of following minutes on:
That precious moment's out of nature fled,
And in the heap of common rubbish laid,
Of things that once have been, and are decayed.

    Almahide. Your passion, like a fright, suspends my pain;
It meets, o'erpowers, and beats mine back again:
But as, when tides against the current flow,
The native stream runs its own course below,
So, though your griefs possess the upper part,
My own have deeper channels in my heart.

    Almanzor. Forgive that fury which my soul does move;
'Tis the essay of an untaught first love:
Yet rude, unfashioned truth it does express;
'Tis love just peeping in a hasty dress.

Retire, fair creature, to your needful rest;
There's something noble labouring in my breast:
This raging fire, which through the mass does move;
Shall purge my dross, and shall refine my love.
                    [*Exeunt* ALMAHIDE *and* ESPERANZA.
She goes, and I like my own ghost appear;
It is not living when she is not here.

To him ABDALLA *as King, attended.*

Abdalla. My first acknowledgments to heaven are due,
My next, Almanzor, let me pay to you.

Almanzor. A poor surprise, and on a naked foe,
Whatever you confess, is all you owe;
And I no merit own, or understand
That fortune did you justice by my hand:
Yet, if you will that little service pay
With a great favour, I can show the way.

Abdalla. I have a favour to demand of you;
That is, to take the thing for which you sue.

Almanzor. Then, briefly, thus: when I the Albayzyn
          won,
I found the beauteous Almahide alone,
Whose sad condition did my pity move;
And that compassion did produce my love.

Abdalla. This needs no suit; in justice, I declare,
She is your captive by the right of war.

Almanzor. She is no captive then; I set her free;
And, rather than I will her jailer be,
I'll nobly lose her in her liberty.

Abdalla. Your generosity I much approve;
But your excess of that shows want of love.

Almanzor. No, 'tis the excess of love which mounts so
          high,
That seen far off, it lessens to the eye.
Had I not loved her, and had set her free,
That, sir, had been my generosity;
But 'tis exalted passion when I show
I dare be wretched, not to make her so:
And, while another passion fills her breast,
I'll be all wretched rather than half blest.

Abdalla. May your heroic act so prosperous be,
That Almahide may sigh you set her free.

Enter Zulema.

Zulema. Of five tall towers which fortify this town
All but the Alhambra your dominion own:
Now, therefore, boldly I confess a flame,
Which is excused in Almahide's name.
If you the merit of this night regard,
In her possession I have my reward.

Almanzor. She your reward! why, she's a gift so great,
That I myself have not deserved her yet;
And therefore, though I won her with my sword,
I have, with awe, my sacrilege restored.

Zulema. What you deserve
I'll not dispute because I do not know;
This only I will say, she shall not go.

Almanzor. Thou, single, art not worth my answering:
But take what friends, what armies thou canst bring;
What worlds; and, when you are united all,
Then will I thunder in your ears,—She shall.

Zulema. I'll not one tittle of my right resign.—
Sir, your implicit promise made her mine;
When I, in general terms, my love did show,
You swore our fortunes should together go.

Abdalla. The merits of the cause I'll not decide,
But, like my love, I would my gift divide.
Your equal titles then no longer plead;
But one of you, for love of me, recede.

Almanzor. I have receded to the utmost line,
When, by my free consent, she is not mine:
Then let him equally recede with me,
And both of us will join to set her free.

Zulema. If you will free your part of her, you may;
But, sir, I love not your romantic way.
Dream on, enjoy her soul, and set that free;
I'm pleased her person should be left for me.

Almanzor. Thou shalt not wish her thine; thou shalt
          not dare
To be so impudent as to despair.

Zulema. The Zegrys, sir, are all concerned to see
How much their merit you neglect in me.

Hamet. Your slighting Zulema, this very hour,
Will take ten thousand subjects from your power.

Almanzor. What are ten thousand subjects such as they?

If I am scorned——I'll take myself away.

Abdalla. Since both can not possess what both pursue,
I grieve, my friend, the chance should fall on you;
But when you hear what reasons I can urge——

Almanzor. None, none that your ingratitude can purge.
Reason's a trick, when it no grant affords;
It stamps the face of majesty on words.

Abdalla. Your boldness to your services I give:
Now take it, as your full reward,—to live.

Almanzor. To live!
If from thy hands alone my death can be,
I am immortal, and a god to thee.
If I would kill thee now, thy fate's so low,
That I must stoop ere I can give the blow:
But mine is fixed so far above thy crown,
That all thy men,
Piled on thy back, can never pull it down.
But at my ease thy destiny I send,
By ceasing from this hour to be thy friend.
Like heaven, I need but only to stand still,
And, not concurring in thy life, I kill.
Thou canst no title to my duty bring;
I'm not thy subject, and my soul's thy king.
Farewell. When I am gone,
There's not a star of thine dare stay with thee:
I'll whistle thy tame fortune after me;
And whirl fate with me wheresoe'er I fly,
As winds drive storms before them in the sky.   [*Exit.*

Zulema. Let not this insolent unpunished go;
Give your commands; your justice is too slow.

[ZULEMA, HAMET, *and others are
going after him.*

Abdalla. Stay, and what part he pleases let him take:
I know my throne's too strong for him to shake.
But my fair mistress I too long forget;
The crown I promised is not offered yet.
Without her presence all my joys are vain,
Empire a curse, and life itself a pain.   [*Exeunt.*

ACT IV

SCENE I

Enter BOABDELIN, ABENAMAR, *and* Guards.

BOABDELIN. Advise, or aid, but do not pity me:
No monarch born can fall to that degree.
Pity descends from kings to all below;
But can, no more than fountains, upward flow.
Witness, just heaven, my greatest grief has been,
I could not make your Almahide a queen.

   Abenamar. I have too long the effects of fortune known,
Either to trust her smiles, or fear her frown.
Since in their first attempt you were not slain,
Your safety bodes you yet a second reign.
The people like a headlong torrent go,
And ev'ry dam they break, or overflow;
But, unopposed, they either lose their force,
Or wind, in volumes, to their former course.

   Boabdelin. In walls we meanly must our hopes enclose,
To wait our friends, and weary out our foes!
While Almahide
To lawless rebels is exposed a prey,
And forced the lustful victor to obey.

   Abenamar. One of my blood, in rules of virtue bred!
Think better of her, and believe she's dead.

Enter ALMANZOR.

   Boabdelin. We are betrayed, the enemy is here;
We have no farther room to hope or fear.

   Almanzor. It is indeed Almanzor whom you see,
But he no longer is your enemy.
You were ungrateful, but your foes were more;
What your injustice lost you, theirs restore.
Make profit of my vengeance while you may,
My two-edged sword can cut the other way.—
I am your fortune, but am swift like her,
And turn my hairy front if you defer:

That hour, when you deliberate, is too late;
I point you the white moment of your fate.
　　Abenamar. Believe him sent as prince Abdalla's spy;
He would betray us to the enemy.
　　Almanzor. Were I, like thee, in cheats of state grown
　　　　old
(Those public markets, where for foreign gold,
The poorer prince is to the richer sold),
Then thou mightst think me fit for that low part;
But I am yet to learn the statesman's art.
My kindness and my hate unmasked I wear;
For friends to trust, and enemies to fear.
My heart's so plain,
That men on every passing thought[11] may look,
Like fishes gliding in a crystal brook;
When troubled most, it does the bottom show,
'Tis weedless all above, and rockless all below.
　　Abenamar. Ere he be trusted, let him then be tried;
He may be false, who once has changed his side.
　　Almanzor. In that you more accuse yourselves than me;
None who are injured can inconstant be.
You were inconstant, you, who did the wrong;
To do me justice does to me belong.
Great souls by kindness only can be tied;
Injured again, again I'll leave your side.
Honour is what myself, and friends, I owe;
And none can lose it who forsake a foe.
Since, then, your foes now happen to be mine,
Though not in friendship, we'll in interest join:
So while my loved revenge is full and high,
I'll give you back your kingdom by the by.
　　Boabdelin. That I so long delayed what you desire,
　　　　　　　　　　　　　　　　[Embracing him.
Was, not to doubt your worth, but to admire.
　　Almanzor. This counsellor an old man's caution shows,
Who fears that little, he has left, to lose:
Age sets a fortune; while youth boldly throws.
But let us first your drooping soldiers cheer;
Then seek out danger, ere it dare appear:
This hour I fix your crown upon your brow;
Next hour fate gives it, but I give it now.　　*[Exeunt.*

---

[11] Folio "through," absurdly.

SCENE II

Enter Lyndaraxa.

Lyndaraxa. O, could I read the dark decrees of fate,
That I might once know whom to love, or hate
For I myself scarce my own thoughts can guess,
So much I find them varied by success.
As in some weather-glass, my love I hold;
Which falls or rises with the heat or cold.—
I will be constant yet, if Fortune can;
I love the king,—let her but name the man.

Enter Halyma.

Halyma. Madam, a gentleman, to me unknown,
Desires that he may speak with you alone.
  Lyndaraxa. Some message from the king—Let him
  appear.

Enter Abdelmelech; *who throws off his disguise.*—
She starts.

Abdelmelech. I see you are amazed that I am here:
But let at once your fear and wonder end.
In the usurper's guards I found a friend,
Who led me to you safe in this disguise.
  Lyndaraxa. Your danger brings this trouble in my
  eyes.—
But what affair this 'venturous visit drew?
  Abdelmelech. The greatest in the world,—the seeing
  you.
  Lyndaraxa. The courage of your love I so admire,
That, to preserve you, you shall straight retire.
                    [*She leads him to the door.*
Go, dear! each minute does new dangers bring;
You will be taken; I expect the king.
  Abdelmelech. The king!—the poor usurper of an hour:
His empire's but a dream of kingly power.—
I warn you, as a lover and a friend,
To leave him, ere his short dominion end:
The soldier I suborned will wait at night,
And shall alone be conscious of your flight.
  Lyndaraxa. I thank you, that you so much care bestow;
But, if his reign be short, I need not go.

For why should I expose my life, and yours,
For what, you say, a little time assures?
   Abdelmelech. My danger in the attempt is very small;
And, if he loves you, yours is none at all.
But, though his ruin be as sure as fate,
Your proof of love to me would come too late.
This trial I in kindness would allow;
'Tis easy: if you love me, show it now.
   Lyndaraxa. It is because I love you, I refuse;
For all the world my conduct would accuse,
If I should go with him I love away:
And, therefore, in strict virtue I will stay.
   Abdelmelech. You would in vain dissemble love to me;
Through that thin veil your artifice I see.
You would expect the event, and then declare;
But do not, do not drive me to despair:
For, if you now refuse with me to fly,
Rather than love you after this, I'll die;
And, therefore, weigh it well before you speak;
My king is safe, his force within not weak.
   Lyndaraxa. The counsel, you have given me, may be wise;
But, since the affair is great, I will advise.
   Abdelmelech. Then that delay I for denial take.

                                    [Is going.
   Lyndaraxa. Stay; you too swift an exposition make.
If I should go, since Zulema will stay,
I should my brother to the king betray.
   Abdelmelech. There is no fear; but, if there were, I see
You value still your brother more than me.—
Farewell! some ease I in your falsehood find;
It lets a beam in, that will clear my mind:
My former weakness I with shame confess,
And, when I see you next, shall love you less.

                                  [Is going again.
   Lyndaraxa. Your faithless dealings you may blush to tell;   *[Weeping.*
This is a maid's reward, who loves too well.—

                                  [He looks back.
Remember that I drew my latest breath,
In charging your unkindness with my death.
   Abdelmelech [*coming back*]. Have I not answered all
you can invent,

Even the least shadow of an argument?

    Lyndaraxa. You want not cunning what you please to
    prove,
But my poor heart knows only how to love;
And, finding this, you tyrannise the more:
'Tis plain, some other mistress you adore;
And now, with studied tricks of subtlety,
You come prepared to lay the fault on me.

                        [Wringing her hands.
But, oh, that I should love so false a man!

    Abdelmelech. Hear me, and then disprove it, if you
    can.

    Lyndaraxa. I'll hear no more; your breach of faith is
    plain:
You would with wit your want of love maintain.
But, by my own experience, I can tell,
They, who love truly, cannot argue well.——
Go, faithless man!
Leave me alone to mourn my misery;
I cannot cease to love you, but I'll die.

               [Leans her head on his arm.

    Abdelmelech. What man but I so long unmoved could
    hear   *[Weeping.*
Such tender passion, and refuse a tear!——
But do not talk of dying any more,
Unless you mean that I should die before.

    Lyndaraxa. I fear your feigned repentance comes too
    late;
I die, to see you still thus obstinate:
But yet, in death my truth of love to show.
Lead me; if I have strength enough, I'll go.

    Abdelmelech. By heaven, you shall not go! I will not be
O'ercome in love or generosity.
All I desire, to end the unlucky strife,
Is but a vow, that you will be my wife.

    Lyndaraxa. To tie me to you by a vow is hard;
It shows, my love you as no tie regard.——
Name anything but that, and I'll agree.

    Abdelmelech. Swear, then, you never will my rival's be.

    Lyndaraxa. Nay, pr'ythee, this is harder than before.——
Name anything, good dear, but that thing more.

    Abdelmelech. Now I too late perceive I am undone;
Living and seeing, to my death I run.

I know you false, yet in your snares I fall;
You grant me nothing, and I grant you all.

    Lyndaraxa. I would grant all; but I must curb my will,
Because I love to keep you jealous still.
In your suspicion I your passion find;
But I will take a time to cure your mind.

    Halyma. O, madam, the new king is drawing near!

    Lyndaraxa. Haste quickly hence, lest he should find
    you here!

    Abdelmelech. How much more wretched than I came,
    I go!
I more my weakness and your falsehood know;
And now must leave you with my greatest foe!

                    [*Exit* ABDELMELECH.

    Lyndaraxa. Go!—How I love thee Heaven can only
    tell:
And yet I love thee, for a subject, well.—
Yet, whatsoever charms a crown can bring,
A subject's greater than a little king.
I will attend till time this throne secure;
And, when I climb, my footing shall be sure.—

                    [*Music without.*

Music! and, I believe, addressed to me.

SONG

I

Wherever I am, and whatever I do,
   My Phyllis is still in my mind;
When angry, I mean not to Phyllis to go,
   My feet, of themselves, the way find;
Unknown to myself I am just at her door,
  And, when I would rail, I can bring out no more,
    Than, Phyllis too fair and unkind!

II

When Phyllis I see, my heart bounds in my breast,
   And the love I would stifle is shown;
But asleep, or awake, I am never at rest,
   When from my eyes Phyllis is gone.
Sometimes a sad dream does delude my sad mind;
But, alas! when I wake, and no Phyllis I find,
    How I sigh to myself all alone!

III

Should a king be my rival in her I adore,
   He should offer his treasure in vain:
O, let me alone to be happy and poor,
   And give me my Phyllis again!
Let Phyllis be mine, and but ever be kind,
I could to a desert with her be confined,
   And envy no monarch his reign.

IV

Alas! I discover too much of my love,
   And she too well knows her own power!
She makes me each day a new martyrdom prove,
   And makes me grow jealous each hour:
But let her each minute torment my poor mind,
I had rather love Phyllis, both false and unkind,
   Than ever be freed from her power.

Enter ABDALLA, *with* Guards.

Abdalla. Now, madam, at your feet a king you see;
Or, rather, if you please, a sceptred slave;
'Tis just you should possess the power you gave.
Had love not made me yours, I yet had been
But the first subject to Boabdelin.
Thus Heaven declares the crown I bring your due;
And had forgot my title, but for you.
   Lyndaraxa. Heaven to your merits will, I hope, be
     kind;
But, sir, it has not yet declared its mind.
'Tis true, it holds the crown above your head;
But does not fix it 'till your brother's dead.
   Abdalla. All, but the Alhambra, is within my power;
And that my forces go to take this hour.
   Lyndaraxa. When, with its keys your brother's head you
     bring,
I shall believe you are indeed a king.
   Abdalla. But since the events of all things doubtful are,
And, of events, most doubtful those of war;
I beg to know before, if fortune frown,
Must I then lose your favour with my crown?
   Lyndaraxa. You'll soon return a conqueror again;
And, therefore, sir, your question is in vain.

Abdalla. I think to certain victory I move;
But you may more assure it, by your love.
That grant will make my arms invincible.

    Lyndaraxa. My prayers and wishes your success fore-
    tell.—
Go then, and fight, and think you fight for me;
I wait but to reward your victory.

    Abdalla. But if I lose it, must I lose you too?

    Lyndaraxa. You are too curious, if you more would
    know.
I know not what my future thoughts will be:
Poor women's thoughts are all *extempore.*
Wise men, indeed,
Beforehand a long chain of thoughts produce;
But ours are only for our present use.

    Abdalla. Those thoughts, you will not know, too well
    declare.
You mean to wait the final doom of war.

    Lyndaraxa. I find you come to quarrel with me now:
Would you know more of me than I allow?
Whence are you grown that great divinity,
That with such ease into my thoughts can pry?
Indulgence does not with some tempers suit;
I see I must become more absolute.

    Abdalla. I must submit,
On what hard terms soe'er my peace be bought.

    Lyndaraxa. Submit!—you speak as you were not in
    fault.—
'Tis evident the injury is mine;
For why should you my secret thoughts divine?

    Abdalla. Yet if we might be judged by reason's laws——

    Lyndaraxa. Then you would have your reason judge
    my cause!—
Either confess your fault, or hold your tongue;
For I am sure I'm never in the wrong.

    Abdalla. Then I acknowledge it.

    Lyndaraxa. Then I forgive.

    Abdalla. Under how hard a law poor lovers live!
Who, like the vanquished, must their right release,
And with the loss of reason buy their peace.—

                          [*Aside.*
Madam, to show that you my power command,
I put my life and safety in your hand:—

Dispose of the Albayzyn as you please,
To your fair hands I here resign the keys.

 Lyndaraxa. I take your gift, because your love it shows,
And faithful Selin for alcalde choose.

 Abdalla. Selin, from her alone your orders take.—
This one request, yet, madam, let me make,
That, from those turrets, you the assault will see;
And crown, once more, my arms with victory.

      [Exeunt, leading her out. SELIN
        remains with GAZUL *and*
        REDUAN, *his servants.*

 Selin. Gazul, go tell my daughter that I wait.—
You, Reduan, bring the prisoner to his fate.

       [Exeunt GAZUL *and* REDUAN.

Ere of my charge I will possession take,
A bloody sacrifice I mean to make:
The manes of my son shall smile this day,
While I, in blood, my vows of vengeance pay.

Enter at one door BENZAYDA, *with* GAZUL; *at the other,*
  OZMYN *bound, with* REDUAN.

 Selin. I sent, Benzayda, to glad your eyes:
These rites we owe your brother's obsequies.—
You two [*To* GAZUL *and* REDUAN.] the cursed Abencer-
rago bind:
You need no more to instruct you in my mind.

     [They bind him to one corner of the stage.

 Benzayda. In what sad object am I called to share?
Tell me, what is it, sir, you here prepare?

 Selin. 'Tis what your dying brother did bequeath;
A scene of vengeance, and a pomp of death!

 Benzayda. The horrid spectacle my soul does fright:
I want the heart to see the dismal sight.

 Selin. You are my principal invited guest,
Whose eyes I would not only feed, but feast:
You are to smile at his last groaning breath,
And laugh to see his eyeballs roll in death;
To judge the lingering soul's convulsive strife,
When thick short breath catches at parting life.

 Benzayda. And of what marble do you think me made?
 Selin. What! can you be of just revenge afraid?
 Benzayda. He killed my brother in his own defence.
Pity his youth, and spare his innocence.

Selin. Art thou so soon to pardon murder won?
Can he be innocent, who killed my son?
Abenamar shall mourn as well as I;
His Ozmyn, for my Tarifa, shall die.
But since thou plead'st so boldly, I will see
That justice thou wouldst hinder done by thee.
Here—[*gives her his sword*]—take the sword, and do a
     sister's part:
Pierce his, fond girl, or I will pierce thy heart.
Ozmyn. To his commands I join my own request;
All wounds from you are welcome to my breast:
Think only, when your hand this act has done,
It has but finished what your eyes begun.
I thought, with silence, to have scorned my doom;
But now your noble pity has o'ercome;
Which I acknowledge with my latest breath,—
The first whoe'er began a love in death.
Benzayda [*to* SELIN]. Alas, what aid can my weak
     hand afford?
You see I tremble when I touch a sword:
The brightness dazzles me, and turns my sight;
Or, if I look, 'tis but to aim less right.
Ozmyn. I'll guide the hand which must my death con-
     vey;
My leaping heart shall meet it half the way.
Selin [*to* BENZAYDA]. Waste not the precious time in
     idle breath.
Benzayda. Let me resign this instrument of death.
     [*Giving the sword to her father, and then pulling
     it back.*
Ah, no! I was too hasty to resign:
'Tis in your hand more mortal than in mine.

Enter HAMET.

Hamet. The king is from the Alhambra beaten back
And now preparing for a new attack;
To favour which, he wills, that instantly
You reinforce him with a new supply.
Selin [*to* BENZAYDA]. Think not, although my duty calls
     me hence,
That with the breach of yours I will dispense.
Ere my return, see my commands you do:
Let me find Ozmyn dead, and killed by you.—

Gazul and Reduan, attend her still;
And, if she dares to fail, perform my will.

> [*Exeunt* SELIN *and* HAMET. BENZAYDA
> *looks languishing on him, with her sword
> down;* GAZUL *and* REDUAN *standing with
> drawn swords by her.*

Ozmyn. Defer not, fair Benzayda, my death:
Looking on you,
I should but live to sigh away my breath.
My eyes have done the work they had to do:
I take your image with me, which they drew;
And, when they close, I shall die full of you.

Benzayda. When parents their commands unjustly lay,
Children are privileged to disobey;
Yet from that breach of duty I am clear,
Since I submit the penalty to bear.
To die, or kill you, is the alternative;
Rather than take your life, I will not live.

Ozmyn. This shows the excess of generosity;
But, madam, you have no pretence to die.
I should defame the Abencerrages' race,
To let a lady suffer in my place.
But neither could that life, you would bestow,
Save mine; nor do you so much pity owe
To me, a stranger, and your house's foe.

Benzayda. From whencesoe'er their hate our houses
drew,
I blush to tell you, I have none for you.
'Tis a confession which I should not make,
Had I more time to give, or you to take:
But, since death's near, and runs with so much force,
We must meet first, and intercept his course.

Ozmyn. Oh, how unkind a comfort do you give!
Now I fear death again, and wish to live.
Life were worth taking, could I have it now;
But 'tis more good than Heaven can e'er allow
To one man's portion, to have life and you.

Benzayda. Sure, at our births,
Death with our meeting planets danced above,
Or we were wounded by a mourning love!—

> [*Shouts within.*

Reduan. The noise returns, and doubles from behind;
It seems as if two adverse armies joined.—

Time presses us.

Gazul. If longer you delay,
We must, though loth, your father's will obey.

Ozmyn. Haste, madam, to fulfill his hard commands,
And rescue me from their ignoble hands.
Let me kiss yours, when you my wound begin,
Then easy death will slide with pleasure in.

Benzayda. Ah, gentle soldiers, some short time allow!
　　　　　　　　　　　　[*To* GAZUL *and* REDUAN.
My father has repented him ere now;
Or will repent him, when he finds me dead.
My clue of life is twined with Ozmyn's thread.

Reduan. 'Tis fatal to refuse her, or obey.—
But where is our excuse? what can we say?

Benzayda. Say anything.
Say, that to kill the guiltless you were loth;
Or if you did, say I would kill you both.

Gazul. To disobey our orders is to die.—
I'll do't,—who dare oppose it?

Reduan. That dare I.

　　　　　[REDUAN *stands before* OZMYN, *and fights with*
　　　　　　GAZUL. BENZAYDA *unbinds* OZMYN, *and gives*
　　　　　　him her sword.

Benzayda. Stay not to see the issue of the fight;
　　　　　　　　　　　　[REDUAN *kills* GAZUL.
But haste to save yourself by speedy flight.
　　　　　　　　　　　　[OZMYN *kneels to kiss her hand.*

Ozmyn. Did all mankind against my life conspire,
Without this blessing I would not retire.—
But, madam, can I go and leave you here?
Your father's anger now for you I fear:
Consider, you have done too much to stay.

Benzayda. Think not of me, but fly yourself away.

Reduan. Haste quickly hence; the enemies are nigh!
From every part I see the soldiers fly.
The foes not only our assailants beat,
But fiercely sally out on their retreat,
And, like a sea broke loose, come on amain.

Enter ABENAMAR, *and a party with their swords drawn,*
　　　driving in some of the enemies.

Abenamar. Traitors, you hope to save yourselves in
　　vain!—

Your forefeit lives shall for your treason pay;
And Ozmyn's blood shall be revenged this day.

   Ozmyn. No, sir, your Ozmyn lives; and lives to own
                       [Kneeling to his father.
A father's piety to free his son.

   Abenamar. My Ozmyn!—O, thou blessing of my age!
                          [Embracing him.
And art thou safe from their deluded rage!—
Whom must I praise for thy deliverance?
Was it thy valour, or the work of chance?

   Ozmyn. Nor chance, nor valour, could deliver me;
But 'twas a noble pity set me free.—
My liberty, and life,
And what your happiness you're pleased to call,
We to this charming beauty owe it all.

   Abenamar. Instruct me, visible divinity!—   *[To her.*
Instruct me by what name to worship thee!
For to thy virtue I would altars raise,
Since thou art much above all human praise.
But see,——

     Enter ALMANZOR, *his sword bloody, leading in*
       ALMAHIDE, *attended by* ESPERANZA.

My other blessing, Almahide, is here!—
I'll to the king, and tell him she is near:
You, Ozmyn, on your fair deliverer wait,
And with your private joys the public celebrate.
       [Exeunt ABENAMAR, OZMYN, *and* BENZAYDA.

   Almanzor. The work is done; now, madam, you are
     free;
At least, if I can give you liberty:
But you have chains which you yourself have chose;
And, O, that I could free you too from those!
But you are free from force, and have full power
To go, and kill my hopes and me, this hour.—
I see, then, you will go; but yet my toil
May be rewarded with a looking-while.

   Almahide. Almanzor can from every subject raise
New matter for our wonder and his praise.
You bound and freed me; but the difference is,
That showed your valour; but your virtue this.

   Almanzor. Madam, you praise a funeral victory,
At whose sad pomp the conqueror must die.

Almahide. Conquest attends Almanzor everywhere;
I am too small a foe for him to fear:
But heroes still must be opposed by some,
Or they would want occasion to o'ercome.

Almanzor. Madam I cannot on bare praises live;
Those, who abound in praises, seldom give.

Almahide. While I to all the world your worth make
    known,
May Heaven reward the pity you have shown!

Almanzor. My love is languishing, and starved to
    death;
And would you give me charity—in breath?
Prayers are the alms of churchmen to the poor:
They send's to heaven, but drive us from their door.

Almahide. Cease, cease a suit
So vain to you, and troublesome to me,
If you will have me think that I am free.
If I am yet a slave, my bonds I'll bear;
But what I cannot grant, I will not hear.

Almanzor. You will not hear!—You must both hear and
    grant;
For, madam, there's an impudence in want.

Almahide. Your way is somewhat strange to ask relief;
You ask with threatening, like a begging thief.—
Once more, Almanzor, tell me, am I free?

Almanzor. Madam, you are, from all the world,—but
    me!—
But as a pirate, when he frees the prize
He took from friends, sees the rich merchandise,
And, after he has freed it, justly buys;
So, when I have restored your liberty—
But then, alas, I am too poor to buy!

Almahide. Nay, now you use me just as pirates do:
You free me; but expect a ransom too.

Almanzor. You've all the freedom that a prince can
    have;
But greatness cannot be without a slave.
A monarch never can in private move,
But still is haunted with officious love.
So small an inconvenience you may bear;
'Tis all the fine Fate sets upon the fair.

Almahide. Yet princes may retire, whene'er they please,
And breathe free air from out their palaces:

They go sometimes unknown, to shun their state;
And then, 'tis manners not to know or wait.

Almanzor. If not a subject then, a ghost I'll be;
And from a ghost, you know, no place is free.
Asleep, awake, I'll haunt you everywhere;
From my white shroud groan love into your ear:
When in your lover's arms you sleep at night,
I'll glide in cold betwixt, and seize my right:
And is't not better, in your nuptial bed,
To have a living lover than a dead?

Almahide. I can no longer bear to be accused,
As if what I could grant you, I refused.
My father's choice I never will dispute;
And he has chosen ere you moved your suit.
You know my case; if equal you can be,
Plead for yourself, and answer it for me.

Almanzor. Then, madam, in that hope you bid me live;
I ask no more than you may justly give:
But in strict justice there may favour be,
And may I hope that you have that for me?

Almahide. Why do you thus my secret thoughts pursue,
Which, known, hurt me, and cannot profit you?
Your knowledge but new troubles does prepare,
Like theirs who curious in their fortunes are.
To say, I could with more content be yours,
Tempts you to hope; but not that hope assures.
For since the king has right,
And favoured by my father in his suit,
It is a blossom which can bear no fruit.
Yet, if you dare attempt so hard a task,
May you succeed; you have my leave to ask.

Almanzor. I can with courage now my hopes pursue,
Since I no longer have to combat you.
That did the greatest difficulty bring;
The rest are small, a father and a king!

Almahide. Great souls discern not when the leap's too
    wide,
Because they only view the farther side.
Whatever you desire, you think is near;
But, with more reason, the event I fear.

Almanzor. No; there is a necessity in fate,
Why still the brave bold man is fortunate:
He keeps his object ever full in sight,

And that assurance holds him firm and right.
True, 'tis a narrow path that leads to bliss,
But right before there is no precipice:
Fear makes men look aside, and then their footing miss.
    Almahide. I do your merit all the right I can;
Admiring virtue in a private man:
I only wish the king may grateful be,
And that my father with my eyes may see.
Might I not make it as my last request,—
Since humble carriage suits a suppliant best,—
That you would somewhat of your fierceness hide—
That inborn fire—I do not call it pride?
    Almanzor. Born, as I am, still to command, not sue,
Yet you shall see that I can beg for you;
And if your father will require a crown,
Let him but name the kingdom, 'tis his own.
I am, but while I please, a private man;
I have that soul which empires first began.
From the dull crowd, which every king does lead,
I will pick out whom I will choose to head:
The best and bravest souls I can select,
And on their conquered necks my throne erect.

                                          [*Exeunt.*

ACT V

SCENE I

Abdalla *alone, under the walls of the Albayzyn.*

Abdalla. While she is mine, I have not yet lost all,
But in her arms shall have a gentle fall:
Blest in my love, although in war o'ercome,
I fly, like Antony from Actium,
To meet a better Cleopatra here.—
You of the watch! you of the watch! appear.
    Soldier [*above*]. Who calls below? What's your demand?
    Abdalla. 'Tis I:
Open the gate with speed; the foe is nigh.
    Soldier. What orders for admittance do you bring?
    Abdalla. Slave, my own orders: look, and know the
    king.

Soldier. I know you; but my charge is so severe,
That none, without exception, enter here.

Abdalla. Traitor, and rebel! thou shalt shortly see
Thy orders are not to extend to me.

Lyndaraxa [*above*]. What saucy slave so rudely does
    exclaim,
And brands my subject with a rebel's name?

Abdalla. Dear Lyndaraxa, haste; the foes pursue.

Lyndaraxa. My lord, the Prince Abdalla, is it you?
I scarcely can believe the words I hear;
Could you so coarsely treat my officer?

Abdalla. He forced me; but the danger nearer draws:
When I am entered, you shall know the cause.

Lyndaraxa. Entered! Why, have you any business here?

Abdalla. I am pursued, the enemy is near.

Lyndaraxa. Are you pursued, and do you thus delay
To save yourself? Make haste, my lord, away.

Abdalla. Give me not cause to think you mock my
    grief:
What place have I, but this, for my relief?

Lyndaraxa. This favour does your handmaid much
    oblige,
But we are not provided for a siege:
My subjects few; and their provision thin;
The foe is strong without, we weak within.
This to my noble lord may seem unkind,
But he will weigh it in his princely mind;
And pardon her, who does assurance want
So much, she blushes when she cannot grant.

Abdalla. Yes, you may blush; and you have cause to
    weep.
Is this the faith you promised me to keep?
Ah yet, if to a lover you will bring
No succour, give your succour to a king.

Lyndaraxa. A king is he, whom nothing can withstand;
Who men and money can with ease command.
A king is he, whom fortune still does bless;
He is a king, who does a crown possess.
If you would have me think that you are he,
Produce to view your marks of sovereignty;
But if yourself alone for proof you bring,
You're but a single person, not a king.

Abdalla. Ungrateful maid, did I for this rebel?

I say no more; but I have loved too well.

Lyndaraxa. Who but yourself did that rebellion move?
Did I e'er promise to receive your love?
Is it my fault you are not fortunate?
I love a king, but a poor rebel hate.

Abdalla. Who follow fortune, still are in the right;
But let me be protected here this night.

Lyndaraxa. The place to-morrow will be circled round;
And then no way will for your flight be found.

Abdalla. I hear my enemies just coming on;

[*Trampling within.*

Protect me but one hour till they are gone.

Lyndaraxa. They'll know you have been here; it cannot
be;
That very hour you stay, will ruin me:
For if the foe behold our interview,
I shall be thought a rebel too, like you.
Haste hence; and, that your flight may prosperous prove
I'll recommend you to the powers above.

[*Exit* LYNDARAXA *from above.*

Abdalla. She's gone: Ah, faithless and ungrateful
maid!—
I hear some tread; and fear I am betrayed.
I'll to the Spanish king; and try if he,
To countenance his own right, will succour me:
There is more faith in Christian dogs, than thee. [*Exit.*

Enter OZMYN, BENZAYDA, *and* ABENAMAR.

Benzayda. I wish
(To merit all these thanks) I could have said,
My pity only did his virtue aid;
'Twas pity, but 'twas of a love-sick maid.
His manly suffering my esteem did move;
That bred compassion, and compassion love.

Ozmyn. O blessing sold me at too cheap a rate!
My danger was the benefit of fate.   [*To his* Father.
But that you may my fair deliverer know,
She was not only born our house's foe,
But to my death by powerful reasons led;
At least, in justice, she might wish me dead.

Abenamar. But why thus long do you her name conceal?

Ozmyn. To gain belief for what I now reveal:

Even thus prepared, you scarce can think it true,
The saver of my life from Selin drew
Her birth; and was his sister whom I slew.

Abenamar. No more; it cannot, was not, must not be:
Upon my blessing, say not it was she.
The daughter of the only man I hate!
Two contradictions twisted in a fate!

Ozmyn. The mutual hate, which you and Selin bore,
Does but exalt her generous pity more.
Could she a brother's death forgive to me,
And cannot you forget her family?
Can you so ill requite the life I owe,
To reckon her, who gave it, still your foe?
It lends too great a lustre to her line,
To let her virtue ours so much outshine.

Abenamar. Thou gav'st her line the advantage which
        they have,
By meanly taking of the life they gave.
Grant that it did in her a pity show;
But would my son be pitied by a foe?
She has the glory of thy act defaced:
Thou kill'dst her brother; but she triumphs last:
Poorly for us our enmity would cease;
When we are beaten, we receive a peace.

Benzayda. If that be all in which you disagree,
I must confess 'twas Ozmyn conquered me.
Had I beheld him basely beg his life,
I should not now submit to be his wife;
But when I saw his courage death control,
I paid a secret homage to his soul;
And thought my cruel father much to blame,
Since Ozmyn's virtue his revenge did shame.

Abenamar. What constancy canst thou e'er hope to find
In that unstable, and soon conquered mind?
What piety canst thou expect from her,
Who could forgive a brother's murderer?
Or, what obedience hop'st thou to be paid,
From one who first her father disobeyed?

Ozmyn. Nature, that bids us parents to obey,
Bids parents their commands by reason weigh;
And you her virtue by your praise did own,
Before you knew by whom the act was done.

Abenamar. Your reasons speak too much of insolence;

Her birth's a crime past pardon or defence.
Know, that as Selin was not won by thee,
Neither will I by Selin's daughter be.
Leave her, or cease henceforth to be my son:
This is my will; and this I will have done.

[*Exit* ABENAMAR.

Ozmyn. It is a murdering will,
That whirls along with an impetuous sway,
And, like chain-shot, sweeps all things in its way.
He does my honour want of duty call;
To that, and love, he has no right at all.

Benzayda. No, Ozmyn, no; it is a much less ill
To leave me, than dispute a father's will:
If I had any title to your love,
Your father's greater right does mine remove:
Your vows and faith I give you back again,
Since neither can be kept without a sin.

Ozmyn. Nothing but death my vows can give me back:
They are not yours to give, nor mine to take.

Benzayda. Nay, think not, though I could your vows
    resign,
My love or virtue could dispense with mine.
I would extinguish your unlucky fire,
To make you happy in some new desire:
I can preserve enough for me and you,
And love, and be unfortunate, for two.

Ozmyn. In all that's good and great
You vanquish me so fast, that in the end
I shall have nothing left me to defend.
From every post you force me to remove;
But let me keep my last entrenchment, love.

Benzayda. Love then, my Ozmyn; I will be content
    [*Giving her hand.*
To make you wretched by your own consent:
Live poor, despised, and banished for my sake,
And all the burden of my sorrows take;
For, as for me, in whatsoe'er estate,
While I have you, I must be fortunate.

Ozmyn. Thus then, secured of what we hold most dear
(Each other's love) we'll go—I know not where.
For where, alas, should we our flight begin?
The foe's without; our parents are within.

Benzayda. I'll fly to you, and you shall fly to me;

Our flight but to each other's arms shall be.
To providence and chance permit the rest;
Let us but love enough, and we are blest.   [*Exeunt.*

SCENE II

Enter BOABDELIN, ABENAMAR, ABDELMELECH,
Guards: ZULEMA *and* HAMET, *prisoners.*

Abdelmelech. They are Lyndaraxa's brothers; for her
sake
Their lives and pardon my request I make.
      Boabdelin. Then, Zulema and Hamet, live; but know,
Your lives to Abdelmelech's suit you owe.
      Zulema. The grace received so much my hope exceeds,
That words come weak and short to answer deeds.
You've made a venture, sir, and time must show,
If this great mercy you did well bestow.
      Boabdelin. You, Abdelmelech, haste before 'tis night,
And close pursue my brother in his flight.
                          [*Exeunt* ABDELMELECH, ZULEMA,
                                    and HAMET.

Enter ALMANZOR, ALMAHIDE, *and* ESPERANZA.

But see, with Almahide
The brave Almanzor comes, whose conquering sword
The crown, it once took from me, has restored.
How can I recompense so great desert!
      Almanzor. I bring you, sir, performed in every part
My promise made; your foes are fled or slain;
Without a rival, absolute you reign.
Yet though, in justice, this enough may be,
It is too little to be done by me:
I beg to go,
Where my own courage and your fortune calls,
To chase these misbelievers from our walls.
I cannot breathe within this narrow space;
My heart's too big, and swells beyond the place.
      Boabdelin. You can perform, brave warrior, what you
            please;
Fate listens to your voice, and then decrees.
Now I no longer fear the Spanish powers;
Already we are free, and conquerors.
      Almanzor. Accept, great king, to-morrow, from my hand,

The captive head of conquered Ferdinand.
You shall not only what you lost regain,
But o'er the Biscayan mountains to the main,
Extend your sway, where never Moor did reign.

   Abenamar. What, in another, vanity would seem,
Appears but noble confidence in him;
No haughty boasting, but a manly pride;
A soul too fiery, and too great to guide:
He moves eccentric, like a wandering star,
Whose motion's just, though 'tis not regular.

   Boabdelin. It is for you, brave man, and only you,
Greatly to speak, and yet more greatly do.
But, if your benefits too far extend,
I must be left ungrateful in the end:
Yet somewhat I would pay,
Before my debts above all reckoning grow,
To keep me from the shame of what I owe.
But you
Are conscious to yourself of such desert,
That of your gift I fear to offer part.

   Almanzor. When I shall have declared my high request,
So much presumption there will be confest,
That you will find your gifts I do not shun;
But rather much o'er-rate the service done.

   Boabdelin. Give wing to your desires, and let 'em fly,
Secure they cannot mount a pitch too high.
So bless me, Allah, both in peace and war,
As I accord, whate'er your wishes are.

   Almanzor. Emboldened by the promise of a prince,
                          [*Putting one knee to the ground.*
I ask this lady now with confidence.

   Boabdelin. You ask the only thing I cannot grant.
          [*The* King *and* ABENAMAR *look amazedly on
                each other.*
But, as a stranger, you are ignorant
Of what by public fame my subjects know;
She is my mistress.

   Abenamar. —And my daughter too.

   Almanzor. Believe, old man, that I her father knew:
What else should make Almanzor kneel to you?—
Nor doubt, sir, but your right to her was known:
For had you had no claim but love alone,
I could produce a better of my own.

Almahide [*softly to him*]. Almanzor, you forget my last
    request:
Your words have too much haughtiness expressed.
Is this the humble way you were to move?
    Almanzor [*to her*]. I was too far transported by my
    love.
Forgive me; for I had not learned to sue
To anything before, but Heaven and you,—
Sir, at your feet, I make it my request—   [*To the* King.
       First line kneeling: second, rising, and boldly.
Though, without boasting, I deserve her best;
For you her love with gaudy titles sought,
But I her heart with blood and dangers bought.
    Boabdelin. The blood, which you have shed in her
    defence,
Shall have in time a fitting recompence:
Or, if you think your services delayed,
Name but your price, and you shall soon be paid.
    Almanzor. My price!—why, king, you do not think you
    deal
With one who sets his services to sale?
Reserve your gifts for those who gifts regard;
And know, I think myself above reward.
    Boabdelin. Then sure you are some godhead; and our
    care
Must be to come with incense and with prayer.
    Almanzor. As little as you think yourself obliged,
You would be glad to do't, when next besieged.
But I am pleased there should be nothing due;
For what I did was for myself, not you.
    Boabdelin. You with contempt on meaner gifts look
    down;
And, aiming at my queen, disdain my crown.
That crown, restored, deserves no recompence,
Since you would rob the fairest jewel thence.
Dare not henceforth ungrateful me to call;
Whate'er I owed you, this has cancelled all.
    Almanzor. I'll call thee thankless, king, and perjured
    both:
Thou swor'st by Allah, and hast broke thy oath.
But thou dost well; thou tak'st the cheapest way;
Not to own services thou canst not pay.

Boabdelin. My patience more than pays thy service past;
But now this insolence shall be thy last.
Hence from my sight! and take it as a grace,
Thou liv'st, and art but banished from the place.

Almanzor. Where'er I go, there can no exile be;
But from Almanzor's sight I banish thee:
I will not now, if thou wouldst beg me, stay;
But I will take my Almahide away.
Stay thou with all thy subjects here; but know,
We leave thy city empty when we go.

> [*Takes* ALMAHIDE's *hand.*

Boabdelin. Fall on; take; kill the traitor.

> [*The* Guards *fall on him; he makes at the* King
> *through the midst of them, and falls upon him;*
> *they disarm him, and rescue the* King.

Almanzor. —Base and poor,
Blush that thou art Almanzor's conqueror.

> [ALMAHIDE *wrings her hands, then turns and*
> *veils her face.*

Farewell, my Almahide!
Life of itself will go, now thou art gone,
Like flies in winter, when they lose the sun.

> [ABENAMAR *whispers the* King *a little, then*
> *speaks aloud.*

Abenamar. Revenge, and taken so secure a way,
Are blessings which Heaven sends not every day.

Boabdelin. I will at leisure now revenge my wrong;
And, traitor, thou shalt feel my vengeance long:
Thou shalt not die just at thy own desire,
But see my nuptials, and with rage expire.

Almanzor. Thou darest not marry her while I'm in sight:
With a bent brow thy priest and thee I'll fright;
And in that scene,
Which all thy hopes and wishes should content,
The thought of me shall make thee impotent.

> [*He is led off by* Guards.

Boabdelin. As some fair tulip, by a storm oppressed,

> [*To* ALMAHIDE.

Shrinks up, and folds its silken arms to rest;
And, bending to the blast, all pale and dead,
Hears, from within, the wind sing round its head,—
So, shrouded up, your beauty disappears:

Unveil, my love, and lay aside your fears.
The storm, that caused your fright, is passed and done.
> [ALMAHIDE *unveiling, and looking round for*
> ALMANZOR.

  Almahide. So flowers peep out too soon, and miss the
sun.   [*Turning from him.*
  Boabdelin. What mystery in this strange behaviour lies?
  Almahide. Let me for ever hide these guilty eyes.
Which lighted my Almanzor to his tomb;
Or, let them blaze, to show me there a room.
  Boabdelin. Heaven lent their lustre for a nobler end;
A thousand torches must their light attend,
To lead you to a temple and a crown.
Why does my fairest Almahide frown?
Am I less pleasing than I was before,
Or, is the insolent Almanzor more?
  Almahide. I justly own that I some pity have,
Not for the insolent, but for the brave.
  Abenamar. Though to your king your duty you neglect
Know, Almahide, I look for more respect:
And, if a parent's charge your mind can move,
Receive the blessing of a monarch's love.
  Almahide. Did he my freedom to his life prefer,
And shall I wed Almanzor's murderer?
No, sir; I cannot to your will submit;
Your way's too rugged for my tender feet.
  Abenamar. You must be driven where you refuse to go;
And taught, by force, your happiness to know.
  Almahide. To force me, sir, is much unworthy you,
                          [*Smiling scornfully.*
And, when you would, impossible to do.
If force could bend me, you might think, with shame,
That I debased the blood from whence I came.
My soul is soft, which you may gently lay
In your loose palm; but, when 'tis pressed to stay,
Like water, it deludes your grasp, and slips away.
  Boabdelin. I find I must revoke what I decreed:
Almanzor's death my nuptials must precede.
Love is a magic which the lover ties;
But charms still end when the magician dies.
Go; let me hear my hated rival's dead;
                          [*To his* Guard.
And, to convince my eyes, bring back his head.

Almahide. Go on: I wish no other way to prove
That I am worthy of Almanzor's love.
We will in death, at least, united be:
I'll show you I can die as well as he,

Boabdelin. What should I do! when equally I dread
Almanzor living and Almanzor dead!—
Yet, by your promise, you are mine alone.

Almahide. How dare you claim my faith, and break
  your own?

Abenamar. This for your virtue is a weak defence:
No second vows can with your first dispense.
Yet, since the king did to Almanzor swear,
And in his death ungrateful may appear,
He ought, in justice, first to spare his life,
And then to claim your promise as his wife.

Almahide. Whate'er my secret inclinations be,
To this, since honour ties me, I agree:
Yet I declare, and to the world will own,
That, far from seeking, I would shun the throne,
And with Almanzor lead a humble life:
There is a private greatness in his wife.

Boabdelin. That little love I have, I hardly buy;
You give my rival all, while you deny:
Yet, Almahide, to let you see your power,
Your loved Almanzor shall be free this hour.
You are obeyed; but 'tis so great a grace,
That I could wish me in my rival's place.

     [*Exeunt* King *and* ABENAMAR.

Almahide. How blessed was I before this fatal day,
When all I knew of love, was to obey!
'Twas life becalmed, without a gentle breath;
Though not so cold, yet motionless as death.
A heavy quiet state; but love, all strife,
All rapid, is the hurricane of life.
Had love not shown me, I had never seen
An excellence beyond Boabdelin.
I had not, aiming higher, lost my rest;
But with a vulgar good been dully blest:
But, in Almanzor, having seen what's rare,
Now I have learnt too sharply to compare;
And, like a favourite quickly in disgrace,
Just knew the value ere I lost the place.

To her ALMANZOR, *bound and guarded.*

Almanzor. I see the end for which I'm hither sent,
To double, by your sight, my punishment.
There is a shame in bonds I cannot bear;
Far more than death, to meet your eyes I fear.

   Almahide. That shame of long continuance shall not
     be: [*Unbinding him.*
The king, at my entreaty, sets you free.

   Almanzor. The king! my wonder's greater than before;
How did he dare my freedom to restore?
He like some captive lion uses me;
He runs away before he sets me free,
And takes a sanctuary in his court:
I'll rather lose my life than thank him for't.

   Almahide. If any subject for your thanks there be,
The king expects them not; you owe them me.
Our freedoms through each other's hands have past;
You give me my revenge in winning last.

   Almanzor. Then fate commodiously for me has done;
To lose mine there where I would have it won.

   Almahide. Almanzor, you too soon will understand,
That what I win is on another's hand.
The king (who doomed you to a cruel fate)
Gave to my prayers both his revenge and hate;
But at no other price would rate your life,
Than my consent and oath to be his wife.

   Almanzor. Would you, to save my life, my love betray?
Here; take me; bind me; carry me away;
Kill me! I'll kill you if you disobey.   [*To the* Guards.

   Almahide. That absolute command your love does give,
I take, and charge you by that power to live.

   Almanzor. When death, the last of comforts, you refuse,
Your power, like heaven upon the damned, you use;
You force me in my being to remain,
To make me last, and keep me fresh for pain.
When all my joys are gone,
What cause can I for living longer give,
But a dull, lazy habitude to live?

   Almahide. Rash men, like you, and impotent of will,
Give chance no time to turn, but urge her still;
She would repent; you push the quarrel on,

And once because she went, she must be gone.

Almanzor. She shall not turn; what is it she can do,
To recompense me for the loss of you?

Almahide. Heaven will reward your worth some better
way:
At least, for me, you have but lost one day.
Nor is't a real loss which you deplore;
You sought a heart that was engaged before.
'Twas a swift love which took you in his way;
Flew only through your heart, but made no stay:
'Twas but a dream, where truth had not a place;
A scene of fancy, moved so swift a pace,
And shifted, that you can but think it was;—
Let, then, the short vexatious vision pass.

Almanzor. My joys, indeed, are dreams; but not my
pain:
'Twas a swift ruin, but the marks remain.
When some fierce fire lays goodly buildings waste,
Would you conclude
There had been none, because the burning's past?

Almahide. It was your fault that fire seized all your
breast;
You should have blown up some to save the rest:
But 'tis, at worst, but so consumed by fire,
As cities are, that by their falls rise higher.
Build love a nobler temple in my place;
You'll find the fire has but enlarged your space.

Almanzor. Love has undone me; I am grown so poor,
I sadly view the ground I had before,
But want a stock, and ne'er can build it more.

Almahide. Then say what charity I can allow;
I would contribute if I knew but how.
Take friendship; or, if that too small appear,
Take love,—which sisters may to brothers bear.

Almanzor. A sister's love! that is so palled a thing,
What pleasure can it to a lover bring?
'Tis like thin food to men in fevers spent;
Just keeps alive, but gives no nourishment.
What hopes, what fears, what transports can it move?
'Tis but the ghost of a departed love.

Almahide. You, like some greedy cormorant, devour
All my whole life can give you in an hour.

What more I can do for you is to die,
And that must follow, if you this deny.
Since I gave up my love, that you might live,
You, in refusing life, my sentence give.

    Almanzor. Far from my breast be such an impious
        thought!
Your death would lose the quiet mine had sought.
I'll live for you, in spite of misery;
But you shall grant that I had rather die.
I'll be so wretched, filled with such despair,
That you shall see, to live was more to dare.

    Almahide. Adieu, then, O my soul's far better part!
Your image sticks so close,
That the blood follows from my rending heart.
A last farewell!
For, since the last must come, the rest are vain,
Like gasps in death, which but prolong our pain.
But, since the king is now a part of me,
Cease from henceforth to be his enemy.
Go now, for pity go! for, if you stay,
I fear I shall have something still to say.
Thus—I for ever shut you from my sight.   [*Veils.*

    Almanzor. Like one thrust out in a cold winter's night,
Yet shivering underneath your gate I stay;
One look—I cannot go before 'tis day.—
            [*She beckons him to be gone.*
Not one—Farewell: Whate'er my sufferings be
Within, I'll speak farewell as loud as she:
I will not be outdone in constancy.—
              [*She turns her back.*
Then like a dying conqueror I go;
At least I have looked last upon my foe.
I go—but if too heavily I move,
I walk encumbered with a weight of love.
Fain I would leave the thought of you behind,
But still, the more I cast you from my mind,
You dash, like water, back, when thrown against the
    wind.   [*Exit.*
    [*As he goes off, the* King *meets him with* ABENA-
        MAR; *they stare at each other without saluting.*

    Boabdelin. With him go all my fears: A guard there
        wait,
And see him safe without the city gate.

To them ABDELMELECH.

Now, Abdelmelech, is my brother dead?

Abdelmelech. The usurper to the Christian camp is fled;
Whom as Granada's lawful king they own,
And vow, by force, to seat him on the throne.
Meantime the rebels in the Albayzyn rest;
Which is in Lyndaraxa's name possest,

Boabdelin. Haste and reduce it instantly by force.

Abdelmelech. First give me leave to prove a milder course.
She will, perhaps, on summons yield the place.

Boabdelin. We cannot to your suit refuse her grace.

[One enters hastily, and whispers
ABENAMAR.

Abenamar. How fortune persecutes this hoary head!
My Ozmyn is with Selin's daughter fled.
But he's no more my son:
My hate shall like a Zegry him pursue,
'Till I take back what blood from me he drew.

Boabdelin. Let war and vengeance be to-morrow's care;
But let us to the temple now repair.
A thousand torches make the mosque more bright:
This must be mine and Almahide's[12] night.
Hence, ye importunate affairs of state,
You should not tyrannise on love, but wait.
Had life no love, none would for business live;
Yet still from love the largest part we give;
And must be forced, in empire's weary toil,
To live long wretched, to be pleased a while.   [*Exeunt.*

---

[12] The folio, when four syllables are required, prints "Almahi*d*a."

EPILOGUE

Success, which can no more than beauty last,
Makes our sad poet mourn your favours past
For, since without desert he got a name,
He fears to lose it now with greater shame.
Fame, like a little mistress of the town,
Is gained with ease, but then she's lost as soon:
For, as those tawdry misses, soon or late,
Jilt such as keep them at the highest rate;
And oft the lacquey, or the brawny clown,
Gets what is hid in the loose-bodied gown,—
So, Fame is false to all that keep her long;
And turns up to the fop that's brisk and young.
Some wiser poet now would leave Fame first;
But elder wits are, like old lovers, cursed:
Who, when the vigour of their youth is spent,
Still grow more fond, as they grow impotent.
This, some years hence, our poet's case may prove:
But yet, he hopes, he's young enough to love.
When forty comes, if e'er he live to see
That wretched, fumbling age of poetry,
'Twill be high time to bid his Muse adieu:—
Well may he please himself, but never you.
Till then, he'll do as well as he began,
And hopes you will not find him less a man.
Think him not duller for this year's delay;
He was prepared, the women were away;
And men, without their parts, can hardly play.
If they, through sickness, seldom did appear,
Pity the virgins of each theatre:
For, at both houses 'twas a sickly year!
And pity us, your servants, to whose cost,
In one such sickness, nine whole months are lost.
Their stay, he fears, has ruined what he writ:
Long waiting both disables love and wit.
They thought they gave him leisure to do well;
But, when they forced him to attend, he fell!
Yet, though he much has failed, he begs, to-day,
You will excuse his unperforming play:
Weakness sometimes great passion does express;
He had pleased better, had he loved you less.

ALMANZOR AND ALMAHIDE

or, the

CONQUEST OF GRANADA

by the

SPANIARDS

A Tragedy

THE SECOND PART

—*Stimulos dedit æmula virtus.*

LUCAN.

PROLOGUE TO THE SECOND PART

THEY, who write ill, and they, who ne'er durst write,
Turn critics, out of mere revenge and spite:
A playhouse gives them fame; and up there starts,
From a mean fifth-rate wit, a man of parts.
(So common faces on the stage appear;
We take them in, and they turn beauties here.)
Our author fears those critics as his fate;
And those he fears, by consequence must hate.
For they the traffic of all wit invade,
As scriveners draw away the bankers' trade.
Howe'er the poet's safe enough to-day,
They cannot censure an unfinished play.
But, as when vizard-mask appears in pit,
Straight every man, who thinks himself a wit,
Perks up, and, managing his comb with grace,
With his white wig sets off his nut-brown face;
That done, bears up to the prize, and views each limb,
To know her by her rigging and her trim;
Then, the whole noise of fops to wagers go,—
"Pox on her, 'tmust be she;" and—"Damme, no!"—
Just so, I prophesy, these wits to-day
Will blindly guess at our imperfect play;
With what new plots our Second Part is filled,
Who must be kept alive, and who be killed.
And as those vizard-masks maintain that fashion,
To soothe and tickle sweet imagination;
So our dull poet keeps you on with masking,
To make you think there's something worth your asking.
But, when 'tis shown, that, which does now delight you,
Will prove a dowdy, with a face to fright you.

ACT I

SCENE I—*A Camp*

Enter KING FERDINAND, QUEEN ISABEL,
ALONZO D'AGUILAR; Attendants, Men *and* Women.

KING FERDINAND. At length the time is come, when Spain
    shall be
From the long yoke of Moorish tyrants free.
All causes seem to second our design,
And heaven and earth in their destruction join.
When empire in its childhood first appears,
A watchful fate o'ersees its tender years;
Till, grown more strong, it thrusts and stretches out,
And elbows all the kingdoms round about.
The place thus made for its first breathing free,
It moves again for ease and luxury;
Till, swelling by degrees, it has possessed
The greater space, and now crowds up the rest;
When, from behind, there starts some petty state,
And pushes on its now unwieldy fate;
Then down the precipice of time it goes,
And sinks in minutes, which in ages rose.
    Queen Isabel. Should bold Columbus in his search
    succeed,
And find those beds in which bright metals breed;
Tracing the sun, who seems to steal away,
That, miser-like, he might alone survey
The wealth which he in western mines did lay,—
Not all that shining ore could give my heart
The joy, this conquered kingdom will impart;
Which, rescued from the misbelievers' hands,
Shall now, at once, shake off its double bands:
At once to freedom and true faith restored,
Its old religion and its ancient lord.
    King Ferdinand. By that assault which last we made, I
    find,

Their courage is with their success declined:
Almanzor's absence now they dearly buy,
Whose conduct crowned their arms with victory.

Alonzo. Their king himself did their last sally guide;
I saw him, glistering in bright armour, ride
To break a lance in honour of his bride:
But other thoughts now fill his anxious breast;
Care of his crown his love has dispossest.

To them ABDELLA.

Queen Isabel. But see, the brother of the Moorish king:
He seems some news of great import to bring.

King Ferdinand. He brings a specious title to our side:
Those, who would conquer, must their foes divide.

Abdalla. Since to my exile you have pity shown,
And given me courage yet to hope a throne;
While you without our common foes subdue,
I am not wanting to myself or you;
But have, within, a faction still alive,
Strong to assist, and secret to contrive,
And watching each occasion to foment
The people's fears into a discontent;
Which, from Almanzor's loss, before were great,
And now are doubled by their late defeat:
These letters from their chiefs the news assures.
                              [*Give letters to the* King
King Ferdinand. Be mine the honour, but the profit
  yours.

To them the DUKE OF ARCOS, *with* OZMYN *and* BENZAYDA, *prisoners.*

King Ferdinand. That tertia[13] of Italians did you guide,
To take their post upon the river side?

Duke of Arcos. All are according to your orders placed:
My cheerful soldiers their entrenchments haste;
The Murcian foot hath ta'en the upper ground,
And now the city is beleaguered round.

King Ferdinand. Why is not then their leader here
  again?

Duke of Arcos. The Master of Alcantara is slain;
But he, who slew him, here before you stands:
It is that Moor whom you behold in bands.

13 Regiment of infantry.

King Ferdinand. A braver man I had not in my host;
His murderer shall not long his conquest boast:
But, Duke of Arcos, say, how was he slain?

Duke of Arcos. Our soldiers marched together on the plain;
We two rode on, and left them far behind,
'Till, coming where we found the valley wind,
We saw these Moors; who, swiftly as they could,
Ran on to gain the covert of the wood.
This we observed; and, having crossed their way,
The lady, out of breath, was forced to stay.
The man then stood, and straight his falchion drew;
Then told us, we in vain did those pursue,
Whom their ill fortune to despair did drive,
And yet, whom we should never take alive.
Neglecting this, the Master straight spurred on;
But the active Moor his horse's shock did shun,
And, ere his rider from his reach could go,
Finished the combat with one deadly blow.
I, to revenge my friend, prepared to fight;
But now our foremost men were come in sight,
Who soon would have despatched him on the place,
Had I not saved him from a death so base,
And brought him to attend your royal doom.

King Ferdinand. A manly face, and in his age's bloom;
But, to content the soldiers, he must die:
Go, see him executed instantly.

Queen Isabel. Stay; I would learn his name before he go:
You, Prince Abdalla, may the prisoner know.

Abdalla. Ozmyn's his name, and he deserves his fate;
His father heads that faction which I hate:
But much I wonder, that I with him see
The daughter of his mortal enemy.

Benzayda. 'Tis true, by Ozmyn's sword my brother fell;
But 'twas a death he merited too well.
I know a sister should excuse his fault;
But you know too, that Ozmyn's death he sought.

Abdalla. Our prophet has declared, by the event,
That Ozmyn is reserved for punishment;
For, when he thought his guilt from danger clear,
He, by new crimes, is brought to suffer here.

Benzayda. In love, or pity, if a crime you find,

We too have sinned above all humankind.

Ozmyn. Heaven in my punishment has done a grace;
I could not suffer in a better place:
That I should die by Christians it thought good,
To save your father's guilt, who sought my blood. [*To her.*

Benzayda. Fate aims so many blows to make us fall,
That 'tis in vain to think to ward them all:
And, where misfortunes great and many are,
Life grows a burden, and not worth our care.

Ozmyn. I cast it from me, like a garment torn,
Ragged, and too indecent to be worn:
Besides, there is contagion in my fate,   [*To* BENZAYDA.
It makes your life too much unfortunate.—
But, since her faults are not allied to mine,
In her protection let your favour shine.
To you, great queen, I make this last request,
(Since pity dwells in every royal breast)
Safe, in your care, her life and honour be:
It is a dying lover's legacy.

Benzayda. Cease, Ozmyn, cease so vain a suit to move;
I did not give you on those terms my love.
Leave me the care of me; for, when you go,
My love will soon instruct me what to do.

Queen Isabel. Permit me, sir, these lovers' doom to give:
My sentence is, they shall together live.
The courts of Kings
To all distressed should sanctuaries be,
But most to lovers in adversity
Castile and Arragon,
Which long against each other war did move,
My plighted lord and I have joined by love;
And, if to add this conquest Heaven thinks good,
I would not have it stained with lovers' blood.

King Ferdinand. Whatever Isabella shall command
Shall always be a law to Ferdinand.

Benzayda. The frowns of fate we will no longer fear:
Ill fate, great queen, can never find us here.

Queen Isabel. Your thanks some other time I will receive
Henceforward safe in my protection live.
Granada is for noble loves renowned:
Her best defence is in her lovers found.
Love's an heroic passion, which can find
No room in any base degenerate mind:

It kindles all the soul with honour's fire,
To make the lover worthy his desire.
Against such heroes I success should fear,
Had we not too an host of lovers here.
An army of bright beauties come with me;
Each lady shall her servant's actions see:
The fair and brave on each side shall contest;
And they shall overcome, who love the best.   [*Exeunt.*

SCENE II—*The Alhambra*

Enter ZULEMA.

Zulema. True, they have pardoned me; but do they
    know
What folly 'tis to trust a pardoned foe?
A blush remains in a forgiven face:
It wears the silent tokens of disgrace.
Forgiveness to the injured does belong;
But they ne'er pardon, who have done the wrong.
My hopeful fortunes lost! and, what's above
All I can name or think, my ruined love!
Feigned honesty shall work me into trust.
And seeming penitence conceal my lust.
Let heaven's great eye of Providence now take
One day of rest, and ever after wake.

Enter BOABDELIN, ABENAMAR, *and* Guards.

Boabdelin. Losses on losses! as if Heaven decreed
Almanzor's valour should alone succeed.
    Abenamar. Each sally we have made, since he is gone,
Serves but to pull our speedy ruin on.
    Boabdelin. Of all mankind, the heaviest fate he bears,
Who the last crown of sinking empire wears.
No kindly planet of his birth took care:
Heaven's outcast, and the dross of every star!
                              [*A tumultuous noise within.*

Enter ABDELMELECH.

What new misfortune do these cries presage?
    Abdelmelech. They are the effects of the mad people's
    rage.
All in despair tumultuously they swarm:
The farthest streets already take the alarm;

The needy creep from cellars under ground;
To them new cries from tops of garrets sound;
The aged from the chimneys seek the cold;
And wives from windows helpless infants hold.

   Boabdelin. See what the many-headed beast demands.—

                                [*Exit* ABDELMELECH.

Cursed is that king, whose honour's in their hands.
In senates, either they too slowly grant,
Or saucily refuse to aid my want;
And, when their thrift has ruined me in war,
They call their insolence my want of care.

   Abenamar. Cursed be their leaders, who that rage
     foment,
And veil, with public good, their discontent:
They keep the people's purses in their hands,
And hector kings to grant their wild demands;
But to each lure a court throws out, descend,
And prey on those they promised to defend.

   Zulema. Those kings, who to their wild demands
     consent,
Teach others the same way to discontent.
Freedom in subjects is not, nor can be;
But still, to please them, we must call them free.
Propriety, which they their idol make,
Or law, or law's interpreters, can shake.

   Abenamar. The name of commonwealth is popular;
But there the people their own tyrants are.

   Boabdelin. But kings, who rule with limited command,
Have players' sceptres put into their hand.
Power has no balance, one side still weighs down,
And either hoists the commonwealth or crown;
And those, who think to set the scale more right,
By various turnings but disturb the weight.

   Abenamar. While people tug for freedom, kings for
     power
Both sink beneath some foreign conqueror:
Then subjects find too late they were unjust,
And want that power of kings they durst not trust.

To them ABDELMELECH.

   Abdelmelech. The tumult now is high, and dangerous
     grown:
The people talk of rendering up the town;

And swear that they will force the king's consent.
   Boabdelin. What counsel can this rising storm prevent?
   Abdelmelech. Their fright to no persuasions will give
    ear:
There's a deaf madness in a people's fear.

Enter a Messenger.

   Messenger. Their fury now a middle course does take;
To yield the town, or call Almanzor back.
   Boabdelin. I'll rather call my death.—
Go, and bring up my guards to my defence:
I'll punish this outrageous insolence.
   Abenamar. Since blind opinion does their reason sway,
You must submit to cure them their own way.
You to their fancies physic must apply;
Give them that chief on whom they most rely.
Under Almanzor prosperously they fought;
Almanzor, therefore, must with prayers be brought.

Enter a second Messenger.

   2 *Messenger.* Haste all you can their fury to assuage:
You are not safe from their rebellious rage.

Enter a third Messenger.

   3 *Messenger.* This minute, if you grant not their desire,
They'll seize your person, and your palace fire.
   Abdelmelech. Your danger, sir, admits of no delay.
   Boabdelin. In tumults people reign, and kings obey.—
Go and appease them with the vow I make,
That they shall have their loved Almanzor back.
                 [*Exit* ABDELMELECH.
Almanzor has the ascendant o'er my fate
I'm forced to stoop to one I fear and hate:
Disgraced, distressed, in exile, and alone,
He's greater than a monarch on his throne:
Without a realm, a royalty he gains;
Kings are the subjects over whom he reigns.
             [*A shout of acclamations within.*
   Abenamar. These shouts proclaim the people satisfied.
   Boabdelin. We for another tempest must provide,
To promise his return as I was loth,
So I want power now to perform my oath.
Ere this, for Afric he is sailed from Spain.

Abenamar. The adverse winds his passage yet detain;
I heard, last night, his equipage did stay
At a small village, short of Malaga.

Boabdelin. Abenamar, this evening thither haste;
Desire him to forget his usage past:
Use all your rhetoric, promise, flatter, pray.

To them ALMAHIDE, *attended.*

Abenamar. Good fortune shows you yet a surer way:
Nor prayers nor promises his mind will move;
'Tis inaccessible to all, but love.

Boabdelin. Oh, thou hast roused a thought within my
   breast,
That will for ever rob me of my rest.
Ah jealousy, how cruel is thy sting!
I, in Almanzor, a loved rival bring!
And now, I think, it is an equal strife,
If I my crown should hazard, or my wife.
Where, marriage, is thy cure, which husbands boast,
That in possession their desire is lost?
Or why have I alone that wretched taste,
Which, gorged and glutted, does with hunger last?
Custom and duty cannot set me free,
Even sin itself has not a charm for me.
Of married lovers I am sure the first,
And nothing but a king could be so curst.

Almahide. What sadness sits upon your royal heart?
Have you a grief, and must not I have part?
All creatures else a time of love possess;
Man only clogs with cares his happiness:
And, while he should enjoy his part of bliss,
With thoughts for what may be, destroys what is.

Boabdelin. You guess aright; I am oppressed with grief,
And 'tis from you that I must seek relief.
                                          [*To the company.*
Leave us; to sorrow there's a reverence due:
Sad kings, like suns eclipsed, withdraw from view.
          [*The* Attendants *go off, and chairs are set for the*
              King *and* Queen.

Almahide. So, two kind turtles, when a storm is nigh,
Look up, and see it gathering in the sky:
Each calls his mate, to shelter in the groves,
Leaving, in murmur, their unfinished loves:

Perched on some drooping branch, they sit alone
And coo, and hearken to each other's moan.

   Boabdelin. Since, Almahide, you seem so kind a wife,
                                [Taking her by the hand.
What would you do to save a husband's life?

   Almahide. When fate calls on that hard necessity,
I'll suffer death, rather than you shall die.

   Boabdelin. Suppose your country should in danger be;
What would you undertake to set it free?

   Almahide. It were too little to resign my breath:
My own free hand should give me nobler death.

   Boabdelin. That hand, which would so much for glory
   do
Must yet do more; for it must kill me too.
You must kill me, for that dear country's sake;
Or, what's all one, must call Almanzor back.

   Almahide. I see to what your speech you now direct;
Either my love or virtue you suspect.
But know, that, when my person I resigned,
I was too noble not to give my mind.
No more the shadow of Almanzor fear;
I have no room, but for your image, here.

   Boabdelin. This, Almahide, would make me cease to
   mourn,
Were that Almanzor never to return:
But now my fearful people mutiny;
Their clamours call Almanzor back, not I.
Their safety, through my ruin, I pursue:
He must return, and must be brought by you.

   Almahide. That hour, when I my faith to you did
   plight,
I banished him for ever from my sight.
His banishment was to my virtue due;
Not that I feared him for myself, but you.
My honour had preserved me innocent:
But I would,[14] your suspicion to prevent;
Which, since I see augmented in your mind,
I yet more reason for his exile find.

   Boabdelin. To your entreaties he will yield alone,
And on your doom depend my life and throne.
No longer, therefore, my desires withstand;
Or, if desires prevail not, my command.

[14] *I.e.* "I chose to do it."

Almahide. In his return, too sadly I foresee
The effects of your returning jealousy.
But your command I prize above my life;
'Tis sacred to a subject and a wife:
If I have power, Almanzor shall return.
    Boabdelin. Cursed be that fatal hour when I was born!
             [Letting go her hand, and starting up.
You love, you love him; and that love reveal,
By your too quick consent to his repeal.
My jealousy had but too just a ground;
And now you stab into my former wound.
    Almahide. This sudden change I do not understand
Have you so soon forgot your own command?
    Boabdelin. Grant that I did the unjust injunction lay,
You should have loved me more than to obey.
I know you did this mutiny design;
But I'll your love-plot quickly countermine.
Let my crown go; he never shall return;
I, like a phœnix, in my nest will burn.
    Almahide. You please me well, that in one common
      fate
You wrap yourself, and me, and all your state.
Let us no more of proud Almanzor hear;
'Tis better once to die, than still to fear;
And better many times to die, than be
Obliged, past payment, to an enemy.
    Boabdelin. 'Tis better; but you wives have still one way:
Whene'er your husbands are obliged, you pay.
    Almahide. Thou, Heaven, who know'st it, judge my
      innocence!—
You, sir, deserve not I should make defence.
Yet, judge my virtue by that proof I gave,
When I submitted to be made your slave.
    Boabdelin. If I have been suspicious or unkind,
Forgive me; many cares distract my mind:
Love, and a crown!
Two such excuses no one man e'er had;
And each of them enough to make me mad:
But now my reason reassumes its throne,
And finds no safety when Almanzor's gone.
Send for him then; I'll be obliged, and sue;
'Tis a less evil than to part with you.

I leave you to your thoughts; but love me still!
Forgive my passion, and obey my will.

         [*Exit* BOABDELIN.

ALMAHIDE *sola*.

My jealous lord will soon to rage return;
That fire, his fear rakes up, does inward burn.
But Heaven, which made me great, has chose for me,
I must the oblation for my people be.
I'll cherish honour, then, and life despise;
What is not pure, is not for sacrifice.
Yet for Almanzor I in secret mourn!
Can virtue, then, admit of his return?
Yes; for my love I will by virtue square;
My heart's not mine, but all my actions are.
I'll like Almanzor act; and dare to be
As haughty, and as wretched too, as he.
What will he think is in my message meant?
I scarcely understand my own intent:
But, silkworm-like, so long within have wrought,
That I am lost in my own web of thought.

         [*Exit* ALMAHIDE.

ACT II

SCENE I—*A Wood*

Enter OZMYN *and* BENZAYDA.

OZMYN. 'Tis true, that our protection here has been
The effect of honour in the Spanish queen;
But, while I as a friend continue here,
I to my country must a foe appear.

 Benzayda. Think not, my Ozmyn, that we here remain
As friends, but prisoners to the power of Spain.
Fortune dispenses with your country's right;
But you desert your honour in your flight.

 Ozmyn. I cannot leave you here, and go away;
My honour's glad of a pretence to stay.

    [*A noise within,*—Follow, follow, follow!—

Enter SELIN, *his sword drawn, as pursued.*

Selin. I am pursued, and now am spent and done;
My limbs suffice me not with strength to run.
And, if I could, alas! what can I save?
A year, the dregs of life too, from the grave.
                                                            [*Sits down on the ground.*
Here will I sit, and here attend my fate,
With the same hoary majesty and state,
As Rome's old senate for the Gauls did wait.
    Benzayda. It is my father; and he seems distressed.
    Ozmyn. My honour bids me succour the oppressed;
That life he sought, for his I'll freely give;
We'll die together, or together live.
    Benzayda. I'll call more succour, since the camp is
        near,
And fly on all the wings of love and fear.
                                                            [*Exit* BENZAYDA.

Enter ABENAMAR, *and four or five Moors.*
He looks and finds SELIN.

    Abenamar. You've lived, and now behold your latest
        hour.
    Selin. I scorn your malice, and defy your power.
A speedy death is all I ask you now;
And that's a favour you may well allow.
    Ozmyn [*showing himself*]. Who gives you death, shall
        give it first to me;
Fate cannot separate our destiny.——   [*Knows his father.*
My father here! then Heaven itself has laid
The snare, in which my virtue is betrayed.
    Abenamar. Fortune, I thank thee! thou hast kindly
        done.
To bring me back that fugitive, my son;
In arms too? fighting for my enemy!——
I'll do a Roman justice,—thou shalt die!
    Ozmyn. I beg not you my forfeit life would save;
Yet add one minute to that breath you gave.
I disobeyed you, and deserved my fate;
But bury in my grave two houses' hate.
Let Selin live; and see your justice done
On me, while you revenge him for his son:
Your mutual malice in my death may cease,

And equal loss persuade you both to peace.

Abenamar. Yes, justice shall be done on him and thee.—
Haste, and despatch them both immediately.

[*To a* Soldier.

Ozmyn. If you have honour,—since you nature want.—
For your own sake my last petition grant;
And kill not a disarmed, defenceless foe,
Whose death your cruelty, or fear, will show.
My father cannot do an act so base:—
My father!—I mistake;—I meant, who was.

Abenamar. Go, then, despatch him first who was my
son!

Ozmyn. Swear but to save his life, I'll yield my own.

Abenamar. Nor tears, nor prayers, thy life, or his, shall
buy.

Ozmyn. Then, sir, Benzayda's father shall not die!—

[*Putting himself before* SELIN.

And, since he'll want defence when I am gone,
I will, to save his life, defend my own.

Abenamar. This justice parricides like thee should
have!—

[ABENAMAR *and his party attack them both.* OZMYN
parries his father's thrusts, and thrusts at the others.

Enter BENZAYDA, *with* ABDALLA, *the* DUKE OF ARCOS,
and Spaniards.

Benzayda. O, help my father! and my Ozmyn save!

Abdalla. Villains, that death you have deserved is near!

Ozmyn. Stay, prince! and know, I have a father here!—

[*Stops* ABDALLA'S *hand.*

I were that parricide, of whom he spoke,
Did not my piety prevent your stroke.

Duke of Arcos [*to* ABENAMAR]. Depart, then, and thank
Heaven you had a son.

Abenamar. I am not with these shows of duty won.

Ozmyn [*to his* Father]. Heaven knows, I would that
life, you seek, resign;
But, while Benzayda lives, it is not mine.
Will you yet pardon my unwilling crime?

Abenamar. By no entreaties, by no length of time,
Will I be won; but, with my latest breath,
I'll curse thee here, and haunt thee after death.

[*Exit* ABENAMAR *with his party.*

Ozmyn. Can you be merciful to that degree,
                  [Kneeling to SELIN.
As to forgive my father's faults in me?
Can you forgive
The death of him I slew in my defence,
And from the malice separate the offence?
I can no longer be your enemy:
In short, now kill me, sir, or pardon me.
                  [Offers him his sword.
In this your silence my hard fate appears.
  Selin. I'll answer you when I can speak for tears.
But, till I can,
Imagine what must needs be brought to pass;
                  [Embraces him.
My heart's not made of marble, nor of brass.
Did I for you a cruel death prepare,
And have you, have you made my life your care!
There is a shame contracted by my faults,
Which hinders me to speak my secret thoughts.
And I will tell you—when the shame's removed—
You are not better by my daughter loved.—
Benzayda be yours.—I can no more.
  Ozmyn. Blessed be that breath which does my life
    restore!   *[Embracing his knees.*
  Benzayda. I hear my father now; these words confess
That name, and that indulgent tenderness.
  Selin. Benzayda, I have been too much to blame;
But let your goodness expiate for my shame:
You Ozmyn's virtue did in chains adore,
And part of me was just to him before.—
My son!—
  Ozmyn. My father!—
  Selin. Since by you I live,
I, for your sake, your family forgive.
Let your hard father still my life pursue,
I hate not him, but for his hate to you;
Even that hard father yet may one day be
By kindness vanquished, as you vanquished me;
Or, if my death can quelch to you his rage,
Heaven makes good use of my remaining age.
  Abdalla. I grieve your joys are mingled with my cares;
But all take interest in their own affairs;
And, therefore, I must ask how mine proceed.

Selin. They now are ripe, and but your presence need:
For Lyndaraxa, faithless as the wind,
Yet to your better fortunes will be kind;
For, hearing that the Christians own your cause,
From thence the assurance of a throne she draws.
And since Almanzor, whom she most did fear,
Is gone, she to no treaty will give ear;
But sent me her unkindness to excuse.

    Abdalla. You much surprise me with your pleasing
    news.

    Selin. But, sir, she hourly does the assault expect,
And must be lost if you her aid neglect:
For Abdelmelech loudly does declare,
He'll use the last extremities of war,
If she refuse the fortress to resign.

    Abdalla. The charge of hastening this relief be mine.

    Selin. This while I undertook, whether beset,
Or else by chance, Abenamar I met;
Who seemed, in haste, returning to the town.

    Abdalla. My love must in my diligence be shown.—
And [*to* ARCOS.] as my pledge of faith to Spain, this hour
I'll put the fortress in your master's power.

    Selin. An open way from hence to it there lies,
And we with ease may send in large supplies,
Free from the shot and sallies of the town.

    Duke of Arcos. Permit me, sir, to share in your renown;
First to my king I will impart the news,
And then draw out what succours we shall use.

                         [*Exit* DUKE OF ARCOS.

    Abdalla [*Aside*]. Grant that she loves me not, at least
    I see
She loves not others, if she loves not me.—
'Tis pleasure, when we reap the fruit of pain:
'Tis only pride, to be beloved again.
How many are not loved, who think they are!
Yet all are willing to believe the fair;
And, though 'tis beauty's known and obvious cheat,
Yet man's self-love still favours the deceit.

                           [*Exit* ABDALLA.

    Selin. Farewell, my children! equally so dear,
That I myself am to myself less near:
While I repeat the dangers of the war,
Your mutual safety be each other's care.

Your father, Ozmyn, till the war be done,
As much as honour will permit, I'll shun:
If by his sword I perish, let him know
It was because I would not be his foe.

Ozmyn. Goodness and virtue all your actions guide;
You only err in choosing of your side.
That party I, with honour, cannot take;
But can much less the care of you forsake:
I must not draw my sword against my prince,
But yet may hold a shield in your defence.
Benzayda, free from danger, here shall stay,
And for a father and a lover pray.

Benzayda. No, no! I gave not on those terms my heart,
That from my Ozmyn I should ever part:
That love I vowed, when you did death attend,
'Tis just that nothing but my death should end.
What merchant is it, who would stay behind,
His whole stock ventured to the waves and wind?
I'll pray for both, but both shall be in sight;
And Heaven shall hear me pray, and see you fight.

Selin. No longer, Ozmyn, combat a design,
Where so much love and so much virtue join.

Ozmyn [*To* BENZAYDA]. Then conquer, and your
    conquest happy be,
Both to yourself, your father, and to me.—
With bended knees our freedom we'll demand
Of Isabel and mighty Ferdinand:
Then while the paths of honour we pursue,
We'll interest Heaven for us, in right of you.   [*Exeunt.*

SCENE II—*The Albayzyn.*

An alarm within; then Soldiers *running over the stage.*
    Enter ABDELMELECH, *victorious, with* Soldiers.

Abdelmelech. 'Tis won, 'tis won! and Lyndaraxa, now,
Who scorned to treat, shall to a conquest bow.
To every sword I free commission give;
Fall on, my friends, and let no rebel live.
Spare only Lyndaraxa; let her be
In triumph led, to grace my victory.
Since by her falsehood she betrayed my love,
Great as that falsehood my revenge shall prove.—

Enter LYNDARAXA, *as affrighted, attended by women.*

Go, take the enchantress, bring her to me bound!

    Lyndaraxa. Force needs not, where resistance is not
      found:
I come, myself, to offer you my hands;
And, of my own accord, invite your bands.
I wished to be my Abdelmelech's slave;
I did but wish,—and easy fortune gave.

    Abdelmelech. O, more than woman false!—but 'tis in
      vain.—
Can you e'er hope to be believed again?
I'll sooner trust the hyæna than your smile;
Or, than your tears, the weeping crocodile.
In war and love none should be twice deceived;
The fault is mine if you are now believed.

    Lyndaraxa. Be overwise, then, and too late repent;
Your crime will carry its own punishment.
I am well pleased not to be justified;
I owe no satisfaction to your pride.
It will be more advantage to my fame,
To have it said, I never owned a flame.

    Abdelmelech. 'Tis true, my pride has satisfied itself:
I have at length escaped the deadly shelf.
The excuses you prepare will be in vain,
Till I am fool enough to love again.

    Lyndaraxa. Am I not loved?

    Abdelmelech. I must with shame avow,
I loved you once;—but do not love you now.

    Lyndaraxa. Have I for this betrayed Abdalla's trust?
You are to me, as I to him, unjust.   [*Angrily.*

    Abdelmelech. 'Tis like you have done much for love of
      me,
Who kept the fortress of my enemy.

    Lyndaraxa. 'Tis true, I took the fortress from his hand;
But, since, have kept it in my own command.

    Abdelmelech. That act your foul ingratitude did show.

    Lyndaraxa. You are the ungrateful, since 'twas kept for
      you.

    Abdelmelech. 'Twas kept indeed; but not by your in-
      tent:
For all your kindness I may thank the event.

Blush, Lyndaraxa, for so gross a cheat:
'Twas kept for me,—when you refused to treat!
                                        [*Ironically.*

   Lyndaraxa. Blind man! I knew the weakness of the
    place:
It was my plot to do your arms this grace.
Had not my care of your renown been great,
I loved enough to offer you to treat.
She, who is loved, must little lets create;
But you bold lovers are to force your fate.
This force you used, my maiden blush will save;
You seemed to take, what secretly I gave.
I knew we must be conquered; but I knew
What confidence I might repose in you.
I knew you were too grateful to expose
My friends and soldiers, to be used like foes.
   Abdelmelech. Well, though I love you not, their lives
    shall be
Spared out of pity and humanity.—
Alferez [*To a* Soldier.] go, and let the slaughter cease.
                                [*Exit the* Alferez.[15]

   Lyndaraxa. Then must I to your pity owe my peace?
Is that the tenderest term you can afford?
Time was, you would have used another word.
   Abdelmelech. Then, for your beauty I your soldiers
    spare:
For, though I do not love you, you are fair.
   Lyndaraxa. That little beauty why did Heaven impart,
To please your eyes, but not to move your heart!
I'll shroud this gorgon from all human view,
And own no beauty, since it charms not you!
Reverse your orders, and your sentence give;
My soldiers shall not from my beauty live.
   Abdelmelech. Then, from your friendship they their lives
    shall gain;
Though love be dead, yet friendship does remain.
   Lyndaraxa. That friendship, which from withered love
    does shoot,
Like the faint herbage on a rock, wants root.
Love is a tender amity, refined:
Grafted on friendship it exalts the kind.
But when the graff no longer does remain,

[15] "Ancient" or "ensign."

The dull stock lives, but never bears again.

 Abdelmelech. Then, that my friendship may not doubt-
ful prove,—
Fool that I am to tell you so!—I love.
You would extort this knowledge from my breast,
And tortured me so long that I confest.
Now I expect to suffer for my sin;
My monarchy must end, and yours begin.

 Lyndaraxa. Confess not love, but spare yourself that
shame,
And call your passion by some other name.
Call this assault, your malice, or your hate;
Love owns no acts so disproportionate.
Love never taught this insolence you show,
To treat your mistress like a conquered foe.
Is this the obedience which my heart should move?
This usage looks more like a rape than love.

 Abdelmelech. What proof of duty would you I should
give?

 Lyndaraxa. 'Tis grace enough to let my subjects live!
Let your rude soldiers keep possession still;
Spoil, rifle, pillage,—anything but kill.
In short, sir, use your fortune as you please;
Secure my castle, and my person seize;
Let your true men my rebels hence remove:
I shall dream on, and think 'tis all your love!

 Abdelmelech. You know too well my weakness and your
power:
Why did Heaven make a fool a conqueror!
She was my slave, 'till she by me was shown
How weak my force was, and how strong her own.
Now she has beat my power from every part,
Made her way open to my naked heart: [*To a* Soldier.
Go, strictly charge my soldiers to retreat:
Those countermand who are not entered yet.
On peril of your lives leave all things free. [*Exit* Soldier.
Now, madam, love Abdalla more than me.
I only ask, in duty you would bring
The keys of our Albayzyn to the king:
I'll make your terms as gentle as you please.
       [*Trumpets sound a charge within, and*
       Soldiers *shout.*
What shouts, and what new sounds of war are these?

Lyndaraxa. Fortune, I hope, has favoured my intent,

　　　　　　　　　　　　　　　　　　　[*Aside.*

Of gaining time, and welcome succours sent.

Enter the *Alferez.*

Alferez. All's lost, and you are fatally deceived:
The foe is entered, and the place relieved.
Scarce from the walls had I drawn off my men,
When, from their camp, the enemy rushed in,
And prince Abdalla entered first the gate.

Abdelmelech. I am betrayed, and find it now too late.
When your proud soul to flatteries did descend,

　　　　　　　　　　　　　　　　　　　[*To her.*

I might have known it did some ill portend.
The wary seaman stormy weather fears,
When winds shift often, and no cause appears.
You by my bounty live—
Your brothers, too, were pardoned for my sake,
And this return your gratitude does make.

Lyndaraxa. My brothers best their own obligement
　　know;
Without your charging me with what they owe.
But, since you think the obligement is so great,
I'll bring a friend to satisfy my debt.　　[*Looking behind.*

Abdelmelech. Thou shalt not triumph in thy base design;
Though not thy fort, thy person shall be mine.

　　　[*He goes to take her: She runs and cries out help.*

Enter ABDALLA, Duke of ARCOS, *and Spaniards.* ABDEL-
　　MELECH *retreats fighting, and is pursued by the*
　　adverse party off the stage. An alarm within. Enter
　　again ABDALLA *and the* DUKE OF ARCOS, *with* LYN-
　　DARAXA.

Duke of Arcos. Bold Abdelmelech twice our Spaniards
　　faced,
Though much outnumbered; and retreated last.

Abdalla. Your beauty, as it moves no common fire,

　　　　　　　　　　　　　　　　　　　[*To* LYNDARAXA.

So it no common courage can inspire.
As he fought well, so had he prospered too,
If, madam, he, like me, had fought for you.

Lyndaraxa. Fortune, at last, has chosen with my eyes;
And, where I would have given it, placed the prize.

You see, sir, with what hardship I have kept
This precious gage, which in my hands you left.
But 'twas the love of you which made me fight,
And gave me courage to maintain your right.
Now, by experience, you my faith may find,
And are to thank me that I seemed unkind.
When your malicious fortune doomed your fall,
My care restrained you then from losing all;
Against your destiny I shut the gate,
And gathered up the shipwrecks of your fate;
I, like a friend, did even yourself withstand,
From throwing all upon a losing hand.

   Abdalla. My love makes all your acts unquestioned go,
And sets a sovereign stamp on all you do.
Your love I will believe with hoodwinked eyes;—
In faith, much merit in much blindness lies.
But now, to make you great as you are fair,
The Spaniards an imperial crown prepare.

   Lyndaraxa. That gift's more welcome, which with you
    I share.
Let us no time in fruitless courtship lose,
But sally out upon our frighted foes.
No ornaments of power so please my eyes,
As purple, which the blood of princes dyes.   [*Exeunt.*

SCENE III—*The Alhambra*

BOABDELIN, ABENAMAR, ALMAHIDE, *and* Guards,
etc. The Queen *wearing a scarf.*

   Abenamar. My little journey has successful been;
The fierce Almanzor will obey the queen.
I found him, like Achilles on the shore,
Pensive, complaining much, but threatening more;
And, like that injured Greek, he heard our woes,
Which, while I told, a gloomy smile arose
From his bent brows: And still, the more he heard,
A more severe and sullen joy appeared.
But, when he knew we to despair were driven,
Betwixt his teeth he muttered thanks to Heaven.

   Boabdelin. How I disdain this aid! which I must take,
Not for my own, but Almahide's sake.

   Abenamar. But when he heard it was the queen who
    sent,

That her command repealed his banishment,
He took the summons with a greedy joy,
And asked me how she would his sword employ:
Then bid me say, her humblest slave would come
From her fair mouth with joy to take his doom.

Boabdelin. Oh that I had not sent you! though it cost
My crown! though I, and it, and all were lost!

Abenamar. While I, to bring this news, came on before,
I met with Selin——

Boabdelin. I can hear no more.

Enter HAMET.

Hamet. Almanzor is already at the gate,
And throngs of people on his entrance wait.

Boabdelin. Thy news does all my faculties surprise;
He bears two basilisks in those fierce eyes;
And that tame demon, which should guard my throne,
Shrinks at a genius greater than his own.

[*Exit* BOABDELIN *with* ABENAMAR *and* Guards.

Enter ALMANZOR; *seeing* ALMAHIDE *approach him, he speaks.*

Almanzor. So Venus moves, when to the Thunderer,
In smiles or tears, she would some suit prefer;
When with her cestus girt,
And drawn by doves, she cuts the liquid skies,
And kindles gentle fires where'er she flies:
To every eye a goddess is confest,
By all the heavenly nation she is blest,
And each with secret joy admits her to his breast.—
Madam, your new commands I come to know,
If yet you can have any where I go.   [*To her bowing.*
If to the regions of the dead they be,
You take the speediest course to send by me.

Almahide. Heaven has not destined you so soon to rest:
Heroes must live to succour the distrest.

Almanzor. To serve such beauty all mankind should live;
And, in our service, our reward you give.
But stay me not in torture, to behold
And ne'er enjoy. As from another's gold
The miser hastens, in his own defence,
And shuns the sight of tempting excellence;

So, having seen you once so killing fair,
A second sight were but to move despair.
I take my eyes from what too much would please,
As men in fevers famish their disease.

    Almahide. No; you may find your cure an easier way,
If you are pleased to seek it,—in your stay.
All objects lose by too familiar view,
When that great charm is gone, of being new;
By often seeing me, you soon will find
Defects so many, in my face and mind,
That to be freed from love you need not doubt;
And, as you looked it in, you'll look it out.

    Almanzor. I rather, like weak armies, should retreat,
And so prevent my more entire defeat.
For your own sake in quiet let me go;
Press not too far on a despairing foe:
I may turn back, and armed against you move,
With all the furious train of hopeless love.

    Almahide. Your honour cannot to ill thoughts give way,
And mine can run no hazard by your stay.

    Almanzor. Do you then think I can with patience see
That sovereign good possessed, and not by me?
No; I all day shall languish at the sight,
And rave on what I did not see all night;
My quick imagination will present
The scenes and images of your content,
When to my envied rival you dispense
Joys too unruly and too fierce for sense.[16]

    Almahide. These are the day-dreams which wild fancy
      yields,
Empty as shadows are, that fly o'er fields.
Oh, whither would this boundless fancy move!
'Tis but the raging calenture of love,
Like a distracted passenger you stand,
And see, in seas, imaginary land,
Cool groves, and flowery meads; and while you think
To walk, plunge in, and wonder that you sink.

    Almanzor. Love's calenture too well I understand;
But sure your beauty is no fairy-land!
Of your own form a judge you cannot be;
For, glow-worm-like, you shine, and do not see.

    Almahide. Can you think this, and would you go away?

Almanzor. What recompence attends me if I stay?

Almahide. You know I am from recompence debarred
But I will grant your merit a reward;
Your flame's too noble to deserve a cheat,
And I too plain to practise a deceit.
I no return of love can ever make,
But what I ask is for my husband's sake;
He, I confess, has been ungrateful too,
But he and I are ruined if you go:
Your virtue to the hardest proof I bring;—
Unbribed, preserve a mistress and a king.

Almanzor. I'll stop at nothing that appears so brave:
I'll do't, and now I no reward will have.
You've given my honour such an ample field,
That I may die, but that shall never yield.
Spite of myself I'll stay, fight, love, despair;
And I can do all this, because I dare.
Yet I may own one suit—
That scarf, which, since by you it has been borne,
Is blessed, like relics which by saints were worn.

Almahide. Presents like this my virtue durst not make,
But that 'tis given you for my husband's sake.

[*Gives the scarf.*

Almanzor. This scarf to honourable rags I'll wear,
As conquering soldiers tattered ensigns bear;
But oh, how much my fortune I despise,
Which gives me conquest, while she love denies!

[*Exeunt.*

ACT III

SCENE I—*The Alhambra*

Enter ALMAHIDE and ESPERANZA.

ESPERANZA. Affected modesty has much of pride;
That scarf he begged, you could not have denied;
Nor does it shock the virtue of a wife,
When given that man to whom you owe your life.

Almahide. Heaven knows from all intent of ill 'twas
free,

Yet it may feed my husband's jealousy;
And for that cause I wish it were not done.

To them BOABDELIN, *and walks apart.*

See, where he comes, all pensive and alone;
A gloomy fury has o'erspread his face:
'Tis so! and all my fears are come to pass.

   Boabdelin. Marriage, thou curse of love, and snare of
      life,   [*Aside.*
That first debased a mistress to a wife!
Love, like a scene, at distance should appear,
But marriage views the gross-daubed landscape near.
Love's nauseous cure! thou cloyest whom thou shouldst
    please;
And, when thou cur'st, then thou art the disease.
When hearts are loose, thy chain our bodies ties;
Love couples friends, but marriage enemies.
If love like mine continues after thee,
'Tis soon made sour, and turned by jealousy;
No sign of love in jealous men remains,
But that which sick men have of life—their pains.

   Almahide. Has my dear lord some new affliction had?
                                [*Walking to him.*
Have I done anything that makes him sad?

   Boabdelin [*sighing and going off*]. You! nothing: You!
But let me walk alone.

   Almahide [*approaching him*]. I will not leave you till
    the cause be known:
My knowledge of the ill may bring relief.

   Boabdelin. Thank ye; you never fail to cure my grief!
Trouble me not, my grief concerns not you.

   Almahide. While I have life, I will your steps pursue.

   Boabdelin. I'm out of humour now; you must not stay.

   Almahide. I fear it is that scarf I gave away.

   Boabdelin. No 'tis not that; but speak of it no more:
Go hence! I am not what I was before.

   Almahide. Then I will make you so; give me your
    hand!
Can you this pressing and these tears withstand?

   Boabdelin. Oh Heaven, were she but mine, or mine
    alone!   [*Sighing, and going off from her.*
Ah, why are not the hearts of women known!

False women to new joys unseen can move;
There are no prints left in the paths of love.
All goods besides by public marks are known;
But what we most desire to keep, has none.

   Almahide. Why will you in your breast your passion
      crowd,   [*Approaching him.*
Like unborn thunder rolling in a cloud?
Torment not your poor heart, but set it free,
And rather let its fury break on me.
I am not married to a god; I know
Men must have passions, and can bear from you.
I fear the unlucky present I have made!

   Boabdelin. O power of guilt! how conscience can up-
      braid!
It forces her not only to reveal,
But to repeat what she would most conceal!

   Almahide. Can such a toy, and given in public too——

   Boabdelin. False woman, you contrived it should be so.
That public gift in private was designed
The emblem of the love you meant to bind.
Hence from my sight, ungrateful as thou art!
And, when I can, I'll banish thee my heart. [*She weeps.*

To them ALMANZOR *wearing the scarf. He sees her weep.*

   Almanzor. What precious drops are those,
Which silently each other's track pursue,
Bright as young diamonds in their infant dew?
Your lustre you should free from tears maintain,
Like Egypt, rich without the help of rain.
Now cursed be he who gave this cause of grief;
And double cursed, who does not give relief!

   Almahide. Our common fears, and public miseries,
Have drawn these tears from my afflicted eyes.

   Almanzor. Madam, I cannot easily believe
It is for any public cause you grieve.
On your fair face the marks of sorrow lie;
But I read fury in your husband's eye:
And, in that passion, I too plainly find
That you're unhappy, and that he's unkind.

   Almahide. Not new-made mothers greater love express
Than he, when with first looks their babes they bless;

Not Heaven is more to dying martyrs kind,
Nor guardian angels to their charge assigned.

Boabdelin. O goodness counterfeited to the life!
O the well-acted virtue of a wife!
Would you with this my just suspicions blind?
You've given me great occasion to be kind!
The marks, too, of your spotless love appear;
Witness the badge of my dishonour there.

[*Pointing to* ALMANZOR's *scarf.*

Almanzor. Unworthy owner of a gem so rare!
Heavens! why must he possess, and I despair?
Why is this miser doomed to all this store;
He, who has all, and yet believes he's poor?

Almahide [*to* ALMANZOR]. You're too much bold, to
    blame a jealousy
So kind in him, and so desired by me.
The faith of wives would unrewarded prove,
Without those just observers of our love.
The greater care the higher passion shows;
We hold that dearest we most fear to lose.
Distrust in lovers is too warm a sun,
But yet 'tis night in love when that is gone;
And in those climes which most his scorching know,
He makes the noblest fruits and metals grow.

Almanzor. Yes; there are mines of treasure in your
    breast,
Seen by that jealous sun, but not possest.
He, like a devil, among the blest above,
Can take no pleasure in your heaven of love.
Go, take her, and thy causeless fears remove;

[*To the* King.

Love her so well, that I with rage may die:
Dull husbands have no right to jealousy:
If that's allowed, it must in lovers be.

Boabdelin. The succour, which thou bring'st me, makes
    thee bold:
But know, without thy aid, my crown I'll hold;
Or, if I cannot, I will fire the place,
Of a full city make a naked space.
Hence, then, and from a rival set me free!
I'll do, I'll suffer anything but thee.

Almanzor. I wonnot go; I'll not be forced away:

I came not for thy sake, nor do I stay.
It was the queen who for my aid did send;
And 'tis I only can the queen defend:
I, for her sake, thy sceptre will maintain:
And thou, by me, in spite of thee, shalt reign.

   Boabdelin. Had I but hope I could defend this place
Three days, thou shouldst not live to my disgrace
So small a time;
Might I possess my Almahide alone,
I would live ages out ere they were gone.
I should not be of love or life bereft;
All should be spent before, and nothing left.

   Almahide [*to* BOABDELIN]. As for your sake I for Alman-
     zor sent,
So, when you please, he goes to banishment.
You shall, at last, my loyalty approve:
I will refuse no trial of my love.

   Boabdelin. How can I think you love me, while I see
That trophy of a rival's victory?
I'll tear it from his side.

   Almanzor.   I'll hold it fast
As life, and when life's gone, I'll hold this last;
And if thou tak'st it after I am slain,
I'll send my ghost to fetch it back again.

   Almahide. When I bestowed that scarf, I had not
     thought,
Or not considered it might be a fault;
But, since my lord's displeased that I should make
So small a present, I command it back.
Without delay the unlucky gift restore;
Or, from this minute, never see me more.

   Almanzor. The shock of such a curse I dare not stand:
      [*Pulling it off hastily, and presenting it to her.*
Thus I obey your absolute command.
                    [*She gives it to the* King.
Must he the spoils of scorn'd Almanzor wear?—
May Turnus' fate be thine, who dared to bear
The belt of murdered Pallas! from afar
Mayst thou be known, and be the mark of war!
Live, just to see it from thy shoulders torn
By common hands, and by some coward worn.
                         [*An alarm within.*

Enter ABDELMELECH, ZULEMA, HAMET, ABENAMAR,
their swords drawn.

Abdelmelech. Is this a time for discord or for grief?
We perish, sir, without your quick relief.
I have been fooled, and am unfortunate;
The foes pursue their fortune and our fate.

    Zulema. The rebels with the Spaniards are agreed.

    Boabdelin. Take breath; my guards shall to the fight
      succeed.

    Abenamar [*to* ALMANZOR]. Why stay you, sir? the con-
      quering foe is near:
Give us their courage, and give them our fear.

    Hamet. Take arms, or we must perish in your sight.

    Almanzor. I care not: perish: for I will not fight.
I wonnot lift an arm in his defence:
And yet I wonnot stir one foot from hence.
I to your king's defence his town resign;
This only spot, whereon I stand, is mine.—
Madam, be safe, and lay aside your fear,—
                      [*To the* Queen.
You are as in a magic circle here.

    Boabdelin. To our own valour our success we'll owe.
Haste, Hamet, with Abenamar to go;
You two draw up, with all the speed you may,
Our last reserves, and yet redeem the day.
        [*Exeunt* HAMET *and* ABENAMAR *one way, the*
          King *the other, with* ABDELMELECH, *etc.*
          Alarm *within.*

Enter ABDELMELECH, *his sword drawn.*

    Abdelmelech. Granada is no more! the unhappy king,
Venturing too far, ere we could succour bring,
Was by the Duke of Arcos prisoner made,
And, past relief, is to the fort conveyed.

    Almanzor. Heaven, thou art just! Go, now despise my
      aid.

    Almahide. Unkind Almanzor, how am I betrayed!
Betrayed by him in whom I trusted most!
But I will ne'er outlive what I have lost.
Is this your succour, this your boasted love?
I will accuse you to the saints above!

Almanzor vowed he would for honour fight,
And lets my husband perish in my sight.

[*Exeunt* ALMAHIDE *and* ESPERANZA.

Almanzor. Oh, I have erred; but fury made me blind;
And, in her just reproach, my fault I find!
I promised even for him to fight, whom I—
But since he's loved by her, he must not die.
Thus, happy fortune comes to me in vain,
When I myself must ruin it again.

To him ABENAMAR, HAMET, ABDELMELECH, ZULEMA,
Soldiers.

Abenamar. The foe has entered the Vermillion towers;
And nothing but the Alhambra now is ours.

Almanzor. Even that's too much, except we may have
    more;
You lost it all to that last stake before.
Fate, now come back; thou canst not further get;
The bounds of thy libration[17] here are set.
Thou know'st this place,
And, like a clock wound up, strik'st here for me;
Now, Chance, assert thy own inconstancy,
And, Fortune, fight, that thou may'st Fortune be!—
They come: here, favoured by the narrow place,

[*A noise within.*

I can, with few, their gross battalion face.
By the dead wall, you, Abdelmelech, wind;
Then charge, and their retreat cut off behind.   [*Exeunt.*

[*An alarm within.*

Enter ALMANZOR *and his Party, with* ABDALLA, *prisoner.*

Almanzor. You were my friend: and to that name I
    owe   [*To* ABDALLA.
The just regard, which you refused to show.
Your liberty I frankly would restore,
But honour now forbids me to do more.
Yet, sir, your freedom in your choice shall be,
When you command to set your brother free.

Abdalla. The exchange, which you propose, with joy I
    take;
An offer easier than my hopes could make.
Your benefits revenge my crimes to you,

17 Swing or variation.

For I my shame in that bright mirror view.

   Almanzor. No more; you give me thanks you do not
     owe:
I have been faulty and repent me now.
But, though our penitence a virtue be,
Mean souls alone repent in misery;
The brave own faults when good success is given,
For then they come on equal terms to heaven.

                                   [Exeunt.

SCENE II—*The Albayzyn*

Enter OZMYN *and* BENZAYDA.

   Benzayda. I see there's somewhat which you fear to tell;
Speak quickly, Ozmyn, is my father well?
Why cross you thus your arms, and shake your head?
Kill me at once, and tell me he is dead.

   Ozmyn. I know not more than you; but fear not less;
Twice sinking, twice I drew him from the press:
But the victorious foe pursued so fast,
That flying throngs divided us at last.
As seamen parting in a general wrack,
When first the loosening planks begin to crack,
Each catches one, and straight are far disjoined,
Some borne by tides, and others by the wind;
So, in this ruin, from each other rent,
With heaved-up hands we mutual farewells sent.
Methought his eyes, when just I lost his view,
Were looking blessings to be sent to you.

   Benzayda. Blind queen of Chance, to lovers too severe,
Thou rulest mankind, but art a tyrant there!
Thy widest empire's in a lover's breast:
Like open seas, we seldom are at rest.
Upon thy coasts our wealth is daily cast;
And thou, like pirates, mak'st no peace to last.

   To them LYNDARAXA, DUKE OF ARCOS, *and* Guards.

   Duke of Arcos. We were surprised when least we did
     suspect,
And justly suffered by our own neglect.

   Lyndaraxa. No; none but I have reason to complain!
So near a kingdom, yet 'tis lost again!
O, how unequally in me were joined

A creeping fortune with a soaring mind!
O lottery of fate! where still the wise
Draw blanks of fortune, and the fools the prize!
These cross, ill-shuffled lots from heaven are sent,
Yet dull Religion teaches us content;
But when we ask it where that blessing dwells,
It points to pedant colleges, and cells;
There shows it rude, and in a homely dress,
And that proud want mistakes for happiness.

        [*A trumpet within.*

Enter ZULEMA.

Brother! what strange adventure brought you here?
 Zulema. The news I bring will yet more strange appear.
The little care you of my life did show,
Has of a brother justly made a foe;
And Abdelmelech, who that life did save,
As justly has deserved that life he gave.
 Lyndaraxa. Your business cools, while tediously it stays
On the low theme of Abdelmelech's praise.
 Zulema. This I present from Prince Abdalla's hands.

    [*Delivers a letter, which she reads.*

 Lyndaraxa. He has proposed (to free him from his
  bands)
That, with his brother, an exchange be made.
 Duke of Arcos. It proves the same design which we had
  laid.
Before the castle let a bar be set;
And when the captives on each side are met,
With equal numbers chosen for their guard,
Just at the time the passage is unbarred,
Let both at once advance, at once be free.
 Lyndaraxa. The exchange I will myself in person see.
 Benzayda. I fear to ask, yet would from doubt be
  freed,—
Is Selin captive, sir, or is he dead?
 Zulema. I grieve to tell you what you needs must
  know,—
He is a prisoner to his greatest foe;
Kept with strong guards in the Alhambra tower;
Without the reach even of Almanzor's power.
 Ozmyn. With grief and shame I am at once opprest.
 Zulema. You will be more when I relate the rest.

To you I from Abenamar am sent,   [*To* OZMYN.
And you alone can Selin's death prevent,
Give up yourself a prisoner in his stead;
Or, ere to-morrow's dawn, believe him dead.

  Benzayda. Ere that appear, I shall expire with grief.
  Zulema. Your action swift, your counsel must be brief.
  Lyndaraxa. While for Abdalla's freedom we prepare,
You in each other's breast unload your care.

                  [*Exeunt all but* OZMYN *and* BENZAYDA.

  Benzayda. My wishes contradictions must imply;
You must not go; and yet he must not die.
Your reason may, perhaps, the extremes unite;
But there's a mist of fate before my sight.

  Ozmyn. The two extremes too distant are, to close;
And human wit can no mid way propose.
My duty therefore shows the nearest way,
To free your father, and my own obey.

  Benzayda. Your father, whom, since yours, I grieve to
        blame,
Has lost, or quite forgot, a parent's name;
And, when at once possessed of him and you,
Instead of freeing one, will murder two.

  Ozmyn. Fear not my life; but suffer me to go:
What cannot only sons with parents do!
'Tis not my death my father does pursue;
He only would withdraw my love from you.

  Benzayda. Now, Ozmyn, now your want of love I see;
For would you go, and hazard losing me?

  Ozmyn. I rather would ten thousand lives forsake;
Nor can you e'er believe the doubt you make.
This night I with a chosen band will go,
And, by surprise, will free him from the foe.

  Benzayda. What foe! ah, whither would your virtue fall!
It is your father whom the foe you call.
Darkness and rage will no distinction make.
And yours may perish for my father's sake.

  Ozmyn. Thus, when my weaker virtue goes astray,
Yours pulls it back, and guides me in the way:
I'll send him word, my being shall depend
On Selin's life, and with his death shall end.

  Benzayda. 'Tis that, indeed, would glut your father's
        rage:
Revenge on Ozmyn's youth, and Selin's age.

Ozmyn. Whate'er I plot, like Sisyphus, in vain
I heave a stone, that tumbles down again.

Benzayda. This glorious work is then reserved for me:
He is my father, and I'll set him free.
These chains my father for my sake does wear:
I made the fault; and I the pains will bear.

Ozmyn. Yes; you no doubt have merited these pains;
Those hands, those tender limbs, were made for chains!
Did I not love you, yet it were too base
To let a lady suffer in my place.
Those proofs of virtue you before did show,
I did admire; but I must envy now.
Your vast ambition leaves no fame for me,
But grasps at universal monarchy.

Benzayda. Yes, Ozmyn, I shall still this palm pursue;
I will not yield my glory even to you.
I'll break those bonds in which my father's tied,
Or, if I cannot break them, I'll divide.
What, though my limbs a woman's weakness show,
I have a soul as masculine as you;
And when these limbs want strength my chains to wear,
My mind shall teach my body how to bear.

[*Exit* BENZAYDA.

Ozmyn. What I resolve, I must not let her know;
But honour has decreed she must not go.
What she resolves, I must prevent with care;
She shall not in my fame or danger share.
I'll give strict order to the guards which wait,
That, when she comes, she shall not pass the gate.
Fortune, at last, has run me out of breath;
I have no refuge but the arms of death:
To that dark sanctuary I will go;
She cannot reach me when I lie so low. [*Exit.*

SCENE III—*The Albayzyn*

Enter, on the one side, ALMANZOR, ABDALLA, ABDEL-
MELECH, ZULEMA, HAMET. *On the other side, the*
DUKE OF ARCOS, BOABDELIN, LYNDARAXA, *and their*
Party. After which the bars are opened; and at the
same time BOABDELIN *and* ABDALLA *pass by each*
other, each to his Party; when ABDALLA *is passed on*

the other side, the DUKE OF ARCOS *approaches the bars, and calls to* ALMANZOR.

Duke of Arcos. The hatred of the brave with battles ends,
And foes, who fought for honour, then are friends.
I love thee, brave Almanzor, and am proud
To have one hour when love may be allowed.
This hand, in sign of that esteem, I plight;
We shall have angry hours enough to fight.

[*Giving his hand.*

Almanzor. The man who dares, like you, in fields appear,
And meet my sword, shall be my mistress here.
If I am proud, 'tis only to my foes;
Rough but to such who virtue would oppose
If I some fierceness from a father drew,
A mother's milk gives me some softness too.

Duke of Arcos. Since first you took, and after set me free,
(Whether a sense of gratitude it be,
Or some more secret motion of my mind,
For which I want a name that's more than kind)
I shall be glad, by whate'er means I can,
To get the friendship of so brave a man;
And would your unavailing valour call,
From aiding those whom Heaven has doomed to fall.
We owe you that respect,
Which to the gods of foes besieged was shown,
To call you out before we take your town.

Almanzor. Those whom we love, we should esteem them too,
And not debauch that virtue which we woo.
Yet, though you give my honour just offence,
I'll take your kindness in the better sense;
And, since you for my safety seem to fear,
I, to return your bribe, should wish you here.
But, since I love you more than you do me,
In all events preserve your honour free;
For that's your own, though not your destiny.

Duke of Arcos. Were you obliged in honour by a trust,
I should not think my own proposals just;

But since you fight for an unthankful king,
What loss of fame can change of parties bring?

    Almanzor. It will, and may with justice too be thought,
That some advantage in that change I sought.
And though I twice have changed for wrongs received,
That it was done for profit none believed.
The king's ingratitude I knew before;
So that can be no cause of changing more.
If now I stand, when no reward can be,
'Twill show the fault before was not in me.

    Duke of Arcos. Yet there is one reward to valour due,
And such it is as may be sought by you;
That beauteous queen, whom you can never gain,
While you secure her husband's life and reign.

    Almanzor. Then be it so; let me have no return
        [*Here* LYNDARAXA *comes near, and hears them.*
From him but hatred, and from her but scorn.
There is this comfort in a noble fate,
That I deserve to be more fortunate.
You have my last resolve; and now, farewell:
My boding heart some mischief does foretell;
But what it is, heaven will not let me know.
I'm sad to death, that I must be your foe.

    Duke of Arcos. Heaven, when we meet, if fatal it must be
To one, spare him, and cast the lot on me.   [*They retire.*

    Lyndaraxa. Ah, what a noble conquest were this heart!
I am resolved I'll try my utmost art:
In gaining him, I gain that fortune too,
Which he has wedded, and which I but woo.
I'll try each secret passage to his mind,
And love's soft bands about his heart-strings wind.
Not his vowed constancy shall 'scape my snare;
While he without resistance does prepare,
I'll melt into him ere his love's aware.
        [*She makes a gesture of invitation to* ALMANZOR,
         who returns again.

    Lyndaraxa. You see, sir, to how strange a remedy
A persecuted maid is forced to fly:
Who, much distressed, yet scarce has confidence
To make your noble pity her defence.

    Almanzor. Beauty, like yours, can no protection need;
Or, if it sues, is certain to succeed.
To whate'er service you ordain my hand,

Name your request, and call it your command.

Lyndaraxa. You cannot, sir, but know that my ill fate
Has made me loved with all the effects of hate:
One lover would, by force, my person gain;
Which one, as guilty, would by force detain.
Rash Abdelmelech's love I cannot prize,
And fond Abdalla's passion I despise.
As you are brave, so you are prudent too;
Advise a wretched woman what to do.

Almanzor. Have courage, fair one, put your trust in me;
You shall, at least, from those you hate, be free.
Resign your castle to the king's command,
And leave your love concernments in my hand.

Lyndaraxa. The king, like them, is fierce, and faithless
        too;
How can I trust him who has injured you?
Keep for yourself, (and you can grant no less)
What you alone are worthy to possess.
Enter, brave sir; for, when you speak the word,
These gates will open of their own accord;
The genius of the place its lord will meet,
And bend its tow'ry forehead to your feet.
That little citadel, which now you see,
Shall, then, the head of conquered nations be;
And every turret, from your coming, rise
The mother of some great metropolis.

Almanzor. 'Tis pity, words, which none but gods should
        hear,
Should lose their sweetness in a soldier's ear:
I am not that Almanzor whom you praise;
But your fair mouth can fair ideas raise:—
I am a wretch, to whom it is denied
To accept, with honour, what I wish with pride;
And, since I fight not for myself must bring
The fruits of all my conquests to the king.

Lyndaraxa. Say rather to the queen, to whose fair name
I know you vow the trophies of your fame.
I hope she is as kind as she is fair;
Kinder than inexperienced virgins are
To their first loves; (though she has loved before,
And that first innocence is now no more:)
But, in revenge, she gives you all her heart,
(For you are much too brave to take a part.)

Though, blinded by a crown, she did not see
Almanzor greater than a king could be,
I hope her love repairs her ill-made choice:
Almanzor cannot be deluded twice.

   Almanzor. No, not deluded; for none count their gains,
Who, like Almanzor, frankly give their pains.

   Lyndaraxa. Almanzor, do not cheat yourself, nor me;
Your love is not refined to that degree:
For, since you have desires, and those not blest,
Your love's uneasy, and at little rest.

   Almanzor. 'Tis true, my own unhappiness I see;
But, who, alas, can my physician be?
Love, like a lazy ague, I endure,
Which fears the water, and abhors the cure.

   Lyndaraxa. 'Tis a consumption, which your life does
     waste,
Still flattering you with hope, till help be past;
But, since of cure from her you now despair,
You, like consumptive men, should change your air:
Love somewhere else; 'tis a hard remedy,
But yet you owe yourself so much, to try.

   Almanzor. My love's now grown so much a part of me,
That life would, in the cure, endangered be:
At least, it like a limb cut off would show;
And better die than like a cripple go.

   Lyndaraxa. You must be brought like madmen to their
     cure,
And darkness first, and next new bonds endure:
Do you dark absence to yourself ordain,
And I, in charity, will find the chain.

   Almanzor. Love is that madness which all lovers have;
But yet 'tis sweet and pleasing so to rave:
'Tis an enchantment, where the reason's bound;
But Paradise is in the enchanted ground;
A palace, void of envy, cares and strife,
Where gentle hours delude so much of life.
To take those charms away, and set me free,
Is but to send me into misery;
And prudence, of whose cure so much you boast,
Restores those pains which that sweet folly lost.

   Lyndaraxa. I would not, like philosophers, remove,
But show you a more pleasing shape of love.
You a sad, sullen, froward Love did see;

I'll show him kind, and full of gaiety.
In short, Almanzor, it shall be my care
To show you love; for you but saw despair.
   Almanzor. I, in the shape of Love, Despair did see;
You, in his shape, would show Inconstancy.
   Lyndaraxa. There's no such thing as constancy you call;
Faith ties not hearts; 'tis inclination all.
Some wit deformed, or beauty much decayed,
First constancy in love a virtue made.
From friendship they that landmark did remove,
And falsely placed it on the bounds of love.
Let the effects of change be only tried;
Court me, in jest, and call me Almahide:
But this is only counsel I impart,
For I, perhaps, should not receive your heart.
   Almanzor. Fair though you are
As summer mornings, and your eyes more bright
Than stars that twinkle in a winter's night;
Though you have eloquence to warm and move
Cold age and praying hermits into love;
Though Almahide with scorn rewards my care,—
Yet, than to change, 'tis nobler to despair.
My love's my soul; and that from fate is free;
'Tis that unchanged and deathless part of me.
   Lyndaraxa. The fate of constancy your love pursue!
Still to be faithful to what's false to you.
               [Turns from him, and goes off angrily.
   Almanzor. Ye gods, why are not hearts first paired
    above,
But some still interfere in others' love?
Ere each for each by certain marks are known.
You mould them up in haste, and drop them down;
And while we seek what carelessly you sort,
You sit in state, and make our pains your sport.
               [Exeunt on both sides.

ACT IV

SCENE I

Enter ABENAMAR *and* Servants.

ABENAMAR. Haste and conduct the prisoner to my sight.
>   [*Exit* Servant, *and immediately enters*
>   *with* SELIN, *bound.*

Abenamar. Did you, according to my orders, write?
>   [*To* SELIN.

And have you summoned Ozmyn to appear?

Selin. I am not yet so much a slave to fear,
Nor has your son deserved so ill of me,
That by his death or bonds I would be free.

Abenamar. Against thy life thou dost the sentence give;
Behold how short a time thou hast to live.

Selin. Make haste, and draw the curtain while you may;
You but shut out the twilight of my day.
Beneath the burden of my age I bend:
You kindly ease me ere my journey's end.

>   [*To them a* Servant *with* OZMYN;
>   OZMYN *kneels.*

Abenamar [*to* SELIN]. It is enough, my promise makes
      you free;
Resign your bonds, and take your liberty.

Ozmyn. Sir, you are just, and welcome are these bands;
'Tis all the inheritance a son demands.

Selin. Your goodness, O my Ozmyn, is too great;
I am not weary of my fetters yet:
Already, when you move me to resign,
I feel them heavier on your feet than mine.

Enter another Soldier *or* Servant.

Soldier. A youth attends you in the outer room,
Who seems in haste, and does from Ozmyn come.

Abenamar. Conduct him in.—

Ozmyn. Sent from Benzayda, I fear, to me.

To them BENZAYDA, *in the habit of a man.*

Benzayda. My Ozmyn here!
Ozmyn. Benzayda! 'tis she!—

Go, youth, I have no business for thee here;
Go to the Albayzyn, and attend me there.
I'll not be long away; I pray thee go,
By all our love and friendship——
  Benzayda. Ozmyn, no:
I did not take on me this bold disguise,
For ends so low, to cheat your watchmen's eyes.
When I attempted this, it was to do
An action, to be envied even by you;
But you, alas, have been too diligent,
And what I purposed fatally prevent!
Those chains, which for my father I would bear,
I take with less content to find you here;
Except your father will that mercy show,
That I may wear them both for him and you.
  Abenamar. I thank thee, fortune! thou hast, in one hour,
Put all I could have asked thee in my power.
My own lost wealth thou giv'st not only back,
But driv'st upon my coast my pirate's wrack.
  Selin. With Ozmyn's kindness I was grieved before,
But yours, Benzayda, has undone me more.
  Abenamar [*to a* Soldier]. Go, fetch new fetters, and the
    daughter bind.
  Ozmyn. Be just at least, sir, though you are not kind:
Benzayda is not as a prisoner brought,
But comes to suffer for another's fault.
  Abenamar. Then, Ozmyn, mark, that justice which I do,
I, as severely, will exact from you:
The father is not wholly dead in me;
Or you may yet revive it, if it be.
Like tapers new blown out, the fumes remain,
To catch the light, and bring it back again.
Benzayda gave you life, and set you free;
For that, I will restore her liberty.
  Ozmyn. Sir, on my knees I thank you.
  Abenamar. Ozmyn, hold;
One part of what I purpose is untold:
Consider, then, it on your part remains,
When I have broke, not to resume your chains.
Like an indulgent father, I have paid
All debts, which you, my prodigal, have made.
Now you are clear, break off your fond design,
Renounce Benzayda, and be wholly mine.

Ozmyn. Are these the terms? Is this the liberty?
Ah, sir, how can you so inhuman be?
My duty to my life I will prefer;
But life and duty must give place to her.

Abenamar. Consider what you say, for, with one breath,
You disobey my will, and give her death.

Ozmyn. Ah, cruel father, what do you propose!
Must I then kill Benzayda, or must lose?
I can do neither; in this wretched state,
The least that I can suffer is your hate;
And yet that's worse than death: Even while I sue
And choose your hatred, I could die for you.
Break quickly, heart, or let my blood be spilt
By my own hand, to save a father's guilt.

Benzayda. Hear me, my lord, and take this wretched
        life,
To free you from the fear of Ozmyn's wife.
I beg but what with ease may granted be,
To spare your son, and kill your enemy;
Or, if my death's a grace too great to give,
Let me, my lord, without my Ozmyn live.
Far from your sight and Ozmyn's let me go,
And take from him a care, from you a foe.

Ozmyn. How, my Benzayda! can you thus resign
That love, which you have vowed so firmly mine?
Can you leave me for life and liberty?

Benzayda. What I have done will show that I dare die;
But I'll twice suffer death, and go away,
Rather than make you wretched by my stay:
By this my father's freedom will be won;
And to your father I restore a son.

Selin. Cease, cease, my children, your unhappy strife,
Selin will not be ransomed by your life.
Barbarian, thy old foe defies thy rage;   [*To* ABENAMAR.
Turn, from their youth, thy malice to my age.

Benzayda. Forbear, dear father! for your Ozmyn's sake,
Do not such words to Ozmyn's father speak.

Ozmyn. Alas, 'tis counterfeited rage; he strives
But to divert the danger from our lives:
For I can witness, sir, and you might see,
How in your person he considered me.
He still declined the combat where you were;
And you well know it was not out of fear.

Benzayda. Alas, my lord, where can your vengeance fall?
Your justice will not let it reach us all.
Selin and Ozmyn both would sufferers be;
And punishment's a favour done to me.
If we are foes, since you have power to kill,
'Tis generous in you not to have the will;
But, are we foes? Look round, my lord, and see;
Point out that face which is your enemy.
Would you your hand in Selin's blood embrue?
Kill him unarmed, who, armed, shunned killing you?
Am I your foe? Since you detest my line,
That hated name of Zegry I resign
For you, Benzayda will herself disclaim:
Call me your daughter, and forget my name.

Selin. This virtue would even savages subdue;
And shall it want the power to vanquish you?

Ozmyn. It has, it has; I read it in his eyes;
'Tis now not anger, 'tis but shame denies;
A shame of error, that great spirits find,
Which keeps down virtue struggling in the mind.

Abenamar. Yes, I am vanquished! The fierce conflict's
past,
And shame itself is now o'ercome at last.
'Twas long before my stubborn mind was won;
But, melting once, I on the sudden run;
Nor can I hold my headlong kindness more,
Than I could curb my cruel rage before.

[*Runs to* BENZAYDA *and embraces her.*

Benzayda, 'twas your virtue vanquished me:
That could alone surmount my cruelty.

[*Runs to* SELIN *and unbinds him.*

Forgive me, Selin, my neglect of you;
But men, just waking, scarce know what to do.

Ozmyn. O father!

Benzayda. Father!

Abenamar. Dare I own that name!
Speak, speak it often, to remove my shame.

[*They all embrace him.*

O Selin, O my children, let me go!
I have more kindness than I yet can show.
For my recovery I must shun your sight;
Eyes used to darkness cannot bear the light.

[*He runs in, they following him.*

SCENE II—*The Albayzyn*

Enter ALMANZOR, ABDELMELECH, Soldiers.

Almanzor. 'Tis war again, and I am glad 'tis so;
Success shall now by force and courage go.
Treaties are but the combat of the brain,
Where still the stronger lose, and weaker gain.
    Abdelmelech. On this assault, brave sir, which we pre-
    pare,
Depends the sum and fortune of the war.
Encamped without the fort the Spaniard lies,
And may, in spite of us, send in supplies.
Consider yet, ere we attack the place,
What 'tis to storm it in an army's face.
    Almanzor. The minds of heroes their own measures are,
They stand exempted from the rules of war.
One loose, one sally of the hero's soul,
Does all the military art control:
While timorous wit goes round, or fords the shore,
He shoots the gulf, and is already o'er;
And, when the enthusiastic fit is spent,
Looks back amazed at what he underwent.   [*Exeunt.*
                                              [*An alarum within.*

Re-enter ALMANZOR *and* ABDELMELECH, *with their*
Soldiers.

    Abdelmelech. They fly, they fly; take breath and charge
    again.
    Almanzor. Make good your entrance, and bring up more
    men.
I feared, brave friend, my aid had been too late.
    Abdelmelech. You drew us from the jaws of certain fate.
At my approach,
The gate was open, and the drawbridge down;
But, when they saw I stood, and came not on,
They charged with fury on my little band.
Who much o'erpowered, could scarce the shock with-
    stand.
    Almanzor. Ere night we shall the whole Albayzyn gain.
But see, the Spaniards march along the plain

To its relief; you, Abdelmelech, go,
And force the rest, while I repulse the foe.

          [*Exit* ALMANZOR.

  Enter ABDALLA, *and some few* Soldiers, *who seem
fearful.*

 Abdalla. Turn, cowards, turn! there is no hope in flight;
You yet may live, if you but dare to fight.
Come, you brave few, who only fear to fly,
We're not enough to conquer, but to die.
 Abdelmelech. No, prince, that mean advantage I refuse;
'Tis in your power a nobler fate to choose.
Since we are rivals, honour does command
We should not die but by each other's hand.
Retire; and, if it prove my destiny   [*To his men.*
To fall, I charge you let the prince go free.

     [*The* Soldiers *depart on both sides.*

 Abdalla. O Abdelmelech, that I knew some way
This debt of honour, which, I owe, to pay!
But fate has left this only means for me,
To die, and leave you Lyndaraxa free.
 Abdelmelech. He, who is vanquished and is slain, is
  blest
The wretched conqueror can ne'er have rest;
But is reserved a harder fate to prove,
Bound in the fetters of dissembled love.
 Abdalla. Now thou art base, and I deserve her more;
Without complaint I will to death adore.
Dar'st thou see faults, and yet dost love pretend?
I will even Lyndaraxa's crimes defend.
 Abdelmelech. Maintain her cause, then, better than thy
  own,—
Than thy ill-got, and worse-defended throne.

     [*They fight,* ABDALLA *falls.*

 Abdelmelech. Now ask your life.
 Abdalla. 'Tis gone; that busy thing,
The soul, is packing up, and just on wing,
Like parting swallows, when they seek the spring:
Like them, at its appointed time, it goes,
And flies to countries more unknown than those.

Enter LYNDARAXA *hastily, sees them, and is going out
again.* ABDELMELECH *stops her.*

Abdelmelech. No, you shall stay, and see a sacrifice,
Not offered by my sword, but by your eyes.
From those he first ambitious poison drew,
And swelled to empire for the love of you.
Accursed fair!
Thy comet-blaze portends a prince's fate;
And suffering subjects groan beneath thy weight.
 Abdalla. Cease, rival, cease!
I would have forced you, but it wonnot be;
I beg you now, upbraid her not for me.
You, fairest, to my memory be kind! [*To* LYNDARAXA.
Lovers like me your sex will seldom find.
When I usurped a crown for love of you,
I then did more than, dying, now I do.
I'm still the same as when my love begun;
And, could I now this fate foresee or shun,
Would yet do all I have already done.   [*Dies.*
   [*She puts her handkerchief to her eyes.*
 Abdelmelech. Weep on, weep on, for it becomes you
  now;
These tears you to that love may well allow.
His unrepenting soul, if it could move
Upward in crimes, flew spotted with your love;
And brought contagion to the blessed above.
 Lyndaraxa. He's gone, and peace go with a constant
  mind!
His love deserved I should have been more kind;
But then your love and greater worth I knew:
I was unjust to him, but just to you.
 Abdelmelech. I was his enemy, and rival too,
Yet I some tears to his misfortune owe:
You owe him more; weep then, and join with me:
So much is due even to humanity.
 Lyndaraxa. Weep for this wretch, whose memory I hate!
Whose folly made us both unfortunate!
Weep for this fool, who did my laughter move!
This whining, tedious, heavy lump of love!
 Abdelmelech. Had fortune favoured him, and frowned
  on me,
I then had been that heavy fool, not he:

Just this had been my funeral elegy.
Thy arts and falsehood I before did know,
But this last baseness was concealed till now;
And 'twas no more than needful to be known;
I could be cured by such an act alone.
My love, half blasted, yet in time would shoot;
But this last tempest rends it to the root.

    Lyndaraxa. These little piques, which now your anger
      move,
Will vanish, and are only signs of love.
You've been too fierce; and, at some other time,
I should not with such ease forgive your crime:
But, in a day of public joy like this,
I pardon, and forget whate'er's amiss.

    Abdelmelech. These arts have oft prevailed, but must
      no more:
The spell is ended, and the enchantment o'er.
You have at last destroyed, with much ado,
That love, which none could have destroyed, but you.
My love was blind to your deluding art;
But blind men feel, when stabbed so near the heart.

    Lyndaraxa. I must confess there was some pity due;
But I concealed it out of love to you.

    Abdelmelech. No, Lyndaraxa; 'tis at last too late;
Our loves have mingled with too much of fate.
I would, but cannot now, myself deceive:
O that you still could cheat, and I believe!

    Lyndaraxa. Do not so light a quarrel long pursue:
You grieve your rival was less loved than you.
'Tis hard, when men of kindness must complain!

    Abdelmelech. I'm now awake, and cannot dream again.

    Lyndaraxa. Yet hear——

    Abdelmelech. No more; nothing my heart can bend:
That queen you scorned, you shall this night attend.
Your life the king has pardoned for my sake;
But on your pride I some revenge must take.
See now the effects of what your arts designed!
Thank your inconstant and ambitious mind.
'Tis just that she, who to no love is true,
Should be forsaken, and contemned, like you.

    Lyndaraxa. All arts of injured women I will try:
First I will be revenged; and then I'll die.
But, like some falling tower,

Whose seeming firmness does the sight beguile,
So hold I up my nodding head a while,
Till they come under; and reserve my fall,
That with my ruins I may reach them all.
    Abdelmelech. Conduct her hence.

                         [Exit LYNDARAXA *guarded.*

Enter a Soldier.

    Soldier. Almanzor is victorious without fight;
The foes retreated when he came in sight.
Under the walls, this night, his men are drawn,
And mean to seek the Spaniard with the dawn.
    Abdelmelech. The sun's declined:
Command the watch be set without delay,
And in the fort let bold Benducar stay.——   *[Exit* Soldier.
I'll haste to court, where solitude I'll fly,
And herd, like wounded deer, in company.
But oh, how hard a passion to remove,
When I must shun myself to 'scape from love!   *[Exit.*

SCENE III—*Gallery in the Alhambra*

ZULEMA, HAMET.

    Hamet. I thought your passion for the queen was dead,
Or that your love had, with your hopes, been fled.
    Zulema. 'Twas like a fire within a furnace pent;
I smothered it, and kept it long from vent;
But, fed with looks, and blown with sighs so fast,
It broke a passage through my lips at last.
    Hamet. Where found you confidence your suit to move?
Our broken fortunes are not fit to love.
Well; you declared your love:—What followed then?
    Zulema. She looked as judges do on guilty men,
When big with fate they triumph in their dooms,
And smile before the deadly sentence comes.
Silent I stood, as I were thunder-struck;
Condemned and executed with a look.
    Hamet. You must, with haste, some remedy prepare:
Now you are in, you must break through the snare.
    Zulema. She said, she would my folly yet conceal;
But vowed my next attempt she would reveal.
    Hamet. 'Tis dark; and in this lonely gallery,
Remote from noise, and shunning every eye,

One hour each evening she in private mourns,
And prays, and to the circle then returns.
Now, if you dare, attempt her passing by.
   Zulema. These lighted tapers show the time is nigh.
Perhaps my courtship will not be in vain:
At least, few women will of force complain.

At the other end of the Gallery enter ALMANZOR *and*
ESPERANZA.

   Hamet. Almanzor, and with him
The favourite slave of the sultana queen.
   Zulema. Ere they approach, let us retire unseen,
And watch our time when they return again:
Then force shall give, if favour does deny;
And, that once done, we'll to the Spaniards fly.

[*Exeunt* ZULEMA *and* HAMET.

   Almanzor. Now stand; the apartment of the queen is
     near,
And, from this place, your voice will reach her ear.

[ESPERANZA *goes out.*

SONG IN TWO PARTS

I

He. How unhappy a lover am I,
     While I sigh for my Phyllis in vain:
   All my hopes of delight
   Are another man's right,
     Who is happy, while I am in pain!

II

She. Since her honour allows no relief,
     But to pity the pains which you bear,
   'Tis the best of your fate,
   In a hopeless estate,
     To give o'er, and betimes to despair.

III

He. I have tried the false med'cine in vain;
     For I wish what I hope not to win:
   From without, my desire
   Has no food to its fire;
     But it burns and consumes me within.

IV

She. Yet, at least 'tis a pleasure to know
            That you are not unhappy alone:
        For the nymph you adore
        Is as wretched, and more;
            And counts all your sufferings her own.

V

He.   O ye gods, let me suffer for both;
            At the feet of my Phyllis I'll lie:
        I'll resign up my breath,
        And take pleasure in death,
            To be pitied by her when I die.

VI

She. What her honour denied you in life,
            In her death she will give to your love.
        Such a flame as is true
        After fate will renew,
            For the souls to meet closer above.

Enter ESPERANZA *again, after the song.*

Almanzor. Accept this diamond, till I can present
Something more worthy my acknowledgment.
And now farewell: I will attend, alone,
Her coming forth; and make my sufferings known.
                                    [*Exit* ESPERANZA.
A hollow wind comes whistling through that door,
And a cold shivering seizes me all o'er;
My teeth, too, chatter with a sudden fright:—
These are the raptures of too fierce delight,
The combat of the tyrants, Hope and Fear;
Which hearts, for want of field-room, cannot bear.
I grow impatient;—this, or that's the room:—
I'll meet her;—now, methinks I hear her come.
        [*He goes to the door; the* Ghost *of his Mother meets
            him: He starts back: The* Ghost *stands in the door.*
Well mayst thou make thy boast whate'er thou art!
Thou art the first e'er made Almanzor start.
My legs
Shall bear me to thee in their own despite:
I'll rush into the covert of thy night,

And pull thee backward, by thy shroud, to light;
Or else I'll squeeze thee, like a bladder, there,
And make thee groan thyself away to air.

> [*The* Ghost *retires.*

So, thou art gone! Thou canst no conquest boast:
I thought what was the courage of a ghost.—
The grudging of my ague yet remains;
My blood, like icicles, hangs in my veins,
And does not drop;—Be master of that door,
We two will not disturb each other more.
I erred a little, but extremes may join;
That door was hell's, but this is heaven's and mine.

> [*Goes to the other door, and is met again by the*
> Ghost.

Again! by Heaven, I do conjure thee, speak!
What art thou, spirit? and what dost thou seek?

> [*The* Ghost *comes on softly after the conjuration; and*
> ALMANZOR *retires to the middle of the stage.*

Ghost. I am the ghost of her who gave thee birth;
The airy shadow of her mouldering earth.
Love of thy father me through seas did guide;
On seas I bore thee, and on seas I died.
I died; and for my winding-sheet a wave
I had, and all the ocean for my grave.
But, when my soul to bliss did upward move,
I wandered round the crystal walls above;
But found the eternal fence so steeply high,
That, when I mounted to the middle sky,
I flagged, and fluttered down, and could not fly.
Then, from the battlements of the heavenly tower,
A watchman angel bid me wait this hour;
And told me, I had yet a task assigned,
To warn that little pledge I left behind;
And to divert him, ere it were too late,
From crimes unknown, and errors of his fate:

> *Almanzor.* Speak, holy shade; thou parent-form, speak
> on!   [*Bowing.*

Instruct thy mortal-elemented son;
For here I wander, to myself unknown.
But O, thou better part of heavenly air,
Teach me, kind spirit, since I'm still thy care,
My parents' names:
If I have yet a father, let me know

To whose old age my humble youth must bow,
And pay its duty, if he mortal be,
Or adoration, if a mind, like thee.

Ghost. Then, what I may, I'll tell.—
From ancient blood thy father's lineage springs,
Thy mother's thou deriv'st from stems of kings.
A Christian born, and born again that day,
When sacred water washed thy sins away.
Yet, bred in errors, thou dost misemploy
That strength Heaven gave thee, and its flock destroy.

Almanzor. By reason, man a godhead may discern,
But how he would be worshipped cannot learn.

Ghost. Heaven does not now thy ignorance reprove,
But warns thee from known crimes of lawless love.
That crime thou knowest, and, knowing, dost not shun,
Shall an unknown and greater crime pull on:
But if, thus warned, thou leav'st this cursed place,
Then shalt thou know the author of thy race.
Once more I'll see thee; then my charge is done.
Far hence, upon the Mountains of the Moon,
Is my abode; where heaven and nature smile,
And strew with flowers the secret bed of Nile.
Blessed souls are there refined, and made more bright,
And, in the shades of heaven, prepared for light.

[*Exit* Ghost.

Almanzor. O Heaven, how dark a riddle's thy decree,
Which bounds our wills, yet seems to leave them free:
Since thy foreknowledge cannot be in vain,
Our choice must be what thou didst first ordain.
Thus, like a captive in an isle confined,
Man walks at large, a prisoner of the mind:
Wills all his crimes, while Heaven the indictment draws,
And, pleading guilty, justifies the laws.
Let fate be fate; the lover and the brave
Are ranked, at least, above the vulgar slave.
Love makes me willing to my death to run;
And courage scorns the death it cannot shun.

Enter ALMAHIDE *with a taper.*

Almahide. My light will sure discover those who talk.—
Who dares to interrupt my private walk?

Almanzor. He, who dares love, and for that love must
die,

And, knowing this, dares yet love on, am I.

    Almahide. That love which you can hope, and I can
      pay,
May be received and given in open day:
My praise and my esteem you had before;
And you have bound yourself to ask no more.

    Almanzor. Yes, I have bound myself; but will you take
The forfeit of that bond, which force did make?

    Almahide. You know you are from recompence de-
      barred;
But purest love can live without reward.

    Almanzor. Pure love had need be to itself a feast;
For, like pure elements, 'twill nourish least.

    Almahide. It therefore yields the only pure content;
For it, like angels, need no nourishment.
To eat and drink can no perfection be;
All appetite implies necessity.

    Almanzor. 'Twere well if I could like a spirit live:
But, do not angels food to mortals give?
What if some demon should my death foreshow,
Or bid me change, and to the Christians go;
Will you not think I merit some reward,
When I my love above my life regard?

    Almahide. In such a case your change must be allowed;
I would myself dispense with what you vowed.

    Almanzor. Were I to die that hour when I possess,
This minute shall begin my happiness.

    Almahide. The thoughts of death your passion would
      remove;
Death is a cold encouragement to love.

    Almanzor. No; from my joys I to my death would run,
And think the business of my life well done:
But I should walk a discontented ghost,
If flesh and blood were to no purpose lost.

    Almahide. You love me not, Almanzor; if you did,
You would not ask what honour must forbid.

    Almanzor. And what is honour, but a love well hid?

    Almahide. Yes, 'tis the conscience of an act well done,
Which gives us power our own desires to shun;
The strong and secret curb of headlong will;
The self-reward of good, and shame of ill.

    Almanzor. These, madam, are the maxims of the day,
When honour's present, and when love's away.

The duty of poor honour were too hard,
In arms all day, at night to mount the guard.
Let him, in pity, now to rest retire;
Let these soft hours be watched by warm desire.

Almahide. Guards, who all day on painful duty keep,
In dangers are not privileged to sleep.

Almanzor. And with what dangers are you threatened
here?
Am I, alas! a foe for you to fear?
See, madam, at your feet this enemy;   [*Kneels*
Without your pity and your love I die.

Almahide. Rise, rise, and do not empty hopes pursue;
Yet think that I deny myself, not you.

Almanzor. A happiness so high I cannot bear:
My love's too fierce, and you too killing fair.
I grow enraged to see such excellence!—
If words, so much disordered, give offence,
My love's too full of zeal to think of sense.
Be you like me; dull reason hence remove,
And tedious forms, and give a loose to love.
Love eagerly; let us be gods to-night;
And do not, with half yielding, dash delight.

Almahide. Thou strong seducer, Opportunity!
Of womankind, half are undone by thee!
Though I resolve I will not be misled,
I wish I had not heard what you have said!
I cannot be so wicked to comply;
And, yet, am most unhappy to deny!
Away!

Almanzor. I will not move me from this place:
I can take no denial from that face!

Almahide. If I could yield,—but think not that I will,—
You and myself I in revenge should kill;
For I should hate us both, when it were done,
And would not to the shame of life be won.

Almanzor. Live but to-night, and trust to-morrow's
mind:
Ere that can come, there's a whole life behind.
Methinks, already crowned with joys I lie,
Speechless and breathless, in an ecstasy!
Not absent in one thought: I am all there:
Still close, yet wishing still to be more near.

Almahide. Deny your own desires: for it will be

Too little now to be denied by me.
Will he, who does all great, all noble seem,
Be lost and forfeit to his own esteem?
Will he, who may with heroes claim a place,
Belie that fame, and to himself be base?
Think how august and godlike you did look,
When my defence, unbribed, you undertook;
But, when an act so brave you disavow,
How little, and how mercenary now!

    Almanzor. Are, then, my services no higher prized?
And can I fall so low to be despised?

    Almahide. Yes; for whatever may be bought, is low;
And you yourself, who sell yourself, are so.
Remember the great act you did this day:
How did your love to virtue then give way!
When you gave freedom to my captive lord,—
That rival who possessed what you adored,—
Of such a deed what price can there be made?
Think well; is that an action to be paid?
It was a miracle of virtue shown;
And wonders are with wonder paid alone.
And would you all that secret joy of mind,
Which great souls only in great actions find,
All that, for one tumultuous minute lose?

    Almanzor. I would that minute before ages choose.
Praise is the pay of heaven for doing good;
But love's the best return for flesh and blood.

    Almahide. You've moved my heart so much, I can deny
No more: but know, Almanzor, I can die.
Thus far my virtue yields; if I have shown
More love than what I ought, let this atone.

                        [*Going to stab herself.*

    Almanzor. Hold, hold!
Such fatal proofs of love you shall not give:
Deny me; hate me; both are just,—but live!
Your virtue I will ne'er disturb again;
Nor dare to ask, for fear I should obtain.

    Almahide. 'Tis generous to have conquered your desire;
You mount above your wish, and lose it higher.
There's pride in virtue, and a kindly heat;
Not feverish, like your love, but full as great.
Farewell; and may our loves hereafter be
But image-like, to heighten piety.

Almanzor. 'Tis time I should be gone.—
Alas! I am but half converted yet;
All I resolve, I with one look forget;
And, like a lion, whom no arts can tame,
Shall tear even those, who would my rage reclaim.
[Exeunt severally.

[ZULEMA *and* HAMET *watch* ALMANZOR; *and when
he is gone, go in after the* Queen.

Enter ABDELMELECH and LYNDARAXA.

Lyndaraxa. It is enough, you've brought me to this
place:
Here stop and urge no further my disgrace.
Kill me; in death your mercy will be seen,
But make me not a captive to the queen.
    Abdelmelech. 'Tis therefore I this punishment provide:
This only can revenge me on your pride.
Prepare to suffer what you shun in vain;
And know, you now are to obey, not reign.

Enter ALMAHIDE, shrieking; her hair loose; she runs over
the stage.

Almahide. Help, help, O heaven, some help!

Enter ZULEMA and HAMET.

Zulema. Make haste before,
And intercept her passage to the door.
    Abdelmelech. Villains, what act are you attempting
here!
    Almahide. I thank thee, heaven! some succour does
appear.
        [*As* ABDELMELECH *is going to help the* Queen,
        LYNDARAXA *pulls out his sword, and holds it.*
    Abdelmelech. With what ill fate my good design is
curst!
    Zulema. We have no time to think; despatch him first.
    Abdelmelech. O for a sword!
        [*They make at* ABDELMELECH; *he goes off at one
        door while the Queen escapes at the other.*
    Zulema. Ruined!
    Hamet. Undone!
    Lyndaraxa. And which is worst of all,

He is escaped.

    Zulema. I hear them loudly call.

    Lyndaraxa. Your fear will lose you; call as loud as they:
I have not time to teach you what to say.
The court will in a moment all be here;
But second what I say, and do not fear.
Call help; run that way; leave the rest to me.

                [ZULEMA *and* HAMET *retire, and within*
                  cry,—Help!

Enter, at several doors, the King, ABENAMAR, SELIN,
    OZMYN, ALMANZOR, *with* Guards *attending* BOAB-
    DELIN.

    Boabdelin. What can the cause of all this tumult be?
And what the meaning of that naked sword?

    Lyndaraxa. I'll tell, when fear will so much breath
afford.—
The queen and Abdelmelech—'Twill not out—
Even I, who saw it, of the truth yet doubt,
It seems so strange.

    Almanzor. Did she not name the queen?
Haste; speak,

    Lyndaraxa. How dare I speak what I have seen?—
With Hamet, and with Zulema I went,
To pay both theirs, and my acknowledgment
To Almahide, and by her mouth implore
Your clemency, our fortunes to restore.
We chose this hour, which we believed most free,
When she retired from noise and company.
The antechamber past, we gently knocked,
Unheard it seems, but found the lodgings locked.
In duteous silence while we waited there,
We first a noise, and then long whispers hear;
Yet thought it was the queen at prayers alone,
Till she distinctly said,—If this were known,
My love, what shame, what danger would ensue!
Yet I,—and sighed,—could venture more for you!

    Boabdelin. O heaven, what do I hear!

    Almanzor. Let her go on.

    Lyndaraxa. And how,—then murmured in a bigger tone
Another voice,—and how should it be known?
This hour is from your court attendants free;

The king suspects Almanzor, but not me.

   Zulema. I find her drift; Hamet, be confident;

[At the door.

Second her words, and fear not the event.

   Zulema *and* Hamet *enter. The* King *embraces them.*

   Boabdelin. Welcome, my only friends;—behold in me,
O kings, behold the effects of clemency!
See here the gratitude of pardoned foes!
That life, I gave them, they for me expose!

   Hamet. Though Abdelmelech was our friend before,
When duty called us, he was so no more.

   Almanzor. Damn your delay—you torturers, proceed!
I will not hear one word but Almahide.

   Boabdelin. When you, within, the traitor's voice did hear,
What did you then?

   Zulema. I durst not trust my ear;
But, peeping through the key-hole I espied
The queen, and Abdelmelech by her side;
She on the couch, he on her bosom lay;
Her hand about his neck his head did stay,
And from his forehead wiped the drops away.

   Boabdelin. Go on, go on, my friends, to clear my doubt;
I hope I shall have life to hear you out.

   Zulema. What had been, sir, you may suspect too well;
What followed, modesty forbids to tell:
Seeing what we had thought beyond belief,
Our hearts so swelled with anger and with grief,
That, by plain force, we strove the door to break.
He, fearful, and with guilt, or love, grown weak,
Just as we entered, 'scaped the other way;
Nor did the amazed queen behind him stay.

   Lyndaraxa. His sword, in so much haste, he could not mind;
But left this witness of his crime behind.

   Boabdelin. O proud, ungrateful, faithless womankind!
How changed, and what a monster am I made!
My love, my honour, ruined and betrayed!

   Almanzor. Your love and honour! mine are ruined worse:—
Furies and hell!—What right have you to curse?
Dull husbands as you are,

What can your love, or what your honour, be?
I am her lover, and she's false to me.

    Boabdelin. Go; when the authors of my shame are
    found,
Let them be taken instantly and bound:
They shall be punished as our laws require:
'Tis just, that flames should be condemned to fire.
This, with the dawn of morning shall be done.

    Abenamar. You haste too much her execution.
Her condemnation ought to be deferred;
With justice, none can be condemned unheard.

    Boabdelin. A formal process tedious is, and long;
Besides, the evidence is full and strong.

    Lyndaraxa. The law demands two witnesses; and she
Is cast, for which heaven knows I grieve, by three.

    Ozmyn. Hold, sir! since you so far insist on law,
We can from thence one just advantage draw:
That law, which dooms adultresses to die,
Gives champions, too, to slandered chastity.

    Almanzor. And how dare you, who from my bounty
    live,
Intrench upon my love's prerogative?
Your courage in your own concernments try;
Brothers are things remote, while I am by.

    Ozmyn. I knew not you thus far her cause would own,
And must not suffer you to fight alone;
Let two to two in equal combat join;
You vindicate her person, I her line.

    Lyndaraxa. Of all mankind, Almanzor has least right
In her defence, who wrong'd his love, to fight.

    Almanzor. 'Tis false: she is not ill, nor can she be;
She must be chaste, because she's loved by me.

    Zulema. Dare you, what sense and reason prove, deny?

    Almanzor. When she's in question, sense and reason lie.

    Zulema. For truth, and for my injured sovereign,
What I have said, I will to death maintain.

    Ozmyn. So foul a falsehood, whoe'er justifies,
Is basely born, and, like a villain, lies.
In witness of that truth, be this my gage.
                    [Takes a ring from his finger.

    Hamet. I take it; and despise a traitor's rage.

    Boabdelin. The combat's yours.—A guard the lists
    surround;

Then raise a scaffold in the encompassed ground,
And, by it, piles of wood; in whose just fire,
Her champions slain, the adultress shall expire.

 Abenamar. We ask no favour, but what arms will yield.

 Boabdelin. Choose, then, two equal judges of the field:
Next morning shall decide the doubtful strife,
Condemn the unchaste, or quit the virtuous wife.

 Almanzor. But I am both ways cursed:
For Almahide must die, if I am slain:
Or for my rival I the conquest gain.   [*Exeunt.*

ACT V

SCENE I

ALMANZOR *solus.*

I HAVE outfaced myself; and justified
What I knew false, to all the world beside.
She was as faithless as her sex could be;
And, now I am alone, she's so to me.
She's fallen! and, now, where shall we virtue find?
She was the last that stood of womankind.
Could she so holily my flames remove,
And fall that hour to Abdelmelech's love?
Yet her protection I must undertake;
Not now for love, but for my honour's sake,
That moved me first, and must oblige me still:
My cause is good, however hers be ill.
I'll leave her, when she's freed; and let it be
Her punishment, she could be false to me.

To him ABDELMELECH, *guarded.*

 Abdelmelech. Heaven is not heaven, nor are there
  deities;
There is some new rebellion in the skies.
All that was good and holy is dethroned,
And lust and rapine are for justice owned.

 Almanzor. 'Tis true; what justice in that heaven can
  be,
Which thus affronts me with the sight of thee?
Why must I be from just revenge debarred?

Chains are thy arms, and prisons are thy guard:
The death, thou diest, may to a husband be
A satisfaction; but 'tis none to me.
My love would justice to itself afford;
But now thou creep'st to death below my sword.

    Abdelmelech. This threatening would show better were
I free.

    Almanzor. No; wert thou freed, I would not threaten
thee;
This arm should then—but now it is too late!
I could redeem thee to a nobler fate,
As some huge rock,
Rent from its quarry, does the waves divide,
So I
Would souse upon thy guards, and dash them wide:
Then, to my rage left naked and alone,
Thy too much freedom thou shouldst soon bemoan;
Dared [18] like a lark, that, on the open plain
Pursued and cuffed, seeks shelter now in vain;
So on the ground wouldst thou expecting lie,
Not daring to afford me victory.
But yet thy fate's not ripe; it is decreed,
Before thou diest, that Almahide be freed.
My honour first her danger must remove,
And then revenge on thee my injured love.

                        [*Exeunt severally.*

SCENE II

The SCENE *changes to the Vivarambla, and appears filled
with* Spectators; *a scaffold hung with black.*

Enter the Queen, *guarded, with* ESPERANZA.

    Almahide. See how the gazing people crowd the place,
All gaping to be filled with my disgrace.

                       [*A shout within.*
That shout, like the hoarse peals of vultures, rings,
When over fighting fields they beat their wings.—
Let never woman trust in innocence,
Or think her chastity its own defence.
Mine has betrayed me to this public shame,
And virtue, which I served, is but a name.

[18] *I.e.* scared with bright objects, or with a hawk.

Esperanza. Leave then that shadow, and for succour
    fly
To Him we serve, the Christian's Deity.
Virtue's no god, nor has she power divine:
But He protects it, who did first enjoin.
Trust then in Him; and from His grace implore
Faith to believe, what rightly we adore.
    Almahide. Thou Power unknown, if I have erred, for-
      give!
My infancy was taught what I believe.
But if the Christians truly worship thee,
Let me thy Godhead in thy succour see:
So shall thy justice in my safety shine,
And all my days, which thou shalt add, be thine!

    Enter the King, ABENAMAR, LYNDARAXA, BENZAYDA:
    then ABDELMELECH, *guarded; and after him* SELIN
    and ALABEZ, *as Judges of the Field.*

    Boabdelin. You, judges of the field, first take your
      place.—
The accusers and accused bring face to face.
Set guards, and let the lists be opened wide;
And may just heaven assist the juster side!
    Almahide. What! not one tender look, one passing word?
Farewell, my much unkind, but still loved lord!
Your throne was for my humble fate too high,
And therefore heaven thinks fit that I should die.
My story be forgot, when I am dead,
Lest it should fright some other from your bed;
And, to forget me, may you soon adore
Some happier maid,—yet none could love you more.
But may you never think me innocent,
Lest it should cause you trouble to repent.
    Boabdelin. 'Tis pity so much beauty should not live;
                           [*Aside.*
Yet I too much am injured, to forgive. [*Goes to his seat.*
    [*Trumpets: Then enter two Moors, bearing two naked
      swords before the accusers* ZULEMA *and* HAMET, *who
      follow them. The Judges seat themselves; the Queen
      and* ABDELMELECH *are led to the scaffold.*
    Alabez. Say for what end you thus in arms appear;
What are your names, and what demand you here?
    Zulema. The Zegrys' ancient race our lineage claims;

And Zulema and Hamet are our names.
Like loyal subjects in these lists we stand,
And justice in our king's behalf demand.

   Hamet. For whom, in witness of what both have seen,
Bound by our duty, we appeach the queen
And Abdelmelech, of adultery.

   Zulema. Which, like true knights, we will maintain, or
      die.

   Alabez. Swear on the Alcoran your cause is right,
And Mahomet so prosper you in fight.
      [*They touch their foreheads with the Alcoran, and bow.*
      [*Trumpets on the other side of the stage; two Moors, as
         before, with bare swords, before* ALMANZOR *and*
         OZMYN.

   Selin. Say for what end you thus in arms appear;
What are your names, and what demand you here?

   Almanzor. Ozmyn is his, Almanzor is my name;
We come as champions of the queen's fair fame.

   Ozmyn. To prove these Zegrys, like false traitors, lie;
Which, like true knights, we will maintain, or die.

   Selin [*to* ALMAHIDE]. Madam, do you for champions
      take these two,
By their success to live or die?

   Almahide. I do.

   Selin. Swear on the Alcoran your cause is right;
And Mahomet so prosper you in fight.
                                    [*They kiss the Alcoran.*
      [OZMYN *and* BENZAYDA *embrace, and take leave in
         dumb show; while* LYNDARAXA *speaks to her
         brother.*

   Lyndaraxa. If you o'ercome, let neither of them live,
But use with care the advantages I give:
One of their swords in fight shall useless be;
The bearer of it is suborned by me.
                              [*She and* BENZAYDA *retire.*

   Alabez. Now, principals and seconds, all advance.
And each of you assist his fellow's chance.

   Selin. The wind and sun we equally divide,
So let the event of arms the truth decide.
The chances of the fight, and every wound,
The trumpets, on the victor's part, resound.
         [*The trumpets sound;* ALMANZOR *and* ZULEMA
            meet and fight; OZMYN *and* HAMET. *After some*

passes, the sword of OZMYN *breaks; he retires,*
defending himself, and is wounded; the Zegrys'
trumpets sound their advantage. ALMANZOR, *in*
the meantime, drives ZULEMA *to the farther end*
of the stage, till hearing the trumpets of the
adverse party, he looks back, and sees OZMYN'S
misfortune; he makes at ZULEMA *just as* OZMYN
falls, in retiring, and HAMET *is thrusting at him.*

Hamet [*to* OZMYN, *thrusting*]. Our difference now shall
soon determined be.

Almanzor. Hold, traitor, and defend thyself from me.
[HAMET *leaves* OZMYN (*who cannot rise*), *and both*
he and ZULEMA *fall on* ALMANZOR, *and press him;*
he retires, and HAMET, *advancing first, is run*
through the body, and falls. The Queen's *trumpets*
sound. ALMANZOR *pursues* ZULEMA.

Lyndaraxa. I must make haste some remedy to find:—
Treason, Almanzor, treason! look behind.
[ALMANZOR *looks behind him to see who calls, and*
ZULEMA *takes the advantage, and wounds him;*
the Zegrys' trumpets sound; ALMANZOR *turns*
upon ZULEMA, *and wounds him; he falls. The*
Queen's *trumpets sound.*

Almanzor. Now triumph in thy sister's treachery,
[*Stabbing him.*

Zulema Hold, hold! I have enough to make me die,
But, that I may in peace resign my breath,
I must confess my crime before my death.
Mine is the guilt; the queen is innocent;
I loved her, and, to compass my intent,
Used force, which Abdelmelech did prevent.
The lie my sister forged; but O! my fate
Comes on too soon, and I repent too late.
Fair queen, forgive; and let my penitence
Expiate some part of——   [*Dies.*

Almahide. Even thy whole offence!

Almanzor [*to the* Judges]. If aught remains in the
sultana's cause,
I here am ready to fulfil the laws.

Selin. The law is fully satisfied, and we
Pronounce the queen and Abdelmelech free.

Abdelmelech. Heaven, thou art just!
[*The* Judges *rise from their seats and go before*

ALMANZOR to the Queen's *scaffold; he unbinds
the* Queen *and* ABDELMELECH; *they all go off,
the People shouting, and the trumpets sounding
the while.*

Boabdelin. Before we pay our thanks, or show our joy,
Let us our needful charity employ.
Some skilful surgeon speedily be found,
To apply fit remedies to Ozmyn's wound.

  Benzayda [*running to* OZMYN]. That be my charge: my
    linen I will tear;
Wash it with tears, and bind it with my hair.

  Ozmyn. With how much pleasure I my pains endure,
And bless the wound which causes such a cure!

      [*Exit* OZMYN *led by* BENZAYDA *and* ABENAMAR.

  Boabdelin. Some from the place of combat bear the
    slain.—
Next Lyndaraxa's death I should ordain:
But let her, who this mischief did contrive,
For ever banished from Granada live.

  Lyndaraxa. Thou shouldst have punished more, or not
    at all:
By her thou hast not ruined, thou shalt fall.
The Zegrys shall revenge their branded line,
Betray their gate, and with the Christians join.   [*Aside.*

      [*Exit* LYNDARAXA *with* ALABEZ; *the bodies of her
      brothers are borne after her.*

ALMANZOR, ALMAHIDE *and* ESPERANZA, *re-enter
to the* King.

  Almahide. The thanks thus paid, which first to heaven
    were due,
My next, Almanzor, let me pay to you:
Somewhat there is of more concernment too,
Which 'tis not fit you should in public know,
First let your wounds be dressed with speedy care,
And then you shall the important secret share.

  Almanzor. Whene'er you speak,
Were my wounds mortal, they should still bleed on;
And I would listen till my life were gone:
My soul should even for your last accent stay,
And then shout out, and with such speed obey,
It should not bait at heaven to stop its way.

      [*Exit* ALMANZOR.

Boabdelin. 'Tis true, Almanzor did her honours save,
But yet what private business can they have?
Such freedom virtue will not sure allow;
I cannot clear my heart, but must my brow.   [*Aside.*
                              [*He approaches* ALMAHIDE.
Welcome, again, my virtuous, loyal wife;
Welcome to love, to honour, and to life!
                    [*Goes to salute her, she starts back.*
You seem
As if you from a loathed embrace did go!
    Almahide. Then briefly will I speak, since you must
         know
What to the world my future acts will show:
But hear me first, and then my reasons weigh.
'Tis known, how duty led me to obey
My father's choice; and how I since did live,
You, sir, can best your testimony give.
How to your aid I have Almanzor brought,
When by rebellious crowds your life was sought;
Then, how I bore your causeless jealousy.
(For I must speak) and after set you free,
When you were prisoner in the chance of war:
These, sure, are proofs of love.
    Boabdelin. I grant they are.
    Almahide. And could you then, O cruelly unkind!
So ill reward such tenderness of mind?
Could you, denying what our laws afford
The meanest subject on a traitor's word,
Unheard, condemn, and suffer me to go
To death, and yet no common pity show!
    Boabdelin. Love filled my heart even to the brim before;
And then, with too much jealousy, boiled o'er.
    Almahide. Be't love or jealousy, 'tis such a crime,
That I'm forewarned to trust a second time.
Know, then, my prayers to heaven shall never cease,
To crown your arms in war, your wars with peace;
But from this day I will not know your bed:
Though Almahide still lives, your wife is dead;
And with her dies a love so pure and true,
It could be killed by nothing but by you. [*Exit* ALMAHIDE.
    Boabdelin. Yes; you will spend your life in prayers for
         me,
And yet this hour my hated rival see.

She might a husband's jealousy forgive;
But she will only for Almanzor live.
It is resolved; I will myself provide
That vengeance, which my useless laws denied;
And, by Almanzor's death, at once remove
The rival of my empire, and my love.   [*Exit* BOABDELIN.

Enter ALMAHIDE, *led by* ALMANZOR, *and followed by*
ESPERANZA; *she speaks, entering.*

Almahide. How much, Almanzor, to your aid I owe,
Unable to repay, I blush to know;
Yet, forced by need, ere I can clear that score,
I, like ill debtors, come to borrow more.

Almanzor. Your new commands I on my knees attend:
I was created for no other end.
Born to be yours, I do by nature serve,
And, like the labouring beast, no thanks deserve.

Almahide. Yet first your virtue to your succour call,
For in this hard command you'll need it all.

Almanzor. I stand prepared; and whatsoe'er it be,
Nothing is hard to him, who loves like me.

Almahide. Then know, I from your love must yet implore
One proof:—that you would never see me more.

Almanzor. I must confess,   [*Starting back.*
For this last stroke I did no guard provide;
I could suspect no foe was near that side.
From winds and thickening clouds we thunder fear,
None dread it from that quarter which is clear;
And I would fain believe, 'tis but your art
To show
You knew where deepest you could wound my heart.

Almahide. So much respect is to your passion due,
That sure I could not practise arts on you.
But that you may not doubt what I have said,
This hour I have renounced my husband's bed:
Judge, then, how much my fame would injured be,
If, leaving him, I should a lover see.

Almanzor. If his unkindness have deserved that curse,
Must I, for loving well, be punished worse?

Almahide. Neither your love nor merits I compare,
But my unspotted name must be my care.

Almanzor. I have this day established its renown.

Almahide. Would you so soon, what you have raised,
    throw down?

    Almanzor. But, madam, is not yours a greater guilt,
To ruin him, who has that fabric built?

    Almahide. No lover should his mistress' prayers with-
    stand,
Yet you contemn my absolute command.

    Almanzor. 'Tis not contempt,
When your command is issued out too late:
'Tis past my power, and all beyond is fate.
I scarce could leave you, when to exile sent,
Much less when now recalled from banishment;
For if that heat your glances cast were strong,
Your eyes, like glasses, fire, when held so long.

    Almahide. Then, since you needs will all my weakness
    know,
I love you; and so well, that you must go.
I am so much obliged, and have withal
A heart so boundless and so prodigal,
I dare not trust myself, or you, to stay,
But, like frank gamesters, must forswear the play.

    Almanzor. Fate, thou art kind to strike so hard a blow:
I am quite stunned, and past all feeling now.
Yet—can you tell me you have power and will
To save my life, and at that instant kill?

    Almahide. This, had you stayed, you never must have
    known;
But, now you go, I may with honour own.

    Almanzor. But, madam, I am forced to disobey:
In your defence my honour bids me stay.
I promised to secure your life and throne,
And, heaven be thanked, that work is yet undone.

    Almahide. I here make void that promise which you
    made,
For now I have no further need of aid.
That vow, which to my plighted lord was given,
I must not break, but may transfer to heaven:
I will with vestals live:
There needs no guard at a religious door;
Few will disturb the praying and the poor.

    Almanzor. Let me but near that happy temple stay,
And through the grates peep on you once a day;
To famished hope I would no banquet give:

I cannot starve, and wish but just to live.
Thus, as a drowning man
Sinks often, and does still more faintly rise,
With his last hold catching whate'er he spies;
So, fallen from those proud hopes I had before,
Your aid I for a dying wretch implore.
    Almahide. I cannot your hard destiny withstand,

BOABDELIN, *and* Guards *above.*

But slip, like bending rushes, from your hand.
Sink all at once, since you must sink at last.
    Almanzor. Can you that last relief of sight remove,
And thrust me out the utmost line of love!
Then, since my hopes of happiness are gone,
Denied all favours, I will seize this one.
                    [*Catches her hand, and kisses it.*
    Boabdelin. My just revenge no longer I'll forbear:
I've seen too much; I need not stay to hear. [*Descends.*
    Almanzor. As a small shower
To the parched earth does some refreshment give,
So, in the strength of this, one day I'll live:
A day,—a year,——an age,—for ever, now;
        [*Betwixt each word he kisses her hand by force:*
            she struggling.
I feel from every touch a new soul flow.
                    [*She snatches her hand away.*
My hoped eternity of joy is past!
'Twas insupportable, and could not last.
Were heaven not made of less, or duller joy,
'Twould break each minute, and itself destroy.

Enter King, *and* Guards, *below.*

    Boabdelin. This, this, is he, for whom thou didst deny
To share my bed:—Let them together die.
    Almahide. Hear me, my lord.
    Boabdelin. Your flattering arts are vain:
Make haste and execute what I ordain. [*To the* Guards.
    Almanzor. Cut piecemeal in this cause,
From every wound I should new vigour take,
And every limb should new Almanzors make.
        [*He puts himself before the* Queen; *the* Guards
            attack him with the King.

Enter ABDELMELECH.

Abdelmelech. What angry god, to exercise his spite,
                                          [*To the* King.
Has arm'd your left hand, to cut off your right?
                            [*The* King *turns; the fight ceases.*
The foes are entered at the Elvira gate:
False Lyndaraxa has the town betrayed,
And all the Zegrys give the Spaniards aid.

Boabdelin. O mischief, not suspected nor foreseen!

Abdelmelech. Already they have gained the Zacatin,
And thence the Vivarambla place possest,
While our faint soldiers scarce defend the rest.
The Duke of Arcos does one squadron head,
The next by Ferdinand himself is led.

Almahide. Now, brave Almanzor, be a god again;
Above our crimes and your own passions reign.
My lord has been by jealousy misled,
To think I was not faithful to his bed.
I can forgive him, though my death he sought,
For too much love can never be a fault.
Protect him, then; and what to his defence
You give not, give to clear my innocence.

Almanzor. Listen, sweet heaven, and all ye blessed
          above,
Take rules of virtue from a mortal love!
You've raised my soul; and if it mount more high,
'Tis as the wren did on the eagle fly.
Yes, I once more will my revenge neglect,
And whom you can forgive, I can protect.

Boabdelin. How hard a fate is mine, still doomed to
          shame!
I make occasions for my rival's fame!
                            [*Exeunt. An alarm within.*

Enter FERDINAND, ISABEL, DON ALONZO D'AGUILAR.
          Spaniards *and* Ladies.

King Ferdinand. Already more than half the town is
          gained,
But there is yet a doubtful fight maintained.

Alonzo. The fierce young king the entered does attack,
And the more fierce Almanzor drives them back.

King Ferdinand. The valiant Moors like raging lions
    fight;
Each youth encouraged by his lady's sight.

Queen Isabel. I will advance with such a shining train,
That Moorish beauties shall oppose in vain.
Into the press of clashing swords we'll go,
And, where the darts fly thickest, seek the foe.

King Ferdinand. May heaven, which has inspired this
    generous thought,
Avert those dangers you have boldly sought!
Call up more troops; the women, to our shame,
Will ravish from the men their part of fame.

                    [*Exeunt* ISABELLA *and* Ladies.

Enter ALABEZ, *and kisses the* King's *hand.*

Alabez. Fair Lyndaraxa, and the Zegry line,
Have led their forces with your troops to join:
The adverse part, which obstinately fought,
Are broke, and Abdelmelech prisoner brought.

King Ferdinand. Fair Lyndaraxa, and her friends, shall
    find
The effects of an obliged and grateful mind.

Alabez. But, marching by the Vivarambla place,
The combat carried a more doubtful face:
In that vast square the Moors and Spaniards met,
Where the fierce conflict is continued yet;
But with advantage on the adverse side,
Whom fierce Almanzor does to conquest guide.

King Ferdinand. With my Castilian foot I'll meet his
    rage;   [*Is going out: Shouts within are heard,—*
                    Victoria! Victoria!
But these loud clamours better news presage.

Enter the DUKE OF ARCOS, *and* Soldiers; *their swords
        drawn and bloody.*

Duke of Arcos. Granada now is yours; and there remain
No Moors, but such as own the power of Spain.
That squadron, which their king in person led,
We charged, but found Almanzor in their head:
Three several times we did the Moors attack,
And thrice with slaughter did he drive us back:
Our troops then shrunk; and still we lost more ground

'Till from our queen we needful succour found:
Her guards to our assistance bravely flew,
And with fresh vigour did the fight renew:
At the same time
Did Lyndaraxa with her troops appear,
And, while we charged the front, engaged the rear:
Then fell the king, slain by a Zegry's hand.

   King Ferdinand. How could he such united force with-
     stand?

   Duke of Arcos. Discouraged with his death, the Moorish
     powers
Fell back, and, falling back, were pressed by ours;
But as, when winds and rain together crowd,
They swell till they have burst the bladdered cloud;
And first the lightning, flashing deadly clear,
Flies, falls, consumes, kills ere it does appear,—
So, from his shrinking troops, Almanzor flew,
Each blow gave wounds, and with each wound he slew:
His force at once I envied and admired,
And rushing forward, where my men retired,
Advanced alone.

   King Ferdinand. You hazarded too far,
Your person, and the fortune of the war.

   Duke of Arcos. Already both our arms for fight did
     bare,
Already held them threatening in the air,
When heaven (it must be heaven) my sight did guide
To view his arm, upon whose wrist I spied
A ruby cross in diamond bracelets tied!
And just above it, in the brawnier part,
By nature was engraved a bloody heart;
Struck with these tokens, which so well I knew,
And staggering back some paces, I withdrew,
He followed, and supposed it was my fear;
When, from above, a shrill voice reached his ear:—
"Strike not thy father!"—it was heard to cry!
Amazed, and casting round his wondering eye,
He stopped; then, thinking that his fears were vain,
He lifted up his thundering arm again:
Again the voice withheld him from my death;
"Spare, spare his life," it cried, "who gave thee breath!"
Once more he stopped; then threw his sword away;

"Blessed shade," he said, "I hear thee, I obey
Thy sacred voice;" then, in the sight of all,
He at my feet, I on his neck did fall.

   King Ferdinand. O blessed event!

   Duke of Arcos. The Moors no longer fought;
But all their safety by submission sought:
Meantime my son grew faint with loss of blood,
And on his bending sword supported stood;
Yet, with a voice beyond his strength, he cried,
"Lead me to live or die by Almahide."

   King Ferdinand. I am not for his wounds less grieved
      than you:
For, if what now my soul divines prove true,
This is that son, whom in his infancy
You lost, when by my father forced to fly.

   Duke of Arcos. His sister's beauty did my passion move
(The crime for which I suffered was my love.)
Our marriage known, to sea we took our flight:
There, in a storm, Almanzor first saw light.
On his right arm a bloody heart was graved,
(The mark by which, this day, my life was saved:)
The bracelets and the cross his mother tied
About his wrist, ere she in childbed died.
How we were captive made, when she was dead,
And how Almanzor was in Afric bred,
Some other hour you may at leisure hear,
For see, the queen in triumph does appear.

     Enter Queen ISABEL, LYNDARAXA, Ladies, *Moors and
      Spaniards mixed as* Guards, ABDELMELECH, ABENA-
      MAR, SELIN, *prisoners.*

   King Ferdinand [*embracing* Queen ISABEL]. All stories
      which Granada's conquest tell,
Shall celebrate the name of Isabel.
Your ladies too, who, in their country's cause,
Led on the men, shall share in your applause;
And, for your sakes, henceforward I ordain,
No lady's dower shall questioned be in Spain.
Fair Lyndaraxa, for the help she lent,
Shall, under tribute, have this government.

   Abdelmelech. O heaven, that I should live to see this
      day!

Lyndaraxa. You murmur now, but you shall soon obey.
I knew this empire to my fate was owed;
Heaven held it back as long as e'er it could.
For thee, base wretch, I want a torture yet—
                                        [*To* ABDELMELECH.
I'll cage thee; thou shalt be my Bajazet,
I on no pavement but on thee will tread;
And, when I mount, my foot shall know thy head.
   Abdelmelech [*stabbing her with a poniard*]. This first
      shall know thy heart.
   Lyndaraxa. O! I am slain!
   Abdelmelech. Now, boast thy country is betrayed to
      Spain.
   King Ferdinand. Look to the lady!—Seize the mur-
      derer!
   Abdelmelech [*stabbing himself*]. I do myself that justice
      I did her.
Thy blood I to thy ruined country give,   [*To* LYNDARAXA.
But love too well thy murder to outlive.
Forgive a love, excused by its excess,
Which, had it not been cruel, had been less.
Condemn my passion, then, but pardon me,
And think I murdered him who murdered thee.   [*Dies.*
   Lyndaraxa. Die for us both; I have not leisure now;
A crown is come, and will not fate allow:
And yet I feel something like death is near.
My guards, my guards,—
Let not that ugly skeleton appear!
Sure destiny mistakes; this death's not mine;
She dotes, and meant to cut another line.
Tell her I am a queen;——but 'tis too late;
Dying, I charge rebellion on my fate,
Bow down, ye slaves:——   [*To the Moors.*
Bow quickly down, and your submission show.—
                                        [*They bow.*
I'm pleased to taste an empire e'er I go.   [*Dies.*
   Selin. She's dead, and here her proud ambition ends.
   Abenamar. Such fortune still such black designs attends.
   King Ferdinand. Remove those mournful objects from
      our eyes,
And see performed their funeral obsequies.
                         [*The bodies are carried off.*

Enter ALMANZOR *and* ALMAHIDE, OZMYN *and* BENZAYDA—
ALMAHIDE *brought in a chair;* ALMANZOR *led betwixt*
Soldiers. ISABEL *salutes* ALMAHIDE *in dumb show.*

    Duke of Arcos [presenting ALMANZOR *to the* King]. See
      here that son, whom I with pride call mine;
And who dishonours not your royal line.
    King Ferdinand. I'm now secure, this sceptre, which I
      gain,
Shall be continued in the power of Spain;
Since he, who could alone my foes defend,
By birth and honour is become my friend.
Yet I can own no joy, nor conquest boast, [*To* ALMANZOR.
While in this blood I see how dear it cost.
    Almanzor. This honour to my veins new blood will
      bring;
Streams cannot fail, fed by so high a spring.
But all court-customs I so little know,
That I may fail in those respects I owe.
I bring a heart which homage never knew;
Yet it finds something of itself in you;
Something so kingly, that my haughty mind
Is drawn to yours, because 'tis of a kind.
    Queen Isabel. And yet that soul, which bears itself so
      high,
If fame be true, admits a sovereignty.
This queen, in her fair eyes, such fetters brings,
As chain that heart, which scorns the power of kings.
    Almahide. Little of charm in these sad eyes appears;
If they had any, now 'tis lost in tears.
A crown, and husband, ravished in one day!—
Excuse a grief I cannot choose but pay.
    Queen Isabel. Have courage, madam; heaven has joys
      in store,
To recompence those losses you deplore.
    Almahide. I know your God can all my woes redress;
To him I made my vows in my distress:
And, what a misbeliever vowed this day,
Though not a queen, a Christian yet shall pay.
    Queen Isabel [embracing her]. That Christian name
      you shall receive from me,
And Isabella of Granada be.
    Benzayda. This blessed change we all with joy receive;

And beg to learn that faith which you believe.

  Queen Isabel. With reverence for those holy rites pre-
    pare;
And all commit your fortunes to my care.

  King Ferdinand [*to* ALMAHIDE]. You, madam, by that
    crown you lose, may gain,
If you accept, a coronet of Spain,
Of which Almanzor's father stands possest.

  Queen Isabel [*to* ALMAHIDE]. May you in him, and he
    in you, be blest!

  Almahide. I owe my life and honour to his sword;
But owe my love to my departed lord.

  Almanzor. Thus, when I have no living force to dread,
Fate finds me enemies amongst the dead.
I'm now to conquer ghosts, and to destroy
The strong impressions of a bridal joy.

  Almahide. You've yet a greater foe than these can
    be,—
Virtue opposes you, and modesty

  Almanzor. From a false fear that modesty does grow,
And thinks true love, because 'tis fierce, its foe.
'Tis but the wax whose seals on virgins stay:
Let it approach love's fire, 'twill melt away.
But I have lived too long; I never knew,
When fate was conquered, I must combat you.
I thought to climb the steep ascent of love;
But did not think to find a foe above.
'Tis time to die, when you my bar must be,
Whose aid alone could give me victory;
Without,
I'll pull up all the sluices of the flood,
And love, within, shall boil out all my blood.

  Queen Isabel. Fear not your love should find so sad
    success,
While I have power to be your patroness.
I am her parent now, and may command
So much of duty as to give her hand.
        [*Gives him* ALMAHIDE's *hand.*

  Almahide Madam, I never can dispute your power;
Or as a parent, or a conqueror;
But, when my year of widowhood expires,
Shall yield to your command, and his desires.

  Almanzor. Move swiftly, sun, and fly a lover's pace;

Leave weeks and months behind thee in thy race!
   King Ferdinand. Meantime, you shall my victories
    pursue,
The Moors in woods and mountains to subdue.
   Almanzor. The toils of war shall help to wear each
    day,
And dreams of love shall drive my nights away.—
Our banners to the Alhambra's turrets bear;
Then, wave our conquering crosses in the air,
And cry, with shouts of triumph,—Live and reign,
Great Ferdinand and Isabel of Spain!   [*Exeunt.*

EPILOGUE

THEY, who have best succeeded on the stage,
Have still conformed their genius to their age.
Thus Jonson did mechanic humour show,
When men were dull, and conversation low.
Then comedy was faultless, but 'twas coarse:
Cobb's tankard was a jest, and Otter's horse.[19]
And, as their comedy, their love was mean;
Except, by chance, in some one laboured scene,
Which must atone for an ill-written play,
They rose, but at their height could seldom stay.
Fame then was cheap, and the first comer sped;
And they have kept it since, by being dead.
But, were they now to write, when critics weigh
Each line, and every word, throughout a play,
None of them, no, not Jonson in his height,
Could pass, without allowing grains for weight.
Think it not envy, that these truths are told;
Our poet's not malicious, though he's bold.
'Tis not to brand them, that their faults are shown,
But, by their errors, to excuse his own.
If love and honour now are higher raised,
'Tis not the poet, but the age is praised.
Wit's now arrived to a more high degree;
Our native language more refined and free.
Our ladies and our men now speak more wit
In conversation, than those poets writ.
Then, one of these is, consequently, true;
That what this poet writes comes short of you,
And imitates you ill (which most he fears),
Or else his writing is not worse than theirs.
Yet, though you judge (as sure the critics will),
That some before him writ with greater skill,
In this one praise he has their fame surpast,
To please an age more gallant than the last.

[19] Cobb, the water-bearer, in *Every Man in his Humour:* and Captain
Otter, in *The Silent Woman*, who calls his drinking-cups, Horse, Bull, and
Bear.

DEFENCE OF THE EPILOGUE

OR

AN ESSAY ON THE DRAMATIC POETRY OF THE LAST AGE

THE promises of authors, that they will write again, are, in effect, a threatening of their readers with some new impertinence; and they, who perform not what they promise, will have their pardon on easy terms. It is from this consideration, that I could be glad to spare you the trouble, which I am now giving you, of a postscript,[1] if I were not obliged, by many reasons, to write somewhat concerning our present plays, and those of our predecessors on the English stage. The truth is, I have so far engaged myself in a bold epilogue to this play, wherein I have somewhat taxed the former writing, that it was necessary for me either not to print it, or to show that I could defend it. Yet I would so maintain my opinion of the present age, as not to be wanting in my veneration for the past: I would ascribe to dead authors their just praises in those things wherein they have excelled us; and in those wherein we contend with them for the pre-eminence, I would acknowledge our advantages to the age, and claim no victory from our wit. This being what I have proposed to myself, I hope I shall not be thought arrogant when I inquire into their errors: For we live in an age so sceptical, that as it determines little, so it takes nothing from antiquity on trust; and I profess to have no other ambition in this essay, than that poetry may not go backward, when all other arts and sciences are advancing. Whoever censures me for this inquiry, let him hear his character from Horace:

> *Ingeniis non ille favet, plauditque sepultis,*
> *Nostra sed impugnat; nos nostraque lividus odit.*

He favours not dead wits, but hates the living.

It was upbraided to that excellent poet, that he was an enemy to the writings of his predecessor, Lucilius, because he had said, *Lucilium lutulentum fluere,* that he ran muddy; and that he ought to have retrenched from his satires many unnecessary verses. But Horace makes Lucilius himself to justify him from the imputation of envy, by telling you that he would have done the same, had he lived in an age which was more refined:

[1] First edit. "preface."

163

Si foret hoc nostrum fato delapsus in ævum,
Detereret sibi multa, recideret omne quod ultra
Perfectum traheretur, etc.

And, both in the whole course of that satire, and in his most
admirable Epistle to Augustus, he makes it his business to
prove, that antiquity alone is no plea for the excellency of a
poem; but that, one age learning from another, the last (if we
can suppose an equality of wit in the writers) has the advantage of knowing more and better than the former. And
this, I think, is the state of the question in dispute. It is there-
for my part to make it clear, that the language, wit, and conversation of our age, are improved and refined above the last;
and then it will not be difficult to infer, that our plays have
received some part of those advantages.

In the first place, therefore, it will be necessary to state, in
general, what this refinement is, of which we treat; and that,
I think, will not be defined amiss, "An improvement of our
Wit, Language, and Conversation; or, an alteration in them for
the better."

To begin with Language. That an alteration is lately made
in ours, or since the writers of the last age (in which I com-
prehend Shakespeare, Fletcher, and Jonson), is manifest. Any
man who reads those excellent poets, and compares their language with what is now written, will see it almost in every
line; but that this is an improvement of the language, or an
alteration for the better, will not so easily be granted. For
many are of a contrary opinion, that the English tongue was
then in the height of its perfection; that from Jonson's time to
ours it has been in a continual declination, like that of the
Romans from the age of Virgil to Statius, and so downward
to Claudian; of which, not only Petronius, but Quintilian himself so much complains, under the person of *Secundus,* in his
famous dialogue *De Causis corruptæ Eloquentiæ.*

But, to show that our language is improved, and that those
people have not a just value for the age in which they live, let
us consider in what the refinement of a language principally
consists: that is, "either in rejecting such old words, or phrases,
which are ill sounding or improper; or in admitting new, which
are more proper, more sounding, and more significant."

The reader will easily take notice, that when I speak of
rejecting improper words and phrases, I mention not such as
are antiquated by custom only, and, as I may say, without any
fault of theirs. For in this case the refinement can be but accidental; that is, when the words and phrases, which are rejected,
happen to be improper. Neither would I be understood, when I
speak of impropriety of language, either wholly to accuse the last
age, or to excuse the present, and least of all myself; for all writers

have their imperfections and failings: but I may safely conclude
in the general, that our improprieties are less frequent, and
less gross than theirs. One testimony of this is undeniable, that
we are the first who have observed them; and, certainly, to
observe errors is a great step to the correcting of them. But,
malice and partiality set apart, let any man, who understands
English, read diligently the works of Shakespeare and Fletcher,
and I dare undertake, that he will find in every page either
some solecism of speech, or some notorious flaw in sense; and
yet these men are reverenced, when we are not forgiven. That
their wit is great, and many times their expressions noble, envy
itself cannot deny.

> *Neque ego illis detrahere ausim*
> *Hærentem capiti multâ cum laude coronam.*

But the times were ignorant in which they lived. Poetry was
then, if not in its infancy among us, at least not arrived to its
vigour and maturity: Witness the lameness of their plots; many
of which, especially those which they writ first (for even that
age refined itself in some measure), were made up of some
ridiculous incoherent story, which in one play many times took
up the business of an age. I suppose I need not name *Pericles,
Prince of Tyre,* nor the historical plays of Shakespeare: besides
many of the rest, as the *Winter's Tale, Love's Labour's Lost,
Measure for Measure,* which were either grounded on impossibilities, or at least so meanly written, that the comedy neither
caused your mirth, nor the serious part your concernment. If
I would expatiate on this subject, I could easily demonstrate,
that our admired Fletcher, who writ after him, neither understood correct plotting nor that which they call "the decorum
of the stage." I would not search in his worst plays for examples:
He who will consider his *Philaster,* his *Humorous Lieutenant,*
his *Faithful Shepherdess,* and many others which I could name,
will find them much below the applause which is now given
them. He will see Philaster wounding his mistress, and afterwards his boy, to save himself; not to mention the Clown, who
enters immediately, and not only has the advantage of the
combat against the hero, but diverts you from your serious concernment, with his ridiculous and absurd raillery. In his *Humorous Lieutenant* you find his Demetrius and Leontius staying
in the midst of a routed army, to hear the cold mirth of the
Lieutenant; and Demetrius afterwards appearing with a pistol
in his hand, in the next age to Alexander the Great. And for
his Shepherd, he falls twice into the former indecency of
wounding women. But these absurdities, which those poets
committed, may more properly be called the age's fault than
theirs. For, besides the want of education and learning (which

was their particular unhappiness), they wanted the benefit of
converse: But of that I shall speak hereafter, in a place more
proper for it. Their audiences knew no better; and therefore
were satisfied with what they brought. Those, who call theirs
the golden age of poetry, have only this reason for it, that they
were then content with acorns before they knew the use of
bread; or that "Αλις δρυός was become a proverb. They had
many who admired them, and few who blamed them; and certainly a severe critic is the greatest help to a good wit: he does
the office of a friend, while he designs that of an enemy; and
his malice keeps a poet within those bounds, which the lux-
uriancy of his fancy would tempt him to overleap.

But it is not their plots which I meant principally to tax; I
was speaking of their sense and language; and I dare almost
challenge any man to show me a page together which is correct
in both. As for Ben Jonson, I am loath to name him, because he
is a most judicious writer; yet he very often falls into these
errors: and I once more beg the reader's pardon for accusing
him of them. Only let him consider, that I live in an age where
my least faults are severely censured; and that I have no way
left to extenuate my failings, but by showing as great in those
whom we admire:

> *Cædimus, inque vicem præbemus crura sagittis.*

I cast my eyes but by chance on *Catiline;* and in the three or
four last pages, found enough to conclude that Jonson writ not
correctly.

> Let the long-hid seeds
> Of treason, in thee, now shoot forth in deeds
> Ranker than horror.

In reading some bombast speeches of Macbeth, which are not
to be understood, he used to say that it was horror; and I am
much afraid that this is so.

> Thy parricide late on thy only son,
> After his mother, to make empty way
> For thy last wicked nuptials, worse than they
> That blaze that act of thy incestuous life,
> Which gained thee at once a daughter and a wife.

The sense is here extremely perplexed; and I doubt the word
they is false grammar.

> And be free
> Not heaven itself from thy impiety.

A synchysis, or ill-placing of words, of which Tully so much
complains in oratory.

> The waves and dens of beasts could not receive
> The bodies that those souls were frighted *from*.

The preposition in the end of the sentence; a common fault with him, and which I have but lately observed in my own writings.

> What all the several ills that visit earth,
> Plague, famine, fire, could not reach *unto,*
> The sword, nor surfeits, let thy fury do.

Here are both the former faults: for, besides that the preposition *unto* is placed last in the verse, and at the half period, and is redundant, there is the former synchysis in the words "the sword, nor surfeits," which in construction ought to have been placed before the other.

Catiline says of Cethegus, that for his sake he would

> *Go on upon* the gods, kiss lightning, wrest
> The engine from the Cyclops, and *give fire*
> *At face of a full cloud,* and stand *his ire.*

To "go on upon," is only to go on twice.[2] To "give fire at face of a full cloud," was not understood in his own time; "and stand *his ire*," besides the antiquated word *ire,* there is the article *his,* which makes false construction! and giving fire at the face of a cloud, is a perfect image of shooting, however it came to be known in those days to Catiline.

> Others there are,
> Whom envy to the state draws and pulls on,
> For contumelies received; and such are sure *ones.*

Ones, in the plural number: but that is frequent with him; for he says, not long after,

> Cæsar and Crassus, if they be ill men,
> Are mighty *ones.*
> Such men, *they* do not succour more the cause, etc.

They redundant.

> Though heaven should speak with all *his* wrath at once,
> We should stand upright and *unfeared.*

His is ill syntax with *heaven;* and by *unfeared* he means *unafraid:* words of a quite contrary signification.

"The ports are open." He perpetually uses ports for gates; which is an affected error in him, to introduce Latin by the

---

[2] Jonson seems, as Scott says, to have used it for to *go on against.*

loss of the English idiom; as, in the translation of Tully's speeches, he usually does.

Well-placing of words, for the sweetness of pronunciation, was not known till Mr. Waller introduced it; and, therefore, it is not to be wondered if Ben Jonson has many such lines as these:

> "But being bred up in his father's needy fortunes;
> Brought up in's sister's prostitution," etc.

But meanness of expression one would think not to be his error in a tragedy, which ought to be more high and sounding than any other kind of poetry; and yet, amongst others in *Catiline* I find these four lines together:

> So Asia, thou art cruelly even
> With us, for all the blows thee given;
> When we, whose virtues conquered thee,
> Thus by thy vices ruined be.

Be there is false English for *are;* though the rhyme hides it.

But I am willing to close the book, partly out of veneration to the author, partly out of weariness to pursue an argument which is so fruitful in so small a compass. And what correctness, after this, can be expected from Shakespeare or from Fletcher, who wanted that learning and care which Jonson had? I will, therefore, spare my own trouble of inquiring into their faults; who, had they lived now, had doubtless written more correctly. I suppose it will be enough for me to affirm (as I think I safely may), that these, and the like errors, which I taxed in the most correct of the last age, are such into which we do not ordinarily fall. I think few of our present writers would have left behind them such a line as this:

> Contain your spirit in more stricter bounds.

But that gross way of two comparatives was then ordinary; and, therefore, more pardonable in Jonson.

As for the other part of refining, which consists in receiving new words and phrases, I shall not insist much on it. It is obvious that we have admitted many, some of which we wanted, and therefore our language is the richer for them, as it would be by importation of bullion: Others are rather ornamental than necessary; yet, by their admission, the language is become more courtly, and our thoughts are better drest. These are to be found scattered in the writers of our age, and it is not my business to collect them. They, who have lately written with most care, have, I believe, taken the rule of Horace for their guide; that is, not to be too hasty in receiving of words, but rather to stay till custom has made them familiar to us:

Quem penes arbitrium est, et jus, et norma loquendi.

For I cannot approve of their way of refining, who corrupt our English idiom by mixing it too much with French: That is a sophistication of language, not an improvement of it; a turning English into French, rather than a refining of English by French. We meet daily with those fops, who value themselves on their travelling, and pretend they cannot express their meaning in English, because they would put off to us some French phrase of the last edition; without considering, that, for aught they know, we have a better of our own. But these are not the men who are to refine us; their talent is to prescribe fashions, not words; at best, they are only serviceable to a writer, so as Ennius was to Virgil. He may *aurum ex stercore colligere:* For it is hard if, amongst many insignificant phrases, there happen not something worth preserving; though they themselves, like Indians, know not the value of their own commodity.

There is yet another way of improving language, which poets especially have practised in all ages; that is, by applying received words to a new signification; and this, I believe, is meant by Horace, in that precept which is so variously construed by expositors:

Dixeris egregie, notum si callida verbum
Reddiderit junctura novum.

And, in this way, he himself had a particular happiness; using all the tropes, and particular metaphors, with that grace which is observable in his Odes, where the beauty of expression is often greater than that of thought; as in that one example, amongst an infinite number of others, *"Et vultus nimium lubricus aspici."*

And therefore, though he innovated little, he may justly be called a great refiner of the Roman tongue. This choice of words, and heightening of their natural signification, was observed in him by the writers of the following ages; for Petronius says of him, *"Et Horatii curiosa felicitas."* By this graffing, as I may call it, on old words, has our tongue been beautified by the three fore-mentioned poets, Shakespeare, Fletcher, and Jonson, whose excellencies I can never enough admire; and in this they have been followed, especially by Sir John Suckling and Mr. Waller, who refined upon them. Neither have they, who succeeded them, been wanting in their endeavours to adorn our mother tongue: but it is not so lawful for me to praise my living contemporaries, as to admire my dead predecessors.

I should now speak of the refinement of Wit; but I have been so large on the former subject, that I am forced to contract myself in this. I will therefore only observe to you, that the wit of the last age was yet more incorrect than their language. Shakespeare, who many times has written better than any poet, in any language, is yet so far from writing wit always, or expressing that wit according to the dignity of the subject, that he writes, in many places, below the dullest writers of ours, or any precedent age. Never did any author precipitate himself from such height of thought to so low expressions, as he often does. He is the very Janus of poets; he wears almost everywhere two faces; and you have scarce begun to admire the one, ere you despise the other. Neither is the luxuriance of Fletcher, which his friends have taxed in him, a less fault than the carelessness of Shakespeare. He does not well always; and, when he does, he is a true Englishman,—he knows not when to give over. If he wakes in one scene, he commonly slumbers in another; and, if he pleases you in the first three acts, he is frequently so tired with his labour, that he goes heavily in the fourth, and sinks under his burden in the fifth.

For Ben Jonson, the most judicious of poets, he always writ properly, and as the character required; and I will not contest farther with my friends, who call that wit: it being very certain, that even folly itself, well represented, is wit in a larger signification; and that there is fancy, as well as judgment, in it, though not so much or noble: because all poetry being imitation, that of folly is a lower exercise of fancy, though perhaps as difficult at the other; for it is a kind of looking downward in the poet, and representing that part of mankind which is below him.

In these low characters of vice and folly, lay the excellency of that inimitable writer; who, when at any time he aimed at wit in the stricter sense, that is, sharpness of conceit, was forced either to borrow from the ancients, as to my knowledge he did very much from Plautus; or when he trusted himself alone, often fell into meanness of expression. Nay, he was not free from the lowest and most grovelling kind of wit, which we call clenches,[3] of which *Every Man in His Humour* is infinitely full; and, which is worse, the wittiest persons in the drama speak them. His other comedies are not exempt from them. Will you give me leave to name some few? Asper,[4] in which character he personates himself (and he neither was nor thought himself a fool), exclaiming against the ignorant judges of the age, speaks thus:

[3] Puns.
[4] In *Every Man out of His Humour*.

> How monstrous and detested is't, to see
> A fellow, that has neither art nor brain,
> Sit like an *Aristarchus*, or, *stark-ass*,
> Taking men's lines, with a *tobacco face*,
> In *snuff*, etc.

And presently after: "I marvel whose wit 'twas to put a prologue in yond Sackbut's mouth. They might well think he
would be out of tune, and yet you'd play upon him too."—
Will you have another of the same stamp? "O, I cannot abide
these limbs of *sattin*, or rather *Satan*."

But, it may be, you will object that this was Asper, Maci-
lente, or Carlo Buffone: you shall, therefore, hear him speak
in his own person, and that in the two last lines, or sting of
an epigram. It is inscribed to *Fine Grand*, who, he says, was
indebted to him for many things which he reckons there; and
concludes thus:

> Forty things more, dear *Grand*, which you know true,
> For which, or pay me quickly, or I'll pay you.

This was then the mode of wit, the vice of the age, and not
Ben Jonson's; for you see, a little before him, that admirable
wit, Sir Philip Sidney, perpetually playing with his words. In
his time, I believe, it ascended first into the pulpit, where
(if you will give me leave to clench too) it yet finds the benefit of its clergy; for they are commonly the first corrupters of
eloquence, and the last reformed from vicious oratory; as a
famous Italian has observed before me, in his Treatise of the
Corruption of the Italian Tongue; which he principally ascribes
to priests and preaching friars.

But, to conclude with what brevity I can, I will only add
this, in defence of our present writers, that, if they reach not
some excellencies of Ben Jonson (which no age, I am confident,
ever shall), yet, at least, they are above that meanness of
thought which I have taxed, and which is frequent in him.

That the wit of this age is much more courtly, may easily
be proved, by viewing the characters of gentlemen which were
written in the last. First, for Jonson:—Truewit, in the *Silent
Woman* was his masterpiece; and Truewit was a scholar-like
kind of man, a gentleman with an allay of pedantry, a man
who seems mortified to the world, by much reading. The best
of his discourse is drawn, not from the knowledge of the town,
but books; and, in short, he would be a fine gentleman in an
university. Shakespeare showed the best of his skill in his Mer-
cutio; and he said himself, that he was forced to kill him in
the third act, to prevent being killed by him. But, for my part,

I cannot find he was so dangerous a person: I see nothing in him but what was so exceeding harmless, that he might have lived to the end of the play, and died in his bed, without offence to any man.

Fletcher's Don John is our only bugbear; and yet I may affirm, without suspicion of flattery, that he now speaks better, and that his character is maintained with much more vigour in the fourth and fifth acts, than it was by Fletcher in the three former. I have always acknowledged the wit of our predecessors, with all the veneration which becomes me; but, I am sure, their wit was not that of gentlemen; there was ever somewhat that was ill-bred and clownish in it, and which confessed the conversation of the authors.

And this leads me to the last and greatest advantage of our writing, which proceeds from conversation. In the age wherein those poets lived, there was less of gallantry than in ours; neither did they keep the best company of theirs.

Their fortune has been much like that of Epicurus, in the retirement of his gardens; to live almost unknown, and to be celebrated after their decease. I cannot find that any of them had been conversant in courts, except Ben Jonson; and his genius lay not so much that way, as to make an improvement by it. Greatness was not then so easy of access, nor conversation so free, as now it is. I cannot, therefore, conceive it any insolence to affirm, that, by the knowledge and pattern of their wit who writ before us, and by the advantage of our own conversation, the discourse and raillery of our comedies excel what has been written by them. And this will be denied by none, but some few old fellows who value themselves on their acquaintance with the Black Friars; who, because they saw their plays, would pretend a right to judge ours. The memory of these grave gentlemen is their only plea for being wits. They can tell a story of Ben Jonson, and, perhaps, have had fancy enough to give a supper in the Apollo, that they might be called his sons: And, because they were drawn in to be laughed at in those times, they think themselves now sufficiently entitled to laugh at ours. Learning I never saw in any of them; and wit no more than they could remember. In short, they were unlucky to have been bred in an unpolished age, and more unlucky to live to a refined one. They have lasted beyond their own, and are cast behind ours; and, not contented to have known little at the age of twenty, they boast of their ignorance at three-score.

Now, if they ask me, whence it is that our conversation is so much refined? I must freely, and without flattery, ascribe it to the court; and, in it, particularly to the king, whose example gives a law to it. His own misfortunes, and the nation's, afforded him an opportunity, which is rarely allowed to sovereign princes, I mean of travelling, and being conversant in the most polished courts of Europe; and, thereby, of cultivating a spirit which was formed by nature to receive the impressions of a gallant and generous education. At his return, he found a nation lost as much in barbarism as in rebellion: And, as the excellency of his nature forgave the one, so the excellency of his manners reformed the other. The desire of imitating so great a pattern first awakened the dull and heavy spirits of the English from their natural reservedness; loosened them from their stiff forms of conversation, and made them easy and pliant to each other in discourse. Thus, insensibly, our way of living became more free; and the fire of the English wit, which was before stifled under a constrained, melancholy way of breeding, began first to display its force, by mixing the solidity of our nation with the air and gaiety of our neighbours. This being granted to be true, it would be a wonder if the poets, whose work is imitation, should be the only persons in three kingdoms who should not receive advantage by it; or, if they should not more easily imitate the wit and conversation of the present age than of the past.

Let us therefore admire the beauties and the heights of Shakespeare, without falling after him into a carelessness, and, as I may call it, a lethargy of thought, for whole scenes together. Let us imitate, as we are able, the quickness and easiness of Fletcher, without proposing him as a pattern to us, either in the redundancy of his matter, or the incorrectness of his language. Let us admire his wit and sharpness of conceit; but let us at the same time acknowledge, that it was seldom so fixed, and made proper to his character, as that the same things might not be spoken by any person in the play. Let us applaud his scenes of love; but let us confess, that he understood not either greatness or perfect honour in the parts of any of his women. In fine, let us allow, that he had so much fancy, as when he pleased he could write wit; but that he wanted so much judgment, as seldom to have written humour, or described a pleasant folly. Let us ascribe to Jonson, the height and accuracy of judgment in the ordering of his plots, his choice of characters, and maintaining what he had chosen to the end: But let us not think him a perfect pattern of imitation, except it be in humour; for love, which is the foundation of all comedies in other languages, is scarcely mentioned in any of his plays: And for humour itself, the poets of this age will be more wary than to imitate the meanness of his persons. Gentlemen will now be entertained with the follies of each other; and, though they allow Cobb and Tib to speak properly, yet they are not much pleased with their tankard, or with their rags: And surely their conversation can be no jest to them on the theatre, when they would avoid it in the street.

To conclude all, let us render to our predecessors what is their due, without confining ourselves to a servile imitation of all they writ; and without assuming to ourselves the title of better poets, let us ascribe to the gallantry and civility of our age the advantage which we have above them, and, to our knowledge of the customs and manners of it, the happiness we have to please beyond them.

✓

MARRIAGE A LA MODE

A Comedy

—*Quicquid sum ego, quamvis
Infra Lucili censum ingeniumque, tamen me
Cum magnis vixisse, invita fatebitur usque
Invidia, et fragili quærens illidere dentem,
Offendet solido.*

HORAT. SERM.

MARRIAGE A LA MODE (1673)

THIS very interesting play has a theatrical history which Scott rather confused in his notice of it. Somebody (who had been guessed and denied to be Southerne), gave in the *Gentleman's Magazine* for 1745 an account of the first presentation, in which Mohun played Rhodophil; Hart, Palamede; Mrs. Marshall, Doralice; and Mrs. Boutell, Melantha. Cibber, in his *Apology,* bestows almost unlimited praise on the *later* rendering of Melantha's part by Mrs. Montfort. And lastly, there is no doubt, that Melantha herself gave more than a hint to Congreve for one of his greatest triumphs, Millamant. Dryden has, after his usual fashion (and the usual fashion of almost every playwright), borrowed scenes and touches from this and from that; while his French snatches are taken partly from the *Bourgeois Gentilhomme,* and partly from French song books. But the whole is very much his own; and, as I have said in the General Introduction, I think it is nearly his best, as far as the comic part is concerned, while the serious part at least gives Rhodophil and Palamede opportunities to prove themselves more than mere carpet knights. As for the women, the contrast of Melantha, the mere coquette and *évaporée,* and Doralice the accomplished, but not heartless or wholly unmoralled, flirt, grows on me every time I read it, as well as the force of each sketch separately. The play was both acted and printed in 1673, the performance taking place, during the rebuilding of Drury Lane (which had been burnt), at a neighboring house in Lincoln's Inn Fields.

THE EARL OF ROCHESTER *John Wilmot*

MY LORD,

I HUMBLY dedicate to your Lordship that poem, of which you were pleased to appear an early patron, before it was acted on the stage. I may yet go farther, with your permission, and say, that it received amendment from your noble hands ere it was fit to be presented. You may please likewise to remember, with how much favour to the author, and indulgence to the play, you commended it to the view of his Majesty, then at Windsor, and, by his approbation of it in writing, made way for its kind reception on the theatre. In this dedication, therefore, I may seem to imitate a custom of the ancients, who offered to their gods the firstlings of the flock (which, I think, they called *Ver sacrum*), because they helped them to increase. I am sure, if there be anything in this play, wherein I have raised myself beyond the ordinary lowness of my comedies, I ought wholly to acknowledge it to the favour of being admitted into your Lordship's conversation. And not only I, who pretend not to this way, but the best comic writers of our age, will join with me to acknowledge, that they have copied the gallantries of courts, the delicacy of expression, and the decencies of behaviour, from your Lordship, with more success, than if they had taken their models from the court of France. But this, my Lord, will be no wonder to the world, which knows the excellency of your natural parts, and those you have acquired in a noble education. That which, with more reason, I admire, is, that being so absolute a courtier, you have not forgot either the ties of friendship, or the practice of generosity. In my little experience of a court (which, I confess, I desire not to improve), I have found in it much of interest, and more of detraction: Few men there have that assurance of a friend, as not to be made ridiculous by him when they are absent. There are a middling sort of courtiers, who become happy by their want of wit; but they supply that want by an excess of malice to those who have it. And there is no such persecution as that of fools: They can never be considerable enough to be talked of themselves; so that they are safe only in their obscurity, and grow mischievous to witty men, by the great diligence of their envy, and by being always present to represent and aggravate their faults. In the meantime, they are forced, when they endeavour to be pleasant, to live on the offals of their wit whom they decry; and either to quote it (which they do unwillingly), or to pass it upon others for their own. These are the men who make it their business to chase wit from the knowledge of princes, lest it should disgrace their ignorance. And this kind of malice your Lordship has not so much avoided, as surmounted. But if by the excellent temper of a royal master, always more ready to hear good than ill; if by his inclination to love you; if by your own merit and address; if by the charms of your conversation, the grace of your behaviour, your knowledge of greatness, and habitude in courts, you have been able to preserve yourself with honour in the midst of so dangerous a course; yet at least the remembrance of those hazards has inspired you with pity for other men, who, being of an inferior wit and quality to you, are yet persecuted, for being that in little, which your lordship is in great. For the quarrel of those people extends itself to anything of sense; and if I may be so vain to own it, amongst the rest of the poets, has sometimes reached to the very borders of it, even to me. So that, if our general good fortune had not raised up your Lordship to defend us, I know not whether anything had been more ridiculous in court than writers. It is to your lordship's favour we generally owe our protection and patronage; and to the nobleness of your nature, which will not suffer the least shadow of your wit to be contemned in other men. You have been often pleased, not only to excuse my imperfections, but to vindicate what was tolerable in my writings from their censures; and, what I never can forget, you have not only been careful of my reputation, but of my fortune. You have been solicitous to supply my neglect of myself; and to overcome the fatal modesty of poets, which submits them to perpetual wants, rather than to become importunate with those people who have the liberality of kings in their disposing, and who, dishonouring the bounty of their master, suffer such to be in necessity who endeavour at least to please him; and for whose entertainment he has generously provided, if the fruits of his royal favour were not often stopped in other hands. But your Lordship has given me occasion, not to complain of courts whilst you are there. I have found the effects of your mediation in all my concernments; and they were so much the more noble in you, because they were wholly voluntary. I became your Lordship's (if I may venture on the similitude) as the world was made, without knowing him who made it; and brought only a passive obedience to be your creature. This nobleness of yours I think myself the rather obliged to own, because otherwise it must have been lost to all remembrance: For you are endued with that excellent quality of a frank nature, to forget the good which you have done.

But, my Lord, I ought to have considered, that you are as

great a judge, as you are a patron; and that in praising you ill, I should incur a higher note of ingratitude, than that I thought to have avoided. I stand in need of all your accustomed goodness for the dedication of this play; which, though perhaps it be the best of my comedies, is yet so faulty, that I should have feared you for my critic, if I had not, with some policy, given you the trouble of being my protector. Wit seems to have lodged itself more nobly in this age, than in any of the former; and people of my mean condition are only writers, because some of the nobility, and your Lordship in the first place, are above the narrow praises which poesy could give you. But, let those who love to see themselves exceeded, encourage your Lordship in so dangerous a quality; for my own part, I must confess, that I have so much of self-interest, as to be content with reading some papers of your verses, without desiring you should proceed to a scene, or play; with the common prudence of those who are worsted in a duel, and declare they are satisfied, when they are first wounded. Your Lordship has but another step to make, and from the patron of wit, you may become its tyrant; and oppress our little reputations with more ease than you now protect them. But these, my Lord, are designs, which I am sure you harbour not, any more than the French king is contriving the conquest of the Swissers. It is a barren triumph, which is not worth your pains; and would only rank him amongst your slaves, who is already,

MY LORD,
Your lordship's most obedient,
And most faithful servant,

JOHN DRYDEN

PROLOGUE

Lord, how reformed and quiet are we grown,
Since all our braves and all our wits are gone!
Fop-corner now is free from civil war,
White-wig and vizard make[1] no longer jar.
France, and the fleet, have swept the town so clear
That we can act in peace, and you can hear.
[2] [Those that durst fight are gone to get renown,
And those that durst not, blush to stand in town.]
'Twas a sad sight, before they marched from home,
To see our warriors in red waistcoats come,
With hair tucked up, into our tiring-room.
But 'twas more sad to hear their last adieu:
The women sobbed, and swore they would be true;
And so they were, as long as e'er they could,
But powerful guinea cannot be withstood,
And they were made of playhouse flesh and blood.
Fate did their friends for double use ordain;
In wars abroad they grinning honour gain,
And mistresses, for all that stay, maintain.
Now they are gone, 'tis dead vacation here,
For neither friends nor enemies appear.
Poor pensive punk now peeps ere plays begin.
Sees the bare bench, and dares not venture in;
But manages her last half-crown with care,
And trudges to the Mall, on foot, for air.
Our city friends so far will hardly come,[3]
They can take up with pleasures nearer home;
And see gay shows and gaudy scenes elsewhere;
For we presume they seldom come to hear.
But they have now ta'en up a glorious trade,
And cutting Morecraft[4] struts in masquerade.
There's all our hope, for we shall show to-day
A masking ball, to recommend our play;
Nay, to endear them more, and let them see
We scorn to come behind in courtesy,
We'll follow the new mode which they begin,
And treat them with a room, and couch within:
For that's one way, howe'er the play fall short,
To oblige the town, the city, and the court.

---

[1] Some ed. "mask."
[2] This couplet is inserted from *Covent Garden Drollery*.
[3] "Roam" in one version.
[4] In Beaumont and Fletcher's play of *The Scornful Lady*.

DRAMATIS PERSONÆ

POLYDAMAS, Usurper of Sicily.
LEONIDAS, the rightful Prince, unknown.
ARGALEON, favourite to POLYDAMAS.
HERMOGENES, foster-father to LEONIDAS.
EUBULUS, his friend and companion.
RHODOPHIL, Captain of the Guards.
PALAMEDE, a Courtier.

PALMYRA, daughter to the Usurper.
AMALTHEA, sister to ARGALEON.
DORALICE, wife to RHODOPHIL.
MELANTHA, an affected Lady.
PHILOTIS, woman to MELANTHA.
BELIZA, woman to DORALICE.
ARTEMUS, a Court Lady.
Attendants, Guards, Ladies, and Gentlemen.

SCENE—SICILY

MARRIAGE A LA MODE

ACT I

SCENE I—*Walks near the Court*

Enter DORALICE *and* BELIZA.

DORALICE. Beliza, bring the lute into this arbour! the walks are empty: I would try the song the princess Amalthea bade me learn.   [*They go in and sing.*

I

Why should a foolish marriage vow,
   Which long ago was made,
Oblige us to each other now,
   When passion is decayed?
We loved, and we loved, as long as we could,
   'Till our love was loved out in us both;
But our marriage is dead, when the pleasure is fled:
   'Twas pleasure first made it an oath.

II

If I have pleasures for a friend,
   And further love in store,
What wrong has he, whose joys did end,
   And who could give no more?
'Tis a madness that he should be jealous of me,
   Or that I should bar him of another:
For all we can gain, is to give ourselves pain,
   When neither can hinder the other.

Enter PALAMEDE, *in riding habit, and hears the song.*
Re-enter DORALICE *and* BELIZA.

Beliza. Madame, a stranger.

Doralice. I did not think to have had witnesses of my bad singing.

Palamede. If I have erred, madam, I hope you'll pardon the curiosity of a stranger; for I may well call myself

185

so, after five years' absence from the court: but you have freed me from one error.

Doralice. What's that, I beseech you?

Palamede. I thought good voices, and ill faces, had been inseparable; and that to be fair, and sing well, had been only the privilege of angels.

Doralice. And how many more of these fine things can you say to me?

Palamede. Very few, madam; for if I should continue to see you some hours longer, you look so killingly, that I should be mute with wonder.

Doralice. This will not give you the reputation of a wit with me. You travelling monsieurs live upon the stock you have got abroad, for the first day or two: to repeat with a good memory, and apply with a good grace, is all your wit; and, commonly, your gullets are sewed up, like cormorants. When you have regorged what you have taken in, you are the leanest things in nature.

Palamede. Then, madam, I think you had best make that use of me; let me wait on you for two or three days together, and you shall hear all I have learnt of extraordinary in other countries; and one thing which I never saw 'till I came home, that is, a lady of a better voice, better face, and better wit, than any I have seen abroad. And, after this, if I should not declare myself most passionately in love with you, I should have less wit than yet you think I have.

Doralice. A very plain, and pithy declaration. I see, sir, you have been travelling in Spain or Italy, or some of the hot countries, where men come to the point immediately. But are you sure these are not words of course? For I would not give my poor heart an occasion of complaint against me, that I engaged it too rashly, and then could not bring it off.

Palamede. Your heart may trust itself with me safely; I shall use it very civilly while it stays, and never turn it away, without fair warning to provide for itself.

Doralice. First, then, I do receive your passion with as little consideration, on my part, as ever you gave it me, on yours. And now, see what a miserable wretch you have made yourself!

Palamede. Who, I miserable? Thank you for that. Give me love enough, and life enough, and I defy Fortune.

Doralice. Know, then, thou man of vain imagination, know, to thy utter confusion, that I am virtuous.

Palamede. Such another word, and I give up the ghost.

Doralice. Then, to strike you quiet dead, know that I am married too.

Palamede. Art thou married? O thou damnable virtuous woman!

Doralice. Yes, married to a gentleman; young, handsome, rich, valiant, and with all the good qualities that will make you despair, and hang yourself.

Palamede. Well, in spite of all that, I'll love you: Fortune has cut us out for one another; for I am to be married within these three days; married, past redemption, to a young, fair, rich, and virtuous lady; and it shall go hard but I will love my wife as little, as, I perceive, you do your husband.

Doralice. Remember, I invade no propriety: my servant you are, only 'till you are married.

Palamede. In the meantime, you are to forget you have a husband.

Doralice. And you, that you are to have a wife.

Beliza [*aside, to her* Lady]. O madam, my lord's just at the end of the walks! and, if you make not haste, will discover you.

Doralice. Some other time, new servant, we'll talk further of the premisses; in the meanwhile, break not my first commandment, that is, not to follow me.

Palamede. But where, then, shall I find you again?

Doralice. At court. Yours, for two days, sir.

Palamede. And nights, I beseech you, madam.

[*Exeunt* DORALICE *and* BELIZA.

Palamede. Well, I'll say that for thee, thou art a very dexterous executioner; thou hast done my business at one stroke: yet I must marry another—and yet I must love this; and if it lead me into some little inconveniencies, as jealousies, and duels, and death, and so forth—yet, while sweet love is in the case, Fortune, do thy worst, and avaunt, mortality!

Enter RHODOPHIL, *who seems speaking to one within.*

Rhodophil. Leave 'em with my lieutenant, while I fetch new orders from the king.—How? Palamede!

[*Sees* PALAMEDE.

Palamede. Rhodophil!

Rhodophil. Who thought to have seen you in Sicily?

Palamede. Who thought to have found the court so far from Syracuse?

Rhodophil. The king best knows the reason of the progress. But, answer me, I beseech you, what brought you home from travel?

Palamede. The commands of an old rich father.

Rhodophil. And the hopes of burying him?

Palamede. Both together, as you see, have prevailed on my good-nature. In few words, my old man has already married me; for he has agreed with another old man, as rich and as covetous as himself; the articles are drawn, and I have given my consent, for fear of being disinherited; and yet know not what kind of woman I am to marry.

Rhodophil. Sure your father intends you some very ugly wife, and has a mind to keep you in ignorance till you have shot the gulf.

Palamede. I know not that; but obey I will, and must.

Rhodophil. Then I cannot choose but grieve for all the good girls and courtesans of France and Italy. They have lost the most kind-hearted, doting, prodigal humble servant, in Europe.

Palamede. All I could do, in these three years I stayed behind you, was to comfort the poor creatures for the loss of you. But what's the reason that, in all this time, a friend could never hear from you?

Rhodophil. Alas, dear Palamede! I have had no joy to write, nor indeed to do anything in the world to please me. The greatest misfortune imaginable is fallen upon me.

Palamede. Pr'ythee, what's the matter?

Rhodophil. In one word, I am married: wretchedly married; and have been above these two years. Yes, faith, the devil has had power over me, in spite of my vows and resolutions to the contrary.

Palamede. I find you have sold yourself for filthy lucre; she's old, or ill conditioned.

Rhodophil. No; none of these: I'm sure she's young; and, for her humour, she laughs, sings, and dances eternally; and, which is more, we never quarrel about it, for I do the same.

Palamede. You're very unfortunate indeed: then the case is plain, she is not handsome.

Rhodophil. A great beauty too, as people say.

Palamede. As people say? why, you should know that best yourself.

Rhodophil. Ask those, who have smelt to a strong perfume two years together, what's the scent.

Palamede. But here are good qualities enough for one woman.

Rhodophil. Ay, too many, Palamede. If I could put them into three or four women, I should be content.

Palamede. O, now I have found it! you dislike her for no other reason but because she's your wife.

Rhodophil. And is not that enough? All that I know of her perfections now, is only by memory. I remember, indeed, that about two years ago I loved her passionately; but those golden days are gone, Palamede: Yet I loved her a whole half year, double the natural term of any mistress; and I think, in my conscience, I could have held out another quarter, but then the world began to laugh at me, and a certain shame, of being out of fashion, seized me. At last, we arrived at that point, that there was nothing left in us to make us new to one another. Yet still I set a good face upon the matter, and am infinite fond of her before company; but when we are alone, we walk like lions in a room; she one way, and I another. And we lie with our backs to each other, so far distant, as if the fashion of great beds was only invented to keep husband and wife sufficiently asunder.

Palamede. The truth is, your disease is very desperate; but, though you cannot be cured, you may be patched up a little: you must get you a mistress, Rhodophil. That, indeed, is living upon cordials; but, as fast as one fails, you must supply it with another. You're like a gamester who has lost his estate; yet, in doing that, you have learned the advantages of play, and can arrive to live upon't.

Rhodophil. Truth is, I have been thinking on't, and have just resolved to take your counsel; and, faith, considering the damned disadvantages of a married man, I have provided well enough, for a poor humble sinner, that is not ambitious of great matters.

Palamede. What is she, for a woman?

Rhodophil. One of the stars of Syracuse, I assure you:
Young enough, fair enough; and, but for one quality,
just such a woman as I could wish.

Palamede. O friend, this is not an age to be critical in
beauty. When we had good store of handsome women,
and but few chapmen, you might have been more curious
in your choice; but now the price is enhanced upon us, and
all mankind set up for mistresses, so that poor little creatures, without beauty, birth, or breeding, but only impudence, go off at unreasonable rates: And a man, in these
hard times, snaps at them, as he does at broad gold;
never examines the weight, but takes light or heavy, as
he can get it.

Rhodophil. But my mistress has one fault, that's almost
unpardonable; for being a town-lady, without any relation to the court, yet she thinks herself undone if she be
not seen there three or four times a day with the princess
Amalthea. And, for the king, she haunts and watches him
so narrowly in a morning, that she prevents even the
chemists, who beset his chamber, to turn their mercury
into his gold.

Palamede. Yet hitherto, methinks, you are no very unhappy man.

Rhodophil. With all this, she's the greatest gossip in
nature; for, besides the court, she's the most eternal visitor
of the town; and yet manages her time so well, that she
seems ubiquitary. For my part, I can compare her to
nothing but the sun; for, like him, she takes no rest, nor
ever sets in one place, but to rise in another.

Palamede. I confess, she had need be handsome, with
these qualities.

Rhodophil. No lady can be so curious of a new fashion,
as she is of a new French word: she's the very mint of the
nation; and as fast as any bullion comes out of France,
coins it immediately into our language.

Palamede. And her name is——

Rhodophil. No naming; that's not like a cavalier: Find
her, if you can, by my description; and I am not so ill a
painter that I need write the name beneath the picture.

Palamede. Well, then, how far have you proceeded in
your love?

Rhodophil. 'Tis yet in the bud, and what fruit it may
bear I cannot tell; for this insufferable humour, of haunt-

ing the court, is so predominant, that she has hitherto
broken all her assignations with me, for fear of missing her
visits there.

Palamede. That's the hardest part of your adventure.
But, for aught I see, fortune has used us both alike: I have
a strange kind of mistress too in court, besides her I am
to marry.

Rhodophil. You have made haste to be in love then; for
if I am not mistaken, you are but this day arrived.

Palamede. That's all one: I have seen the lady already,
who has charmed me; seen her in these walks, courted
her, and received, for the first time, an answer that does
not put me into despair.

To them ARGALEON, AMALTHEA, *and* ARTEMIS.

I'll tell you at more leisure my adventures. The walks
fill apace, I see. Stay, is not that the young lord Argaleon,
the king's favourite?

Rhodophil. Yes, and as proud as ever, as ambitious and
as revengeful.

Palamede. How keeps he the king's favour with these
qualities?

Rhodophil. Argaleon's father helped him to the crown:
besides, he gilds over all his vices to the king, and, standing in the dark to him, sees all his inclinations, interests,
and humours, which he so times and soothes, that, in
effect, he reigns.

Palamede. His sister Amalthea, who, I guess, stands by
him, seems not to be of his temper.

Rhodophil. O, she's all goodness and generosity.

Argaleon. Rhodophil, the king expects you earnestly.

Rhodophil. 'Tis done, my lord, what he commanded: I
only waited his return from hunting. Shall I attend your
lordship to him?

Argaleon. No; I go first another way.   [*Exit hastily.*

Palamede. He seems in haste, and discomposed.

Amalthea [*to* RHODOPHIL *after a short whisper*]. Your
friend? then he must needs be of much merit.

Rhodophil. When he has kissed the king's hand, I know
he'll beg the honour to kiss yours. Come, Palamede.

[*Exeunt* RHODOPHIL *and* PALAMEDE
bowing to AMALTHEA.

Artemis. Madam, you tell me most surprising news.

    Amalthea. The fear of it, you see,
Has discomposed my brother; but to me,
All, that can bring my country good, is welcome.

    Artemis. It seems incredible, that this old king,
Whom all the world thought childless,
Should come to search the farthest parts of Sicily,
In hope to find an heir.

    Amalthea. To lessen your astonishment, I will
Unfold some private passages of state,
Of which you are yet ignorant: Know, first,
That this Polydamas, who reigns, unjustly
Gained the crown.

    Artemis. Somewhat of this I have confusedly heard.

    Amalthea. I'll tell you all in brief: Theagenes,
Our last great king,
Had, by his queen, one only son, an infant
Of three years old, called, after him, Theagenes.
The general, this Polydamas, then married;
The public feasts for which were scarcely past,
When a rebellion in the heart of Sicily
Called out the king to arms.

    Artemis. Polydamas
Had then a just excuse to stay behind.

    Amalthea. His temper was too warlike to accept it.
He left his bride, and the new joys of marriage,
And followed to the field. In short, they fought,
The rebels were o'ercome; but in the fight
The too bold king received a mortal wound.
When he perceived his end approaching near,
He called the general, to whose care he left
His widow queen, and orphan son! then died.

    Artemis. Then false Polydamas betrayed his trust?

    Amalthea. He did; and with my father's help,—for
      which
Heaven pardon him!—so gained the soldiers' hearts,
That, in few days, he was saluted king:
And when his crimes had impudence enough
To bear the eye of day,
He marched his army back to Syracuse.
But see how heaven can punish wicked men,
In granting their desires: The news was brought him,

That day he was to enter it, that Eubulus,
Whom his dead master had left governor,
Was fled, and with him bore away the queen,
And royal orphan; but, what more amazed him,
His wife, now big with child, and much detesting
Her husband's practices, had willingly
Accompanied their flight.

   Artemis. How I admire her virtue!

   Amalthea. What became
Of her, and them, since that, was never known;
Only, some few days since, a famous robber
Was taken with some jewels of vast price,
Which, when they were delivered to the king,
He knew had been his wife's; with these, a letter,
Much torn and sullied, but which yet he knew
To be her writing.

   Artemis. Sure, from hence he learned
He had a son?

   Amalthea. It was not left so plain:
The paper only said, she died in child-bed;
But when it should have mentioned son or daughter,
Just there it was torn off.

   Artemis. Madam, the king.

To them POLYDAMAS, ARGALEON, Guard and
Attendants.

   Argaleon. The robber, though thrice racked, confessed
no more,
But that he took those jewels near this place.

   Polydamas. But yet the circumstances strongly argue,
That those, for whom I search, are not far off.

   Argaleon. I cannot easily believe it.

   Artemis. No,
You would not have it so.   [*Aside.*

   Polydamas. Those, I employed, have in the neighbouring
hamlet,
Amongst the fishers' cabins, made discovery
Of some young persons, whose uncommon beauty,
And graceful carriage, make it seem suspicious
They are not what they seem: I therefore sent
The captain of my guards, this morning early,
With orders to secure and bring them to me.

Enter RHODOPHIL *and* PALAMEDE.

O, here he is.—Have you performed my will?
   Rhodophil. Sir, those whom you commanded me to bring,
Are waiting in the walks.
   Polydamas. Conduct them hither.
   Rhodophil. First, give me leave
To beg your notice of this gentleman.
   Polydamas. He seems to merit it. His name and quality?
   Rhodophil. Palamede, son to lord Cleodemus of Palermo,
And new returned from travel.
               [PALAMEDE *approaches, and kneels to kiss the* King's *hand.*
   Polydamas. You are welcome.
I knew your father well, he was both brave
And honest; we two once were fellow-soldiers
In the last civil wars.
   Palamede. I bring the same unquestion'd honesty
And zeal to serve your majesty; the courage
You were pleased to praise in him,
Your royal prudence, and your people's love,
Will never give me leave to try, like him,
In civil wars; I hope it may in foreign.
   Polydamas. Attend the court, and it shall be my care
To find out some employment, worthy you.
Go, Rhodophil, and bring in those without.
               [*Exeunt* RHODOPHIL *and* PALAMEDE.

RHODOPHIL *returns again immediately, and with him*   *enter* HERMOGENES, LEONIDAS, *and* PALMYRA.

Behold two miracles!
               [*Looking earnestly on* LEONIDAS *and* PALMYRA.
Of different sexes, but of equal form:
So matchless both, that my divided soul
Can scarcely ask the gods a son or daughter,
For fear of losing one. If from your hands,
You powers, I shall this day receive a daughter,
Argaleon, she is yours; but if a son,
Then Amalthea's love shall make him happy.
   Argaleon. Grant, heaven, this admirable nymph may prove

That issue, which he seeks!

Amalthea. Venus Urania, if thou art a goddess,
Grant that sweet youth may prove the prince of Sicily!

Polydamas. Tell me, old man, and tell me true, from
whence   [*To* HERMOGENES.
Had you that youth and maid?

Hermogenes. From whence you had
Your sceptre, sir: I had them from the gods.

Polydamas. The gods then have not such another gift.
Say who their parents were.

Hermogenes. My wife, and I.

Argaleon. It is not likely, a virgin, of so excellent a
beauty,
Should come from such a stock.

Amalthea. Much less, that such a youth, so sweet, so
graceful,
Should be produced from peasants.

Hermogenes. Why, nature is the same in villages,
And much more fit to form a noble issue,
Where it is least corrupted.

Polydamas. He talks too like a man that knew the
world,
To have been long a peasant. But the rack
Will teach him other language. Hence with him!

             [*As the* Guards *are carrying him away, his
                  peruke falls off.*
Sure I have seen that face before. Hermogenes!
'Tis he, 'tis he, who fled away with Eubulus,
And with my dear Eudoxia?

Hermogenes. Yes, sir, I am Hermogenes!
And if to have been loyal be a crime,
I stand prepared to suffer.

Polydamas. If thou wouldst live, speak quickly,
What is become of my Eudoxia?
Where is the queen and young Theagenes?
Where Eubulus: and which of these is mine?

                    [*Pointing to* LEONIDAS *and* PALMYRA.
Hermogenes. Eudoxia is dead, so is the queen,
The infant king, her son, and Eubulus.

Polydamas. Traitor, 'tis false: Produce them, or——
Hermogenes. Once more
I tell you, they are dead; but leave to threaten,
For you shall know no further.

Polydamas. Then prove indulgent to my hopes, and be
My friend for ever. Tell me, good Hermogenes,
Whose son is that brave youth?

Hermogenes. Sir, he is yours.

Polydamas. Fool that I am! thou see'st that so I wish it,
And so thou flatter'st me.

Hermogenes. By all that's holy!

Polydamas. Again. Thou canst not swear too deeply.—
Yet hold, I will believe thee:—Yet I doubt.

Hermogenes. You need not, sir.

Argaleon. Believe him not; he sees you credulous,
And would impose his own base issue on you,
And fix it to your crown.

Amalthea. Behold his goodly shape and feature, sir;
Methinks he much resembles you.

Argaleon. I say, if you have any issue here,
It must be that fair creature;
By all my hopes I think so.

Amalthea. Yes, brother, I believe you by your hopes,
For they are all for her.

Polydamas. Call the youth nearer.

Hermogenes. Leonidas, the king would speak with you.

Polydamas. Come near, and be not dazzled with the
        splendour,
And greatness of a court.

Leonidas. I need not this encouragement;
I can fear nothing but the gods.
And, for this glory, after I have seen
The canopy of state spread wide above
In the abyss of heaven, the court of stars,
The blushing morning, and the rising sun,
What greater can I see?

Polydamas. This speaks thee born a prince; thou art,
        thyself,   [*Embracing him.*
That rising sun, and shalt not see, on earth,
A brighter than thyself. All of you witness,
That for my son I here receive this youth,
This brave, this——but I must not praise him further,
Because he now is mine.

Leonidas. I wonnot, sir, believe   [*Kneeling.*
That I am made your sport;
For I find nothing in myself, but what
Is much above a scorn. I dare give credit

To whatsoe'er a king, like you, can tell me.
Either I am, or will deserve to be, your son.

Argaleon. I yet maintain it is impossible
This young man should be yours; for, if he were,
Why should Hermogenes so long conceal him,
When he might gain so much by his discovery?

Hermogenes. I stayed a while to make him worthy, sir,
Of you.   [*To the* King.
But in that time I found
Somewhat within him, which so moved my love,
I never could resolve to part with him.

Leonidas. You ask too many questions, and are
                                    [*To* ARGALEON.
Too saucy for a subject

Argaleon. You rather over-act your part, and are
Too soon a prince.

Leonidas. Too soon you'll find me one.

Polydamas. Enough, Argaleon!
I have declared him mine; and you, Leonidas,
Live well with him I love.

Argaleon. Sir, if he be your son, I may have leave
To think your queen had twins. Look on this virgin;
Hermogenes would enviously deprive you
Of half your treasure.

Hermogenes. Sir, she is my daughter.
I could, perhaps, thus aided by this lord,
Prefer her to be yours; but truth forbid
I should procure her greatness by a lie!

Polydamas. Come hither, beauteous maid: Are you not
     sorry
Your father will not let you pass for mine?

Palmyra. I am content to be what heaven has made me.

Polydamas. Could you not wish yourself a princess then?

Palmyra. Not to be sister to Leonidas.

Polydamas. Why, my sweet maid?

Palmyra. Indeed I cannot tell;
But I could be content to be his handmaid.

Argaleon. I wish I had not seen her.   [*Aside.*

Palmyra. I must weep for your good fortune;
                                    [*To* LEONIDAS.
Pray, pardon me, indeed I cannot help it.

Leonidas,—alas! I had forgot,
Now I must call you prince,—but must I leave you?

Leonidas. I dare not speak to her; for, if I should,
I must weep too.   [*Aside.*

Polydamas. No, you shall live at court, sweet innocence,
And see him there. Hermogenes,
Though you intended not to make me happy,
Yet you shall be rewarded for the event.
Come, my Leonidas, let's thank the gods;
Thou for a father, I for such a son.

[*Exeunt all but* LEONIDAS *and* PALMYRA.

Leonidas. My dear Palmyra, many eyes observe me,
And I have thoughts so tender, that I cannot
In public speak them to you: Some hours hence,
I shall shake off these crowds of fawning courtiers,
And then——   [*Exit* LEONIDAS.

Palmyra. Fly swift, you hours! you measure time for me
in vain,
Till you bring back Leonidas again.
Be shorter now; and, to redeem that wrong,
When he and I are met, be twice as long!   [*Exit.*

clever

ACT II

SCENE I

Enter MELANTHA *and* PHILOTIS.   *woman to Melantha*

PHILOTIS. Count Rhodophil's a fine gentleman indeed,
madam; and, I think, deserves your affection.

Melantha. Let me die but he's a fine man; he sings and
dances *en Français*, and writes the *billets-doux* to a
miracle.

Philotis. And those are no small talents, to a lady that
understands, and values the French air, as your ladyship
does.

Melantha. How charming is the French air, and what an
étourdi bête is one of our untravelled islanders! When he
would make his court to me, let me die but he is just
Æsop's ass, that would imitate the courtly French in his
addresses; but, instead of those, comes pawing upon me,
and doing all things so *maladroitly*.

Philotis. 'Tis great pity Rhodophil's a married man, that
you may not have an honourable intrigue with him.

Melantha. Intrigue, Philotis! that's an old phrase; I have laid that word by; amour sounds better. But thou art heir to all my cast words, as thou art to my old wardrobe. Oh, Count Rhodophil! Ah *mon cher!* I could live and die with him.

Enter PALAMEDE, *and a* Servant.

Servant. Sir, this is my lady.

Palamede. Then this is she that is to be divine, and nymph, and goddess, and with whom I am to be desperately in love. [*Bows to her, delivering a letter.*] This letter, madam, which I present you from your father, has given me both the happy opportunity, and the boldness, to kiss the fairest hands in Sicily.

Melantha. Came you lately from Palermo, sir?

Palamede. But yesterday, madam.

Melantha [*reading the letter*]. *Daughter, receive the bearer of this letter, as a gentleman whom I have chosen to make you happy.* [O Venus, a new servant sent me! and let me die but he has the air of a *galant homme!*] *His father is the rich lord Cleodemus, our neighbour: I suppose you'll find nothing disagreeable in his person or his converse; both which he has improved by travel. The treaty is already concluded, and I shall be in town within these three days; so that you have nothing to do but to obey your careful father.*

[*To* PALAMEDE.] Sir, my father, for whom I have a blind obedience, has commanded me to receive your passionate addresses; but you must also give me leave to avow, that I cannot merit them from so accomplished a cavalier.

Palamede. I want many things, madam, to render me accomplished; and the first and greatest of them is your favour.

Melantha. Let me die, Philotis, but this is extremely French; but yet Count Rhodophil—A gentleman, sir, that understands the *grand monde* so well, who has haunted the best conversations, and who, in short, has voyaged, may pretend to the good graces of a lady.

Palamede [*aside*]. Hey-day! *Grand monde! Conversation! voyaged!* and *good graces!* I find my mistress is one of those that run mad in new French words.

Melantha. I suppose, sir, you have made the tour of France; and, having seen all that's fine there, will make

a considerable reformation in the rudeness of our court:
For let me die, but an unfashioned, untravelled, mere
Sicilian, is a *bête;* and has nothing in the world of an
honnête homme.

Palamede. I must confess, madam, that——

Melantha. And what new minuets have you brought
over with you? their minuets are to a miracle! and our
Sicilian jigs are so dull and sad to them!

Palamede. For minuets, madam——

Melantha. And what new plays are there in vogue? And
who danced best in the last grand ballet? Come, sweet
servant, you shall tell me all.

Palamede [*aside*]. Tell her all? Why she asks all, and
will hear nothing.—To answer in order, madam, to your
demands——

Melantha. I am thinking what a happy couple we shall
be! For you shall keep up your correspondence abroad,
and everything that's new writ, in France, and fine, I mean
all that's delicate, and *bien tourné,* we will have first.

Palamede. But, madam, our fortune——

Melantha. I understand you, sir; you'll leave that to
me: For the *ménage* of a family, I know it better than any
lady in Sicily.

Palamede. Alas, madam, we——

Melantha. Then, we will never make visits together, nor
see a play, but always apart; you shall be every day at
the king's levee, and I at the queen's; and we will never
meet, but in the drawing-room.

Philotis. Madam, the new prince is just passed by the
end of the walk.

Melantha. The new prince, sayest thou? Adieu, dear
servant; I have not made my court to him these two
long hours. O, it is the sweetest prince! so *obligant,
charmant, ravissant,* that——Well, I'll make haste to kiss
his hands, and then make half a score visits more, and be
with you again in a twinkling.

                         [*Exit running, with* PHILOTIS.

Palamede [*solus*]. Now heaven, of thy mercy, bless me
from this tongue! it may keep the field against a whole
army of lawyers, and that in their own language, French
gibberish. It is true, in the daytime, it is tolerable, when
a man has field-room to run from it; but to be shut up in a
bed with her, like two cocks in a pit, humanity cannot

support it. I must kiss all night in my own defence, and
hold her down, like a boy at cuffs, and give her the rising
blow every time she begins to speak.

Enter RHODOPHIL.

But here comes Rhodophil. It is pretty odd that my mistress should so much resemble his: the same newsmonger,
the same passionate lover of a court, the same——But,
Basta, since I must marry her, I'll say nothing, because
he shall not laugh at my misfortune.

Rhodophil. Well, Palamede, how go the affairs of love?
You have seen your mistress?

Palamede. I have so.

Rhodophil. And how, and how? has the old Cupid, your
father, chosen well for you? is he a good woodman?

Palamede. She's much handsomer than I could have
imagined: In short, I love her, and will marry her.

Rhodophil. Then you are quite off from your other mistress?

Palamede. You are mistaken; I intend to love them both,
as a reasonable man ought to do: For, since all women
have their faults and imperfections, it is fit that one of
them should help out the other.

Rhodophil. This were a blessed doctrine, indeed, if our
wives would hear it; but they are their own enemies: If
they would suffer us but now and then to make excursions,
the benefit of our variety would be theirs; instead of one
continued, lazy, tired love, they would, in their turns,
have twenty vigorous, fresh, and active lovers.

Palamede. And I would ask any of them, whether a poor
narrow brook, half dry the best part of the year, and
running ever one way, be to be compared to a lusty stream,
that has ebbs and flows?

Rhodophil. Ay, or is half so profitable for navigation?

Enter DORALICE, *walking by, and reading.*

Palamede. Ods my life, Rhodophil, will you keep my
counsel?

Rhodophil. Yes: Where's the secret?

Palamede. There it is:—[*showing* DORALICE]—I may
tell you, as my friend, *sub sigillo,* etc., this is that very nu-
merical [1] lady, with whom I am in love.

[1] *I.e.* "identical."

Rhodophil. By all that's virtuous, my wife!   [*Aside.*

Palamede. You look strangely: How do you like her?
Is she not very handsome?

Rhodophil. Sure he abuses me. [*Aside.*]—Why the devil
do you ask my judgment?

Palamede. You are so dogged now, you think no man's
mistress handsome but your own. Come, you shall hear
her talk too; she has wit, I assure you.

Rhodophil. This is too much, Palamede.   [*Going back.*

Palamede. Pr'ythee do not hang back so: Of an old tried
lover, thou art the most bashful fellow!

                            [*Pulling him forward.*

Doralice. Were you so near, and would not speak, dear
husband?   [*Looking up.*

Palamede. Husband, quoth a! I have cut out a fine piece
of work for myself.

Rhodophil. Pray, spouse, how long have you been acquainted with this gentleman?

Doralice. Who? I acquainted with this stranger? To
my best knowledge, I never saw him before.

            Enter MELANTHA *at the other end.*

Palamede. Thanks, fortune, thou hast helped me. [*Aside.*

Rhodophil. Palamede, this must not pass so. I must
know your mistress a little better.

Palamede. It shall be your own fault else. Come, I'll
introduce you.

Rhodophil. Introduce me! where?

Palamede. There. To my mistress.

            [*Pointing to* MELANTHA, *who swiftly passes
            over the stage.*

Rhodophil. Who? Melantha! O heavens, I did not see
her.

Palamede. But I did: I am an eagle where I love; I have
seen her this half hour.

Doralice [*aside*]. I find he has wit, he has got off so
readily; but it would anger me, if he should love Melantha.

Rhodophil [*aside*]. Now, I could even wish it were my
wife he loved; I find he's to be married to my mistress.

Palamede. Shall I run after, and fetch her back again,
to present you to her?

Rhodophil. No, you need not; I have the honour to have
some small acquaintance with her.

Palamede [*aside*]. O Jupiter! what a blockhead was I, not to find it out! my wife, that must be, is his mistress. I did a little suspect it before. Well, I must marry her, because she's handsome, and because I hate to be disinherited for a younger brother, which I am sure I shall be, if I disobey; and yet I must keep in with Rhodophil, because I love his wife.—[*To* Rhodophil.] I must desire you to make my excuse to your lady, if I have been so unfortunate to cause any mistake; and, withal, to beg the honour of being known to her.

Rhodophil. O, that is but reason.—Hark you, spouse, pray look upon this gentleman as my friend; whom, to my knowledge, you have never seen before this hour.

Doralice. I am so obedient a wife, sir, that my husband's commands shall ever be a law to me.

Enter Melantha *again, hastily, and runs to embrace* Doralice.

Melantha. O, my dear, I was just going to pay my devoirs to you; I had not time this morning, for making my court to the king, and our new prince. Well, never nation was so happy, and all that, in a young prince; and he is the kindest person in the world to me, let me die if he is not.

Doralice. He has been bred up far from court, and therefore——

Melantha. That imports not: Though he has not seen the *grand monde*, and all that, let me die but he has the air of the court most absolutely.

Palamede. But yet, madam, he——

Melantha. O, servant, you can testify that I am in his good graces. Well, I cannot stay long with you, because I have promised him this afternoon to——But hark you, my dear, I'll tell you a secret. [*Whispers to* Doralice.

Rhodophil. The devil's in me, that I must love this woman. [*Aside.*

Palamede. The devil's in me, that I must marry this woman. [*Aside.*

Melantha [*raising her voice*]. So the prince and I—But you must make a secret of this, my dear; for I would not for the world your husband should hear it, or my tyrant, there, that must be.

Palamede. Well, fair impertinent, your whisper is not
lost, we hear you.   [*Aside.*

Doralice. I understand then that——

Melantha. I'll tell you, my dear, the prince took me by
the hand, and pressed it *à la dérobée* because the king was
near, made the *doux yeux* to me, and, *ensuite,* said a
thousand gallantries, or let me die, my dear.

Doralice. Then I am sure you——

Melantha. You are mistaken, my dear.

Doralice. What, before I speak?

Melantha. But I know your meaning. You think, my
dear, that I assumed something of *fierté* into my countenance, to *rebute* him; but, quite contrary, I regarded him,
—I know not how to express it in our dull, Sicilian language,—*d'un air enjoué;* and said nothing but *à d'autres, à
d'autres*, and that it was all *grimace*, and would not pass
upon me.

Enter ARTEMIS: MELANTHA *sees her, and runs away
from* DORALICE.

[*To* ARTEMIS.] My dear, I must beg your pardon, I was
just making a loose from Doralice, to pay my respects to
you. Let me die, if I ever pass time so agreeably as in
your company, and if I would leave it for any lady's in
Sicily.

Artemis. The princess Amalthea is coming this way.

Enter AMALTHEA: MELANTHA *runs to her.*

Melantha. O, dear madam! I have been at your lodging,
in my new *calèche*, so often, to tell you of a new amour,
betwixt two persons whom you would little suspect for
it, that, let me die if one of my coach-horses be not dead,
and another quite tired, and sunk under the fatigue.

Amalthea. O, Melantha, I can tell you news; the prince
is coming this way.

Melantha. The prince? O sweet prince! He and I are
to—and I forgot it.—Your pardon, sweet madam, for
my abruptness.—Adieu, my dears.—Servant, Rhodophil.
—Servant, servant, servant all.   [*Exit running.*

Amalthea. Rhodophil, a word with you.   [*Whispers.*

Doralice [*to* PALAMEDE]. Why do you not follow your
mistress, sir?

Palamede. Follow her? Why, at this rate she'll be at the Indies within this half hour.

Doralice. However, if you cannot follow her all day, you will meet her at night, I hope?

Palamede. But can you, in charity, suffer me to be so mortified, without affording me some relief? If it be but to punish that sign of a husband there, that lazy matrimony, that dull insipid taste, who leaves such delicious fare at home, to dine abroad on worse meat, and pay dear for it into the bargain.

Doralice. All this is in vain: Assure yourself, I will never admit of any visit from you in private.

Palamede. That is to tell me, in other words, my condition is desperate.

Doralice. I think you in so ill a condition, that I am resolved to pray for you, this very evening, in the close walk behind the terrace; for that's a private place, and there I am sure nobody will disturb my devotions. And so, good-night, sir.   [*Exit.*

Palamede. This is the newest way of making an appointment I ever heard of. Let women alone to contrive the means; I find we are but dunces to them. Well, I will not be so profane a wretch as to interrupt her devotions; but, to make them more effectual, I'll down upon my knees, and endeavour to join my own with them.   [*Exit.*

Amalthea [*to* RHODOPHIL]. I know already they do not love each other; and that my brother acts but a forced obedience to the king's commands; so that if a quarrel should arise betwixt the prince and him, I were most miserable on both sides.

Rhodophil. There shall be nothing wanting in me, madam, to prevent so sad a consequence.

Enter the King *and* LEONIDAS; *the* King *whispers* AMALTHEA.

[*To himself.*] I begin to hate this Palamede, because he is to marry my mistress: Yet break with him I dare not, for fear of being quite excluded from her company. It is a hard case, when a man must go by his rival to his mistress: But it is, at worst, but using him like a pair of heavy boots in a dirty journey; after I have fouled him all day, I'll throw him off at night.   [*Exit.*

Amalthea [*to the* King]. This honour is too great for me
to hope.

Polydamas. You shall this hour have the assurance of
   it.——

Leonidas, come hither; you have heard,
I doubt not, that the father of this princess
Was my most faithful friend, while I was yet
A private man; and when I did assume
This crown, he served me in the high attempt.
You see, then, to what gratitude obliges me;
Make your addresses to her.

   Leonidas. Sir, I am yet too young to be a courtier;
I should too much betray my ignorance,
And want of breeding to so fair a lady.

   Amalthea. Your language speaks you not bred up in
      deserts,
But in the softness of some Asian court,
Where luxury and ease invent kind words,
To cozen tender virgins of their hearts.

   Polydamas. You need not doubt,
But in what words soe'er a prince can offer
His crown and person, they will be received.
You know my pleasure, and you know your duty.

   Leonidas. Yes, sir, I shall obey, in what I can.

   Polydamas. In what you can, Leonidas? Consider,
He's both your king, and father, who commands you.
Besides, what is there hard in my injunction?

   Leonidas. 'Tis hard to have my inclination forced.
I would not marry, sir; and, when I do,
I hope you'll give me freedom in my choice.

   Polydamas. View well this lady,
Whose mind as much transcends her beauteous face,
As that excels all others.

   Amalthea. My beauty, as it ne'er could merit love,
So neither can it beg: And, sir, you may
Believe, that what the king has offered you,
I should refuse, did I not value more
Your person than your crown.

   Leonidas. Think it not pride,
Or my new fortunes swell me to contemn you;
Think less, that I want eyes to see your beauty;
And, least of all, think duty wanting in me
To obey a father's will: But——

Polydamas. But what, Leonidas?
For I must know your reason; and be sure
It be convincing too.

   Leonidas. Sir, ask the stars,
Which have imposed love on us, like a fate,
Why minds are bent to one, and fly another?
Ask, why all beauties cannot move all hearts?
For though there may
Be made a rule for colour, or for feature,
There can be none for liking.

   Polydamas. Leonidas, you owe me more
Than to oppose your liking to my pleasure.

   Leonidas. I owe you all things, sir; but something, too,
I owe myself.

   Polydamas. You shall dispute no more; I am a king,
And I will be obeyed.

   Leonidas. You are a king, sir, but you are no god;
Or, if you were, you could not force my will.

   Polydamas [*aside*]. But you are just, you gods; O, you
      are just.
In punishing the crimes of my rebellion
With a rebellious son!
Yet I can punish him, as you do me.—
Leonidas, there is no jesting with
My will: I ne'er had done so much to gain
A crown, but to be absolute in all things.

   Amalthea. O, sir, be not so much a king, as to
Forget you are a father: Soft indulgence
Becomes that name. Tho' nature gives you power
To bind his duty, 'tis with silken bonds:
Command him, then, as you command yourself;
He is as much a part of you, as are
Your appetite and will, and those you force not,
But gently bend, and make them pliant to your reason.

   Polydamas. It may be I have used too rough a way.——
Forgive me, my Leonidas; I know
I lie as open to the gusts of passion,
As the bare shore to every beating surge:
I will not force thee now; but I entreat thee,
Absolve a father's vow to this fair virgin;
A vow, which hopes of having such a son
First caused.

   Leonidas. Show not my disobedience by your prayers;

For I must still deny you, though I now
Appear more guilty to myself, than you:
I have some reasons, which I cannot utter,
That force my disobedience; yet I mourn
To death, that the first thing, you e'er enjoined me,
Should be that only one command in nature,
Which I could not obey.

    Polydamas. I did descend too much below myself,
When I entreated him.—Hence, to thy desert!
Thou'rt not my son, or art not fit to be.

    Amalthea. Great sir, I humbly beg you, make not me
                                                  [Kneeling.
The cause of your displeasure. I absolve
Your vow; far, far from me be such designs;
So wretched a desire of being great,
By making him unhappy. You may see
Something so noble in the prince's nature,
As grieves him more, not to obey, than you,
That you are not obeyed.

    Polydamas. Then, for your sake,
I'll give him one day longer to consider,
Not to deny; for my resolves are firm
As fate, that cannot change, *[Exeunt* King *and* AMALTHEA

    Leonidas. And so are mine.
This beauteous princess, charming as she is,
Could never make me happy: I must first
Be false to my Palmyra, and then wretched.
But, then, a father's anger!
Suppose he should recede from his own vow,
He never would permit me to keep mine.

    Enter PALMYRA; ARGALEON *following her a little after.*

See, she appears!
I'll think no more of anything, but her.
Yet I have one good hour ere I am wretched.
But, oh! Argaleon follows her! so night
Treads on the footsteps of a winter's sun,
And stalks all black behind him.

    Palmyra. O, Leonidas,
For I must call you still by that dear name,
Free me from this bad man.

    Leonidas. I hope he dares not be injurious to you.

    Argaleon. I rather was injurious to myself,

Than her.

    Leonidas. That must be judged, when I hear what you
    said.

    Argaleon. I think you need not give yourself that
    trouble:

It concerned us alone.

    Leonidas. You answer saucily, and indirectly:

What interest can you pretend in her?

    Argaleon. It may be, sir, I made her some expressions

Which I would not repeat, because they were

Below my rank, to one of hers.

    Leonidas. What did he say, Palmyra?

    Palmyra. I'll tell you all: First, he began to look,

And then he sighed, and then he looked again;

At last, he said, my eyes wounded his heart:

And, after that, he talked of flames and fires,

And such strange words, that I believed he conjured.

    Leonidas. O my heart!—Leave me, Argaleon.

    Argaleon. Come, sweet Palmyra,

I will instruct you better in my meaning:

You see he would be private.

    Leonidas. Go yourself,

And leave her here.

    Argaleon. Alas, she's ignorant,

And is not fit to entertain a prince.

    Leonidas. First learn what's fit for you; that's to obey.

    Argaleon. I know my duty is to wait on you.

A great king's son, like you, ought to forget

Such mean converse.

    Leonidas. What? a disputing subject?

Hence, or my sword shall do me justice on thee.

    Argaleon. Yet I may find a time——   [*Going.*

    Leonidas. What's that you mutter,—   [*Going after him.*

To find a time?——

    Argaleon. To wait on you again——

In the meanwhile I'll watch you.   [*Softly.*

               [*Exit, and watches during the scene.*

    Leonidas. How precious are the hours of love in courts!

In cottages, where love has all the day,

Full, and at ease, he throws it half away.

Time gives himself, and is not valued, there;

But sells at mighty rates, each minute, here:

There, he is lazy, unemployed, and slow;

Here, he's more swift; and yet has more to do.
So many of his hours in public move,
That few are left for privacy and love.

    Palmyra. The sun, methinks, shines faint and dimly, here;
Light is not half so long, nor half so clear:
But, oh! when every day was yours and mine,
How early up! what haste he made to shine!

    Leonidas. Such golden days no prince must hope to see,
Whose every subject is more blessed than he.

    Palmyra. Do you remember, when their tasks were done,
How all the youth did to our cottage run?
While winter-winds were whistling loud without,
Our cheerful hearth was circled round about:
With strokes in ashes, maids their lovers drew;
And still you fell to me, and I to you.

    Leonidas. When love did of my heart possession take,
I was so young, my soul was scarce awake:
I cannot tell when first I thought you fair;
But sucked in love, insensibly as air.

    Palmyra. I know too well when first my love began,
When at our wake you for the chaplet ran:
Then I was made the lady of the May,
And, with the garland, at the goal did stay:
Still, as you ran, I kept you full in view;
I hoped, and wished, and ran, methought, for you.
As you came near, I hastily did rise,
And stretched my arm outright, that held the prize.
The custom was to kiss whom I should crown;
You kneeled, and in my lap your head laid down:
I blushed, and blushed, and did the kiss delay;
At last my subjects forced me to obey:
But, when I gave the crown, and then the kiss,
I scarce had breath to say, Take that,—and this.

    Leonidas. I felt, the while, a pleasing kind of smart;
That kiss went, tingling, to my very heart.
When it was gone, the sense of it did stay;
The sweetness clinged upon my lips all day,
Like drops of honey, loth to fall away.

    Palmyra. Life, like a prodigal, gave all his store
To my first youth, and now can give no more.
You are a prince; and, in that high degree,
No longer must converse with humble me.

Leonidas. 'Twas to my loss the gods that title gave;
A tyrant's son is doubly born a slave:
He gives a crown; but, to prevent my life
From being happy, loads it with a wife.
    Palmyra. Speak quickly; what have you resolved to do?
    Leonidas. To keep my faith inviolate to you.
He threatens me with exile, and with shame,
To lose my birthright, and a prince's name;
But there's a blessing which he did not mean,
To send me back to love and you again.
    Palmyra. Why was not I a princess for your sake?
But heaven no more such miracles can make:
And, since that cannot, this must never be;
You shall not lose a crown for love of me.
Live happy, and a nobler choice pursue;
I shall complain of fate, but not of you.
    Leonidas. Can you so easily without me live?
Or could you take the counsel, which you give?
Were you a princess, would you not be true?
    Palmyra. I would; but cannot merit it from you.
    Leonidas. Did you not merit, as you do, my heart,
Love gives esteem, and then it gives desert.
But if I basely could forget my vow,
Poor helpless innocence, what would you do?
    Palmyra. In woods, and plains, where first my love
        began,
There would I live, retired from faithless man:
I'd sit all day within some lonely shade,
Or that close arbour which your hands have made:
I'd search the groves, and every tree, to find
Where you had carved our names upon the rind:
Your hook, your scrip, all that was yours I'd keep,
And lay them by me when I went to sleep.
Thus would I live: And maidens, when I die,
Upon my hearse white true-love-knots should tie;
And thus my tomb should be inscribed above,
Here the forsaken Virgin rests from love.
    Leonidas. Think not that time or fate shall e'er divide
Those hearts, which love and mutual vows have tied.
But we must part; farewell, my love.
    Palmyra. Till when?
    Leonidas. Till the next age of hours we meet again.
Meantime, we may,

When near each other we in public stand,
Contrive to catch a look, or steal a hand:
Fancy will every touch and glance improve;
And draw the most spirituous parts of love.
Our souls sit close, and silently within,
And their own web from their own entrails spin;
And when eyes meet far off, our sense is such,
That, spider-like, we feel the tenderest touch.   [*Exeunt.*

ACT III

SCENE I

Enter RHODOPHIL, *meeting* DORALICE *and* ARTEMIS.
RHODOPHIL *and* DORALICE *embrace.*

RHODOPHIL. My own dear heart!

Doralice. My own true love! [*She starts back.*] I had
forgot myself to be so kind; indeed, I am very angry with
you, dear; you are come home an hour after you appointed: if you had stayed a minute longer, I was just
considering whether I should stab, hang, or drown myself.
                                        [*Embracing him.*

Rhodophil. Nothing but the king's business could have
hindered me; and I was so vexed, that I was just laying
down my commission, rather than have failed my dear.
                                        [*Kisses her hand.*

Artemis. Why, this is love as it should be betwixt man
and wife: such another couple would bring marriage into
fashion again. But is it always thus betwixt you?

Rhodophil. Always thus! this is nothing. I tell you, there
is not such a pair of turtles in Sicily; there is such an
eternal cooing and kissing betwixt us, that indeed it is
scandalous before civil company.

Doralice. Well, if I had imagined I should have been
this fond fool, I would never have married the man I
loved: I married to be happy, and have made myself
miserable by over-loving. Nay, and now my case is desperate; for I have been married above these two years,
and find myself every day worse and worse in love: nothing but madness can be the end on't.

Artemis. Doat on, to the extremity, and you are happy.

Doralice. He deserves so infinitely much, that, the truth is, there can be no doating in the matter; but, to love well, I confess, is a work that pays itself: 'Tis telling gold, and, after, taking it for one's pains.

Rhodophil. By that I should be a very covetous person; for I am ever pulling out my money, and putting it into my pocket again.

Doralice. O dear Rhodophil!

Rhodophil. O sweet Doralice!   [*Embracing each other.*

Artemis [*aside*]. Nay, I am resolved, I'll never interrupt lovers: I'll leave them as happy as I found them.

[*Steals away.*

Rhodophil. What, is she gone?   [*Looking up.*

Doralice. Yes; and without taking leave.

Rhodophil. Then there's enough for this time.

[*Parting from her.*

Doralice. Yes, sure, the scene is done, I take it.

[*They walk contrary ways on the stage; he, with his hands in his pockets, whistling; she singing a dull melancholy tune.*

Rhodophil. Pox o' your dull tune, a man can't think for you.

Doralice. Pox o' your damned whistling; you can neither be company to me yourself, nor leave me to the freedom of my own fancy.

Rhodophil. Well, thou art the most provoking wife!

Doralice. Well, thou art the dullest husband, thou art never to be provoked.

Rhodophil. I was never thought dull till I married thee; and now thou hast made an old knife of me; thou hast whetted me so long, till I have no edge left.

Doralice. I see you are in the husband's fashion; you reserve all your good humours for your mistresses, and keep your ill for your wives.

Rhodophil. Pr'ythee leave me to my own cogitations; I am thinking over all my sins, to find for which of them it was I married thee.

Doralice. Whatever your sin was, mine's the punishment.

Rhodophil. My comfort is, thou art not immortal; and, when that blessed, that divine day comes of thy departure, I'm resolved I'll make one holiday more in the almanac for thy sake.

Doralice. Ay, you had need make a holiday for me, for I am sure you have made me a martyr.

Rhodophil. Then, setting my victorious foot upon thy head, in the first hour of thy silence, (that is, the first hour thou art dead, for I despair of it before,) I will swear by thy ghost,—an oath as terrible to me as Styx is to the gods,—never more to be in danger of the banes of matrimony.

Doralice. And I am resolved to marry the very same day thou diest, if it be but to show how little I'm concerned for thee.

Rhodophil. Pray thee, Doralice, why do we quarrel thus a-days? ha! this is but a kind of heathenish life, and does not answer the ends of marriage. If I have erred, propound what reasonable atonement may be made before we sleep, and I will not be refractory; but withal consider, I have been married these three years, and be not too tyrannical.

Doralice. What should you talk of a peace a-bed, when you can give no security for performance of articles?

Rhodophil. Then, since we must live together, and both of us stand upon our terms, as to matters of dying first, let us make ourselves as merry as we can with our misfortunes. Why, there's the devil on't! if thou couldst make my enjoying thee but a little easy, or a little more unlawful, thou shouldst see what a termagant lover I would prove. I have taken such pains to enjoy thee, Doralice, that I have fancied thee all the fine women of the town—to help me out: But now there's none left for me to think on, my imagination is quite jaded. Thou art a wife, and thou wilt be a wife, and I can make thee another no longer.

[*Exit* RHODOPHIL.

Doralice. Well, since thou art a husband, and wilt be a husband, I'll try if I can find out another. 'Tis a pretty time we women have on't, to be made widows while we are married. Our husbands think it reasonable to complain, that we are the same, and the same to them, when we have more reason to complain, that they are not the same to us. Because they cannot feed on one dish, therefore we must be starved. 'Tis enough that they have a sufficient ordinary provided, and a table ready spread for them: If they cannot fall-to and eat heartily, the fault is theirs; and 'tis pity, methinks, that the good creature should be lost, when many a poor sinner would be glad on't.

Enter MELANTHA *and* ARTEMIS *to her.*

Melantha. Dear, my dear, pity me, I am so *chagrin* to-day, and have had the most signal affront at court! I went this afternoon to do my devoir to princess Amalthea, found her, conversed with her, and helped to make her court some half an hour; after which, she went to take the air, chose out two ladies to go with her, that came in after me, and left me most barbarously behind her.

Artemis. You are the less to be pitied, Melantha, because you subject yourself to these affronts, by coming perpetually to court, where you have no business nor employment.

Melantha. I declare, I had rather of the two be rallied, nay, *mal traitée* at court, than be defied in the town; for, assuredly, nothing can be so *ridicule* as a mere town lady.

Doralice. Especially at court. How I have seen them crowd and sweat in the drawing-room on a holiday-night! For that's their time to swarm and invade the presence. O, how they catch at a bow, or any little salute from a courtier, to make show of their acquaintance! and, rather than be thought to be quite unknown, they court'sy to one another; but they take true pains to come near the circle, and press and peep upon the princess, to write letters into the country how she was dressed, while the ladies that stand about, make their court to her with abusing them.

Artemis. These are sad truths, Melantha; and therefore I would e'en advise you to quit the court, and live either wholly in the town, or, if you like not that, in the country.

Doralice. In the country! nay, that's to fall beneath the town, for they live upon our offals here. Their entertainment of wit is only the remembrance of what they had when they were last in town;—they live this year upon the last year's knowledge, as their cattle do all night, by chewing the cud of what they eat in the afternoon.

Melantha. And they tell, for news, such unlikely stories! A letter from one of us is such a present to them, that the poor souls wait for the carrier's-day with such devotion, that they cannot sleep the night before.

Artemis. No more than I can, the night before I am to go a journey.

Doralice. Or I, before I am to try on a new gown.

Melantha. A song, that's stale here, will be new there a twelvemonth hence; and if a man of the town by chance come amongst them, he's reverenced for teaching them the tune.

Doralice. A friend of mine, who makes songs sometimes, came lately out of the west, and vowed he was so put out of countenance with a song of his; for, at the first country gentleman's he visited, he saw three tailors cross-legged upon the table in the hall, who were tearing out as loud as ever they could sing.

———After the pangs of a desperate lover, etc.[2]

And that all day he heard of nothing else, but the daughters of the house, and the maids, humming it over in every corner, and the father whistling it.

Artemis. Indeed, I have observed of myself, that when I am out of town but a fortnight, I am so humble, that I would receive a letter from my tailor or mercer for a favour.

Melantha. When I have been at grass in the summer, and am new come up again, methinks I'm to be turned into ridicule by all that see me; but when I have been once or twice at court, I begin to value myself again, and to despise my country acquaintance.

Artemis. There are places where all people may be adored, and we ought to know ourselves so well as to choose them.

Doralice. That's very true; your little courtier's wife, who speaks to the king but once a month, need but go to a town lady, and there she may vapour and cry,—"The king and I," at every word. Your town lady, who is laughed at in the circle, takes her coach into the city, and there's she's called Your honour, and has a banquet from the merchant's wife, whom she laughs at for her kindness. And, as for my finical cit, she removes but to her country house, and there insults over the country gentlewoman that never comes up, who treats her with furmity and custard, and opens her dear bottle of *mirabilis* beside, for a gill-glass of it at parting.

[2] A song of Dryden's own in *An Evening's Love*.

Artemis. At last, I see, we shall leave Melantha where we found her; for, by your description of the town and country, they are become more dreadful to her than the court, where she was affronted. But you forget we are to wait on the princess Amalthea. Come, Doralice.

Doralice. Farewell, Melantha.

Melantha. Adieu, my dear.

Artemis. You are out of charity with her, and therefore I shall not give your service.

Melantha. Do not omit it, I beseech you; for I have such a *tendre* for the court, that I love it even from the drawing-room to the lobby, and can never be *rebutée* by any usage. But hark you, my dears; one thing I had forgot, of great concernment.

Doralice. Quickly then, we are in haste.

Melantha. Do not call it my service, that's too vulgar; but do my *baise-mains* to the princess Amalthea; that is *spirituelle!*

Doralice. To do your service, then, we will *prendre* the *carosse* to court, and do your *baise-mains* to the princess Amalthea, in your phrase *spirituelle.*

[*Exeunt* ARTEMIS *and* DORALICE.

Enter PHILOTIS *with a paper in her hand.*

Melantha. O, are you there, minion? And, well, are not you a most precious damsel, to retard all my visits for want of language, when you know you are paid so well for furnishing me with new words for my daily conversation? Let me die, if I have not run the risk already to speak like one of the vulgar, and if I have one phrase left in all my store, that is not threadbare *et usé,* and fit for nothing but to be thrown to peasants.

Philotis. Indeed, madam, I have been very diligent in my vocation; but you have so drained all the French plays and romances, that they are not able to supply you with words for your daily expense.

Melantha. Drained? What a word's there! *Epuisée,* you sot you. Come, produce your morning's work.

Philotis. 'Tis here, madam.   [*Shows the paper.*

Melantha. O, my Venus! fourteen or fifteen words to serve me a whole day! Let me die, at this rate I cannot last till night. Come, read your works: Twenty to one, half of them will not pass muster neither.

Philotis. Sottises.   [*Reads.*

Melantha. Sottises: bon. That's an excellent word to
begin withal; as, for example, he or she said a thousand
Sottises to me. Proceed.

Philotis. Figure: As, what a *figure* of a man is there!
Naïve and *naïveté.*

Melantha. Naïve! as how?

Philotis. Speaking of a thing that was naturally said, it
was so *naïve;* or such an innocent piece of simplicity 'twas
such a *naïveté.*

Melantha. Truce with your interpretations. Make haste.

*Philotis. Foible, chagrin, grimace, embarrassé, double
entendre, équivoque, éclaircissement, suite, bévue, façon,
penchant, coup d'étourdi,* and *ridicule.*

Melantha. Hold, hold; how did they begin?

Philotis. They began at *sottises,* and ended *en ridicule.*

Melantha. Now, give me your paper in my hand, and
hold you my glass, while I practise my postures for the
day. [MELANTHA *laughs in the glass.*] How does that
laugh become my face?

Philotis. Sovereignly well, madam.

Melantha. Sovereignly? Let me die, that's not amiss.
That word shall not be yours; I'll invent it, and bring it
up myself. My new point gorget shall be yours upon't. Not
a word of the word, I charge you.

Philotis. I am dumb, madam.

Melantha. That glance, how suits it with my face?
                          [*Looking in the glass again.*

Philotis. 'Tis so *languissant!*

Melantha. Languissant! that word shall be mine too, and
my last Indian gown thine for't. That sigh? [*Looks again.*

Philotis. 'Twill make a man sigh, madam. 'Tis a mere
incendiary.

Melantha. Take my gimp petticoat for that truth. If
thou hast more of these phrases, let me die but I could
give away all my wardrobe, and go naked for them.

Philotis. Go naked? Then you would be a Venus,
madam. O Jupiter! what had I forgot? This paper was
given me by Rhodophil's page.

Melantha [*reading the letter*]. Beg the favour from you.
—Gratify my passion—so far—assignation—in the grotto
—behind the terrace—clock this evening——Well, for the
billets-doux there is no man in Sicily must dispute with

Rhodophil; they are so French, so *gallant*, and so *tendre*,
that I cannot resist the temptation of the assignation.
Now, go you away, Philotis; it imports me to practise what
to say to my servant when I meet him. [*Exit* PHILOTIS.]
Rhodophil, you'll wonder at my assurance to meet you
here;—let me die, I am so out of breath with coming,
that I can render you no reason of it.—Then he will make
this *repartee;* Madam, I have no reason to accuse you for
that which is so great a favour to me.—Then I reply, But
why have you drawn me to this solitary place? Let me die,
but I am apprehensive of some violence from you.—Then
says he, Solitude, madam, is most fit for lovers; but by
this fair hand——Nay, now I vow you're rude, sir. O fy,
fy, fy; I hope you'll be honourable?—You'd laugh at me
if I should, madam—What, do you mean to throw me
down thus? Ah me! ah! ah! ah!

Enter POLYDAMAS, LEONIDAS, *and* Guards.

O Venus! the king and court. Let me die, but I fear they
have found my *foible,* and will turn me into *ridicule.*

[*Exit running.*

Leonidas. Sir, I beseech you.
Polydamas. Do not urge my patience.
Leonidas. I'll not deny,
But what your spies informed you of is true:
I love the fair Palmyra; but I loved her
Before I knew your title to my blood.

Enter PALMYRA, *guarded.*

See, here she comes, and looks, amidst her guards,
Like a weak dove under the falcon's gripe.
O heaven, I cannot bear it.
Polydamas. Maid, come hither.
Have you presumed so far, as to receive
My son's affections?
Palmyra. Alas, what shall I answer? To confess it
Will raise a blush upon a virgin's face;
Yet I was ever taught 'twas base to lie.
Polydamas. You've been too bold, and you must love no
    more.
Palmyra. Indeed I must; I cannot help my love;
I was so tender when I took the bent,
That now I grow that way.

Polydamas. He is a prince, and you are meanly born.

Leonidas. Love either finds equality, or makes it:
Like death, he knows no difference in degrees,
But plains, and levels all.

Palmyra. Alas! I had not rendered up my heart,
Had he not loved me first; but he preferred me
Above the maidens of my age and rank,—
Still shunned their company, and still sought mine.
I was not won by gifts, yet still he gave;
And all his gifts, though small, yet spake his love.
He picked the earliest strawberries in woods,
The clustered filberts, and the purple grapes;
He taught a prating stare[3] to speak my name;
And, when he found a nest of nightingales,
Or callow linnets, he would show them me,
And let me take them out.

Polydamas. This is a little mistress, meanly born,
Fit only for a prince's vacant hours,
And then, to laugh at her simplicity,
Not fix a passion there. Now hear my sentence.

Leonidas. Remember, ere you give it, 'tis pronounced
Against us both.

Polydamas. First, in her hand
There shall be placed a player's painted sceptre,
And, on her head, a gilded pageant crown:
Thus shall she go,
With all the boys attending on her triumph;
That done, be put alone into a boat,
With bread and water only for three days;
So on the sea she shall be set adrift,
And who relieves her dies.

Palmyra. I only beg that you would execute
The last part first: Let me be put to sea;
The bread and water for my three days' life
I give you back, I would not live so long;
But let me 'scape the shame.

Leonidas Look to me, piety; and you, O gods, look to
my piety!
Keep me from saying that, which misbecomes a son;
But let me die before I see this done.

Polydamas. If you for ever will abjure her sight,
I can be yet a father; she shall live.

[3] Starling.

Leonidas. Hear, O you powers! is this to be a father?
I see 'tis all my happiness and quiet
You aim at, sir; and take them:
I will not save even my Palmyra's life
At that ignoble price; but I'll die with her.

Palmyra. So had I done by you,
Had fate made me a princess.—Death, methinks,
Is not a terror now:
He is not fierce, or grim, but fawns, and soothes me,
And slides along, like Cleopatra's aspick,
Offering his service to my troubled breast.

Leonidas. Begin what you have purposed when you
    please:
Lead her to scorn, your triumph shall be doubled.
As holy priests,
In pity, go with dying malefactors,
So I will share her shame.

Polydamas. You shall not have your will so much; first
    part them,
Then execute your office.

Leonidas. No; I'll die
In her defence.   [*Draws his sword.*

Palmyra. Ah, hold, and pull not on
A curse, to make me worthy of my death:
Do not by lawless force oppose your father,
Whom you have too much disobeyed for me.

Leonidas. Here, take it, sir, and with it pierce my
    heart:
[*Presenting his sword to his* Father *upon his knees.*
You have done more in taking my Palmyra.
You are my father; therefore I submit.

Polydamas. Keep him from anything he may design
Against his life, while the first fury lasts;
And now perform what I commanded you.

Leonidas. In vain; if sword and poison be denied me,
I'll hold my breath and die.

Palmyra. Farewell, my lost[4] Leonidas; yet live,
I charge you, live, 'till you believe me dead.
I cannot die in peace, if you die first;
If life's a blessing, you shall have it last.

Polydamas. Go on with her, and lead him after me.

4 Ed. "last," which *may* be right.

Enter ARGALEON, *hastily, with* HERMOGENES.

Argaleon. I bring you, sir, such news as must amaze you,
And such as will prevent you from an action,
Which would have rendered all your life unhappy.
                              [HERMOGENES *kneels.*

Polydamas. Hermogenes, you bend your knees in vain,
My doom's already past.

Hermogenes. I kneel not for Palmyra, for I know
She will not need my prayers; but for myself:
With a feigned tale I have abused your ears,
And, therefore, merit death: but since, unforced,
I first accuse myself, I hope your mercy.

Polydamas. Haste to explain your meaning.

Hermogenes. Then, in few words, Palmyra is your
        daughter.

Polydamas. How can I give belief to this impostor?
He, who has once abused me, often may.
I'll hear no more.

Argaleon. For your own sake, you must.

Hermogenes. A parent's love,—for I confess my crime,—
Moved me to say, Leonidas was yours;
But when I heard Palmyra was to die,
The fear of guiltless blood so stung my conscience,
That I resolved, even with my shame, to save
Your daughter's life.

Polydamas. But how can I be certain, but that interest,
Which moved you first to say your son was mine,
Does not now move you too, to save your daughter!

Hermogenes. You had but then my word; I bring you
        now
Authentic testimonies. Sir, in short,
                    [*Delivers on his knees a jewel, and letter.*
If this will not convince you, let me suffer.

Polydamas. I know this jewel well; 'twas once my
        mother's,   [*Looking first on the jewel.*
Which, marrying, I presented to my wife.
And this, O this, is my Eudocia's hand.
This was the pledge of love given to Eudocia,   [*Reads.*
Who, dying, to her young Palmyra leaves it;
And this, when you, my dearest lord, receive,
Own her, and think on me, dying Eudocia.
Take it; 'tis well there is no more to read. [*To* ARGALEON.

My eyes grow full, and swim in their own light.

[He embraces PALMYRA.

Palmyra. I fear, sir, this is your intended pageant.
You sport yourself at poor Palmyra's cost;
But if you think to make me proud,
Indeed I cannot be so: I was born
With humble thoughts, and lowly, like my birth.
A real fortune could not make me haughty,
Much less a feigned.

Polydamas. This was her mother's temper.
I have too much deserved thou shouldst suspect
That I am not thy father; but my love
Shall henceforth show I am. Behold my eyes,
And see a father there begin to flow:
This is not feigned, Palmyra.

Palmyra. I doubt no longer, sir; you are a king,
And cannot lie: Falsehood's a vice too base
To find a room in any royal breast.
I know, in spite of my unworthiness,
I am your child; for when you would have killed me,
Methought I loved you then.

Argaleon. Sir, we forget the prince Leonidas;
His greatness should not stand neglected thus.

Polydamas. Guards, you may now retire; Give him his
sword,
And leave him free.

Leonidas. Then the first use I make of liberty
Shall be, with your permission, mighty sir,
To pay that reverence to which nature binds me.

[Kneels to HERMOGENES.

Argaleon. Sure you forget your birth, thus to misplace
This act of your obedience; you should kneel
To nothing but to heaven, and to a king,

Leonidas. I never shall forget what nature owes,
Nor be ashamed to pay it; though my father
Be not a king, I know him brave and honest,
And well deserving of a worthier son.

Polydamas. He bears it gallantly.

Leonidas. Why would you not instruct me, sir, before,

[To HERMOGENES.

Where I should place my duty?
From which, if ignorance have made me swerve,
I beg your pardon for an erring son.

Palmyra. I almost grieve I am a princess, since
It makes him lose a crown.

Leonidas. And next, to you, my king, thus low I kneel,
To implore your mercy; if in that small time
I had the honour to be thought your son,
I paid not strict obedience to your will.
I thought, indeed, I should not be compelled,
But thought it as your son; so what I took
In duty from you, I restored in courage:
Because your son should not be forced.

Polydamas. You have my pardon for it.

Leonidas. To you, fair princess, I congratulate
Your birth; of which I ever thought you worthy:
And give me leave to add, that I am proud
The gods have picked me out to be the man,
By whose dejected fate yours is to rise;
Because no man could more desire your fortune,
Or franklier part with his, to make you great.

Palmyra. I know the king, though you are not his son,
Will still regard you as my foster-brother,
And so conduct you downward from a throne,
By slow degrees, so unperceived and soft,
That it may seem no fall: Or, if it be,
May fortune lay a bed of down beneath you!

Polydamas. He shall be ranked with my nobility,
And kept from scorn by a large pension given him.

Leonidas. You are all great and royal in your gifts;
                                        [*Bowing.*

But at the donor's feet I lay them down:
Should I take riches from you, it would seem
As I did want a soul to bear that poverty,
To which the gods design my humble birth:
And should I take your honours without merit,
It would appear, I wanted manly courage
To hope them, in your service, from my sword.

Polydamas. Still brave, and like yourself.
The court shall shine this night in its full splendour,
And celebrate this new discovery.
Argaleon, lead my daughter: As we go,
I shall have time to give her my commands,
In which you are concerned.   [*Exeunt all but* LEONIDAS.

Leonidas. Methinks, I do not want
That huge long train of fawning followers,

That swept a furlong after me.
'Tis true I am alone;
So was the Godhead, ere he made the world,
And better served himself, than served by nature.
And yet I have a soul
Above this humble fate. I could command,
Love to do good, give largely to true merit,
All that a king should do: But though these are not
My province, I have scene enough within,
To exercise my virtue.
All that a heart, so fixed as mine, can move,
Is, that my niggard fortune starves my love.   [*Exit.*

SCENE II

PALAMEDE *and* DORALICE *meet: She, with a book in
her hand, seems to start at the sight of him.*

Doralice. 'Tis a strange thing that no warning will serve
your turn; and that no retirement will secure me from
your impertinent addresses! Did I not tell you, that I was
to be private here at my devotions?

Palamede. Yes; and you see I have observed my cue
exactly: I am come to relieve you from them. Come, shut
up, shut up your book; the man's come who is to supply
all your necessities.

Doralice. Then, it seems, you are so impudent to think
it was an assignation? This, I warrant, was your lewd
interpretation of my innocent meaning.

Palamede. Venus forbid, that I should harbour so unreasonable a thought of a fair young lady, that you should
lead me hither into temptation. I confess, I might think
indeed it was a kind of honourable challenge to meet
privately without seconds, and decide the difference
betwixt the two sexes; but heaven forgive me, if I thought
amiss.

Doralice. You thought too, I'll lay my life on't, that
you might as well make love to me, as my husband does
to your mistress.

Palamede. I was so unreasonable to think so too.

Doralice. And then you wickedly inferred, that there
was some justice in the revenge if it; or, at least, but little
injury for a man to endeavour to enjoy that, which he
counts a blessing, and which is not valued as it ought by

the dull possessor. Confess your wickedness,—did you not think so?

Palamede. I confess I was thinking so, as fast as I could; but you think so much before me, that you will let me think nothing.

Doralice. 'Tis the very thing that I designed; I have forestalled all your arguments, and left you without a word more, to plead for mercy. If you have anything farther to offer, ere sentence pass——Poor animal, I brought you hither only for my diversion.

Palamede. That you may have, if you'll make use of me the right way; but I tell thee, woman, I am now past talking.

Doralice. But it may be, I came hither to hear what fine things you could say for yourself.

Palamede. You would be very angry, to my knowledge, if I should lose so much time to say many of them.—By this hand you would!

Doralice. Fie, Palamede, I am a woman of honour.

Palamede. I see you are; you have kept touch with your assignation: And before we part, you shall find that I am a man of honour. Yet I have one scruple of conscience——

Doralice. I warrant you will not want some naughty argument, or other, to satisfy yourself.—I hope you are afraid of betraying your friend?

Palamede. Of betraying my friend! I am more afraid of being betrayed by you to my friend. You women now are got into the way of telling first yourselves: A man, who has any care of his reputation, will be loth to trust it with you.

Doralice. O, you charge your faults upon our sex! You men are like clocks; you never make love, but you clap your wings, and crow when you have done.

Palamede. Nay, rather you women are like hens; you never lay, but you cackle an hour after, to discover your nest—But I'll venture it for once.

Doralice. To convince you that you are in the wrong, I'll retire into the dark grotto to my devotion, and make so little noise, that it shall be impossible for you to find me.

Palamede. But if I find you——

Doralice. Ay, if you find me—But I'll put you to search in more corners than you imagine.

[*She runs in, and he after her.*

Enter RHODOPHIL *and* MELANTHA.

Melantha. Let me die, but this solitude, and that grotto are scandalous; I'll go no further; besides, you have a sweet lady of your own.

Rhodophil. But a sweet mistress, now and then, makes my sweet lady so much more sweet.

Melantha. I hope you will not force me?

Rhodophil. But I will, if you desire it.

Palamede [*within*]. Where the devil are you, madam? 'Sdeath, I begin to be weary of this hide and seek: If you stay a little longer, till the fit's over, I'll hide in my turn, and put you to the finding me, [*He enters and sees* RHODOPHIL *and* MELANTHA.] How! Rhodophil and my mistress!

Melantha. My servant, to apprehend me! this is *surprenant au dernier.*

Rhodophil. I must on; there's nothing but impudence can help me out.

Palamede. Rhodophil, how came you hither in so good company?

Rhodophil. As you see, Palamede; an effect of pure friendship; I was not able to live without you.

Palamede. But what makes my mistress with you?

Rhodophil. Why I heard you were here alone, and could not in civility but bring her to you.

Melantha. You'll pardon the effects of a passion which I may now avow for you, if it transported me beyond the rules of *bienséance.*

Palamede. But, who told you I was here? they, that told you that, may tell you more, for aught I know.

Rhodophil. O, for that matter, we had intelligence.

Palamede. But let me tell you, we came hither so very privately, that you could not trace us.

Rhodophil. Us! what us? you are alone.

Palamede. Us! the devil's in me for mistaking:—me, I meant. Or us, that is, you are me, or I you, as we are friends: That's us.

Doralice. Palamede, Palamede!   [*Within.*

Rhodophil. I should know that voice; who's within there, that calls you?

Palamede. Faith, I can't imagine; I believe the place is haunted.

Doralice. Palamede, Palamede, all cocks hidden.

[*Within.*

Palamede. Lord, Lord, what shall I do?—Well, dear friend, to let you see I scorn to be jealous, and that I dare trust my mistress with you, take her back, for I would not willingly have her frighted, and I am resolved to see who's there; I'll not be daunted with a bugbear, that's certain:— Prithee, dispute it not, it shall be so; nay, do not put me to swear, but go quickly: There's an effort of pure friendship for you now.

Enter DORALICE, *and looks amazed, seeing them.*

Rhodophil. Doralice! I am thunder-struck to see you here.

Palamede. So am I! quite thunder-struck. Was it you that called me within?—I must be impudent.

Rhodophil. How came you hither, spouse?

Palamede. Ay, how came you hither? And which is more, how could you be here without my knowledge?

Doralice [*to her husband*]. O, gentleman, have I caught you i' faith! have I broke forth in ambush upon you! I thought my suspicions would prove true.

Rhodophil. Suspicions! this is very fine, spouse! Prithee, what suspicions?

Doralice. O, you feign ignorance: Why, of you, and Melantha; here have I stayed these two hours, waiting with all the rage of a passionate, loving wife, but infinitely jealous, to take you two in the manner; for hither I was certain you would come.

Rhodophil. But you are mistaken, spouse, in the oc- casion; for we came hither on purpose to find Palamede, on intelligence he was gone before.

Palamede. I'll be hanged then, if the same party, who gave you intelligence I was here, did not tell your wife you would come hither. Now I smell the malice on't on both sides.

Doralice. Was it so, think you? nay, then I'll confess my part of the malice too. As soon as ever I spied my husband and Melantha come together, I had a strange temptation to make him jealous in revenge; and that made me call Palamede, Palamede, as though there had been an intrigue between us.

Melantha. Nay, I avow, there was an appearance of
an intrigue between us too.

Palamede. To see how things will come about!

Rhodophil. And was it only thus, my dear Doralice?
　　　　　　　　　　　　　　　　　　　[*Embrace.*

Doralice. And did I wrong n'own[5] Rhodophil, with a
false suspicion?　　　　　　　　　　　[*Embracing him.*

Palamede [*aside*]. Now I am confident we had all four
the same design: 'Tis a pretty odd kind of game this,
where each of us plays for double stakes: This is just thrust
and parry with the same motion; I am to get his wife, and
yet to guard my own mistress. But I am vilely suspicious,
that, while I conquer in the right wing, I shall be routed
in the left; for both our women will certainly betray their
party, because they are each of them for gaining of two,
as well as we; and I much fear,
If their necessities and ours were known,
They have more need of two, than we of one.

　　　　　　　　　　[*Exeunt, embracing one another.*

ACT IV

SCENE I

Enter LEONIDAS, *musing;* AMALTHEA, *following him.*

AMALTHEA. Yonder he is; and I must speak or die:
And yet 'tis death to speak! yet he must know
I have a passion for him, and may know it
With a less blush; because to offer it
To his low fortunes, shows I loved before,
His person, not his greatness.

Leonidas. First scorned, and now commanded from
　　　the court!
The king is good; but he is wrought to this
By proud Argaleon's malice.
What more disgrace can love and fortune join
To inflict upon one man? I cannot now
Behold my dear Palmyra: She, perhaps, too,
Is grown ashamed of a mean ill-placed love.

[5] *I.e.* "mine own."

Amalthea. Assist me, Venus, for I tremble when
I am to speak, but I must force myself.　　　　[*Aside.*
Sir, I would crave but one short minute with you,
And some few words.

    Leonidas. The proud Argaleon's sister!　　　[*Aside.*

    Amalthea. Alas! it will not out; Shame stops my mouth.
                                     [*Aside.*

Pardon my error, sir; I was mistaken,
And took you for another.

    Leonidas. In spite of all his guards, I'll see Palmyra;
                                       [*Aside.*

Though meanly born, I have a kingly soul.

    Amalthea. I stand upon a precipice, where fain
I would retire, but love still thrusts me on:
Now I grow bolder, and will speak to him.　　　[*Aside.*
Sir, 'tis indeed to you that I would speak,
And if——

    Leonidas. O, you are sent to scorn my fortunes?
Your sex and beauty are your privilege;
But should your brother——

    Amalthea. Now he looks angry, and I dare not speak.
I had some business with you, sir,
But 'tis not worth your knowledge.

    Leonidas. Then 'twill be charity to let me mourn
My griefs alone, for I am much disordered.

    Amalthea. 'Twill be more charity to mourn them with
    you:
Heaven knows I pity you.

    Leonidas. Your pity, madam,
Is generous, but 'tis unavailable.

    Amalthea. You know not till 'tis tried.
Your sorrows are no secret; you have lost
A crown, and mistress.

    Leonidas. Are not these enough?
Hang two such weights on any other soul,
And see if it can bear them.

    Amalthea. More; you are banished, by my brother's
    means,
And ne'er must hope again to see your princess;
Except as prisoners view fair walks and streets,
And careless passengers going by their grates,
To make them feel the want of liberty.
But, worse than all,

The king this morning has enjoined his daughter
To accept my brother's love.
   Leonidas. Is this your pity?
You aggravate my griefs, and print them deeper,
In new and heavier stamps.
   Amalthea. 'Tis as physicians show the desperate ill,
To endear their art, by mitigating pains
They cannot wholly cure: When you despair
Of all you wish, some part of it, because
Unhoped for, may be grateful; and some other——
   Leonidas. What other?
   Amalthea. Some other may——
My shame again has seized me, and I can go
No farther.   [*Aside.*
   Leonidas. These often failing sighs and interruptions
Make me imagine you have grief like mine;
Have you ne'er loved
   Amalthea. I? never!—'Tis in vain:
I must despair in silence.   [*Aside.*
   Leonidas. You come, as I suspected then, to mock,
At least observe, my griefs: Take it not ill,
That I must leave you.   [*Is going.*
   Amalthea. You must not go with these unjust opinions.
Command my life and fortunes: you are wise;
Think, and think well, what I can do to serve you.
   Leonidas. I have but one thing in my thoughts and
     wishes:
If, by your means, I can obtain the sight
Of my adored Palmyra; or, what's harder,
One minute's time, to tell her, I die hers—
                     [*She starts back.*
I see I am not to expect it from you;
Nor could, indeed, with reason.
   Amalthea. Name any other thing! Is Amalthea
So despicable, she can serve your wishes
In this alone?
   Leonidas. If I should ask of heaven,
I have no other suit.
   Amalthea. To show you, then, I can deny you nothing,
Though 'tis more hard to me than any other,
Yet I will do it for you.
   Leonidas. Name quickly, name the means! speak, my
     good angel!

Amalthea. Be not so much o'erjoyed; for, if you are,
I'll rather die than do't. This night the court
Will be in masquerade;
You shall attend on me; in that disguise
You may both see and speak to her,
If you dare venture it.

    Leonidas. Yes; were a god her guardian,
And bore in each hand thunder, I would venture.

    Amalthea. Farewell, then; two hours hence I will expect
      you:—
My heart's so full, that I can stay no longer.   [*Exit.*

    Leonidas. Already it grows dusky: I'll prepare
With haste for my disguise. But who are these?

Enter HERMOGENES *and* EUBULUS.

    Hermogenes. 'Tis he; we need not fear to speak to him.

    Eubulus. Leonidas?

    Leonidas. Sure I have known that voice.

    Hermogenes. You have some reason, sir: 'tis Eubulus,
Who bred you with the princess: and, departing,
Bequeathed you to my care.

    Leonidas. My foster-father! let my knees express
My joys for your return!   [*Kneeling.*

    Eubulus. Rise, sir; you must not kneel.

    Leonidas. E'er since you left me,
I have been wandering in a maze of fate,
Led by false fires of a fantastic glory,
And the vain lustre of imagined crowns.
But, ah! why would you leave me? or how could you
Absent yourself so long?

    Eubulus. I'll give you a most just account of both:
And something more I have to tell you, which
I know must cause your wonder; but this place,
Though almost hid in darkness, is not safe.
Already I discern some coming towards us
                      [*Torches appear.*
With lights, who may discover me. Hermogenes,
Your lodgings are hard by, and much more private.

    Hermogenes. There you may freely speak.

    Leonidas. Let us make haste;
For some affairs, and of no small importance,
Call me another way.   [*Exeunt.*

SCENE II

Enter Palamede *and* Rhodophil, *with vizor-masques
in their hands, and torches before them.*

Palamede. We shall have noble sport to-night, Rhodophil; this masquerading is a most glorious invention.

Rhodophil. I believe it was invented first by some jealous lover, to discover the haunts of his jilting mistress; or
perhaps, by some distressed servant, to gain an opportunity with a jealous man's wife.

Palamede. No, it must be the invention of a woman, it
has so much of subtilty and love in it.

Rhodophil. I am sure 'tis extremely pleasant; for to go
unknown, is the next degree to going invisible.

Palamede. What with our antic habits and feigned
voices,—*Do you know me?* and—*I know you,*—methinks
we move and talk just like so many overgrown puppets.

Rhodophil. Masquerade is only vizor-mask[6] improved;
a heightening of the same fashion.

Palamede. No, masquerade is vizor-mask in debauch,
and I like it the better for't: for, with a vizor-mask, we
fool ourselves into courtship, for the sake of an eye that
glanced; or a hand that stole itself out of the glove, sometimes, to give us a sample of the skin: But in masquerade
there is nothing to be known, she's all *terra incognita;*
and the bold discoverer leaps ashore, and takes his lot
among the wild Indians and savages without the vile
consideration of safety to his person, or of beauty, or
wholesomeness in his mistress.

Enter Beliza.

Rhodophil. Beliza, what make you here?

Beliza. Sir, my lady sent me after you, to let you know,
she finds herself a little indisposed; so that she cannot
be at court, but is retired to rest in her own apartment,
where she shall want the happiness of your dear embraces
to-night.

Rhodophil. A very fine phrase, Beliza, to let me know
my wife desires to lie alone.

[6] The sign of a courtesan.—Ed.

Palamede. I doubt, Rhodophil, you take the pains sometimes to instruct your wife's woman in these elegancies.

Rhodophil. Tell my dear lady, that since I must be so unhappy as not to wait on her to-night, I will lament bitterly for her absence. 'Tis true I shall be at court, but I will take no divertisement there; and when I return to my solitary bed, if I am so forgetful of my passion as to sleep, I will dream of her; and betwixt sleep and waking, put out my foot towards her side, for midnight consolation; and, not finding her I will sigh, and imagine myself a most desolate widower.

Beliza. I shall do your commands, sir.   [*Exit.*

Rhodophil [*aside*]. She's sick as aptly for my purpose, as if she had contrived it so. Well, if ever woman was a help mate for man, my spouse is so; for within this hour I received a note from Melantha, that she would meet me this evening in masquerade, in boy's habit, to rejoice with me before she entered into fetters; for I find she loves me better than Palamede, only because he's to be her husband. There's something of antipathy in the word *marriage* to the nature of love; marriage is the mere ladle of affection, that cools it when 'tis never so fiercely boiling over.

Palamede. Dear Rhodophil, I must needs beg your pardon; there is an occasion fallen out which I had forgot: I cannot be at court to-night.

Rhodophil. Dear Palamede, I am sorry we shall not have one course together at the herd; but I find your game lies single: Good fortune to you with your mistress.   [*Exit.*

Palamede. He has wished me good fortune with his wife; there's no sin in this then, there's fair leave given. Well, I must go visit the sick; I cannot resist the temptations of my charity. O what a difference will she find betwixt a dull resty husband, and a quick vigorous lover! He sets out like a carrier's horse, plodding on, because he knows he must, with the bells of matrimony chiming so melancholy about his neck, in pain till he's at his journey's end; and, despairing to get thither, he is fain to fortify imagination with the thoughts of another woman: I take heat after heat, like a well-breathed courser, and—But hark, what noise is that? Swords! [*Clashing of swords within.*] Nay, then, have with you.   [*Exit* PALAMEDE.

Re-enter PALAMEDE, *with* RHODOPHIL; *and* DORALICE *in man's habit.*

Rhodophil. Friend, your relief was timely, otherwise I had been oppressed.

Palamede. What was the quarrel?

Rhodophil. What I did was in rescue of this youth.

Palamede. What cause could he give them?

Doralice. The cause was nothing but only the common cause of fighting in masquerades: They were drunk, as I was sober.

Rhodophil. Have they not hurt you?

Doralice. No; but I am exceeding ill with the fright on't.

Palamede. Let's lead him to some place, where he may refresh himself.

Rhodophil. Do you conduct him then.

Palamede [*aside*]. How cross this happens to my design of going to Doralice! for I am confident she was sick on purpose that I should visit her. Hark you, Rhodophil, could not you take care of the stripling? I am partly engaged to-night.

Rhodophil. You know I have business; but come, youth, if it must be so.

Doralice [*to* RHODOPHIL]. No, good sir, do not give yourself that trouble; I shall be safer, and better pleased with your friend here.

Rhodophil. Farewell, then; once more I wish you a good adventure.

Palamede. Damn this kindness! now must I be troubled with this young rogue, and miss my opportunity with Doralice.

[*Exit* RHODOPHIL *alone;* PALAMEDE *with* DORALICE.

SCENE III

Enter POLYDAMAS.

Polydamas. Argaleon counselled well to banish him;
He has, I know not what,
Of greatness in his looks, and of high fate,
That almost awes me; but I fear my daughter,
Who hourly moves me for him; and I marked,
She sighed when I but named Argaleon to her.

But see, the maskers: Hence, my cares, this night!
At least take truce, and find me on my pillow.

> *Enter the* Princess *in masquerade, with* Ladies. *At the
> other end,* ARGALEON *and* Gentlemen *in masquer-
> ade; then* LEONIDAS *leading* AMALTHEA. *The* King
> *sits. A Dance. After the Dance*

Amalthea [*to* LEONIDAS]. That's the princess;
I saw the habit ere she put it on.
    Leonidas. I know her by a thousand other signs;
She cannot hide so much divinity,
Disguised, and silent, yet some graceful motion
Breaks from her, and shines round her like a glory.
                                        [*Goes to* PALMYRA.
    Amalthea. Thus she reveals herself, and knows it not:
Like love's dark lanthorn, I direct his steps,
And yet he sees not that, which gives them light.
    Palmyra. I know you; but, alas! Leonidas,
Why should you tempt this danger on yourself?
    Leonidas. Madam, you know me not, if you believe
I would not hazard greater for your sake.
But you, I fear, are changed.
    Palmyra. No, I am still the same;
But there are many things became Palmyra,
Which ill become the princess.
    Leonidas. I ask nothing
Which honour will not give you leave to grant:
One hour's short audience, at my father's house,
You cannot sure refuse me.
    Palmyra. Perhaps I should, did I consult strict virtue;
But something must be given to love and you.
When would you I should come?
    Leonidas. This evening, with the speediest opportunity.
I have a secret to discover to you,
Which will surprise and please you.
    Palmyra. 'Tis enough.
Go now; for we may be observed and known.
I trust your honour; give me not occasion
To blame myself or you.
    Leonidas. You never shall repent your good opinion.
                          [*Kisses her hand, and exit.*
    Argaleon. I cannot be deceived; that is the princess:
One of her maids betrayed the habit to me.

But who was he with whom she held discourse?
'Tis one she favours, for he kissed her hand.
Our shapes are like, our habits near the same;
She may mistake, and speak to me for him.
I am resolved; I'll satisfy my doubts,
Though to be more tormented.

SONG

bawdy song

I

Whilst Alexis lay prest
  In her arms he loved best,
With his hands round her neck,
  And his head on her breast,
He found the fierce pleasure too hasty to stay,
And his soul in the tempest just flying away.

II

When Cælia saw this,
With a sigh and a kiss,
She cried,—O, my dear, I am robbed of my bliss!
'Tis unkind to your love, and unfaithfully done,
To leave me behind you, and die all alone.

III

The youth, though in haste,
And breathing his last,
In pity died slowly, while she died more fast;
Till at length she cried,—Now, my dear, now let us
  go;
Now die, my Alexis, and I will die too!

IV

Thus entranced they did lie,
Till Alexis did try
To recover new breath, that again he might die:
Then often they died; but the more they did so,
The nymph died more quick, and the shepherd more
  slow.

Another Dance. After it, ARGALEON *re-enters, and
stands by the* Princess.

Palmyra. Leonidas, what means this quick return?
                            [*To* ARGALEON.

Argaleon. O heaven! 'tis what I feared.

Palmyra. Is aught of moment happened since you went?

Argaleon. No, madam; but I understood not fully
Your last commands.

Palmyra. And yet you answered to them.
Retire; you are too indiscreet a lover:
I'll meet you where I promised.   [*Exit.*

Argaleon. O my curst fortune! what have I discovered!
But I will be revenged.   [*Whispers to the* King.

Polydamas. But are you certain you are not deceived?

Argaleon. Upon my life.

Polydamas. Her honour is concerned.
Somewhat I'll do; but I am yet distracted,
And know not where to fix. I wished a child,
And heaven, in anger, granted my request.
So blind we are, our wishes are so vain,
That what we most desire, proves most our pain.
                                             [*Exeunt.*

SCENE IV

An Eating-house. Bottles of wine on the table.
PALAMEDE, *and* DORALICE, *in man's habit.*

Doralice [*aside*]. Now cannot I find in my heart to discover myself, though I long he should know me.

Palamede. I tell thee, boy, now I have seen thee safe, I
must be gone: I have no leisure to throw away on thy
raw conversation; I am a person that understands better
things, I.

Doralice. Were I a woman, oh how you would admire
me! cry up every word I said, and screw your face into
a submissive smile; as I have seen a dull gallant act wit,
and counterfeit pleasantness, when he whispers to a great
person in a play-house; smile, and look briskly, when the
other answers, as if something of extraordinary had past
betwixt them, when, heaven knows, there was nothing
else but—What a clock does your lordship think it is?
And my lord's *repartee* is,—It is almost park-time: or, at
most,—Shall we out of the pit, and go behind the scenes
for an act or two? And yet such fine things as these
would be wit in a mistress's mouth.

Palamede. Ay, boy; there dame Nature's in the case:
He, who cannot find wit in a mistress, deserves to find

nothing else, boy. But these are riddles to thee, child, and I have not leisure to instruct thee; I have affairs to despatch, great affairs; I am a man of business.

Doralice. Come, you shall not go: You have no affairs but what you may despatch here, to my knowledge.

Palamede. I find now, thou art a boy of more understanding than I thought thee; a very lewd wicked boy: O' my conscience, thou wouldst debauch me, and hast some evil designs upon my person.

Doralice. You are mistaken, sir; I would only have you show me a more lawful reason why you would leave me, than I can why you should not, and I'll not stay you; for I am not so young, but I understand the necessities of flesh and blood, and the pressing occasions of mankind, as well as you.

Palamede. A very forward and understanding boy! thou art in great danger of a page's wit, to be brisk at fourteen, and dull at twenty. But I'll give thee no further account; I must, and will go.

Doralice. My life on it, your mistress is not at home.

Palamede. This imp will make me very angry.—I tell thee, young sir, she is at home, and at home for me; and which is more, she is a-bed for me, and sick for me.

Doralice. For you only?

Palamede. Ay, for me only.

Doralice. But how do you know she's sick a-bed?

Palamede. She sent her husband word so.

Doralice. And are you such a novice in love, to believe a wife's message to her husband?

Palamede. Why, what the devil should be her meaning else?

Doralice. It may be, to go in masquerade, as well as you; to observe your haunts, and keep you company without your knowledge.

Palamede. Nay, I'll trust her for that: She loves me too well, to disguise herself from me.

Doralice. If I were she, I would disguise on purpose to try your wit; and come to my servant like a riddle,— Read me, and take me.

Palamede. I could know her in any shape: My good genius would prompt me to find out a handsome woman: There's something that would attract me to her without my knowledge.

Doralice. Then you make a load-stone of your mistress?

Palamede. Yes, and I carry steel about me, which has been so often touched that it never fails to point to the north pole.

Doralice. Yet still my mind gives me, that you have met her disguised to-night, and have not known her.

Palamede. This is the most pragmatical conceited little fellow, he will needs understand my business better than myself. I tell thee, once more, thou dost not know my mistress.

Doralice. And I tell you once more, that I know her better than you do.

Palamede. The boy's resolved to have the last word. I find I must go without reply.   [*Exit.*

Doralice. Ah mischief, I have lost him with my fooling. Palamede, Palamede!

He returns. She plucks off her peruke, and puts it on again, when he knows her.

Palamede. O heavens! is it you, madam?

Doralice. Now, where was your good genius, that would prompt you to find me out?

Palamede. Why, you see I was not deceived; you yourself were my good genius.

Doralice. But where was the steel, that knew the load-stone? Ha?

Palamede. The truth is, madam, the steel has lost its virtue: and, therefore, if you please, we'll new touch it.

Enter RHODOPHIL; *and* MELANTHA *in boy's habit.* RHODOPHIL *sees* PALAMEDE *kissing* DORALICE'S *hand.*

Rhodophil. Palamede again! am I fallen into your quarters? What? Engaging with a boy? Is all honourable?

Palamede. Oh, very honourable on my side. I was just chastising this young villain; he was running away, without paying his share of the reckoning.

Rhodophil. Then I find I was deceived in him.

Palamede. Yes, you are deceived in him: 'tis the archest rogue, if you did but know him.

Melantha. Good Rhodophil, let us get off *à la dérobée,* for fear I should be discovered.

Rhodophil. There's no retiring now; I warrant you for discovery. Now have I the oddest thought, to entertain you before your servant's face, and he never the wiser: it will be the prettiest juggling trick, to cheat him when he looks upon us.

Melantha. This is the strangest caprice in you.

Palamede [*to* DORALICE]. This Rhodophil's the unluckiest fellow to me! this is now the second time he has barred the dice when we were just ready to have nicked him; but if ever I get the box again—

Doralice. Do you think he will not know me? Am I like myself?

Palamede. No more than a picture in the hangings.

Doralice. Nay, then he can never discover me, now the wrong side of the arras is turned towards him.

Palamede. At least, it will be some pleasure to me, to enjoy what freedom I can while he looks on; I will storm the outworks of matrimony even before his face.

Rhodophil. What wine have you there, Palamede?

Palamede. Old Chios, or the rogue's damn'd that drew it.

Rhodophil. Come,—to the most constant of mistresses! that, I believe, is yours, Palamede.

Doralice. Pray spare your seconds; for my part I am but a weak brother.

Palamede. Now,—to the truest of turtles! that is your wife, Rhodophil, that lies sick at home, in the bed of honour.

Rhodophil. Now let us have one common health, and so have done.

Doralice. Then, for once, I'll begin it. Here's to him that has the fairest lady of Sicily in masquerade to-night.

Palamede. This is such an obliging health, I'll kiss thee, dear rogue, for thy invention.   [*Kisses her.*

Rhodophil. He, who has this lady, is a happy man, without dispute,—I'm most concerned in this, I am sure.

                                                      [*Aside.*

Palamede. Was it not well found out, Rhodophil?

Melantha. Ay, this was *bien trouvée* indeed.

Doralice [*to* MELANTHA]. I suppose I shall do you a kindness, to inquire if you have not been in France, sir?

Melantha. To do you service, sir.

Doralice. O, monsieur, *votre valet bien humble.*
> [*Saluting her.*

Melantha. Votre esclave, monsieur, de tout mon cœur.
> [*Returning the salute.*

Doralice. I suppose, sweet sir, you are the hope and joy of some thriving citizen, who has pinched himself at home, to breed you abroad, where you have learned your exercises, as it appears, most awkwardly, and are returned, with the addition of a new-laced bosom and a clap, to your good old father, who looks at you with his mouth, while you spout French with your man monsieur.

Palamede. Let me kiss thee again for that, dear rogue.

Melantha. And you, I imagine, are my young master, whom your mother durst not trust upon salt-water, but left you to be your own tutor at fourteen, to be very brisk and *entreprenant,* to endeavour to be debauched ere you have learned the knack of it, to value yourself upon a clap before you can get it, and to make it the height of your ambition to get a player for your mistress.

Rhodophil [*embracing* MELANTHA]. O dear young bully, thou hast tickled him with a *repartee,* i'faith.

Melantha. You are one of those that applaud our country plays, where drums, and trumpets, and blood, and wounds, are wit.

Rhodophil. Again, my boy? Let me kiss thee most abundantly.

Doralice. You are an admirer of the dull French poetry, which is so thin, that it is the very leaf-gold of wit, the very wafers and whipped cream of sense, for which a man opens his mouth, and gapes, to swallow nothing: And to be an admirer of such profound dulness, one must be endowed with a great perfection of impudence and ignorance.

Palamede. Let me embrace thee most vehemently.

Melantha. I'll sacrifice my life for French poetry.
> [*Advancing.*

Doralice. I'll die upon the spot for our country wit.

Rhodophil [*to* MELANTHA]. Hold, hold, young Mars! Palamede, draw back your hero.

Palamede. 'Tis time; I shall be drawn in for a second else at the wrong weapon.

Melantha. O that I were a man, for thy sake!

Doralice. You'll be a man as soon as I shall.

Enter a Messenger *to* RHODOPHIL.

Messenger. Sir, the king has instant business with you.
I saw the guard drawn up by your lieutenant,
Before the palace gate, ready to march.

Rhodophil. 'Tis somewhat sudden; say that I am coming.
                                                    [*Exit* Messenger.
Now, Palamede, what think you of this sport?
This is some sudden tumult; will you along?

Palamede. Yes, yes, I will go; but the devil take me if
ever I was less in humour. Why the pox could they not
have stayed their tumult, till to-morrow? Then I had done
my business, and been ready for them. Truth is, I had a
little transitory crime to have committed first; and I am
the worst man in the world at repenting, till a sin be
thoroughly done: But what shall we do with the two
boys?

Rhodophil. Let them take a lodging in the house, 'till the
business be over.

Doralice. What, lie with a boy? For my part, I own it,
I cannot endure to lie with a boy.

Palamede. The more's my sorrow, I cannot accommodate
you with a better bedfellow.

Melantha. Let me die, if I enter into a pair of sheets
with him that hates the French.

Doralice. Pish, take no care for us, but leave us in the
streets; I warrant you, as late as it is, I'll find my lodging
as well as any drunken bully of them all.

Rhodophil. I'll fight in mere revenge, and wreak my
         passion,
On all that spoil this hopeful assignation.   [*Aside.*

Palamede. I'm sure we fight in a good quarrel:
Rogues may pretend religion, and the laws;
But a kind mistress is the Good Old Cause.   [*Exeunt.*

SCENE V

Enter PALMYRA, EUBULUS, *and* HERMOGENES.

Palmyra. You tell me wonders; that Leonidas
Is prince Theagenes, the late king's son.

Eubulus. It seemed as strange to him, as now to you,
Before I had convinced him; but, besides
His great resemblance to the king his father,

The queen his mother lives, secured by me
In a religious house, to whom, each year,
I brought the news of his increasing virtues.
My last long absence from you both was caused
By wounds, which in my journey I received,
When set upon by thieves; I lost those jewels
And letters, which your dying mother left.

    Hermogenes. The same he means, which, since, brought
      to the king,
Made him first know he had a child alive:
'Twas then my care of prince Leonidas,
Caused me to say he was the usurper's son;
Till after, forced by your apparent danger,
I made the true discovery of your birth,
And once more hid my prince's.

Enter LEONIDAS.

    Leonidas. Hermogenes, and Eubulus, retire;
Those of our party, whom I left without,
Expect your aid and council.

                [*Exeunt* HERMOGENES *and* EUBULUS.

    Palmyra. I should, Leonidas, congratulate
This happy change of your exalted fate;
But, as my joy, so you my wonder move.
Your looks have more of business than of love;
And your last words some great design did show.

    Leonidas. I frame not any to be hid from you;
You, in my love, all my designs may see.
But what have love and you designed for me?
Fortune, once more, has set the balance right;
First, equalled us in lowness; then, in height.
Both of us have so long, like gamesters, thrown,
Till fate comes round, and gives to each his own.
As fate is equal, so may love appear:
Tell me, at least, what I must hope, or fear.

    Palmyra. After so many proofs, how can you call
My love in doubt? Fear nothing, and hope all.
Think what a prince, with honour, may receive,
Or I may give, without a parent's leave.

    Leonidas. You give, and then restrain the grace you
      show;
As ostentatious priests, when souls they woo,
Promise their heaven to all, but grant to few.

But do for me, what I have dared for you:
I did no argument from duty bring:
Duty's a name, and love's a real thing.

Palmyra. Man's love may, like wild torrents, overflow;
Woman's as deep, but in its banks must go,
My love is mine, and that I can impart;
But cannot give my person, with my heart.

Leonidas. Your love is then no gift:
For, when the person it does not convey,
'Tis to give gold, and not to give the key.

Palmyra. Then ask my father.

Leonidas. He detains my throne;
Who holds back mine, will hardly give his own.

Palmyra. What then remains?

Leonidas. That I must have recourse
To arms, and take my love and crown, by force.
Hermogenes is forming the design;
And with him all the brave and loyal join.

Palmyra. And is it thus you court Palmyra's bed?
Can she the murderer of her parent wed?
Desist from force: So much you well may give
To love, and me, to let my father live.

Leonidas. Each act of mine my love to you has shown;
But you, who tax my want of it, have none.
You bid me part with you, and let him live;
But they should nothing ask, who nothing give.

Palmyra. I give what virtue, and what duty can,
In vowing ne'er to wed another man.

Leonidas. You will be forced to be Argaleon's wife.

Palmyra. I'll keep my promise, though I lose my life.

Leonidas. Then you lose love, for which we both contend;
For life is but the means, but love's the end.

Palmyra. Our souls shall love hereafter.

Leonidas. I much fear,
That soul, which could deny the body here
To taste of love, would be a niggard there.

Palmyra. Then 'tis past hope: our cruel fate, I see,
Will make a sad divorce 'twixt you and me.
For, if you force employ, by heaven I swear,
And all blessed beings——

Leonidas. Your rash oath forbear.

Palmyra. I never——

Leonidas. Hold once more. But yet, as he,
Who 'scapes a dangerous leap, looks back to see;
So I desire, now I am past, my fear,
To know what was that oath you meant to swear.
  Palmyra. I meant, that if you hazarded your life,
Or sought my father's, ne'er to be your wife.
  Leonidas. See now, Palmyra, how unkind you prove!
Could you, with so much ease, forswear my love?
  Palmyra. You force me with your ruinous design.
  Leonidas. Your father's life is more your care, than mine.
  Palmyra. You wrong me: 'Tis not, though it ought to
    be;
You are my care, heaven knows, as well as he.
  Leonidas. If now the execution I delay,
My honour, and my subjects, I betray.
All is prepared for the just enterprise;
And the whole city will to-morrow rise.
The leaders of the party are within,
And Eubulus has sworn that he will bring,
To head their arms, the person of their king.
  Palmyra. In telling this, you may be guilty too;
I therefore must discover what I know:
What honour bids you do, nature bids me prevent;
But kill me first, and then pursue your black intent.
  Leonidas. Palmyra, no; you shall not need to die;
Yet I'll not trust so strict a piety.
Within there!

                    Enter EUBULUS.

Eubulus, a guard prepare;
Here, I commit this prisoner to your care.
            [*Kisses* PALMYRA's *hand, then gives it to*
                    EUBULUS.
  Palmyra. Leonidas, I never thought these bands
Could e'er be given me by a lover's hands.
  Leonidas. Palmyra, thus your judge himself arraigns;
                                    [*Kneeling.*
He, who imposed these bands, still wears your chains:
When you to love or duty false must be,
Or to your father guilty, or to me,
These chains, alone, remain to set you free.
                    [*Noise of swords clashing.*

Polydamas [*within*]. Secure these, first: then search the
  inner room.

Leonidas. From whence do these tumultuous clamours
  come?

Enter HERMOGENES, *hastily.*

Hermogenes. We are betrayed; and there remains alone
This comfort, that your person is not known.

Enter the King, ARGALEON, RHODOPHIL, PALAMEDE,
  Guards; *some like citizens, as prisoners.*

Polydamas. What mean these midnight consultations
  here,
Where I like an unsummoned guest appear?
  Leonidas. Sir——
  Argaleon. There needs no excuse; 'tis understood;
You were all watching for your prince's good.
  Polydamas. My reverend city friends, you are well met!
On what great work were your grave wisdoms set?
Which of my actions were you scanning here?
What French invasion have you found to fear?
  Leonidas. They are my friends; and come, sir, with
    intent,
To take their leaves, before my banishment.
  Polydamas. Your exile in both sexes friends can find:
I see the ladies, like the men, are kind. [*Seeing* PALMYRA.
  Palmyra. Alas, I came but——   [*Kneeling.*
  Polydamas. Add not to your crime
A lie: I'll hear you speak some other time.
How? Eubulus! nor time, nor thy disguise,
Can keep thee undiscovered from my eyes.
A guard there! seize them all.
  Rhodophil. Yield, sir; what use of valour can be shown?
  Palamede. One, and unarmed, against a multitude?
  Leonidas. Oh for a sword!

      [*He reaches at one of the* Guards' *halberds, and
        is seized behind.*

I wonnot lose my breath
In fruitless prayers; but beg a speedy death.
  Palmyra. O spare Leonidas, and punish me!
  Polydamas. Mean girl, thou want'st an advocate for
    thee.

Now the mysterious knot will be untied;
Whether the young king lives, or where he died:
To-morrow's dawn shall the dark riddle clear,
Crown all my joys, and dissipate my fear.   [*Exeunt.*

ACT V

SCENE I

PALAMEDE, STRATO. PALAMEDE *with a letter
in his hand.*

PALAMEDE. This evening, sayest thou? will they both be
here?

Strato. Yes, sir, both my old master, and your mistress's
father. The old gentlemen ride hard this journey; they
say, it shall be the last time they will see the town; and
both of them are so pleased with this marriage, which
they have concluded for you, that I am afraid they will
live some years longer to trouble you, with the joy of it.

Palamede. But this is such an unreasonable thing, to
impose upon me to be married to-morrow; 'tis hurrying a
man to execution, without giving him time to say his
prayers.

Strato. Yet, if I might advise you, sir, you should not
delay it; for your younger brother comes up with them,
and is got already into their favours. He has gained much
upon my old master, by finding fault with innkeepers'
bills, and by starving us, and our horses, to show his
frugality; and he is very well with your mistress's father,
by giving him recipes for the spleen, gout and scurvy,
and other infirmities of old age.

Palamede. I'll rout him, and his country education: Pox
on him, I remember him before I travelled, he had nothing in him but mere jockey; used to talk loud, and make
matches, and was all for the crack of the field: Sense and
wit were as much banished from his discourse, as they are
when the court goes out of town to a horse race. Go now
and provide your master's lodgings.

Strato. I go, sir.   [*Exit.*

Palamede. It vexes me to the heart, to leave all my
designs with Doralice unfinished; to have flown her so
often to a mark, and still to be bobbed at retrieve: If I

had once enjoyed her, though I could not have satisfied my stomach with the feast, at least I should have relished my mouth a little; but now——

Enter PHILOTIS.

Philotis. Oh, sir, you are happily met; I was coming to find you.

Palamede. From your lady, I hope.

Philotis. Partly from her; but more especially from myself: She has just now received a letter from her father, with an absolute command to dispose herself to marry you to-morrow.

Palamede. And she takes it to the death?

Philotis. Quite contrary: The letter could never have come in a more lucky minute; for it found her in an ill-humour with a rival of yours, that shall be nameless, about the pronunciation of a French word.

Palamede. Count Rhodophil? never disguise it, I know the amour: But I hope you took the occasion to strike in for me?

Philotis. It was my good fortune to do you some small service in it: for your sake I discommended him all over, —clothes, person, humour, behaviour, everything; and, to sum up all, told her, it was impossible to find a married man that was otherwise; for they were all so mortified at home with their wives' ill humours, that they could never recover themselves to be company abroad.

Palamede. Most divinely urged!

Philotis. Then I took occasion to commend your good qualities; as the sweetness of your humour, the comeliness of your person, your good mien, your valour; but, above all, your liberality.

Palamede. I vow to Gad I had like to have forgot that good quality in myself, if thou hadst not remembered me of it: Here are five pieces for thee.

Philotis. Lord, you have the softest hand, sir, it would do a woman good to touch it: Count Rhodophil's is not half so soft; for I remember I felt it once, when he gave me ten pieces for my new-year's-gift.

Palamede. O, I understand you, madam; you shall find my hand as soft again as Count Rhodophil's: There are twenty pieces for you. The former was but a retaining fee; now I hope you'll plead for me.

Philotis. Your own merits speak enough. Be sure only
to ply her with French words, and I'll warrant you'll do
your business. Here are a list of her phrases for this day:
Use them to her upon all occasions, and foil her at her
own weapon; for she's like one of the old Amazons, she'll
never marry, except it be the man who has first conquered
her.

Palamede. I'll be sure to follow your advice: But you'll
forget to further my design.

Philotis. What, do you think I'll be ungrateful?—But,
however, if you distrust my memory, put some token on
my finger to remember it by: That diamond there would
do admirably.

Palamede. There 'tis; and I ask your pardon heartily for
calling your memory into question: I assure you I'll trust
it another time, without putting you to the trouble of another token.

Enter PALMYRA *and* ARTEMIS.

Artemis. Madam, this way the prisoners are to pass;
Here you may see Leonidas.

Palmyra. Then here I'll stay, and follow him to death.

Enter MELANTHA, *hastily.*

Melantha. O, here's her highness! Now is my time to
introduce myself, and to make my court to her, in my
new French phrases. Stay, let me read my catalogue—
Suite, figure, chagrin, naïveté, and *let me die,* for the
parenthesis of all.

Palamede [*aside*]. Do, persecute her; and I'll persecute
thee as fast in thy own dialect.

Melantha. Madam, the princess! let me die, but this is a
most horrid spectacle, to see a person who makes so
grand a figure in the court, without the *suite* of a princess,
and entertaining your *chagrin* all alone:—*Naïveté* should
have been there, but the disobedient word would not come
in.   [*Aside.*

Palmyra. What is she, Artemis?

Artemis. An impertinent lady, madam; very ambitious
of being known to your highness.

Palamede [*to* MELANTHA]. Let me die, madam, if I have
not waited you here these two long hours, without so much

as the *suite* of a single servant to attend me: entertaining myself with my own *chagrin,* till I had the honour of seeing your ladyship, who are a person that makes so considerable a figure in the court.

Melantha. Truce with your *douceurs,* good servant; you see I am addressing to the princess; pray do not *embarrass* me—*Embarrass* me! what a delicious French word do you make me lose upon you too! [*To the* Princess.] Your highness, madam, will please to pardon the *bévue* which I made, in not sooner finding you out to be a princess: But let me die if this *éclaircissement,* which is made this day of your quality, does not ravish me; and give me leave to tell you——

Palamede. But first give me leave to tell you, madam, that I have so great a *tendre* for your person, and such a *penchant* to do you service, that——

Melantha. What, must I still be troubled with your *sottises?* (There's another word lost, that I meant for the princess, with a mischief to you!) But your highness, madam——

Palamede. But your ladyship, madam——

Enter LEONIDAS, *guarded, and led over the stage.*

Melantha. Out upon him, how he looks, madam! now he's found no prince, he is the strangest figure of a man; how could I make that *coup d'étourdi* to think him one?

Palmyra. Away, impertinent!—my dear Leonidas!

Leonidas. My dear Palmyra!

Palmyra. Death shall never part us; my destiny is yours.
                                    [*He is led off, she follows.*

Melantha. Impertinent! Oh I am the most unfortunate person this day breathing: That the princess should thus *rompre en visière,* without occasion. Let me die, but I'll follow her to death, till I make my peace.

Palamede [*holding her*]. And let me die, but I'll follow you to the infernals, till you pity me.

Melantha [*turning towards him angrily*]. Ay, 'tis long of you that this *malheur* is fallen upon me; your impertinence has put me out of the good graces of the princess, and all that, which has ruined me, and all that, and, therefore, let me die, but I'll be revenged, and all that.

Palamede. Façon, façon, you must and shall love me,

and all that; for my old man is coming up, and all that; and I am *désespéré au dernier*, and will not be disinherited, and all that.

Melantha. How durst you interrupt me so *mal à propos*, when you knew I was addressing to the princess?

Palamede. But why would you address yourself so much *à contretemps* then?

Melantha. Ah, *male peste!*

Palamede. Ah, *j'enrage!*

Philotis. Radoucissez vous, de grâce, madame; vous êtes bien en colère pour peu de chose. Vous n'entendez pas la raillerie galante.

Melantha. A d'autres, à d'autres: He mocks himself of me, he abuses me: Ah me unfortunate! [*Cries.*

Philotis. You mistake him, madam, he does but accommodate his phrase to your refined language. *Ah qu'il est un cavalier accompli!* Pursue your point, sir—— [*To him.*

Palamede. Ah qu'il fait beau dans ces bocages;[7]

[*Singing.*

Ah que le ciel donne un beau jour! There I was with you, with a *minuet.*

Melantha. Let me die now, but this singing is fine, and extremely French in him: [*Laughs.*] But then, that he should use my own words, as it were in contempt of me, I cannot bear it. [*Crying.*

Palamede. Ces beaux séjours, ces doux ramages——

[*Singing.*

Melantha. Ces beaux séjours, ces doux ramages. [*Singing after him.*] *Ces beaux séjours nous invitent à l'amour!* Let me die, but he sings *en cavalier,* and so humours the cadence! [*Laughing.*

Palamede. Vois, ma Climène, vois sous ce chêne. [*Singing again.*] *S' entrebaiser ces oiseaux amoureux!* Let me die now, but that was fine. Ah, now, for three or four brisk Frenchmen, to be put into masking habits, and to sing it on a theatre, how witty it would be! and then to dance helter-skelter to a *chanson à boire: Toute la terre, toute la terre est à moi!* What's matter though it were made and sung two or three years ago in *cabarets,* how it would attract the admiration, especially of every one that's an *éveillé!*

[7] This, as well as *Vois, ma Climène,* is from the *Bourgeois Gentilhomme.*

Melantha. Well; I begin to have a *tendre* for you; but yet, upon condition, that—when we are married, you——

[PALAMEDE *sings, while she speaks.*

Philotis. You must drown her voice: If she makes her French conditions, you are a slave for ever.

Melantha. First, you will engage—that——

Palamede. Fa, la, la, la, etc.   [*Louder.*

Melantha. Will you hear the conditions?

Palamede. No; I will hear no conditions! I am resolved to win you *en Français:* To be very airy, with abundance of noise, and no sense: Fa, la, la, la, etc.

Melantha. Hold, hold; I am vanquished with your *gaîté d'esprit.* I am yours, and will be yours, *sans nulle réserve, ni condition:* And let me die, if I do not think myself the happiest nymph in Sicily—My dear French dear, stay but a *minute,* till I *raccommode* myself with the princess; and then I am yours, *jusqu'à la mort. Allons donc*——

[*Exeunt* MELANTHA *and* PHILOTIS.

Palamede [*solus, fanning himself with his hat*]. I never thought before that wooing was so laborious an exercise! If she were worth a million, I have deserved her; and now, methinks too, with taking all this pains for her, I begin to like her. 'Tis so; I have known many, who never cared for hare nor partridge, but those they caught themselves would eat heartily: The pains, and the story a man tells of the taking them, makes the meat go down more pleasantly. Besides, last night I had a sweet dream of her, and, gad, she I have once dreamed of, I am stark mad till I enjoy her, let her be never so ugly.

Enter DORALICE.

Doralice. Who's that you are so mad to enjoy, Palamede?

Palamede. You may easily imagine that, sweet Doralice.

Doralice. More easily than you think I can: I met just now with a certain man, who came to you with letters from a certain old gentleman, y'cleped your father; whereby I am given to understand, that to-morrow you are to take an oath in the church to be grave henceforward, to go ill-dressed and slovenly, to get heirs for your estate, and to dandle them for your diversion; and, in short, that love and courtship are to be no more.

Palamede. Now have I so much shame to be thus apprehended in the manner, that I can neither speak nor look upon you; I have abundance of grace in me, that I find: But if you have any spark of true friendship in you, retire with me a little into the next room, that hath a couch or bed in it, and bestow your charity upon a dying man! A little comfort from a mistress, before a man is going to give himself in marriage, is as good as a lusty dose of strong-water to a dying malefactor: it takes away the sense of hell and hanging from him.

Doralice. No, good Palamede, I must not be so injurious to your bride: 'Tis ill drawing from the bank to-day, when all your ready money is payable to-morrow.

Palamede. A wife is only to have the ripe fruit, that falls of itself; but a wise man will always preserve a shaking for a mistress.

Doralice. But a wife for the first quarter is a mistress.

Palamede. But when the second comes——

Doralice. When it does come, you are so given to variety, that you would make a wife of me in another quarter.

Palamede. No, never, except I were married to you: married people can never oblige one another; for all they do is duty, and consequently there can be no thanks: But love is more frank and generous than he is honest; he's a liberal giver, but a cursed pay-master.

Doralice. I declare I will have no gallant; but, if I would, he should never be a married man; a married man is but a mistress's half-servant, as a clergyman is but the king's half-subject. For a man to come to me that smells of the wife! 'Slife, I would as soon wear her old gown after her, as her husband.

Palamede. Yet 'tis a kind of fashion to wear a princess's cast shoes; you see the country ladies buy them, to be fine in them.

Doralice. Yes, a princess's shoes may be worn after her, because they keep their fashion, by being so very little used. But generally a married man is the creature of the world the most out of fashion; his behaviour is dumpish; his discourse, his wife and family; his habit so much neglected, it looks as if that were married too; his hat is married, his peruke is married, his breeches are married, —and, if we could look within his breeches, we should find him married there too.

Palamede. Am I then to be discarded for ever? pray do but mark how that word sounds; for ever! it has a very damn'd sound, Doralice.

Doralice. Ay, for ever! it sounds as hellishly to me, as it can do to you, but there's no help for it.

Palamede. Yet, if we had but once enjoyed one another! —but then once only is worse than not at all: It leaves a man with such a lingering after it.

Doralice. For aught I know, 'tis better that we have not; we might upon trial have liked each other less, as many a man and woman, that have loved as desperately as we, and yet, when they came to possession, have sighed and cried to themselves, Is this all?

Palamede. That is only, if the servant were not found a man of this world; but if, upon trial, we had not liked each other, we had certainly left loving; and faith, that's the greater happiness of the two.

Doralice. 'Tis better as 'tis; we have drawn off already as much of our love as would run clear; after possessing, the rest is but jealousies, and disquiets, and quarreling, and piecing.

Palamede. Nay, after one great quarrel, there's never any sound piecing; the love is apt to break in the same place again.

Doralice. I declare I would never renew a love; that's like him, who trims an old coach for ten years together; he might buy a new one better cheap.

Palamede. Well, madam, I am convined, that 'tis best for us not to have enjoyed; but, gad, the strongest reason is, because I can't help it.

Doralice. The only way to keep us new to one another, is never to enjoy, as they keep grapes, by hanging them upon a line; they must touch nothing, if you would preserve them fresh.

Palamede. But then they whither, and grow dry in the very keeping. However, I shall have a warmth for you, and an eagerness, every time I see you; and, if I chance to outlive Melantha——

Doralice. And if I chance to outlive Rhodophil——

Palamede. Well, I'll cherish my body as much as I can, upon that hope. 'Tis true, I would not directly murder the wife of my bosom; but, to kill her civilly, by the way of kindness, I'll put as fair as another man: I'll begin to-morrow night, and be very wrathful with her; that's resolved on.

Doralice. Well, Palamede, here's my hand, I'll venture to be your second wife, for all your threatenings.

Palamede. In the meantime I'll watch you hourly, as I would the ripeness of a melon; and I hope you'll give me leave now and then to look on you, and to see if you are not ready to be cut yet.

Doralice. No, no, that must not be, Palamede, for fear the gardener should come and catch you taking up the glass.

Enter RHODOPHIL.

Rhodophil [*aside*]. Billing so sweetly! now I am confirmed in my suspicions; I must put an end to this ere it go further—[*To* DORALICE.] Cry you mercy, spouse, I fear I have interrupted your recreations.

Doralice. What recreations?

Rhodophil. Nay, no excuses, good spouse; I saw fair hand conveyed to lip, and prest, as though you had been squeezing soft wax together for an indenture. Palamede, you and I must clear this reckoning: why would you have seduced my wife?

Palamede. Why would you have debauched my mistress?

Rhodophil. What do you think of that civil couple, that played at a game, called Hide and Seek, last evening, in the grotto?

Palamede. What do you think of that innocent pair, who made it their pretence to seek for others, but came, indeed, to hide themselves there?

Rhodophil. All things considered, I begin vehemently to suspect, that the young gentleman I found in your company last night, was a certain youth of my acquaintance.

Palamede. And I have an odd imagination, that you could never have suspected my small gallant, if your little villainous Frenchman had not been a false brother.

Rhodophil. Further arguments are needless; draw off; I shall speak to you now by the way of *bilbo*.

[*Claps his hands to his sword.*

Palamede. And I shall answer you by the way of Dangerfield.   [*Claps his hands on his.*

Doralice. Hold, hold; are not you two a couple of mad

fighting fools, to cut one another's throats for nothing?

Palamede. How for nothing? He courts the woman I must marry.

Rhodophil. And he courts you, whom I have married.

Doralice. But you can neither of you be jealous of what you love not.

Rhodophil. Faith, I am jealous, and this makes me partly suspect that I love you better than I thought.

Doralice. Pish! a mere jealousy of honour.

Rhodophil. Gad, I am afraid there's something else in't; for Palamede has wit, and, if he loves you, there's something more in ye than I have found: Some rich mine, for aught I know, that I have not yet discovered.

Palamede. 'Slife, what's this? Here's an argument for me to love Melantha; for he has loved her, and he has wit too, and, for aught I know, there may be a mine; but if there be, I am resolved I'll dig for it.

Doralice [*to* RHODOPHIL]. Then I have found my account in raising your jealousy. O! 'tis the most delicate sharp sauce to a cloyed stomach; it will give you a new edge, Rhodophil.

Rhodophil. And a new point too, Doralice, if I could be sure thou art honest.

Doralice. If you are wise, believe me for your own sake: Love and religion have but one thing to trust to; that's a good sound faith. Consider, if I have played false, you can never find it out by any experiment you can make upon me.

Rhodophil. No? Why, suppose I had a delicate screwed [8] gun; if I left her clean, and found her foul, I should discover, to my cost, she had been shot in.

Doralice. But if you left her clean, and found her only rusty, you would discover, to your shame, she was only so for want of shooting.

Palamede. Rhodophil, you know me too well to imagine I speak for fear; and therefore, in consideration of our past friendship, I will tell you, and bind it by all things holy, that Doralice is innocent.

Rhodophil. Friend, I will believe you, and vow the same for your Melantha; but the devil on't is, how shall we keep them so?

Palamede. What dost think of a blessed community

8 Scoured?

betwixt us four, for the solace of the women, and relief of the men? Methinks it would be a pleasant kind of life: Wife and husband for the standing dish, and mistress and gallant for the dessert.

Rhodophil. But suppose the wife and mistress should both long for the standing dish, how should they be satisfied together?

Palamede. In such a case they must draw lots; and yet that would not do neither, for they would both be wishing for the longest cut.

Rhodophil. Then I think, Palamede, we had as good make a firm league, not to invade each other's propriety.[9]

Palamede. Content, say I. From henceforth let all acts of hostility cease betwixt us; and that, in the usual form of treaties, as well by sea as land, and in all fresh waters.

Doralice. I will add but one *proviso,* that whoever breaks the league, either by war abroad, or neglect at home, both the women shall revenge themselves by the help of the other party.

Rhodophil. That's but reasonable. Come away, Doralice: I have a great temptation to be sealing articles in private.

Palamede. Hast thou so?   [*Claps him on the shoulder.*
"Fall on, Macduff,
And cursed be he that first cries, Hold, enough."

Enter POLYDAMAS, PALMYRA, ARTEMIS, ARGALEON;
After them EUBULUS *and* HERMOGENES, *guarded.*

Palmyra. Sir, on my knees I beg you—
Polydamas. Away, I'll hear no more.
Palmyra. For my dead mother's sake; you say you loved her,
And tell me I resemble her. Thus she
Had begged.
Polydamas. And thus I had denied her.
Palmyra. You must be merciful.
Argaleon. You must be constant.
Polydamas. Go, bear them to the torture; you have boasted
You have a king to head you; I would know
To whom I must resign.
Eubulus. This is our recompence
For serving thy dead queen.

---

[9] As often = "property."

Hermogenes. And education
Of thy daughter.

Argaleon. You are too modest, in not naming all
His obligations to you: Why did you
Omit his son, the prince Leonidas?

Polydamas. That imposture
I had forgot; their tortures shall be doubled.

Hermogenes. You please me; I shall die the sooner.

Eubulus. No; could I live an age, and still be racked,
I still would keep the secret.   [*As they are going off.*

                Enter LEONIDAS, *guarded.*

Leonidas. O, whither do you hurry innocence!
If you have any justice, spare their lives;
Or, if I cannot make you just, at least
I'll teach you to more purpose to be cruel.

Palmyra. Alas, what does he seek!

Leonidas. Make me the object of your hate and venge-
        ance.
Are those decrepid bodies, worn to ruin,
Just ready of themselves to fall asunder,
And to let drop the soul,—
Are these fit subjects for a rack and tortures?
Where would you fasten any hold upon them?
Place pains on me,—united fix them here,—
I have both youth, and strength, and soul to bear them;
And, if they merit death, then I much more,
Since 'tis for me they suffer.

Hermogenes. Heaven forbid
We should redeem our pains, or worthless lives,
By our exposing yours.

Eubulus. Away with us. Farewell, sir:
I only suffer in my fears for you.

Argaleon. So much concerned for him! Then my
                                    [*Aside.*
Suspicion's true.   [*Whispers the* King.

Palmyra. Hear yet my last request for poor Leonidas,
Or take my life with his.

Argaleon. Rest satisfied, Leonidas is he.   [*To the* King.

Polydamas. I am amazed: What must be done?

Argaleon. Command his execution instantly:
Give him not leisure to discover it;
He may corrupt the soldiers.

Polydamas. Hence with that traitor, bear him to his
  death:
Haste there, and see my will performed.
  Leonidas. Nay, then, I'll die like him the gods have
  made me.
Hold, gentlemen, I am——[ARGALEON *stops his mouth.*
  Argaleon. Thou art a traitor; 'tis not fit to hear thee.
  Leonidas. I say, I am the——   [*Getting loose a little.*
  Argaleon. So; gag him, and lead him off.
                              [*Again stopping his mouth.*
              [LEONIDAS, HERMOGENES, EUBULUS, *led off;*
                  POLYDAMAS *and* ARGALEON *follow.*

Palmyra. Duty and love, by turns, possess my soul,
And struggle for a fatal victory.
I will discover he's the king:—Ah, no!
That will perhaps save him;
But then I'm guilty of a father's ruin.
What shall I do, or not do? Either way
I must destroy a parent, or a lover.
Break heart; for that's the least of ills to me,
And death the only cure.   [*Swoons.*
  Artemis. Help, help the princess.
  Rhodophil. Bear her gently hence, where she may
Have more succour.
                  [*She is borne off;* ARTEMIS *follows her.*
                  Shouts within, and clashing of swords.
  Palamede. What noise it that?

                 Enter AMALTHEA, *running.*

  Amalthea. Oh, gentlemen, if you have loyalty,
Or courage, show it now! Leonidas,
Broke on the sudden from his guards, and snatching
A sword from one, his back against the scaffold,
Bravely defends himself, and owns aloud
He is our long-lost king; found for this moment,
But, if your valour helps not, lost for ever.
Two of his guards, moved by the sense of virtue,
Are turned for him, and there they stand at bay.
Against an host of foes.
  Rhodophil. Madam, no more
We lose time; my command, or my example,
May move the soldiers to the better cause.
You'll second me?   [*To* PALAMEDE.

Palamede. Or die with you: No subject e'er can meet
A nobler fate, than at his sovereign's feet.   [*Exeunt.*
          [*Clashing of swords within, and shouts.*

Enter LEONIDAS, RHODOPHIL, PALAMEDE, EUBULUS, HER-
     MOGENES, *and their Party, victorious;* POLYDAMAS *and*
     ARGALEON, *disarmed.*

Leonidas. That I survive the dangers of the day,
Next to the gods, brave friends, be yours the honour;
And, let heaven witness for me, that my joy
Is not more great for this my right restored,
Than 'tis, that I have power to recompence
Your loyalty and valour. Let mean princes,
Of abject souls, fear to reward great actions;
I mean to show,
That whatsoe'er subjects, like you, dare merit,
A king like me, dares give.
     Rhodophil. You make us blush, we have deserved so
          little.
     Palamede. And yet instruct us how to merit more.
     Leonidas. And as I would be just in my rewards,
So should I in my punishments; these two,
This, the usurper of my crown, the other,
Of my Palmyra's love, deserve that death,
Which both designed for me.
     Polydamas. And we expect it.
     Argaleon. I have too long been happy, to live wretched.
     Polydamas. And I too long have governed, to desire
A life without an empire.
     Leonidas. You are Palmyra's father; and as such,
Though not a king, shall have obedience paid
From him who is one. Father, in that name
All injuries forgot, and duty owned.   [*Embraces him.*
     Polydamas. O, had I known you could have been this
          king,
Thus god-like, great and good, I should have wished
To have been dethroned before. 'Tis now I live,
And more than reign; now all my joys flow pure,
Unmixed with cares, and undisturbed by conscience.

Enter PALMYRA, AMALTHEA, ARTEMIS, DORALICE,
          and MELANTHA.

     Leonidas. See, my Palmyra comes! the frighted blood
Scarce yet recalled to her pale cheeks,

Like the first streaks of light broke loose from darkness,
And dawning into blushes.—Sir, you said [*To* POLYDAMAS.
Your joys were full; Oh, would you make mine so!
I am but half restored without this blessing.

   Polydamas. The gods, and my Palmyra, make you
      happy,
As you make me!   [*Gives her hand to* LEONIDAS.

   Palmyra. Now all my prayers are heard:
I may be dutiful, and yet may love.
Virtue and patience have at length unravelled
The knots, which fortune tied.

   Melantha. Let me die, but I'll congratulate his majesty:
How admirably well his royalty becomes him! Becomes!
that is *lui sed,* but our damned language expresses nothing.

   Palamede. How? Does it become him already? 'Twas
but just now you said, he was such a figure of a man.

   Melantha. True, my dear, when he was a private man he
was a figure; but since he is a king, methinks he has
assumed another figure: He looks so grand, and so august!

                    [*Going to the* King.

   Palamede. Stay, stay; I'll present you when it is more
convenient. I find I must get her a place at court; and
when she is once there, she can be no longer ridiculous; for
she is young enough, and pretty enough, and fool enough,
and French enough, to bring up a fashion there to be
affected.

   Leonidas [*to* RHODOPHIL]. Did she then lead you to
      this brave attempt?
[*To* AMALTHEA.] To you, fair Amalthea, what I am,
And what all these, from me, we jointly owe:
First, therefore, to your great desert we give
Your brother's life; but keep him under guard
Till our new power be settled. What more grace
He may receive, shall from his future carriage
Be given, as he deserves.

   Argaleon. I neither now desire, nor will deserve it;
My loss is such as cannot be repaired,
And, to the wretched, life can be no mercy.

   Leonidas. Then be a prisoner always: Thy ill fate
And pride will have it so; But since in this I cannot,
Instruct me, generous Amalthea, how
A king may serve you.

Amalthea. I have all I hope,
And all I now must wish; I see you happy.
Those hours I have to live, which heaven in pity
Will make but few, I vow to spend with vestals:
The greatest part in prayers for you; the rest
In mourning my unworthiness.
Press me not further to explain myself;
'Twill not become me, and may cause your trouble.
    Leonidas. Too well I understand her secret grief,
                                              [*Aside.*
But dare not seem to know it.—Come, my fairest;
                                              [*To* PALMYRA.
Beyond my crown I have one joy in store,
To give that crown to her whom I adore.   [*Exeunt.*

EPILOGUE [10]

THUS have my spouse and I informed the nation,
And led you all the way to reformation;
Not with dull morals, gravely writ, like those,
Which men of easy phlegm with care compose,—
Your poets, of stiff words and limber sense,
Born on the confines of indifference;
But by examples drawn, I dare to say,
From most of you who hear and see the play.
There are more Rhodophils in this theatre,
More Palamedes, and some few wives, I fear:
But yet too far our poet would not run;
Though 'twas well offered, there was nothing done.
He would not quite the women's frailty bare,
But stript them to the waist, and left them there:
And the men's faults are less severely shown,
For he considers that himself is one.—
Some stabbing wits, to bloody satire bent,
Would treat both sexes with less compliment;
Would lay the scene at home; of husbands tell,
For wenches taking up their wives i' the Mall;
And a brisk bout, which each of them did want,
Made by mistake of mistress and gallant.
Our modest author thought it was enough
To cut you off a sample of the stuff:
He spared my shame, which you, I'm sure, would not,
For you were all for driving on the plot:
You sighed when I came in to break the sport,
And set your teeth when each design fell short.
To wives and servants all good wishes lend,
But the poor cuckold seldom finds a friend.
Since, therefore, court and town will take no pity
I humbly cast myself upon the city.

[10] Spoken by Rhodophil.

AURENG-ZEBE

A Tragedy

—*Sed, cum fregit subsellia versu,*
Esurit, intactam Paridi nisi vendat Agaven.

JUV.

AURENG-ZEBE [1]

THE play which follows, in addition to the points of interest noticed in the General Introduction, has that of being the only one of Dryden's serious plays dealing with a contemporary subject. He must have relied chiefly on the account of Bernier (1670-1671), for that of Tavernier, generally quoted as his authority, had not, I think, yet been printed in 1675; but the merely historical part of the scenario is of no great importance. The play was exceedingly popular, as it deserved to be, both at its first appearance, and at intervals for many years afterwards. Mohun, Hart, Kynaston, and Mrs. Marshall created the parts of the Emperor, Aurengzebe, Morat, and Nourmahal; while long afterwards, in 1726, the greatest stars of that later day, Wilkes, Booth, and Mrs. Oldfield, took the three principal characters, and it became customary to debate whether Kynaston in his more "huffing" representation of Morat, or Booth in his tamer, had hit the white. Between the two dates (*Aureng-Zebe* was acted and printed in 1675), but nearer the later, the *Spectator's* diary-writing lady kept *Aureng-Zebe* beside her bed, and "Miss Kitty repeated the eight best lines in the play [the Life passage, iv. i. p. 320] without book." Nearly seventy years later Dr. Johnson echoed the approval of this great purple patch, which, to those who consider poetry "criticism of life," ought to be poetry in the very highest, and which certainly is *The Vanity of Human Wishes* in a nutshell. Nor will those who read the play complain that it stands alone.

[1] The folio gives an alternative title "or The Great Mogul," which is not in ed. 1.

JOHN, EARL OF MULGRAVE,

Gentlemen of His Majesty's Bedchamber, and Knight of the Most Noble Order of the Garter.

MY LORD,

IT IS a severe reflection which Montaigne has made on princes, that we ought not, in reason, to have any expectations of favour from them; and that it is kindness enough, if they leave us in possession of our own. The boldness of the censure shows the free spirit of the author: And the subjects of England may justly congratulate to themselves, that both the nature of our government, and the clemency of our king, secure us from any such complaint. I, in particular, who subsist wholly by his bounty, am obliged to give posterity a far other account of my royal master, than what Montaigne has left of his. Those accusations had been more reasonable, if they had been placed on inferior persons: For in all courts, there are too many, who make it their business to ruin wit; and Montaigne, in other places, tells us what effects he found of their good natures. He describes them such, whose ambition, lust, or private interest, seem to be the only end of their creation. If good accrue to any from them, it is only in order to their own designs: conferred most commonly on the base and infamous; and never given, but only happening sometimes on well-deservers. Dulness has brought them to what they are; and malice secures them in their fortunes. But somewhat of specious they must have, to recommend themselves to princes (for folly will not easily go down in its own natural form with discerning judges), and diligence in waiting is their gilding of the pill; for that looks like love, though it is only interest. It is that which gains them their advantage over witty men; whose love of liberty and ease makes them willing too often to discharge their burden of attendance on these officious gentlemen. It is true, that the nauseousness of such company is enough to disgust a reasonable man; when he sees, he can hardly approach greatness, but as a moated castle; he must first pass through the mud and filth with which it is encompassed. These are they, who, wanting wit, affect gravity, and go by the name of solid men; and a solid man is, in plain English, a solid, solemn fool. Another disguise they have (for fools as well as knaves, take other names, and pass by an *alias*), and that is, the title of honest fellows. But this honesty of theirs ought to have many grains for its allowance; for certainly they are no further honest, than they are silly: They are naturally mischievous to their power; and if they speak not maliciously, or sharply, of witty men, it is only because God has not bestowed on them the gift of utterance. They fawn and crouch to men of parts, whom they cannot ruin; quote their wit when they are present, and, when they are absent, steal their jests; but to those who are under them, and whom they can crush with ease, they show themselves in their natural antipathy; there they treat wit like the common enemy; and giving no more quarter, than a Dutchman would to an English vessel in the Indies, they strike sail where they know they shall be mastered and murder where they can with safety.

This, my lord, is the character of a courtier without wit; and therefore that which is a satire to other men, must be a panegyric to your lordship, who are a master of it. If the least of these reflections could have reached your person, no necessity of mine could have made me to have sought so earnestly, and so long, to have cultivated your kindness. As a poet, I cannot but have made some observations on mankind; the lowness of my fortune has not yet brought me to flatter vice; and it is my duty to give testimony to virtue. It is true, your lordship is not of that nature, which either seeks a commendation, or wants it. Your mind has always been above the wretched affectation of popularity. A popular man is, in truth, no better than a prostitute to common fame, and to the people. He lies down to every one he meets for the hire of praise; and his humility is only a disguised ambition. Even Cicero himself, whose eloquence deserved the admiration of mankind, yet, by his insatiable thirst of fame, he has lessened his character with succeeding ages; his action against Catiline may be said to have ruined the consul, when it saved the city; for it so swelled his soul, which was not truly great, that ever afterwards it was apt to be overset with vanity. And this made his virtue so suspected by his friends, that Brutus, whom of all men he adored, refused him a place in his conspiracy. A modern wit has made this observation on him: that, coveting to recommend himself to posterity, he begged it as an alms of all his friends, the historians, to remember his consulship. And observe, if you please, the oddness of the event; all their histories are lost, and the vanity of his request stands yet recorded in his own writings. How much more great and manly in your lordship, is your contempt of popular applause, and your retired virtue, which shines only to a few; with whom you live so easily and freely, that you make it evident, you have a soul which is capable of all the tenderness of friendship, and that you only retire yourself from those, who are not capable of returning it.

Your kindness, where you have once placed it, is inviolable;
and it is to that only I attribute my happiness in your love.
This makes me more easily forsake an argument, on which I
could otherwise delight to dwell; I mean your judgment in
your choice of friends; because I have the honour to be one.
After which I am sure you will more easily permit me to be
silent, in the care you have taken of my fortune; which you have
rescued, not only from the power of others, but from my worst
of enemies, my own modesty and laziness; which favour, had
it been employed on a more deserving subject, had been an
effect of justice in your nature; but, as placed on me, is only
charity. Yet, withal, it is conferred on such a man, as prefers
your kindness itself, before any of its consequences; and who
values, as the greatest of your favours, those of your love, and
of your conversation. From this constancy to your friends, I
might reasonably assume, that your resentments would be as
strong and lasting, if they were not restrained by a nobler
principle of good nature and generosity; for certainly, it is the
same composition of mind, the same resolution and courage,
which makes the greatest friendships, and the greatest enmities.
And he who is too lightly reconciled, after high provocations,
may recommend himself to the world for a Christian, but I
should hardly trust him for a friend. The Italians have a proverb to that purpose, "To forgive the first time, shows me a
good Catholic; the second time, a fool." To this firmness in all
your actions, though you are wanting in no other ornaments
of mind and body, yet to this I principally ascribe the interest
your merits have acquired you in the royal family. A prince,
who is constant to himself, and steady in all his undertakings;
one with whom that character of Horace will agree—

> *Si fractus illabatur orbis,*
> *Impavidum ferient ruinæ;—*

such an one cannot but place an esteem, and repose a confidence on him, whom no adversity, no change of courts, no
bribery of interests, or cabals of factions, or advantages of
fortune, can remove from the solid foundations of honour and
fidelity—

> *Ille meos, primus qui me sibi junxit, amores*
> *Abstulit; ille habeat secum, servetque sepulcro.*

How well your lordship will deserve that praise, I need no
inspiration to foretell. You have already left no room for
prophecy: Your early undertakings have been such, in the
service of your king and country, when you offered yourself

to the most dangerous employment, that of the sea; when you chose to abandon those delights, to which your youth and fortune did invite you, to undergo the hazards, and, which was worse, the company of common seamen, that you have made it evident, you will refuse no opportunity of rendering yourself useful to the nation, when either your courage or conduct shall be required. The same zeal and faithfulness continue in your blood, which animated one of your noble ancestors to sacrifice his life in the quarrels of his sovereign; though I hope, both for your sake and the public tranquillity, the same occasion will never be offered to your lordship, and that a better destiny will attend you. But I make haste to consider you as abstracted from a court, which (if you will give me leave to use a term of logic) is only an adjunct, not a propriety of happiness. The Academics, I confess, were willing to admit the goods of fortune into their notion of felicity; but I do not remember, that any of the sects of old philosophers did ever leave a room for greatness. Neither am I formed to praise a court, who admire and covet nothing, but the easiness and quiet of retirement. I naturally withdraw my sight from a precipice; and, admit the prospect be never so large and goodly, can take no pleasure even in looking on the downfall, though I am secure from the danger. Methinks, there is something of a malignant joy in that excellent description of Lucretius—

> Suave, mari magno turbantibus æquora ventis,
> E terrâ magnum alterius spectare laborem;
> Non quia vexari quenquam est jucunda voluptas,
> Sed, quibus ipse malis careas, quia cernere suave est.

I am sure his master Epicurus, and my better master Cowley, preferred the solitude of a graden, and the conversation of a friend, to any consideration, so much as a regard, of those unhappy people, whom, in our own wrong, we call the great. True greatness, if it be anywhere on earth, is in a private virtue; removed from the notion of pomp and vanity, confined to a contemplation of itself, and centring on itself—

> Omnis enim per se Divûm natura necesse est
> Immortali ævo summâ cum pace fruatur;
> ———curâ semota, metuque,
> Ipsa suis pollens opibus.

If this be not the life of a deity, because it cannot consist with Providence, it is, at least, a god-like life. I can be contented (and I am sure I have your lordship of my opinion) with an humbler station in the temple of virtue, than to be set on the pinnacle of it—

Despicere unde queas alios, passimque videre
Errare, atque viam palantes quærere vitæ.

The truth is, the consideration of so vain a creature as man,
is not worth our pains. I have fool enough at home, without
looking for it abroad; and am a sufficient theatre to myself of
ridiculous actions, without expecting company, either in a court,
a town, or a playhouse. It is on this account that I am weary
with drawing the deformities of life, and lazars of the people,
where every figure of imperfection more resembles me than it
can do others. If I must be condemned to rhyme, I should
find some ease in my change of punishment. I desire to be no
longer the Sisyphus of the stage; to roll up a stone with endless
labour (which, to follow the proverb, gathers no moss), and
which is perpetually falling down again. I never thought myself
very fit for an employment, where many of my predecessors
have excelled me in all kinds; and some of my contemporaries,
even in my own partial judgment, have outdone me in Comedy.
Some little hopes I have yet remaining, and those too, considering my abilities, may be vain, that I may make the world
some part of amends, for many ill plays, by an heroic poem.
Your lordship has been long acquainted with my design; the
subject of which you know is great, the story English, and
neither too far distant from the present age, nor too near approaching it. Such it is in my opinion, that I could not have
wished a nobler occasion to do honour by it to my king, my
country, and my friends; most of our ancient nobility being
concerned in the action. And your lordship has one particular
reason to promote this undertaking, because you were the first
who gave me the opportunity of discoursing it to his Majesty,
and his Royal Highness: They were then pleased, both to
commend the design, and to encourage it by their commands.
But the unsettledness of my condition has hitherto put a stop
to my thoughts concerning it. As I am no successor to Homer
in his wit, so neither do I desire to be in his poverty. I can
make no rhapsodies, nor go a-begging at the Grecian doors,
while I sing the praises of their ancestors. The times of Virgil
please me better, because he had an Augustus for his patron;
and, to draw the allegory nearer you, I am sure I shall not
want a Mæcenas with him. It is for your lordship to stir up that
remembrance in his Majesty, which his many avocations of
business have caused him, I fear, to lay aside; and, as himself
and his royal brother are the heroes of the poem, to represent
to them the images of their warlike predecessors; as Achilles
is said to be roused to glory with the sight of the combat
before the ships. For my own part, I am satisfied to have offered
the design, and it may be to the advantage of my reputation
to have it refused me.

In the meantime, my lord, I take the confidence to present you with a tragedy, the characters of which are the nearest to those of an heroic poem. It was dedicated to you in my heart, before it was presented on the stage. Some things in it have passed your approbation, and many your amendment. You were likewise pleased to recommend it to the king's perusal, before the last hand was added to it, when I received the favour from him, to have the most considerable event of it modelled by his royal pleasure. It may be some vanity in me to add his testimony then, and which he graciously confirmed afterwards, that it was the best of all my tragedies; in which he has made authentic my private opinion of it; at least, he has given it a value by his commendation, which it had not by my writing.

That which was not pleasing to some of the fair ladies in the last act of it, as I dare not vindicate, so neither can I wholly condemn, till I find more reason for their censures. The procedure of Indamora and Melesinda seems yet, in my judgment, natural, and not unbecoming of their characters. If they, who arraign them fail not more, the world will never blame their conduct; and I shall be glad, for the honour of my country, to find better images of virtue drawn to the life in their behaviour, than any I could feign to adorn the theatre. I confess, I have only represented a practicable virtue mixed with the frailties and imperfections of human life. I have made my heroine fearful of death, which neither Cassandra nor Cleopatra would have been; and they themselves, I doubt it not, would have outdone romance in that particular. Yet their Mandana (and the Cyrus was written by a lady) was not altogether so hardhearted: For she sat down on the cold ground by the king of Assyria, and not only pitied him, who died in her defence, but allowed him some favours, such, perhaps, as they would think, should only be permitted to her Cyrus. I have made my Melesinda, in opposition to Nourmahal, a woman passionately loving of her husband, patient of injuries and contempt, and constant in her kindness, to the last; and in that, perhaps, I may have erred, because it is not a virtue much in use. Those Indian wives are loving fools and may do well to keep themselves in their own country, or, at least, to keep company with the Arrias and Portias of old Rome: Some of our ladies know better things. But it may be, I am partial to my own writings; yet I have laboured as much as any man, to divest myself of the self-opinion of an author; and am too well satisfied of my own weakness, to be pleased with anything I have written. But, on the other side, my reason tells me, that in probability, what I have seriously and long considered may be as likely to be just and natural, as what an ordinary judge (if there be any such among those ladies) will think fit, in a transient

presentation, to be placed in the room of that which they
condemn. The most judicious writer is sometimes mistaken,
after all his care; but the hasty critic, who judges on a view,
is full as liable to be deceived. Let him first consider all the
arguments, which the author had, to write this, or to design the
other, before he arraigns him of a fault; and then perhaps, on
second thoughts, he will find his reason oblige him to revoke
his censure. Yet, after all, I will not be too positive. *Homo
sum, humani à me nihil alienum puto.* As I am a man, I must
be changeable: and sometimes the gravest of us all are so,
even upon ridiculous accidents. Our minds are perpetually
wrought on by the temperament of our bodies; which makes
me suspect, they are nearer allied, than either our philosophers
or school-divines will allow them to be. I have observed, says
Montaigne, that when the body is out of order, its companion
is seldom at his ease. An ill dream, or a cloudy day, has power
to change this wretched creature, who is so proud of a reasonable soul, and make him think what he thought not yesterday. And Homer was of this opinion, as Cicero is pleased to
translate him for us—

> *Tales sunt hominum mentes, quali pater ipse*
> *Jupiter auctiferâ lustravit lampade terras.*

Or, as the same author, in his *Tusculan Questions*, speaks, with
more modesty than usual, of himself: *Nos in diem vivimus;
quodcunque animos nostros probabilitate percussit, id dicimus.*
It is not therefore impossible, but that I may alter the conclu-
sion of my play, to restore myself into the good graces of my
fair critics; and your lordship, who is so well with them, may
do me the office of a friend and patron, to intercede with them
on my promise of amendment. The impotent lover in Petronius,
though his was a very unpardonable crime, yet was received
to mercy on the terms I offer. *Summa excusationis meæ hæc
est: Placebo tibi, si culpam emendare permiseris.*

But I am conscious to myself of offering at a greater boldness, in presenting to your view what my meanness can produce,
than in any other error of my play; and therefore make haste
to break off this tedious address, which has, I know not how,
already run itself into so much of pedantry, with an excuse of
Tully's, which he sent with his books *De Finibus* to his friend
Brutus: *De ipsis rebus autem, sæpenumerò, Brute, vereor ne rep-
rehendar, cum hæc ad te scribam, qui tum in poesi* (I change it
from *philosophiâ*), *tum in optimo genere poeseos tantum pro-
cesseris. Quod si facerem quasi te erudiens, jure reprehen-
derer. Sed ab eo plurimùm absum: Nec, ut ea cognoscas quæ
tibi notissima sunt, ad te mitto; sed quià facillimè in nomine*

*tuo acquiesco, et quia te habeo æquissimum eorum studiorum,
quæ mihi communia tecum sunt, æstimatorem et judicem.*
Which you may please, my lord, to apply to yourself, from him,
who is,

> Your Lordship's
>> Most obedient,
>>> Humble servant,
>>>> DRYDEN

PROLOGUE

Our author, by experience, finds it true,
'Tis much more hard to please himself than you;
And out of no feigned modesty, this day
Damns his laborious trifle of a play:
Not that it's worse than what before he writ,
But he has now another taste of wit;
And, to confess a truth, though out of time,
Grows weary of his long-loved mistress, Rhyme.
Passion's too fierce to be in fetters bound,
And nature flies him like enchanted ground:
What verse can do, he has performed in this,
Which he presumes the most correct of his;
But spite of all his pride, a secret shame
Invades his breast at Shakespeare's sacred name:
Awed when he hears his god-like Romans rage,
He, in a just despair, would quit the stage;
And to an age less polished, more unskilled,
Does, with disdain, the foremost honours yield.
As with the greater dead he dares not strive,
He would not match his verse with those who live:
Let him retire, betwixt two ages cast,
The first of this, and hindmost of the last.
A losing gamester, let him sneak away;
He bears no ready money from the play.
The fate, which governs poets, thought it fit
He should not raise his fortunes by his wit.
The clergy thrive, and the litigious bar;
Dull heroes fatten with the spoils of war:
All southern vices, Heaven be praised, are here:
But wit's a luxury you think too dear.
When you to cultivate the plant are loth,
'Tis a shrewd sign 'twas never of your growth;
And wit in northern climates will not blow,
Except, like orange-trees, 'tis housed from snow.
There needs no care to put a playhouse down,
'Tis the most desert place of all the town:
We and our neighbours, to speak proudly, are,
Like monarchs, ruined with expensive war;
While, like wise English, unconcerned you sit,
And see us play the tragedy of wit.

DRAMATIS PERSONÆ

The old Emperor.
AURENG-ZEBE, his Son.
MORAT, his younger Son.
ARIMANT, Governor of Agra.
DIANET,
SOLYMAN,
MIR BABA,⎫ Indian Lords, or Omrahs, of
ABBAS, ⎰ several Factions.
ASAPH KHAN,
FAZEL KHAN,

NOURMAHAL, the Empress.
INDAMORA, a Captive Queen.
MELESINDA, Wife to MORAT.
ZAYDA, favourite Slave to the Empress.
Ambassador, Attendants, Guards, and Soldiers.

SCENE—AGRA, in the year 1660

ACT I

SCENE I

Enter ARIMANT, ASAPH KHAN, *and* FAZEL KHAN.

ARIMANT. Heaven seems the empire of the east to lay
On the success of this important day:
Their arms are to the last decision bent,
And Fortune labours with the vast event:
She now has in her hand the greatest stake,
Which for contending monarchs she can make.
Whate'er can urge ambitious youth to fight,
She pompously displays before their sight;
Laws, empire, all permitted to the sword,
And fate could ne'er an ampler scene afford.

    Asaph Khan. Four several armies to the field are led,
Which, high in equal hopes, four princes head:
Indus and Ganges, our wide empire's bounds,
Swell their dyed currents with their natives' wounds:
Each purple river winding, as he runs,
His bloody arms about his slaughtered sons.

    Fazel Khan. I well remember you foretold the storm,
When first the brothers did their factions form:
When each, by cursed cabals of women, strove
To draw the indulgent king to partial love.

    Arimant. What Heaven decrees, no prudence can prevent.
To cure their mad ambition, they were sent
To rule a distant province each alone:
What could a careful father more have done?
He made provision against all, but fate,
While, by his health, we held our peace of state.
The weight of seventy winters press'd him down,
He bent beneath the burden of a crown:
Sickness, at last, did his spent body seize,
And life almost sunk under the disease:
Mortal 'twas thought, at least by them desired,
Who, impiously, into his years inquired:

As at a signal, straight the sons prepare
For open force, and rush to sudden war:
Meeting, like winds broke loose upon the main,
To prove, by arms, whose fate it was to reign.

Asaph Khan. Rebels and parricides!

Arimant. Brand not their actions with so foul a name:
Pity at least what we are forced to blame.
When death's cold hand has closed the father's eye,
You know the younger sons are doomed to die.
Less ills are chosen greater to avoid,
And nature's laws are by the state's destroyed.
What courage tamely could to death consent,
And not, by striking first, the blow prevent?
Who falls in fight, cannot himself accuse,
And he dies greatly, who a crown pursues.

To them SOLYMAN AGA.

Solyman. A new express all Agra does affright:
Darah and Aureng-Zebe are joined in fight;
The press of people thickens to the court,
The impatient crowd devouring the report.

Arimant. T' each changing news the changed affections
          bring,
And servilely from fate expect a king.

Solyman. The ministers of state, who gave us law,
In corners, with selected friends, withdraw:
There, in deaf murmurs, solemnly are wise;
Whispering, like winds, ere hurricanes arise.
The most corrupt are most obsequious grown,
And those they scorned, officiously they own.

Asaph Khan. In change of government,
The rabble rule their great oppressors' fate;
Do sovereign justice, and revenge the state.

Solyman. The little courtiers, who ne'er come to know
The depth of factions, as in mazes go,
Where interests meet and cross so oft, that they,
With too much care, are wildered in their way.

Arimant. What of the emperor?

Solyman. Unmoved, and brave, he like himself appears,
And, meriting no ill, no danger fears:
Yet mourns his former vigour lost so far,
To make him now spectator of a war:

Repining that he must preserve his crown
By any help or courage but his own:
Wishes, each minute, he could unbeget
Those rebel sons, who dare t' usurp his seat;
To sway his empire with unequal skill,
And mount a throne, which none but he can fill.

   Arimant. Oh, had he still that character maintained,
Of valour, which, in blooming youth, he gained!
He promised in his east a glorious race;
Now, sunk from his meridian, sets apace.
But as the sun, when he from noon declines,
And, with abated heat, less fiercely shines,
Seems to grow milder as he goes away,
Pleasing himself with the remains of day;
So he, who, in his youth, for glory strove,
Would recompence his age with ease and love.

   Asaph Khan. The name of father hateful to him grows,
Which, for one son, produces him three foes.

   Fazel Khan. Darah, the eldest, bears a generous mind,
But to implacable revenge inclined:
Too openly does love and hatred show;
A bounteous master, but a deadly foe.

   Solyman. From Sujah's valour I should much expect,
But he's a bigot of the Persian sect;
And by a foreign interest seeks to reign,
Hopeless by love the sceptre to obtain.

   Asaph Khan. Morat's too insolent, too much a brave;
His courage to his envy is a slave.
What he attempts, if his endeavours fail
To effect, he is resolved no other shall.

   Arimant. But Aureng-Zebe, by no strong passion swayed,
Except his love, more temperate is, and weighed:
This Atlas must our sinking state uphold;
In council cool, but in performance bold:
He sums their virtues in himself alone,
And adds the greatest, of a loyal son:
His father's cause upon his sword he wears,
And with his arms, we hope, his fortune bears.

   Solyman. To vast rewards may well his courage move,
A parent's blessing, and a mistress' love.
If he succeed, his recompence, we hear,
Must be the captive queen of Cassimere.

To them ABBAS.

Abbas. Mischiefs on mischiefs, greater still, and more!
The neighbouring plain with arms is covered o'er:
The vale an iron harvest seems to yield,
Of thick-sprung lances in a waving field.
The polished steel gleams terribly from far,
And every moment nearer shows the war.
The horses' neighing by the wind is blown,
And castled elephants o'erlook the town.

Arimant. If, as I fear, Morat these powers commands,
Our empire on the brink of ruin stands:
The ambitious empress with her son is joined,
And, in his brother's absence, has designed
The unprovided town to take with ease,
And then the person of the king to seize.

Solyman. To all his former issue she has shown
Long hate, and laboured to advance her own.

Abbas. These troops are his.
Surat he took; and thence, preventing fame,
By quick and painful marches hither came.
Since his approach, he to his mother sent,
And two long hours in close debate were spent.

Arimant. I'll to my charge, the citadel, repair,
And show my duty by my timely care.

To them the Emperor, *with a letter in his hand:*
After him an Ambassador, *with a train following.*

Asaph Khan. But see, the emperor! a fiery red
His brows and glowing temples does o'erspread;
Morat has some displeasing message sent.

Ambassador. Do not, great sir, misconstrue his intent,
Nor call rebellion what was prudent care,
To guard himself by necessary war.
While he believed you living, he obeyed;
His governments but as your viceroy swayed:
But, when he thought you gone
To augment the number of the bless'd above,
He deemed them legacies of royal love:
Nor armed his brothers' portions to invade,
But to defend the present you had made.

Emperor. By frequent messages, and strict commands,
He knew my pleasure to discharge his bands:

Proof of my life my royal signet made;
Yet still he armed, came on, and disobeyed.

    Ambassador. He thought the mandate forged, your
       death concealed;
And but delayed, till truth should be revealed.

    Emperor. News of my death from rumour he received;
And what he wished he easily believed:
But long demurred, though from my hand he knew
I lived, so loth he was to think it true
Since he pleads ignorance to that command,
Now let him show his duty, and disband.

    Ambassador. His honour, sir, will suffer in the cause;
He yields his arms unjust, if he withdraws:
And begs his loyalty may be declared,
By owning those he leads to be your guard.

    Emperor. I, in myself, have all the guard I need!
Bid the presumptuous boy draw off with speed:
If his audacious troops one hour remain,
My cannon from the fort shall scour the plain.

    Ambassador. Since you deny him entrance, he demands
His wife, whom cruelly you hold in bands:
Her, if unjustly you from him detain,
He justly will, by force of arms, regain.

    Emperor. O'er him and his a right from Heaven I have;
Subject and son, he's doubly born my slave.
But whatsoe'er his own demerits are,
Tell him, I shall not make on women war.
And yet I'll do her innocence the grace,
To keep her here, as in the safer place.
But thou, who dar'st this bold defiance bring,
May'st feel the rage of an offended king.
Hence, from my sight, without the least reply!
One word, nay one look more, and thou shalt die.

                        [*Exit* Ambassador.

Re-enter ARIMANT.

    Arimant. May Heaven, great monarch, still augment
       your bliss
With length of days, and every day like this!
For, from the banks of Jumna news is brought,
Your army has a bloody battle fought:
Darah from loyal Aureng-Zebe is fled,
And forty thousand of his men lie dead.

To Sujah next your conquering army drew:
Him they surprised, and easily o'erthrew.
    Emperor. 'Tis well.
    Arimant. But well! what more could at your wish be
      done,
Than two such conquests gained by such a son?
Your pardon, mighty sir;
You seem not high enough your joys to rate;
You stand indebted a vast sum to fate,
And should large thanks for the great blessing pay.
    Emperor. My fortune owes me greater every day;
And should my joy more high for this appear,
It would have argued me, before, of fear.
How is Heaven kind, where I have nothing won,
And fortune only pays me with my own?
    Arimant. Great Aureng-Zebe did duteous care express,
And durst not push too far his good success;
But, lest Morat the city should attack,
Commanded his victorious army back;
Which left to march as swiftly as they may,
Himself comes first, and will be here this day,
Before a close-formed siege shut up his way.
    Emperor. Prevent his purpose! hence, with all thy
      speed!
Stop him; his entrance to the town forbid.
    Arimant. How, sir? your loyal, your victorious son?
    Emperor. Him would I, more than all the rebels, shun.
    Arimant. Whom with your power and fortune, sir, you
      trust,
Now to suspect is vain, as 'tis unjust.
He comes not with a train to move your fear,
But trusts himself to be a prisoner here.
You knew him brave, you know him faithful now:
He aims at fame, but fame from serving you.
'Tis said, ambition in his breast does rage:
Who would not be the hero of an age?
All grant him prudent: Prudence interest weighs,
And interest bids him seek your love and praise.
I know you grateful; when he marched from hence,
You bade him hope an ample recompence:
He conquered in that hope; and, from your hands,
His love, the precious pledge he left, demands.

Emperor. No more; you search too deep my wounded
mind,
And show me what I fear, and would not find.
My son has all the debts of duty paid:
Our prophet sends him to my present aid.
Such virtue to distrust were base and low:
I'm not ungrateful—or I was not so!
Inquire no further, stop his coming on:
I will not, cannot, dare not, see my son.
 Arimant. 'Tis now too late his entrance to prevent,
Nor must I to your ruin give consent;
At once your people's heart, and son's, you lose,
And give him all, when you just things refuse.
 Emperor. Thou lov'st me, sure; thy faith has oft been
tried,
In ten pitched fields not shrinking from my side,
Yet giv'st me no advice to bring me ease.
 Arimant. Can you be cured, and tell not your disease?
I asked you, sir.
 Emperor. Thou shouldst have asked again:
There hangs a secret shame on guilty men.
Thou shouldst have pulled the secret from my breast,
Torn out the bearded [1] steel, to give me rest;
At least, thou shouldst have guessed——
Yet thou art honest, thou couldst ne'er have guessed.
Hast thou been never base? did love ne'er bend
Thy frailer virtue, to betray thy friend?
Flatter me, make thy court, and say, It did;
Kings in a crowd would have their vices hid.
We would be kept in count'nance, saved from shame,
And owned by others who commit the same.
Nay, now I have confessed.
Thou seest me naked, and without disguise:
I look on Aureng-Zebe with rival's eyes.
He has abroad my enemies o'ercome,
And I have sought to ruin him at home.
 Arimant. This free confession shows you long did
strive;
And virtue, though oppress'd, is still alive.
But what success did your injustice find?
 Emperor. What it deserved, and not what I designed.
Unmoved she stood, and deaf to all my prayers,

---

[1] = "Barbed."

As seas and winds to sinking mariners.
But seas grow calm, and winds are reconciled:
Her tyrant beauty never grows more mild;
Prayers, promises, and threats, were all in vain.

Arimant. Then cure yourself, by generous disdain.

Emperor. Virtue, disdain, despair, I oft have tried,
And, foiled, have with new arms my foe defied.
This made me with so little joy to hear
The victory, when I the victor fear.

Arimant. Something you swiftly must resolve to do,
Lest Aureng-Zebe your secret love should know.
Morat without does for your ruin wait;
And would you lose the buckler of your state?
A jealous empress lies within your arms,
Too haughty to endure neglected charms.
Your son is duteous, but, as man, he's frail,
And just revenge o'er virtue may prevail.

Emperor. Go then to Indamora; say, from me,
Two lives depend upon her secresy.
Bid her conceal my passion from my son.
Though Aureng-Zebe return a conqueror,
Both he and she are still within my power.
Say, I'm a father, but a lover too;
Much to my son, more to myself I owe.
When she receives him, to her words give law,
And even the kindness of her glances awe.
See, he appears!
            [*After a short whisper* ARIMANT *departs.*

Enter AURENG-ZEBE, DIANET, *and* Attendants.—AURENG-
    ZEBE *kneels to his* Father, *and kisses his hand.*

Aureng-Zebe. My vows have been successful as my
            sword;
My prayers are heard, you have your health restored.
Once more 'tis given me to behold your face;
The best of kings and fathers to embrace.
Pardon my tears; 'tis joy which bids them flow,
A joy which never was sincere[2] till now.
That, which my conquest gave, I could not prize;
Or 'twas imperfect till I saw your eyes.

Emperor. Turn the discourse: I have a reason why
I would not have you speak so tenderly.

[2] In the Latin sense, "unmixed."

Knew you what shame your kind expressions bring,
You would, in pity, spare a wretched king.

Aureng-Zebe. A king! you rob me, sir, of half my due;
You have a dearer name,—a father too.

Emperor. I had that name.

Aureng-Zebe. What have I said or done,
That I no longer must be called your son?
'Tis in that name, Heaven knows, I glory more,
Than that of prince, or that of conqueror.

Emperor. Then you upbraid me; I am pleased to see
You're not so perfect, but can fail, like me.
I have no God to deal with.

Aureng-Zebe. Now I find,
Some sly court-devil has seduced your mind;
Filled it with black suspicions not your own,
And all my actions through false optics shown.
I ne'er did crowns ambitiously regard;
Honour I sought, the generous mind's reward.
Long may you live! while you the sceptre sway,
I shall be still most happy to obey.

Emperor. O Aureng-Zebe! thy virtues shine too bright.
They flash too fierce: I, like a bird of night,
Shut my dull eyes, and sicken at the sight.
Thou hast deserved more love than I can show;
But 'tis thy fate to give, and mine to owe.
Thou seest me much distempered in my mind;
Pulled back, and then pushed forward to be kind.
Virtue, and——fain I would my silence break,
But have not yet the confidence to speak.
Leave me, and to thy needful rest repair.

Aureng-Zebe. Rest is not suiting with a lover's care.
I have not yet my Indamora seen.   [*Is going.*

Emperor. Somewhat I had forgot; come back again:
So weary of a father's company?

Aureng-Zebe. Sir, you were pleased yourself to licence[3]
me.

Emperor. You made me no relation of the fight;
Besides, a rebel's army is in sight.
Advise me first: Yet go——
He goes to Indamora; I should take   [*Aside.*
A kind of envious joy to keep him back.
Yet to detain him makes my love appear;—

[3] Dismiss.

I hate his presence and his absence fear.　　　　　[*Exit.*

　　Aureng-Zebe. To some new clime, or to thy native sky,
O friendless and forsaken Virtue, fly!
Thy Indian air is deadly to thee grown:
Deceit and cankered malice rule thy throne.
Why did my arms in battle prosperous prove,
To gain the barren praise of filial love?
The best of kings by women is misled,
Charmed by the witchcraft of a second bed.
Against myself I victories have won,
And by my fatal absence am undone.

To him INDAMORA, *with* ARIMANT.

But here she comes!
In the calm harbour of whose gentle breast,
My tempest-beaten soul may safely rest.
O my heart's joy! whate'er my sorrows be,
They cease and vanish in beholding thee!
Care shuns thy walks; as at the cheerful light,
The groaning ghosts and birds obscene take flight.
By this one view, all my past pains are paid;
And all I have to come more easily made.

　　Indamora. Such sullen planets at my birth did shine,
They threaten every fortune mixed with mine.
Fly the pursuit of my disastrous love,
And from unhappy neighbourhood remove.

　　Aureng-Zebe. Bid the laborious hind,
Whose hardened hands did long in tillage toil,
Neglect the promised harvest of the soil.
Should I, who cultivated love with blood,
Refuse possession of approaching good?

　　Indamora. Love is an airy good, opinion makes;
Which he, who only thinks he has, partakes:
Seen by a strong imagination's beam,
That tricks and dresses up the gaudy dream:
Presented so, with rapture 'tis enjoyed;
Raised by high fancy, and by low destroyed.

　　Aureng-Zebe. If love be vision, mine has all the fire,
Which, in first dreams, young prophets does inspire.
I dream, in you, our promised paradise:
An age's tumult of continued bliss.
But you have still your happiness in doubt;
Or else 'tis past, and you have dreamt it out.

Indamora. Perhaps not so.

Aureng-Zebe. Can Indamora prove
So altered? Is it but *perhaps,* you love?
Then farewell all! I thought in you to find
A balm, to cure my much distempered mind.
I came to grieve a father's heart estranged;
But little thought to find a mistress changed.
Nature herself is changed to punish me;
Virtue turned vice, and faith inconstancy.

Indamora. You heard me not inconstancy confess:
'Twas but a friend's advice to love me less.
Who knows what adverse fortune may befall?
Arm well your mind: hope little, and fear all.
Hope, with a goodly prospect, feeds your eye;
Shows, from a rising ground, possession nigh;
Shortens the distance, or o'erlooks it quite;
So easy 'tis to travel with the sight.

Aureng-Zebe. Then to despair you would my love
        betray,
By taking hope, its last kind friend, away.
You hold the glass, but turn the perspective,
And farther off the lessened object drive.
You bid me fear: In that your change I know;
You would prepare me for the coming blow.
But, to prevent you, take my last adieu;
I'll sadly tell myself you are untrue,
Rather than stay to hear it told by you.   [*Going.*

Indamora. Stay, Aureng-Zebe, I must not let you go,—
And yet believe yourself your own worst foe;
Think I am true, and seek no more to know.
Let in my breast the fatal secret lie;
'Tis a sad riddle, which, if known, we die.

                                 [*Seeming to pause.*

Aureng-Zebe. Fair hypocrite, you seek to cheat in vain;
Your silence argues you ask time to feign.
Once more, farewell! The snare in sight is laid,
'Tis my own fault if I am now betrayed.   [*Going again.*

Indamora. Yet once more stay; you shall believe me
        true,
Though in one fate I wrap myself and you.
Your absence—

Arimant. Hold! you know the hard command,
I must obey: You only can withstand

Your own mishap. I beg you, on my knee,
Be not unhappy by your own decree.
   Aureng-Zebe. Speak, madam; by (if that be yet an
     oath)
Your love, I'm pleased we should be ruined both.
Both is a sound of joy.
In death's dark bowers our bridals we will keep;
And his cold hand
Shall draw the curtain, when we go to sleep.
   Indamora. Know then, that man, whom both of us did
     trust,
Has been to you unkind, to me unjust.
The guardian of my faith so false did prove,
As to solicit me with lawless love:
Prayed, promised, threatened, all that man could do;
Base as he's great; and need I tell you who?
   Aureng-Zebe. Yes; for I'll not believe my father meant:
Speak quickly, and my impious thoughts prevent.
   Indamora. You've said; I wish I could some other name!
   Arimant. My duty must excuse me, sir, from blame.
A guard there!

Enter Guards.

   Aureng-Zebe. Slave, for me?
   Arimant. My orders are
To seize this princess, whom the laws of war
Long since made prisoner.
   Aureng-Zebe. Villain!
   Arimant. Sir, I know
Your birth, nor durst another call me so.
   Aureng-Zebe. I have redeemed her; and, as mine, she's
     free.
   Arimant. You may have right to give her liberty;
But with your father, sir, that right dispute;
For his commands to me were absolute;
If she disclosed his love, to use the right
Of war, and to secure her from your sight.
   Aureng-Zebe. I'll rescue her, or die.   [*Draws.*
And you, my friends, though few, are yet too brave,
To see your general's mistress made a slave.   [*All draw.*
   Indamora. Hold, my dear love! if so much power there
     lies,
As once you owned, in Indamora's eyes,

Lose not the honour you have early won,
But stand the blameless pattern of a son.
My love your claim inviolate secures;
'Tis writ in fate, I can be only yours.
My sufferings for you make your heart my due;
Be worthy me, as I am worthy you.

    Aureng-Zebe. I've thought, and blessed be you who gave
      me time;   *[Putting up his sword.*
My virtue was surprised into a crime.
Strong virtue, like strong nature, struggles still;
Exerts itself, and then throws off the ill.
I to a son's and lover's praise aspire,
And must fulfill the parts which both require.
How dear the cure of jealousy has cost!
With too much care and tenderness y' are lost.
So the fond youth from hell redeemed his prize,
Till looking back, she vanished from his eyes!
                            [Exeunt severally.

ACT II

SCENE I

*Betwixt the Acts a warlike Tune is played, shooting of
Guns and shouts of Soldiers are heard, as in an Assault.*

AURENG-ZEBE, ARIMANT, ASAPH KHAN, FAZEL KHAN,
            and SOLYMAN.

AURENG-ZEBE. What man could do, was by Morat per-
    formed;
The fortress thrice himself in person stormed.
Your valour bravely did the assault sustain,
And filled the moats and ditches with the slain;
Till, mad with rage, into the breach he fired,
Slew friends and foes, and in the smoke retired.

    Arimant. To us you give what praises are not due;
Morat was thrice repulsed, but thrice by you.
High, over all, was your great conduct shown;
You sought our safety, but forgot your own.

    Asaph Khan. Their standard planted on the battlement.
Despair and death among the soldiers sent;

You the bold Omrah tumbled from the wall,
And shouts of victory pursued his fall.

    Fazel Khan. To you alone we owe this prosperous day;
Our wives and children rescued from the prey:
Know your own interest, sir; where'er you lead,
We jointly vow to own no other head.

    Solyman. Your wrongs are known. Impose but your
      commands,
This hour shall bring you twenty thousand hands.

    Aureng-Zebe. Let them, who truly would appear my
      friends,
Employ their swords, like mine, for noble ends.
No more: Remember you have bravely done;
Shall treason end what loyalty begun?
I own no wrongs; some grievance I confess;
But kings, like gods, at their own time redress.
Yet, some becoming boldness I may use;
I've well deserved, nor will he now refuse.   [*Aside.*
I'll strike my fortunes with him at a heat,
And give him not the leisure to forget.
            [*Exit, attended by the* Omrahs.

    Arimant. O Indamora, hide these fatal eyes!
Too deep they wound whom they too soon surprise;
My virtue, prudence, honour, interest, all
Before this universal monarch fall.
Beauty, like ice, our footing does betray;
Who can tread sure on the smooth slippery way?
Pleased with the passage, we slide swiftly on,
And see the dangers which we cannot shun.

To him INDAMORA.

    Indamora. I hope my liberty may reach thus far;
These terrace walks within my limits are.
I came to seek you, and to let you know,
How much I to your generous pity owe.
The king, when he designed you for my guard,
Resolved he would not make my bondage hard:
If otherwise, you have deceived his end;
And whom he meant a guardian, made a friend.

    Arimant. A guardian's title I must own with shame;
But should be prouder of another name.

    Indamora. And therefore 'twas I changed that name
      before;

I called you friend, and could you wish for more?

    Arimant. I dare not ask for what you would not grant
But wishes, madam, are extravagant;
They are not bounded with things possible:
I may wish more than I presume to tell.
Desire's the vast extent of human mind;
It mounts above, and leaves poor hope behind.
I could wish——

    Indamora. What?

    Arimant. Why did you speak? you've dashed my fancy quite,
Even in the approaching minute of delight.
I must take breath,
Ere I the rapture of my wish renew,
And tell you then,—it terminates in you.

    Indamora. Have you considered what the event would be?
Or know you, Arimant, yourself, or me?
Were I no queen, did you my beauty weigh,
My youth in bloom, your age in its decay?

    Arimant. I, my own judge, condemned myself before
For pity aggravate my crime no more!
So weak I am, I with a frown am slain;
You need have used but half so much disdain.

    Indamora. I am not cruel yet to that degree;
Have better thoughts both of yourself and me.
Beauty a monarch is,
Which kingly power magnificently proves,
By crowds of slaves, and peopled empire loves:
And such a slave as you what queen would lose?
Above the rest, I Arimant would choose,
For counsel, valour, truth, and kindness too;
All I could wish in man, I find in you.

    Arimant. What lover could to greater joy be raised?
I am, methinks, a god, by you thus praised.

    Indamora. To what may not desert like yours pretend?
You have all qualities, that fit a friend.

    Arimant. So mariners mistake the promised coast;
And, with full sails, on the blind rocks are lost.
Think you my aged veins so faintly beat,
They rise no higher than to friendship's heat?
So weak your charms, that, like a winter's night,
Twinkling with stars, they freeze me, while they light?

Indamora. Mistake me not, good Arimant; I know
My beauty's power, and what my charms can do.
You your own talent have not learned so well;
But practise one, where you can ne'er excel.
You can, at most,
To an indifferent lover's praise pretend;
But you would spoil an admirable friend.

Arimant. Never was amity so highly prized,
Nor ever any love so much despised.
Even to myself ridiculous I grow,
And would be angry, if I knew but how.

Indamora. Do not. Your anger, like your love, is vain;
Whene'er I please, you must be pleased again.
Knowing what power I have your will to bend,
I'll use it; for I need just such a friend.
You must perform, not what you think is fit;
But to whatever I propose submit.

Arimant. Madam, you have a strange ascendant gained;
You use me like a courser, spurred and reined:
If I fly out, my fierceness you command,
Then soothe, and gently stroke me with your hand.
Impose; but use your power of taxing well;
When subjects cannot pay, they soon rebel.

Enter the Emperor, *unseen by them.*

Indamora. My rebel's punishment would easy prove;
You know you're in my power, by making love.

Arimant. Would I, without dispute, your will obey,
And could you, in return, my life betray?

Emperor. What danger, Arimant, is this you fear?
Or what love-secret, which I must not hear?
These altered looks some inward motion show:
His cheeks are pale, and yours with blushes glow.
                                        [*To her.*

Indamora. 'Tis what, with justice, may my anger move;
He has been bold, and talked to me of love.

Arimant. I am betrayed, and shall be doomed to die.
                                        [*Aside.*

Emperor. Did he, my slave, presume to look so high?
That crawling insect, who from mud began,
Warmed by my beams, and kindled into man?
Durst he, who does but for my pleasure live,

Intrench on love, my great prerogative?
Print his base image on his sovereign's coin?
'Tis treason if he stamp his love with mine.

Arimant. 'Tis true, I have been bold, but if it be
A crime——

Indamora. He means, 'tis only so to me.
You, sir, should praise, what I must disapprove.
He insolently talked to me of love;
But, sir, 'twas yours, he made it in your name;
You, if you please, may all he said disclaim.

Emperor. I must disclaim whate'er he can express;
His grovelling sense will show my passion less:
But stay,—if what he said my message be,
What fear, what danger, could arrive from me?
He said, he feared you would his life betray.

Indamora. Should he presume again, perhaps I may.
Though in your hands he hazard not his life,
Remember, sir, your fury of a wife;
Who, not content to be revenged on you,
The agents of your passion will pursue.

Emperor. If I but hear her named, I'm sick that day;
The sound is mortal, and frights life away.—
Forgive me, Arimant, my jealous thought:
Distrust in lovers is the tenderest fault.
Leave me, and tell thyself, in my excuse,
Love, and a crown, no rivalship can bear;
And precious things are still possess'd with fear.

                    [*Exit* ARIMANT, *bowing.*
This, madam, my excuse to you may plead;
Love should forgive the faults, which love has made.

Indamora. From me, what pardon can you hope to have,
Robbed of my love, and treated as a slave?

Emperor. Force is the last relief which lovers find;
And 'tis the best excuse of womankind.

Indamora. Force never yet a generous heart did gain;
We yield on parley, but are stormed in vain.
Constraint in all things makes the pleasure less;
Sweet is the love which comes with willingness.

Emperor. No; 'tis resistance that inflames desire,
Sharpens the darts of love, and blows his fire.
Love is disarmed, that meets with too much ease;
He languishes, and does not care to please:

And therefore 'tis, your golden fruit you guard
With so much care,—to make possession hard.
    Indamora. Was't not enough, you took my crown away,
But cruelly you must my love betray?
I was well pleased to have transferred my right,
And better changed your claim of lawless might,
By taking him, whom you esteemed above
Your other sons, and taught me first to love.
    Emperor. My son by my command his course must
    steer:
I bade him love, I bid him now forbear.
If you have any kindness for him still,
Advise him not to shock a father's will.
    Indamora. Must I advise?
Then let me see him, and I'll try to obey.
    Emperor. I had forgot, and dare not trust your way.
But send him word,
He has not here an army to command:
Remember, he and you are in my hand.
    Indamora. Yes, in a father's hand, whom he has served,
And, with the hazard of his life, preserved.
But piety to you, unhappy prince,
Becomes a crime, and duty an offence:
Against yourself you with your foes combine,
And seem your own destruction to design.
    Emperor. You may be pleased your politics to spare;
I'm old enough, and can myself take care.
    Indamora. Advice from me was, I confess, too bold:
Y'are old enough; it may be, sir, too old.
    Emperor. You please yourself with your contempt of
    age;
But love, neglected, will convert to rage.
If on your head my fury does not turn,
Thank that fond dotage which so much you scorn;
But, in another's person, you may prove,
There's warmth for vengeance left, though not for love.

Re-enter ARIMANT.

    Arimant. The empress has the ante-chambers past,
And this way moves with a disordered haste:
Her brows the stormy marks of anger bear.
    Emperor. Madam, retire; she must not find you here.
                  [*Exit* INDAMORA *with* ARIMANT.

Enter NOURMAHAL, *hastily.*

Nourmahal. What have I done, that Nourmahal must prove
The scorn and triumph of a rival's love?
My eyes are still the same; each glance, each grace,
Keep their first lustre, and maintain their place;
Not second yet to any other face.

　　Emperor. What rage transports you? Are you well awake?
Such dreams distracted minds in fevers make.

　　Nourmahal. Those fevers you have given, those dreams have bred,
By broken faith, and an abandoned bed.
Such visions hourly pass before my sight,
Which from my eyes their balmy slumbers fright
In the severest silence of the night;
Visions, which in this citadel are seen,—
Bright glorious visions of a rival queen.

　　Emperor. Have patience,—my first flames can ne'er decay;
These are but dreams, and soon will pass away;
Thou know'st my heart, my empire, all is thine.
In thy own heaven of love serenely shine;
Fair as the face of nature did appear,
When flowers first peep'd, and trees did blossoms bear,
And winter had not yet deformed the inverted year;
Calm as the breath which fans our eastern groves,
And bright as when thy eyes first lighted up our loves
Let our eternal peace be sealed by this,
With the first ardour of a nuptial kiss. [*Offers to kiss her.*

　　Nourmahal. Me would you have—me your faint kisses prove,
The dregs and droppings of enervate love?
Must I your cold long-labouring age sustain,
And be to empty joys provoked in vain?
Receive you, sighing after other charms,
And take an absent husband in my arms?

　　Emperor. Even these reproaches I can bear from you;
You doubted of my love, believe it true:
Nothing but love this patience could produce,
And I allow your rage that kind excuse.

Nourmahal. Call it not patience; 'tis your guilt stands
    mute;
You have a cause too foul to bear dispute.
You wrong me first, and urge my rage to rise:
Then I must pass for mad; you meek and wise.
Good man! plead merit by your soft replies.
Vain privilege poor women have of tongue;
Men can stand silent, and resolve on wrong.

Emperor. What can I more? my friendship you refuse,
And even my mildness, as my crime, accuse.

Nourmahal. Your sullen silence cheats not me, false man;
I know you think the bloodiest things you can.
Could you accuse me, you would raise your voice,
Watch for my crimes, and in my guilt rejoice:
But my known virtue is from scandal free,
And leaves no shadow for your calumny.

Emperor. Such virtue is the plague of human life;
A virtuous woman, but a cursed wife.
In vain of pompous chastity y' are proud;
Virtue's adultery of the tongue, when loud.
I, with less pain, a prostitute could bear,
Than the shrill sound of—"*Virtue! virtue!*" hear.
In unchaste wives
There's yet a kind of recompensing ease;
Vice keeps them humble, gives them care to please
But against clamorous virtue, what defence?
It stops our mouths, and gives your noise pretence.

Nourmahal. Since virtue does your indignation raise,
'Tis pity but you had that wife you praise:
Your own wild appetites are prone to range,
And then you tax our humours with your change.

Emperor. What can be sweeter than our native home?
Thither for ease and soft repose we come:
Home is the sacred refuge of our life;
Secured from all approaches, but a wife.
If thence we fly, the cause admits no doubt;
None but an inmate foe could force us out;
Clamours our privacies uneasy make;
Birds leave their nest disturbed, and beasts their haunts
    forsake.

Nourmahal. Honour's my crime, that has your loathing
    bred;
You take no pleasure in a virtuous bed.

Emperor. What pleasure can there be in that estate,
Which your unquietness has made me hate?
I shrink far off,
Dissembling sleep, but wakeful with the fright;
The day takes off the pleasure of the night.

    Nourmahal. My thoughts no other joys but power
      pursue;
Or, if they did, they must be lost in you.
And yet the fault's not mine,
Though youth and beauty cannot warmth command!
The sun in vain shines on the barren sand.

    Emperor. 'Tis true, of marriage-bands I'm weary grown;
Love scorns all ties, but those that are his own.
Chains, that are dragged, must needs uneasy prove,
For there's a godlike liberty in love.

    Nourmahal. What's love to you?
The bloom of beauty other years demands,
Nor will be gathered by such withered hands:
You importune it with a false desire,
Which sparkles out, and makes no solid fire.
This impudence of age, whence can it spring?
All you expect, and yet you nothing bring:
Eager to ask, when you are past a grant;
Nice in providing what you cannot want.
Have conscience; give not her you love this pain;
Solicit not yourself and her in vain;
All other debts may compensation find;
But love is strict, and will be paid in kind.

    Emperor. Sure, of all ills, domestic are the worst;
When most secure of blessings, we are curst.
When we lay next us what we hold most dear,
Like Hercules, envenomed shirts we wear,
And cleaving mischiefs.

    Nourmahal. What you merit, have;
And share, at least, the miseries you gave.
Your days I will alarm, I'll haunt your nights,
And, worse than age, disable your delights.
May your sick fame still languish till it die,
All offices of power neglected lie,
And you grow cheap in every subject's eye!
Then, as the greatest curse that I can give,
Unpitied be deposed, and, after, live!   [*Going off.*

    Emperor. Stay, and now learn,

How criminal soe'er we husbands are,
'Tis not for wives to push our crimes too far.
Had you still mistress of your temper been,
I had been modest, and now owned my sin.
Your fury hardens me; and whate'er wrong
You suffer, you have cancelled by your tongue.
A guard there! Seize her; she shall know this hour,
What is a husband's and a monarch's power.

         [Guard *seizes her.*

Enter AURENG-ZEBE.

 Nourmahal. I see for whom your charter you maintain;
I must be fettered, and my son be slain,
That Zelyma's ambitious race may reign.
Not so you promised, when my beauty drew
All Asia's vows; when, Persia left for you,
The realm of Candahar for dower I brought;
That long-contended prize for which you fought.

 Aureng-Zebe. The name of stepmother, your practised art,
By which you have estranged my father's heart,
All you have done against me, or design,
Shows your aversion, but begets not mine.
Long may my father India's empire guide,
And may no breach your nuptial vows divide!

 Emperor. Since loves obliges not, I from this hour
Assume the right of man's despotic power;
Man is by nature formed your sex's head,
And is himself the canon of his bed:
In bands of iron fettered you shall be,—
An easier yoke than what you put on me.

 Aureng-Zebe. Though much I fear my interest is not great,
Let me your royal clemency intreat.   [*Kneeling.*
Secrets of marriage still are sacred held;
Their sweet and bitter by the wise concealed.
Errors of wives reflect on husbands still,
And, when divulged, proclaim you've chosen ill,
And the mysterious power of bed and throne
Should always be maintained, but rarely shown.

 Emperor. To so perverse a sex all grace is vain;
It gives them courage to offend again:
For with feigned tears they penitence pretend,

Again are pardoned, and again offend;
Fathom our pity when they seem to grieve,
Only to try how far we can forgive;
Till, launching out into a sea of strife,
They scorn all pardon, and appear all wife.
But be it as you please! for your loved sake,
This last and fruitless trial I will make:
In all requests your right of merit use;
And know, there is but one I can refuse.

> [*He signs to the* Guards, *and they remove from
> the* Empress.

Nourmahal. You've done enough, for you designed my
  chains;
The grace is vanished, but the affront remains.
Nor is't a grace, or for his merit done;
You durst no farther, for you feared my son.
This you have gained by the rough course you prove:
I'm past repentance, and you past my love.   [*Exit.*

Emperor. A spirit so untamed the world ne'er bore.

Aureng-Zebe. And yet worse usage had incensed her
  more.
But since by no obligement she is tied,
You must betimes for your defence provide.
I cannot idle in your danger stand,
But beg once more I may your arms command:
Two battles your auspicious cause has won;
My sword can perfect what it has begun,
And from your walls dislodge that haughty son.

Emperor. My son, your valour has this day been such,
None can enough admire, or praise too much:
But now, with reason, your success I doubt;
Her faction's strong within, his arms without.

Aureng-Zebe. I left the city in a panic fright;
Lions they are in council, lambs in fight.
But my own troops, by Mirza led, are near;
I, by to-morrow's dawn, expect them here:
To favour them, I'll sally out ere day,
And through our slaughtered foes enlarge their way.

Emperor. Age has not yet
So shrunk my sinews, or so chilled my veins,
But conscious virtue in my breast remains:
But had I now
That strength, with which my boiling youth was fraught,

When in the vale of Balasor I fought,
And from Bengal their captive monarch brought;
When elephant 'gainst elephant did rear
His trunk, and castles jostled in the air;
My sword thy way to victory had shown,
And owed the conquest to itself alone.

    Aureng-Zebe. Those fair ideas to my aid I'll call,
And emulate my great original;
Or, if they fail, I will invoke, in arms,
The power of love, and Indamora's charms.

    Emperor. I doubt the happy influence of your star;
To invoke a captive's name bodes ill in war.

    Aureng-Zebe. Sir, give me leave to say, whatever now
The omen prove, it boded well to you.
Your royal promise, when I went to fight,
Obliged me to resign a victor's right:
Her liberty I fought for, and I won,
And claim it, as your general, and your son.

    Emperor. My ears still ring with noise; I'm vexed to
      death,
Tongue-killed, and have not yet recovered breath;
Nor will I be prescribed my time by you.
First end the war, and then your claim renew;
While to your conduct I my fortune trust,
To keep this pledge of duty is but just.

    Aureng-Zebe. Some hidden cause your jealousy does
      move,
Or you could ne'er suspect my loyal love.

    Emperor. What love soever by an heir is shown,
He waits but time to step into the throne;
You're neither justified, nor yet accused;
Meanwhile, the prisoner with respect is used.

    Aureng-Zebe. I know the kindness of her guardian
      such,
I need not fear too little, but too much.
But, how, sir, how have you from virtue swerved?
Or what so ill return have I deserved?
You doubt not me, nor have I spent my blood,
To have my faith no better understood:
Your soul's above the baseness of distrust:
Nothing but love could make you so unjust.

    Emperor. You know your rival then; and know 'tis fit,
The son should to the father's claim submit.

Aureng-Zebe. Sons may have rights which they can
    never quit.
Yourself first made that title which I claim:
First bade me love, and authorised my flame.
    Emperor. The value of my gift I did not know:
If I could give, I can resume it too.
    Aureng-Zebe. Recall your gift, for I your power con-
    fess:
But first take back my life, a gift that's less.
Long life would now but a long burthen prove:
You're grown unkind, and I have lost your love.
My grief lets unbecoming speeches fall:
I should have died, and not complained at all.
    Emperor. Witness, ye powers,
How much I suffered, and how long I strove
Against the assaults of this imperious love!
I represented to myself the shame
Of perjured faith, and violated fame;
Your great deserts, how ill they were repaid;
All arguments, in vain, I urged and weighed:
For mighty love, who prudence does despise,
For reason showed me Indamora's eyes.
What would you more? my crime I sadly view,
Acknowledge, am ashamed, and yet pursue.
    Aureng-Zebe. Since you can love, and yet your error
    see,
The same resistless power may plead for me.
With no less ardour I my claim pursue:
I love, and cannot yield her even to you.
    Emperor. Your elder brothers, though o'ercome, have
    right:
The youngest['s] yet in arms prepared to fight.
But, yielding her, I firmly have decreed,
That you alone to empire shall succeed.
    Aureng-Zebe. To after-ages let me stand a shame,
When I exchange for crowns my love or fame!
You might have found a mercenary son,
To profit of the battles he had won.
Had I been such, what hindered me to take
The crown? nor had the exchange been yours to make.
While you are living, I no right pretend;
Wear it, and let it where you please descend.
But from my love, 'tis sacrilege to part:

There, there's my throne, in Indamora's heart.

 Emperor. 'Tis in her heart alone that you must reign;
You'll find her person difficult to gain.
Give willingly what I can take by force:
And know, obedience is your safest course.

 Aureng-Zebe. I'm taught, by honour's precepts, to
  obey:
Fear to obedience is a slavish way.
If aught my want of duty could beget,
You take the most prevailing means, to threat.
Pardon your blood, that boils within my veins;
It rises high, and menacing disdains.
Even Death's become to me no dreadful name:
I've often met him, and have made him tame:
In fighting fields, where our acquaintance grew,
I saw him, and contemned him first for you.

 Emperor. Of formal duty make no more thy boast:
Thou disobey'st where it concerns me most.
Fool! with both hands thus to push back a crown,
And headlong cast thyself from empire down!
Though Nourmahal I hate, her son shall reign:
Inglorious thou, by thy own fault remain.
Thy younger brother I'll admit this hour:
So mine shall be thy mistress, his thy power. [*Exit.*

 Aureng-Zebe. How vain is virtue, which directs our
  ways
Through certain danger to uncertain praise!
Barren, and airy name! thee Fortune flies,
With thy lean train, the pious and the wise.
Heaven takes thee at thy word, without regard,
And lets thee poorly be thy own reward.
The world is made for the bold impious man,
Who stops at nothing, seizes all he can.
Justice to merit does weak aid afford;
She trusts her balance, and neglects her sword.
Virtue is nice to take what's not her own;
And, while she long consults, the prize is gone.

To him DIANET.

 Dianet. Forgive the bearer of unhappy news:
Your altered father openly pursues
Your ruin; and, to compass his intent,

For violent Morat in haste has sent.
The gates he ordered all to be unbarred,
And from the market-place to draw the guard.
    Aureng-Zebe. How look the people in this turn of
      state?
    Dianet. They mourn your ruin as their proper fate;
Cursing the empress: For they think it done
By her procurement, to advance her son.
Him too, though awed, they scarcely can forbear:
His pride they hate, his violence they fear.
All bent to rise, would you appear their chief,
Till your own troops come up to your relief.
    Aureng-Zebe. Ill treated, and forsaken, as I am,
I'll not betray the glory of my name:
'Tis not for me, who have preserved a state,
To buy an empire at so base a rate.
    Dianet. The points of honour poets may produce;
Trappings of life, for ornament, not use:
Honour, which only does the name advance,
Is the mere raving madness of romance.
Pleased with a word, you may sit tamely down;
And see your younger brother force the crown.
    Aureng-Zebe. I know my fortune in extremes does lie;
The sons of Indostan must reign, or die;
That desperate hazard courage does create,
As he plays frankly who has least estate:
And that the world the coward will despise,
When life's a blank, who pulls not for a prize.
    Dianet. Of all your knowledge, this vain fruit you
      have,
To walk with eyes broad open to your grave.
    Aureng-Zebe. From what I've said, conclude, without
      reply,
I neither would usurp, nor tamely die.
The attempt to fly would guilt betray, or fear:
Besides, 'twere vain; the fort's our prison here.
Somewhat I have resolved.
Morat, perhaps, has honour in his breast;
And, in extremes, both counsels are the best.
Like emp'ric remedies, they last are tried;
And by the event condemned, or justified.
Presence of mind, and courage in distress,
Are more than armies, to procure success.   [*Exeunt.*

ACT III

SCENE I

ARIMANT, *with a letter in his hand:* INDAMORA.

ARIMANT. And I the messenger to him from you?
Your empire you to tyranny pursue:
You lay commands, both cruel and unjust,
To serve my rival, and betray my trust.
  Indamora. You first betrayed your trust, in loving me;
And should not I my own advantage see?
Serving my love, you may my friendship gain;
You know the rest of your pretences vain.
You must, my Arimant, you must be kind:
'Tis in your nature, and your noble mind.
  Arimant. I'll to the king, and straight my trust resign.
  Indamora. His trust you may, but you shall never mine.
Heaven made you love me for no other end,
But to become my confidant and friend:
As such, I keep no secret from your sight,
And therefore make you judge how ill I write:
Read it, and tell me freely then your mind;
It 'tis indited, as I meant it, kind.
  Arimant. I ask not Heaven my freedom to restore.
                                                        [*Reading.*
But only for your sake——I'll read no more:
And yet I must——
Less for my own, than for your sorrows sad——
                                                        [*Reading.*
Another line, like this, would make me mad——
Heaven! she goes on—yet more—and yet more kind!
                                                        [*As reading.*
Each sentence is a dagger to my mind.
See me this night——   [*Reading.*
Thank fortune, who did such a friend provide,
For faithful Arimant shall be your guide.
Not only to be made an instrument,
But pre-engaged without my own consent!

Indamora. Unknown to engage you still augments my
score,
And gives you scope of meriting the more.

Arimant. The best of men
Some interest in their actions must confess;
None merit, but in hope they may possess.
The fatal paper rather let me tear,
Than, like Bellerophon, my own sentence bear.

Indamora. You may; but 'twill not be your best advice:
'Twill only give me pains of writing twice.
You know you must obey me, soon or late:
Why should you vainly struggle with your fate?

Arimant. I thank thee, Heaven, thou hast been won-
drous kind!
Why am I thus to slavery designed,
And yet am cheated with a freeborn mind?
Or make thy orders with my reason suit,
Or let me live by sense, a glorious brute——

[*She frowns.*

You frown, and I obey with speed, before
That dreadful sentence comes, *See me no more:*
See me no more! that sound, methinks, I hear
Like the last trumpet thundering in my ear.

Enter SOLYMAN.

Solyman. The princess Melesinda, bathed in tears,
And tossed alternately with hopes and fears,
If your affairs such leisure can afford,
Would learn from you the fortunes of her lord.

Arimant. Tell her, that I some certainty may bring,
I go this minute to attend the king.

Indamora. This lonely turtle I desire to see:
Grief, though not cured, is eased by company.

Arimant [*to* SOLYMAN]. Say, if she please, she hither
may repair,
And breathe the freshness of the open air.

[*Exit* SOLYMAN.

Indamora. Poor princess! how I pity her estate,
Wrapt in the ruins of her husband's fate!
She mourned Morat should in rebellion rise;
Yet he offends, and she's the sacrifice.

Arimant. Not knowing his design, at court she stayed;

Till, by command, close prisoner she was made.
Since when,
Her chains with Roman constancy she bore,
But that, perhaps, an Indian wife's is more.

    Indamora. Go, bring her comfort; leave me here alone.
    Arimant. My love must still be in obedience shown.

                          [*Exit* ARIMANT.

   Enter MELESINDA, *led by* SOLYMAN, *who retires
afterwards.*

    Indamora. When graceful Sorrow in her pomp appears,
Sure she is dressed in Melesinda's tears.
Your head reclined (as hiding grief from view),
Droops, like a rose, surcharged with morning dew.

    Melesinda. Can flowers but droop in absence of the sun,
Which waked their sweets? And mine, alas! is gone.
But you the noblest charity express:
For they, who shine in courts, still shun distress.

    Indamora. Distressed myself, like you, confined, I live:
And, therefore, can compassion take and give.
We've both love's captives, but with fate so cross,
One must be happy by the other's loss.
Morat, or Aureng-Zebe, must fall this day.

    Melesinda. Too truly Tamerlane's successors they;
Each thinks a world too little for his sway.
Could you and I the same pretences bring,
Mankind should with more ease receive a king:
I would to you the narrow world resign,
And want no empire while Morat was mine.

    Indamora. Wished freedom, I presage, you soon will find:
If Heaven be just, and be to virtue kind.

    Melesinda. Quite otherwise my mind foretells my fate:
Short is my life, and that unfortunate.
Yet should I not complain, would Heaven afford
Some little time, ere death, to see my lord.

    Indamora. These thoughts are but your melancholy's food;
Raised from a lonely life, and dark abode:
But whatsoe'er our jarring fortunes prove,
Though our lords hate, methinks we two may love.

Melesinda. Such be our loves as may not yield to fate;
I bring a heart more true than fortunate.

                    [Giving their hands.

To them ARIMANT.

Arimant. I come with haste surprising news to bring:
In two hours' time, since last I saw the king,
The affairs of court have wholly changed their face:
Unhappy Aureng-Zebe is in disgrace;
And your Morat, proclaimed the successor,
Is called, to awe the city with his power.
Those trumpets his triumphant entry tell,
And now the shouts waft near the citadel.

    Indamora. See, madam, see the event by me fore-
        shown:
I envy not your chance, but grieve my own.

    Melesinda. A change so unexpected must surprise:
And more, because I am unused to joys.

    Indamora. May all your wishes ever prosperous be!
But I'm too much concerned the event to see.
My eyes too tender are,
To view my lord become the public scorn.—
I came to comfort, and I go to mourn.

                    [Taking her leave.

    Melesinda. Stay, I'll not see my lord,
Before I give your sorrow some relief;
And pay the charity you lent my grief.
Here he shall see me first, with you confined;
And, if your virtue fail to move his mind,
I'll use my interest that he may be kind.
Fear not, I never moved him yet in vain.

    Indamora. So fair a pleader any cause may gain.

    Melesinda. I have no taste, methinks, of coming joy;
For black presages all my hopes destroy.
"Die!" something whispers,—"Melesinda, die!
Fulfil, fulfil, thy mournful destiny!"—
Mine is a gleam of bliss, too hot to last;
Wat'ry it shines, and will be soon o'ercast.

        *[*INDAMORA *and* MELESINDA *retire.*

    Arimant. Fortune seems weary grown of Aureng-Zebe,
While to her new-made favourite Morat,
Her lavish hand is wastefully profuse:
With fame and flowing honours tided in,

Borne on a swelling current smooth beneath him.
The king, and haughty empress, to our wonder,
If not atoned, yet seemingly at peace,
As fate for him that miracle reserved.

Enter in triumph, Emperor, MORAT, *and* Train.

Emperor. I have confessed I love.
As I interpret fairly your design,
So look not with severer eyes on mine.
Your fate has called you to the imperial seat:
In duty be, as you in arms are, great;
For Aureng-Zebe a hated name is grown,
And love less bears a rival than the throne.

Morat. To me, the cries of fighting fields are charms:
Keen be my sabre, and of proof my arms,
I ask no other blessing of my stars:
No prize but fame, nor mistress but the wars.
I scarce am pleased I tamely mount the throne:—
Would Aureng-Zebe had all their souls in one!
With all my elder brothers I would fight,
And so from partial nature force my right.

Emperor. Had we but lasting youth, and time to
                                          spare
Some might be thrown away on fame and war;
But youth, the perishing good, runs on too fast,
And, unenjoyed will spend itself to waste;
Few know the use of life before 'tis past.
Had I once more thy vigour to command,
I would not let it die upon my hand:
No hour of pleasure should pass empty by;
Youth should watch joys, and shoot them as they fly.

Morat. Methinks, all pleasure is in greatness found.
Kings, like heaven's eye, should spread their beams
                                          around,
Pleased to be seen, while glory's race they run:
Rest is not for the chariot of the sun.
Subjects are stiff-necked animals; they soon
Feel slackened reins, and pitch their rider down.

Emperor. To thee that drudgery of power I give:
Cares be thy lot: Reign thou, and let me live.
The fort I'll keep for my security;
Business and public state resign to thee.

Morat. Luxurious kings are to their people lost:

They live, like drones, upon the public cost.
My arms from pole to pole the world shall shake,
And, with myself, keep all mankind awake.

Emperor. Believe me, son, and needless trouble spare;
'Tis a base world, and is not worth our care:
The vulgar, a scarce animated clod,
Ne'er pleased with aught above them, prince or God.
Were I a god, the drunken globe should roll,
The little emmets with the human soul
Care for themselves, while at my ease I sat,
And second causes did the work of fate;
Or, if I would take care, that care should be
For wit that scorned the world, and lived like me.

To them NOURMAHAL, ZAYDA, *and* Attendants.

Nourmahal. My dear Morat,   [*Embracing her son.*
This day propitious to us all has been:
You're now a monarch's heir, and I a queen.
Your youthful [4] father now may quit the state,
And find the ease he sought, indulged by fate.
Cares shall not keep him on the throne awake,
Nor break the golden slumbers he would take.

Emperor. In vain I struggled to the goal of life,
While rebel sons, and an imperious wife,
Still dragged me backward into noise and strife.

Morat. Be that remembrance lost; and be it my pride
To be your pledge of peace on either side.

To them AURENG-ZEBE.

Aureng-Zebe. With all the assurance innocence can
     bring,
Fearless without, because secure within,
Armed with my courage, unconcerned I see
This pomp; a shame to you, a pride to me.
Shame is but where with wickedness 'tis joined;
And, while no baseness in this breast I find,
I have not lost the birthright of my mind.

Emperor. Children, the blind effect of love and chance,
Formed by their sportive parents' ignorance,
Bear from their birth the impressions of a slave;
Whom Heaven for play-games first, and then for service
     gave.

---

[4] Ironic if correct. Scott read "faithful."

One then may be displaced, and one may reign,
And want of merit render birthright vain.

   Morat. Comes he to upbraid us with his innocence?
Seize him, and take the preaching Brahman hence.

   Aureng-Zebe. Stay, sir!—I from my years no merit
      plead: [*To his* Father.
All my designs and acts to duty lead.
Your life and glory are my only end;
And for that prize I with Morat contend.

   Morat. Not him alone: I all mankind defy.
Who dares adventure more for both than I?

   Aureng-Zebe. I know you brave, and take you at your
      word:
That present service, which you vaunt, afford.
Our two rebellious brothers are not dead:
Though vanquished, yet again they gather head.
I dare you, as your rival in renown,
March out your army from the imperial town:
Choose whom you please, the other leave to me;
And set our father absolutely free.
This, if you do, to end all future strife,
I am content to lead a private life;
Disband my army, to secure the state,
Nor aim at more, but leave the rest to fate.

   Morat. I'll do it.—Draw out my army on the plain?
War is to me a pastime, peace a pain.

   Emperor. Think better first.—   [*To* MORAT.
You see yourself inclosed beyond escape,
                       [*To* AURENG-ZEBE.
And, therefore, Proteus-like, you change your shape;
Of promise prodigal, while power you want,
And preaching in the self-denying cant.

   Morat. Plot better; for these arts too obvious are,
Of gaining time, the master-piece of war.
Is Aureng-Zebe so known?

   Aureng-Zebe. If acts like mine,
So far from interest, profit, or design,
Can show my heart, by those I would be known:
I wish you could as well defend your own.
My absent army for my father fought:
Yours, in these walls, is to enslave him brought.
If I come singly, you an armed guest,
The world with ease may judge whose cause is best.

Morat. My father saw you ill designs pursue;
And my admission showed his fear of you.

    Aureng-Zebe. Himself best knows why he his love
        withdraws
I owe him more than to declare the cause.
But still I press, our duty may be shown
By arms.

    Morat. I'll vanquish all his foes alone.

    Aureng-Zebe. You speak, as if you could the fates
        command,
And had no need of any other hand.
But, since my honour you so far suspect,
'Tis just I should on your designs reflect.
To prove yourself a loyal son, declare
You'll lay down arms when you conclude the war.

    Morat. No present answer your demand requires;
The war once done, I'll do what Heaven inspires;
And while this sword this monarchy secures,
'Tis managed by an abler arm than yours.

    Emperor. Morat's design a doubtful meaning bears:
                                         [Aside.
In Aureng-Zebe true loyalty appears.
He, for my safety, does his own despise;
Still, with his wrongs, I find his duty rise.
I feel my virtue struggling in my soul,
But stronger passion does its power control.—
Yet be advised your ruin to prevent:
                      [To AURENG-ZEBE, *aside.*
You might be safe, if you would give consent.

    Aureng-Zebe. So to your welfare I of use may be,
My life or death are equal both to me.

    Emperor. The people's hearts are yours; the fort yet
        mine:
Be wise, and Indamora's love resign.
I am observed: Remember, that I give
This my last proof of kindness—die, or live.

    Aureng-Zebe. Life, with my Indamora, I would choose;
But, losing her, the end of living lose.
I had considered all I ought before;
And fear of death can make me change no more.
The people's love so little I esteem,
Condemned by you, I would not live by them.
May he, who must your favour now possess,

Much better serve you, and not love you less.
    Emperor. I've heard you; and, to finish the debate,
                                       [Aloud.
Commit that rebel prisoner to the state.
    Morat. The deadly draught he shall begin this day:
And languish with insensible decay.
    Aureng-Zebe. I hate the lingering summons to attend;
Death all at once would be the nobler end.
Fate is unkind! methinks, a general
Should warm, and at the head of armies fall;
And my ambition did that hope pursue,
That so I might have died in fight for you.
                               [To his Father.
    Morat. Would I had been disposer of thy stars!
Thou shouldst have had thy wish, and died in wars.
'Tis I, not thou, have reason to repine,
That thou shouldst fall by any hand but mine.
    Aureng-Zebe. When thou wert formed, Heaven did a
        man begin;
But the brute soul, by chance, was shuffled in.
In woods and wilds thy monarchy maintain,
Where valiant beasts, by force and rapine, reign.
In life's next scene, if transmigration be,
Some bear, or lion, is reserved for thee.
    Morat. Take heed thou com'st not in that lion's way!
I prophesy, thou wilt thy soul convey
Into a lamb, and be again my prey.——
Hence with that dreaming priest!
    Nourmahal. Let me prepare
The poisonous draught: His death shall be my care
Near my apartment let him prisoner be,
That I his hourly ebbs of life may see.
    Aureng-Zebe. My life I would not ransom with a
        prayer:
'Tis vile, since 'tis not worth my father's care.
I go not, sir, indebted to my grave:
You paid yourself, and took the life you gave.   *[Exit.*
    Emperor. O that I had more sense of virtue left,
                                    [Aside.
Or were of that, which yet remains, bereft!
I've just enough to know how I offend,
And, to my shame, have not enough to mend.
Lead to the mosque.——

Morat. Love's pleasures why should dull devotion
   stay?
Heaven to my Melesinda's but the way.
                    [*Exeunt* Emperor, MORAT, *and* Train.

Zayda. Sure Aureng-Zebe has somewhat of divine,
Whose virtue through so dark a cloud can shine.
Fortune has from Morat this day removed
The greatest rival, and the best beloved.

Nourmahal. He is not yet removed.

Zayda. He lives, 'tis true;
But soon must die, and, what I mourn, by you.

Nourmahal. My Zayda, may thy words prophetic be!
                    [*Embracing her eagerly.*
I take the omen; let him die by me!
He, stifled in my arms, shall lose his breath;
And life itself shall envious be of death.

Zayda. Bless me, you powers above!

Nourmahal. Why dost thou start?
Is love so strange? Or have not I a heart?
Could Aureng-Zebe so lovely seem to thee,
And I want eyes that noble worth to see?
Thy little soul was but to wonder moved:
My sense of it was higher, and I loved.
That man, that god-like man, so brave, so great—
But these are thy small praises I repeat.
I'm carried by a tide of love away:
He's somewhat more than I myself can say.

Zayda. Though all the ideas you can form be true,
He must not, cannot, be possest by you.
If contradicting interests could be mixt,
Nature herself has cast a bar betwixt;
And, ere you reach to this incestuous love,
You must divine and human rights remove.

Nourmahal. Count this among the wonders love has
   done:
I had forgot he was my husband's son.

Zayda. Nay, more, you have forgot who is your own:
For whom your care so long designed the throne.
Morat must fall, if Aureng-Zebe should rise.

Nourmahal. 'Tis true; but who was e'er in love, and
   wise?
Why was that fatal knot of marriage tied,
Which did, by making us too near, divide?

Divides me from my sex! for Heaven, I find,
Excludes but me alone of womankind.
I stand with guilt confounded, lost with shame,
And yet made wretched only by a name.
If names have such command on human life,
Love sure's a name that's more divine than wife.
That sovereign power all guilt from action takes,
At least the stains are beautiful it makes.

Zayda. The encroaching ill you early should oppose:
Flattered, 'tis worse, and by indulgence grows.

Nourmahal. Alas! and what have I not said or done?
I fought it to the last,—and love has won.
A bloody conquest, which destruction brought,
And ruined all the country where he fought.
Whether this passion from above was sent,
The fate of him Heaven favours to prevent;
Or as the curse of fortune in excess,
That, stretching, would beyond its reach possess;
And, with a taste which plenty does deprave,
Loathes lawful good, and lawless ill does crave——

Zayda. But yet, consider——

Nourmahal. No, 'tis loss of time:
Think how to further, not divert my crime.
My artful engines instantly I'll move,
And choose the soft and gentlest hour of love.
The under-provost of the fort is mine.—
But see, Morat! I'll whisper my design.

Enter MORAT *with* ARIMANT, *as talking:* Attendants.

Arimant. And for that cause was not in public seen,
But stays in prison with the captive queen.

Morat. Let my attendants wait; I'll be alone:
Where least of state, there most of love is shown.

Nourmahal. My son, your business is not hard to
            guess;   [*To* MORAT.
Long absence makes you eager to possess:
I will not importune you by my stay;
She merits all the love which you can pay.
                                      [*Exit with* ZAYDA.

Re-enter ARIMANT, *with* MELESINDA; *then exit.* MORAT
    runs to MELESINDA, *and embraces her.*

Morat. Should I not chide you, that you chose to stay
In gloomy shades, and lost a glorious day?

Lost the firstfruits of joy you should possess
In my return, and made my triumph less?
   Melesinda. Should I not chide, that you could stay and
    see
Those joys, preferring public pomp to me?
Through my dark cell your shouts of triumph rung:
I heard with pleasure, but I thought them long.
   Morat. The public will in triumphs rudely share,
And kings the rudeness of their joys must bear:
But I made haste to set my captive free,
And thought that work was only worthy me.
The fame of ancient matrons you pursue,
And stand a blameless pattern to the new.
I have not words to praise such acts as these:
But take my heart, and mould it as you please.
   Melesinda. A trial of your kindness I must make.
Though not for mine so much as virtue's sake.
The queen of Cassimere——
   Morat. No more, my love;
That only suit I beg you not to move.
That she's in bonds for Aureng-Zebe I know,
And should, by my consent, continue so;
The good old man, I fear, will pity show.
My father dotes, and let him still dote on;
He buys his mistress dearly, with his throne.
   Melesinda. See her; and then be cruel if you can.
   Morat. 'Tis not with me as with a private man.
Such may be swayed by honour or by love;
But monarchs only by their interest move.
   Melesinda. Heaven does a tribute for your power
    demand:
He leaves the opprest and poor upon your hand;
And those, who stewards of his pity prove,
He blesses in return with public love:
In his distress some miracle is shown;
If exiled, Heaven restores him to his throne:
He needs no guard, while any subject's near,
Nor, like his tyrant neighbours, lives in fear:
No plots the alarm to his retirement give:
'Tis all mankind's concern that he should live.
   Morat. You promised friendship in your low estate,
And should forget it in your better fate.
Such maxims are more plausible than true;

But somewhat must be given to love and you.
I'll view this captive queen; to let her see,
Prayers and complaints are lost on such as me.

 Melesinda. I'll bear the news: Heaven knows how
  much I'm pleased,
That, by my care, the afflicted may be eased.

   As she is going off, enter INDAMORA.

 Indamora. I'll spare your pains, and venture out alone,
Since you, fair princess, my protection own,
But you, brave prince, a harder task must find;
    [*To* MORAT, *kneeling, who takes her up.*
In saving me, you would but half be kind.
An humble suppliant at your feet I lie;
You have condemned my better part to die,
Without my Aureng-Zebe I cannot live;
Revoke his doom, or else my sentence give.

 Melesinda. If Melesinda in your love have part,—
Which, to suspect, would break my tender heart,—
If love, like mine, may for a lover plead,
By the chaste pleasures of our nuptial bed,
By all the interest my past sufferings make,
And all I yet would suffer for your sake;
By you yourself, the last and dearest tie——

 Morat. You move in vain; for Aureng-Zebe must die.

 Indamora. Could that decree from any brother come?
Nature herself is sentenced in your doom.
Piety is no more, she sees her place
Usurped by monsters, and a savage race.
From her soft eastern climes you drive her forth,
To the cold mansions of the utmost north.
How can our prophet suffer you to reign,
When he looks down, and sees your brother slain?
Avenging furies will your life pursue:
Think there's a heaven, Morat, though not for you.

 Melesinda. Her words imprint a terror on my mind.
What if this death, which is for him designed,
Had been your doom (far be that augury!)
And you, not Aureng-Zebe, condemned to die?
Weigh well the various turns of human fate,
And seek, by mercy, to secure your state.

 Indamora. Had Heaven the crown for Aureng-Zebe
  designed,

Pity for you had pierced his generous mind.
Pity does with a noble nature suit:
A brother's life had suffered no dispute.
All things have right in life; our prophet's care
Commands the beings even of brutes to spare.
Though interest his restraint has justified,
Can life, and to a brother, be denied?

Morat. All reasons, for his safety urge, are weak:
And yet, methinks, 'tis heaven to hear you speak.

Melesinda. 'Tis part of your own being to invade——

Morat. Nay, if she fail to move, would you persuade?
                    [*Turning to* INDAMORA.
My brother does a glorious fate pursue;
I envy him, that he must fall for you,
He had been base, had he released his right:
For such an empire none but kings should fight.
If with a father he disputes this prize,
My wonder ceases when I see those eyes.

Melesinda. And can you, then, deny those eyes you
      praise?
Can beauty wonder, and not pity raise?

Morat. Your intercession now is needless grown:
Retire, and let me speak with her alone.

          [MELESINDA *retires, weeping, to the side of the
          Stage.*
Queen, that you may not fruitless tears employ,
                    [*Taking* INDAMORA's *hand.*
I bring you news to fill your heart with joy:
Your lover, king of all the east shall reign;
For Aureng-Zebe to-morrow shall be slain.

Indamora. The hopes you raised, y' have blasted with
      a breath: [*Starting back.*
With triumphs you began, but end with death,
Did you not say my lover should be king?

Morat. I, in Morat, the best of lovers bring.
For one, forsaken both of earth and heaven,
Your kinder stars a nobler choice have given:
My father, while I please, a king appears;
His power is more declining than his years.
An emperor and lover, but in show;
But you, in me, have youth and fortune too:
As Heaven did to your eyes, and form divine,
Submit the fate of all the imperial line;

So was it ordered by its wise decree,
That you should find them all comprised in me.

   Indamora. If, sir, I seem not discomposed with rage,
Feed not your fancy with a false presage.
Further to press your courtship is but vain;
A cold refusal carries more disdain.
Unsettled virtue stormy may appear;
Honour, like mine, serenely is severe;
To scorn your person, and reject your crown,
Disorder not my face into a frown.   [*Turns from him.*

   Morat. Your fortune you should reverently have used:
Such offers are not twice to be refused.
I go to Aureng-Zebe, and am in haste
For your commands; they're like to be the last.

   Indamora. Tell him,
With my own death I would his life redeem;
But less than honour both our lives esteem.

   Morat. Have you no more?

   Indamora. What shall I do or say?
He must not in this fury go away.—   [*Aside.*
Tell him, I did in vain his brother move;
And yet he falsely said, he was in love:
Falsely, for, had he truly loved, at least
He would have given one day to my request.

   Morat. A little yielding may my love advance:
She darted from her eyes a sidelong glance,
Just as she spoke; and, like her words, it flew:
Seemed not to beg, what yet she bid me do.   [*Aside.*
A brother, madam, cannot give a day;   [*To her.*
A servant, and who hopes to merit, may.

   Melesinda. If, sir——   [*Coming to him.*

   Morat. No more—set speeches, and a formal tale
With none but statesmen and grave fools prevail.
Dry up your tears, and practise every grace,
That fits the pageant of your royal place.   [*Exit.*

   Melesinda. Madam, the strange reverse of fate you see:
I pitied you, now you may pity me.   [*Exit after him.*

   Indamora. Poor princess! thy hard fate I could bemoan,
Had I not nearer sorrows of my own.
Beauty is seldom fortunate, when great:
A vast estate, but overcharged with debt.
Like those, whom want to baseness does betray,

I'm forced to flatter him I cannot pay.
O would he be content to seize the throne!
I beg the life of Aureng-Zebe alone.
Whom Heaven would bless, from pomp it will remove,
And make their wealth in privacy and love.

ACT IV

SCENE I

AURENG-ZEBE *alone.*

DISTRUST, and darkness of a future state,
Make poor mankind so fearful of their fate.
Death, in itself, is nothing; but we fear,
To be we know not what, we know not where.

[*Soft music.*

This is the ceremony of my fate:
A parting treat; and I'm to die in state.
They lodge me, as I were the Persian king:
And with luxuriant pomp my death they bring.

To him NOURMAHAL.

Nourmahal. I thought, before you drew your latest
   breath,
To smooth your passage, and to soften death;
For I would have you, when you upward move,
Speak kindly of me, to our friends above:
Nor name me there the occasion of your fate;
Or what my interest does, impute to hate.
   Aureng-Zebe. I ask not for what end your pomp's
      designed;
Whether to insult, or to compose my mind:
I marked it not.
But, knowing death would soon the assault begin,
Stood firm collected in my strength within:
To guard that breach did all my forces guide,
And left unmanned the quiet sense's side.
   Nourmahal. Because Morat from me his being took,
All I can say will much suspected look:
'Tis little to confess, your fate I grieve;
Yet more than you would easily believe.

Aureng-Zebe. Since my inevitable death you know,
You safely unavailing pity show:
'Tis popular to mourn a dying foe.

Nourmahal. You made my liberty your late request;
Is no return due from a grateful breast?
I grow impatient, till I find some way,
Great offices, with greater, to repay.

Aureng-Zebe. When I consider life, 'tis all a cheat;
Yet, fooled with hope, men favour the deceit;
Trust on, and think to-morrow will repay:
To-morrow's falser than the former day;
Lies worse, and, while it says, we shall be blest
With some new joys, cuts off what we possest.
Strange cozenage! None would live past years again,
Yet all hope pleasure in what yet remain;
And, from the dregs of life, think to receive,
What the first sprightly running could not give.
I'm tired with waiting for this chemic gold,
Which fools us young, and beggars us when old.

Nourmahal. 'Tis not for nothing that we life pursue;
It pays our hopes with something still that's new:
Each day's a mistress, unenjoyed before;
Like travellers, we're pleased with seeing more.
Did you but know what joys your way attend,
You would not hurry to your journey's end.

Aureng-Zebe. I need not haste the end of life to meet;
The precipice is just beneath my feet.

Nourmahal. Think not my sense of virtue is so small.
I'll rather leap down first, and break your fall.
My Aureng-Zebe (may I not call you so?)
                              [*Taking him by the hand.*
Behold me now no longer for your foe;
I am not, cannot be your enemy:
Look, is there any malice in my eye?
Pray, sit.——   [*Both sit.*
That distance shows too much respect, or fear;
You'll find no danger in approaching near.

Aureng-Zebe. Forgive the amazement of my doubtful
          state:
This kindness from the mother of Morat!
Or is't some angel, pitying what I bore,
Who takes that shape, to make my wonder more?

Nourmahal. Think me your better genius in disguise;

Or anything that more may charm your eyes.
Your guardian angel never could excel
In care, nor could he love his charge so well.

 Aureng-Zebe. Whence can proceed so wonderful a
  change?

 Nourmahal. Can kindness to desert, like yours, be
  strange?
Kindness by secret sympathy is tied;
For noble souls in nature are allied.
I saw with what a brow you braved your fate;
Yet with what mildness bore your father's hate.
My virtue, like a string, wound up by art
To the same sound, when yours was touched, took part,
At distance shook, and trembled at my heart.

 Aureng-Zebe. I'll not complain, my father is unkind,
Since so much pity from a foe I find.
Just Heaven reward this act!

 Nourmahal. 'Tis well the debt no payment does demand;
You turn me over to another hand.
But happy, happy she,
And with the blest above to be compared,
Whom you yourself would, with yourself, reward:
The greatest, nay, the fairest of her kind,
Would envy her that bliss, which you designed.

 Aureng-Zebe. Great princes thus, when favourites they
  raise,
To justify their grace, their creatures praise.

 Nourmahal. As love the noblest passion we account,
So to the highest object it should mount.
It shows you brave when mean desires you shun;
An eagle only can behold the sun:
And so must you, if yet presage divine
There be in dreams,—or was't a vision, mine?

 Aureng-Zebe. Of me?

 Nourmahal. And who could else employ my thought?
I dreamed, your love was by love's goddess sought;
Officious Cupids, hovering o'er your head,
Held myrtle wreaths; beneath your feet were spread
What sweets soe'er Sabæan springs disclose,
Our Indian jasmine, or the Syrian rose;
The wanton ministers around you strove
For service, and inspired their mother's love:
Close by your side, and languishing, she lies,

With blushing cheeks, short breath, and wishing eyes;
Upon your breast supinely lay her head,
While on your face her famished sight she fed.
Then, with a sigh, into these words she broke
(And gathered humid kisses as she spoke),
Dull, and ungrateful! Must I offer love?
Desired of gods, and envied even by Jove:
And dost thou ignorance or fear pretend?
Mean soul! and dar'st not gloriously offend?
Then, pressing thus his hand——

   Aureng-Zebe. I'll hear no more.   [*Rising up.*
'Twas impious to have understood before:
And I, till now, endeavoured to mistake
The incestuous meaning, which too plain you make.

   Nourmahal. And why this niceness to that pleasure
     shown,
Where Nature sums up all her joys in one;
Gives all she can, and, labouring still to give,
Makes it so great, we can but taste and live:
So fills the senses, that the soul seems fled,
And thought itself does, for the time, lie dead;
Till, like a string screwed up with eager haste,
It breaks, and is too exquisite to last?

   Aureng-Zebe. Heavens! can you this, without just
     vengeance, hear?
When will you thunder, if it now be clear?
Yet her alone let not your thunder seize:
I, too, deserve to die, because I please.[5]

   Nourmahal. Custom our native royalty does awe;
Promiscuous love is Nature's general law:
For whosoever the first lovers were,
Brother and sister made the second pair,
And doubled, by their love, their piety.

   Aureng-Zebe. Hence, hence, and to some barbarous
     climate fly,
Which only brutes in human form does yield,
And man grows wild in Nature's common field.
Who eat their parents, piety pretend;
Yet there no sons their sacred bed ascend.
To veil great sins, a greater crime you choose;
And, in your incest, your adultery lose.

   Nourmahal. In vain this haughty fury you have shown.

[5] This speech is pretty closely paraphrased from Seneca's *Hippolytus.*

How I adore a soul, so like my own!
You must be mine, that you may learn to live;
Know joys, which only she who loves can give,
Nor think that action you upbraid, so ill;
I am not changed, I love my husband still;[6]
But love him as he was, when youthful grace,
And the first down began to shade his face:
That image does my virgin-flames renew,
And all your father shines more bright in you.

   Aureng-Zebe. In me a horror of myself you raise;
Cursed by your love, and blasted by your praise.
You find new ways to prosecute my fate;
And your least guility passion was your hate.

   Nourmahal. I beg my death, if you can love deny.
                       [*Offering him a dagger.*

   Aureng-Zebe. I'll grant you nothing; no, not even to
die.

   Nourmahal. Know then, you are not half so kind as I.
                       [*Stamps with her foot.*

Enter Mutes, *some with swords drawn, one with a cup.*

You've chosen, and may now repent too late.
Behold the effect of what you wished,—my hate.
               [*Taking the cup to present him.*
This cup a cure for both our ills has brought;
You need not fear a philtre in the draught.

   Aureng-Zebe. All must be poison which can come from
thee: [*Receiving it from her.*
But this the least. To immortal liberty
This first I pour, like dying Socrates;
               [*Spilling a little of it.*
Grim though he be, Death pleases, when he frees.

As he is going to drink, enter MORAT, *attended.*

   Morat. Make not such haste, you must my leisure stay;
Your fate's deferred, you shall not die to-day.
               [*Taking the cup from him.*
   Nourmahal. What foolish pity has possessed your mind,
To alter what your prudence once designed?
   Morat. What if I please to lengthen out his date
A day, and take a pride to cozen fate?

[6] Again a paraphrase from Seneca.

Nourmahal. 'Twill not be safe to let him live an hour.

Morat. I'll do't, to show my arbitrary power.

Nourmahal. Fortune may take him from your hands
again,

And you repent the occasion lost in vain.

Morat. I smile at what your female fear foresees;

I'm in Fate's place, and dictate her decrees.—

Let Arimant be called.   [*Exit one of his* Attendants.

Aureng-Zebe. Give me the poison, and I'll end your
strife;

I hate to keep a poor precarious life.

Would I my safety on base terms receive,

Know, sir, I could have lived without your leave.

But those I could accuse, I can forgive;

By my disdainful silence, let them live.

Nourmahal. What am I, that you dare to bind my
hand?   [*To* MORAT.

So low, I've not a murder at command!

Can you not one poor life to her afford,

Her, who gave up whole nations to your sword?

And from the abundance of whose soul and heat,

The o'erflowing served to make your mind so great?

Morat. What did that greatness in a woman's mind?

Ill lodged, and weak to act what it designed?

Pleasure's your portion, and your slothful ease:

When man's at leisure, study how to please,

Soften his angry hours with servile care,

And, when he calls, the ready feast prepare.

From wars, and from affairs of state abstain;

Women emasculate a monarch's reign;

And murmuring crowds, who see them shine with gold,

That pomp, as their own ravished spoils, behold.

Nourmahal. Rage chokes my words: 'Tis womanly to
weep: [*Aside.*

In my swollen breast my close revenge I'll keep;

I'll watch his tenderest part and there strike deep. [*Exit.*

Aureng-Zebe. Your strange proceeding does my wonder
move;

Yet seems not to express a brother's love.

Say, to what cause my rescued life I owe.

Morat. If what you ask would please, you should not
know.

But since that knowledge, more than death, will grieve,
Know, Indamora gained you this reprieve.

    Aureng-Zebe. And whence had she the power to work
      your change?

    Morat. The power of beauty is not new or strange.
Should she command me more, I could obey;
But her request was bounded with a day.
Take that; and, if you spare my further crime,
Be kind, and grieve to death against your time.

Enter ARIMANT.

Remove this prisoner to some safer place:
He has, for Indamora's sake, found grace;
And from my mother's rage must guarded be,
Till you receive a new command from me.

    Arimant. Thus love, and fortune, persecute me still,
And make me slave to every rival's will.   [*Aside.*

    Aureng-Zebe. How I disdain a life, which I must buy
With your contempt, and her inconstancy!
For a few hours my whole content I pay:
You shall not force on me another day.

[Exit with ARIMANT.

Enter MELESINDA.

    Melesinda. I have been seeking you this hour's long
      space,
And feared to find you in another place;
But since you're here, my jealousy grows less:
You will be kind to my unworthiness.
What shall I say? I love to that degree,
Each glance another way is robbed from me.
Absence, and prisons, I could bear again;
But sink, and die, beneath your least disdain.

    Morat. Why do you give your mind this needless care,
And for yourself, and me, new pains prepare?
I ne'er approved this passion in excess:
If you would show your love, distrust me less.
I hate to be pursued from place to place;
Meet, at each turn, a stale domestic face.
The approach of jealousy love cannot bear;
He's wild, and soon on wing, if watchful eyes come near.

    Melesinda. From your loved presence how can I depart?

My eyes pursue the object of my heart.

Morat. You talk as if it were our bridal night:
Fondness is still the effect of new delight,
And marriage but the pleasure of a day:
The metal's base, the gilding worn away.

Melesinda. I fear I'm guilty of some great offence,
And that has bred this cold indifference.

Morat. The greatest in the world to flesh and blood:
You fondly love much longer than you should.

Melesinda. If that be all which makes your discontent,
Of such a crime I never can repent.

Morat. Would you force love upon me, which I shun?
And bring coarse fare, when appetite is gone?

Melesinda. Why did I not in prison die, before
My fatal freedom made me suffer more?
I had been pleased to think I died for you,
And doubly pleased, because you then were true:
Then I had hope; but now, alas! have none.

Morat. You say you love me; let that love be shown.
'Tis in your power to make my happiness.

Melesinda. Speak quickly! To command me is to bless.

Morat. To Indamora you my suit must move:
You'll sure speak kindly of the man you love.

Melesinda. Oh, rather let me perish by your hand,
Than break my heart, by this unkind command!
Think, 'tis the only one I could deny;
And that 'tis harder to refuse, than die.
Try, if you please, my rival's heart to win;
I'll bear the pain, but not promote the sin.
You own whate'er perfections man can boast,
And, if she view you with my eyes, she's lost.

Morat. Here I renounce all love, all nuptial ties:
Henceforward live a stranger to my eyes:
When I appear, see you avoid the place,
And haunt me not with that unlucky face.

Melesinda. Hard as it is, I this command obey,
And haste, while I have life, to go away:
In pity stay some hours, till I am dead,
That blameless you may court my rival's bed.
My hated face I'll not presume to show;
Yet I may watch your steps where'er you go.
Unseen, I'll gaze; and, with my latest breath,
Bless, while I die, the author of my death.   [*Weeping.*

Enter Emperor.

Emperor. When your triumphant fortune high appears
What cause can draw these unbecoming tears?
Let cheerfulness on happy fortune wait,
And give not thus the counter-time to fate.

    Melesinda. Fortune long frowned, and has but lately
        smiled:
I doubt a foe so newly reconciled.
You saw but sorrow in its waning form,
A working sea remaining from a storm;
When the now weary waves roll o'er the deep,
And faintly murmur ere they fall asleep.

    Emperor. Your inward griefs you smother in your
        mind;
But Fame's loud voice proclaims your lord unkind.

    Morat. Let Fame be busy, where she has to do;
Tell of fought fields, and every pompous show.
Those tales are fit to fill the people's ears;
Monarchs, unquestioned, move in higher spheres.

    Melesinda. Believe not rumour, but yourself; and see
The kindness 'twixt my plighted lord and me.
                    [*Kissing* MORAT.
This is our state; thus happily we live;
These are the quarrels which we take and give.
I had no other way to force a kiss: [*Aside to* MORAT.
Forgive my last farewell to you and bliss.   [*Exit.*

    Emperor. Your haughty carriage shows too much of
        scorn,
And love, like hers, deserves not that return.

    Morat. You'll please to leave me judge of what I do,
And not examine by the outward show.
Your usage of my mother might be good:
I judged it not.

    Emperor. Nor was it fit you should.

    Morat. Then, in as equal balance weigh my deeds.

    Emperor. My right and my authority, exceeds.
Suppose (what I'll not grant) injustice done;
Is judging me the duty of a son?

    Morat. Not of a son, but of an emperor:
You cancelled duty when you gave me power.
If your own actions on your will you ground,
Mine shall hereafter know no other bound.

What meant you when you called me to a throne?
Was it to please me with a name alone?

    Emperor. 'Twas that I thought your gratitude would
    know
What to my partial kindness you did owe;
That what your birth did to your claim deny,
Your merit of obedience might supply.

    Morat. To your own thoughts such hope you might
    propose;
But I took empire not on terms like those.
Of business you complained; now take your ease;
Enjoy whate'er decrepit age can please;
Eat, sleep, and tell long tales of what you were
In flower of youth,—if any one will hear.

    Emperor. Power, like new wine, does your weak brain
    surprise,
And its mad fumes, in hot discourses, rise:
But time these giddy vapours will remove;
Meanwhile, I'll taste the sober joys of love.

    Morat. You cannot love, nor pleasures take, or give;
But life begin, when 'tis too late to live.
On a tired courser you pursue delight,
Let slip your morning, and set out at night.
If you have lived, take thankfully the past;
Make, as you can, the sweet remembrance last.
If you have not enjoyed what youth could give,
But life sunk through you, like a leaky sieve,
Accuse yourself, you lived not while you might
But, in the captive queen resign your right.
I've now resolved to fill your useless place;
I'll take that post, to cover your disgrace,
And love her, for the honour of my race.

    Emperor. Thou dost but try how far I can forbear,
Nor art that monster which thou wouldst appear:
But do not wantonly my passion move;
I pardon nothing that relates to love.
My fury does, like jealous forts, pursue
With death, even strangers who but come to view.

    Morat. I did not only view, but will invade.
Could you shed venom from your reverend shade,
Like trees, beneath whose arms 'tis death to sleep;
Did rolling thunder your fenced fortress keep,
Thence would I snatch my Semele, like Jove,

And 'midst the dreadful wrack enjoy my love.

Emperor. Have I for this, ungrateful as thou art!
When right, when nature, struggled in my heart;
When Heaven called on me for thy brother's claim,
Broke all, and sullied my unspotted fame?
Wert thou to empire, by my baseness, brought,
And wouldst thou ravish what so dear I bought?
Dear! for my conscience and its peace I gave;
Why was my reason made my passion's slave?
I see Heaven's justice; thus the powers divine
Pay crimes with crimes, and punish mine by thine.

Morat. Crimes let them pay, and punish as they please,
What power makes mine, by power I mean to seize.
Since 'tis to that they their own greatness owe
Above, why should they question mine below?   [*Exit.*

Emperor. Prudence, thou vainly in our youth art sought,
And, with age purchased, art too dearly bought:
We're past the use of wit, for which we toil;
Late fruit, and planted in too cold a soil.
My stock of fame is lavished and decayed;
No profit of the vast profusion made.
Too late my folly I repent; I know
My Aureng-Zebe would ne'er have used me so.
But, by his ruin, I prepared my own;
And, like a naked tree, my shelter gone,
To winds and winter-storms must stand exposed alone.
                                                    [*Exit.*

Enter AURENG-ZEBE *and* ARIMANT.

Arimant. Give me not thanks, which I will ne'er de-
    serve;
But know, 'tis for a noble price I serve.
By Indamora's will you're hither brought:
All my reward in her command I sought,
The rest your letter tells you.——See, like light,
She comes, and I must vanish, like the night.   [*Exit.*

Enter INDAMORA.

Indamora. 'Tis now, that I begin to live again;
Heavens, I forgive you all my fear and pain:
Since I behold my Aureng-Zebe appear,
I could not buy him at a price too dear.
His name alone afforded me relief,

Repeated as a charm to cure my grief.
I that loved name did, as some god, invoke,
And printed kisses on it, while I spoke.

    Aureng-Zebe. Short ease, but long, long pains from you I
    find;
Health to my eyes; but poison to my mind.
Why are you made so excellently fair?
So much above what other beauties are,
That, even in cursing, you new-form my breath;
And make me bless those eyes which give me death!

    Indamora. What reason for your curses can you find?
My eyes your conquest, not your death, designed.
If they offend, 'tis that they are too kind.

    Aureng-Zebe. The ruins they have wrought, you will
    not see;
Too kind they are, indeed, but not to me.

    Indamora. Think you, base interest souls like mine can
    sway?
Or that, for greatness, I can love betray?
No, Aureng-Zebe, you merit all my heart,
And I'm too noble but to give a part.
Your father, and an empire! Am I known
No more? Or have so weak a judgment shown,
In choosing you, to change you for a throne?

    Aureng-Zebe. How, with a truth, you would a falsehood
    blind!
'Tis not my father's love you have designed;
Your choice is fix'd where youth and power are joined.

    Indamora. Where youth and power are joined!—has he
    a name?

    Aureng-Zebe. You would be told; you glory in your
    shame;
There's music in the sound; and, to provoke
Your pleasure more, by me it must be spoke.
Then, then it ravishes, when your pleased ear
The sound does from a wretched rival hear.
Morat's the name your heart leaps up to meet,
While Aureng-Zebe lies dying at your feet.

    Indamora. Who told you this?

    Aureng-Zebe. Are you so lost to shame;
Morat, Morat, Morat! You love the name
So well, your every question ends in that;
You force me still to answer you, Morat.

Morat, who best could tell what you revealed;
Morat, too proud to keep his joy concealed.

   Indamora. Howe'er unjust your jealousy appear,
It shows the loss of what you love, you fear;
And does my pity, not my anger move:
I'll fond it, as the froward child of love.
To show the truth of my unaltered breast,
Know, that your life was given at my request,
At last reprieved. When Heaven denied you aid,
She brought it, she, whose falsehood you upbraid.

   Aureng-Zebe. And 'tis by that you would your falsehood
     hide?
Had you not asked, how happy had I died!
Accurst reprieve! not to prolong my breath;
It brought a lingering, and more painful death.
I have not lived since first I heard the news;
The gift the guilty giver does accuse.
You knew the price, and the request did move,
That you might pay the ransom with your love.

   Indamora. Your accusation must, I see, take place;—
And am I guilty, infamous, and base?

   Aureng-Zebe. If you are false, those epithets are small;
You're then the things, the abstract of them all.
And you are false: You promised him your love,—
No other price a heart so hard could move.
Do not I know him? Could his brutal mind
Be wrought upon? Could he be just, or kind?
Insultingly, he made your love his boast;
Gave me my life, and told me what it cost.
Speak; answer. I would fain yet think you true:
Lie; and I'll not believe myself, but you.
Tell me you love; I'll pardon the deceit,
And, to be fooled, myself assist the cheat.

   Indamora. No; 'tis too late; I have no more to say:
If you'll believe I have been false, you may.

   Aureng-Zebe. I would not; but your crimes too plain
     appear:
Nay, even that I should think you true, you fear.
Did I not tell you, I would be deceived?

   Indamora. I'm not concerned to have my truth believed.
You would be cozened! would assist the cheat!
But I'm too plain to join in the deceit:
I'm pleased you think me false,

And, whatsoe'er my letter did pretend,
I made this meeting for no other end.

    Aureng-Zebe. Kill me not quite with this indifference!
When you are guiltless, boast not an offence.
I know you better than yourself you know:
Your heart was true, but did some frailty show:
You promised him your love, that I might live;
But promised what you never meant to give.
Speak, was't not so? confess; I can forgive.

    Indamora. Forgive! what dull excuses you prepare,
As if your thoughts of me were worth my care!

    Aureng-Zebe. Ah traitress! Ah ingrate! Ah faithless mind!
Ah sex, invented first to damn mankind!
Nature took care to dress you up for sin;
Adorned, without; unfinished left, within.
Hence, by no judgment you your loves direct;
Talk much, ne'er think, and still the wrong affect.
So much self-love in your composure's mixed,
That love to others still remains unfixed:
Greatness, and noise, and show, are your delight;
Yet wise men love you, in their own despite:
And finding in their native wit no ease,
Are forced to put your folly on, to please.

    Indamora. Now you shall know what cause you have to
        rage;
But to increase your fury, not assuage:
I found the way your brother's heart to move,
Yet promised not the least return of love.
His pride and brutal fierceness I abhor;
But scorn your mean suspicions of me more.
I owed my honour and my fame this care:
Know what your folly lost you, and despair.
                        [*Turning from him.*

    Aureng-Zebe. Too cruelly your innocence you tell;
Show Heaven, and damn me to the pit of hell.
Now I believe you; 'tis not yet too late:
You may forgive, and put a stop to fate;
Save me, just sinking, and no more to rise. [*She frowns.*
How can you look with such relentless eyes?
Or let your mind by penitence be moved,
Or I'm resolved to think you never loved.
You are not cleared, unless you mercy speak:
I'll think you took the occasion thus to break.

Indamora. Small jealousies, 'tis true, inflame desire;
Too great, not fan, but quite blow out the fire:
Yet I did love you, till such pains I bore,
That I dare trust myself and you no more.
Let me not love you; but here end my pain:
Distrust may make me wretched once again.
Now, with full sails, into the port I move,
And safely can unlade my breast of love;
Quiet, and calm: Why should I then go back,
To tempt the second hazard of a wrack?
    Aureng-Zebe. Behold these dying eyes, see their submissive awe;
These tears, which fear of death could never draw:
Heard you that sigh? from my heaved heart it past,
And said, "If you forgive not, 'tis my last."
Love mounts, and rolls about my stormy mind,
Like fire, that's borne by a tempestuous wind.
Oh, I could stifle you, with eager haste!
Devour your kisses with my hungry taste!
Rush on you! eat you! wander o'er each part,
Raving with pleasure, snatch you to my heart!
Then hold you off, and gaze! then, with new rage,
Invade you till my conscious limbs presage
Torrents of joy, which all their banks o'erflow!
So lost, so blest, as I but then could know!
    Indamora. Be no more jealous! [*Giving him her hand.*
    Aureng-Zebe. Give me cause no more:
The danger's greater after, than before;
If I relapse, to cure my jealousy,
Let me (for that's the easiest parting) die.
    Indamora. My life!
    Aureng-Zebe. My soul!
    Indamora. My all that Heaven can give!
Death's life with you; without you, death to live.

        To them ARIMANT, *hastily.*

Arimant. Oh, we are lost, beyond all human aid!
The citadel is to Morat betrayed.
The traitor, and the treason, known too late;
The false Abbas delivered up the gate:
Even while I speak, we're compassed round with fate.
The valiant cannot fight, or coward fly;
But both in undistinguished crowds must die.

Aureng-Zebe. Then my prophetic fears are come to pass:
Morat was always bloody; now he's base:
And has so far in usurpation gone,
He will by parricide secure a throne.

To them the Emperor.

Emperor. Am I forsaken, and betrayed, by all?
Not one brave man dare, with a monarch, fall?
Then, welcome death, to cover my disgrace!
I would not live to reign o'er such a race.
My Aureng-Zebe!   [*Seeing* AURENG-ZEBE.
But thou no more art mine; my cruelty
Has quite destroyed the right I had in thee.
I have been base,
Base even to him from whom I did receive
All that a son could to a parent give:
Behold me punished in the selfsame kind;
The ungrateful does a more ungrateful find.

Aureng-Zebe. Accuse yourself no more; you could not
     be
Ungrateful; could commit no crime to me.
I only mourn my yet uncancelled score:
You put me past the power of paying more.
That, that's my grief, that I can only grieve,
And bring but pity, where I would relieve;
For had I yet ten thousand lives to pay,
The mighty sum should go no other way.

Emperor. Can you forgive me? 'tis not fit you should.
Why will you be so excellently good?
'Twill stick too black a brand upon my name:
The sword is needless; I shall die with shame.
What had my age to do with love's delight,
Shut out from all enjoyments but the sight?

Arimant. Sir, you forget the danger's imminent:
This minute is not for excuses lent.

Emperor. Disturb me not;—
How can my latest hour be better spent?
To reconcile myself to him is more,
Than to regain all I possessed before.
Empire and life are now not worth a prayer,
His love, alone, deserves my dying care.

Aureng-Zebe. Fighting for you, my death will glorious
     be.

Indamora. Seek to preserve yourself, and live for me.
Arimant. Lose then no further time.
Heaven has inspired me with a sudden thought,
Whence your unhoped for safety may be wrought
Though with the hazard of my blood 'tis bought.
But since my life can ne'er be fortunate,
'Tis so much sorrow well redeemed from fate.
You, madam, must retire
(Your beauty is its own security),
And leave the conduct of the rest to me.
Glory will crown my life, if I succeed;
If not, she may afford to love me dead.   [*Aside.*
  Aureng-Zebe. My father's kind, and, madam, you for-
    give;
Were Heaven so pleased, I now could wish to live.
And I shall live.
With glory and with love, at once, I burn:
I feel the inspiring heat, and absent god return. [*Exeunt.*

ACT V

SCENE I

INDAMORA *alone.*

INDAMORA. The night seems doubled with the fear she
    brings,
And o'er the citadel new spreads her wings.
The morning, as mistaken, turns about,
And all her early fires again go out.
Shouts, cries, and groans, first pierce my ears, and then
A flash of lightning draws the guilty scene,
And shows me arms, and wounds, and dying men.
Ah, should my Aureng-Zebe be fighting there,
And envious winds, distinguished to my ear,
His dying groans and his last accents bear!

To her MORAT, *attended.*

  Morat. The bloody business of the night is done,
And in the citadel, an empire won.
Our swords so wholly did the fates employ,
That they, at length, grew weary to destroy,

Refused the work we brought, and, out of breath,
Made sorrow and despair attend for death.
But what of all my conquest can I boast?
My haughty pride, before your eyes, is lost:
And victory but gains me to present
That homage, which our eastern world has sent.

    Indamora. Your victory, alas! begets my fears.
Can you not then triumph without my tears?
Resolve me (for you know my destiny
Is Aureng-Zebe's); say, do I live or die?

    Morat. Urged by my love, by hope of empire fired,
'Tis true, I have performed what both required:
What fate decreed; for when great souls are given,
They bear the marks of sovereignty from Heaven.
My elder brothers my forerunners came;
Rough-draughts of nature, ill designed, and lame:
Blown off, like blossoms never made to bear;
Till I came, finished, her last-laboured care.

    Indamora. This prologue leads to your succeeding sin:
Blood ended what ambition did begin.

    Morat. 'Twas rumour'd,—but by whom I cannot tell,—
My father 'scaped from out the citadel;
My brother too may live.

    Indamora. He may?

    Morat. He must:
I kill'd him not: and a less fate's unjust.
Heaven owes it me, that I may fill his room,
A phœnix-lover, rising from his tomb;
In whom you'll lose your sorrows for the dead;
More warm, more fierce, and fitter for your bed.

    Indamora. Should I from Aureng-Zebe my heart divide,
To love a monster, and a parricide?
These names your swelling titles cannot hide.
Severe decrees may keep our tongues in awe;
But to our thoughts, what edict can give law?
Even you yourself, to your own breast, shall tell
Your crimes; and your own conscience be your hell.

    Morat. What business has my conscience with a crown?
She sinks in pleasures, and in bowls will drown.
If mirth should fail, I'll busy her with cares,
Silence her clamorous voice with louder wars:
Trumpets and drums shall fright her from the throne,
As sounding cymbals aid the labouring moon.

   Indamora. Repelled by these, more eager she will grow,
Spring back more strongly than a Scythian bow.
Amidst your train, this unseen judge will wait;
Examine how you came by all your state;
Upbraid your impious pomp; and, in your ear,
Will hollo, "Rebel, tyrant, murderer!"
Your ill-got power wan looks and care shall bring,
Known but by discontent to be a king.
Of crowds afraid, yet anxious when alone,
You'll sit and brood your sorrows on a throne.
   Morat. Birthright's a vulgar road to kingly sway;
'Tis every dull-got elder brother's way.
Dropt from above he lights into a throne;
Grows of a piece with that he sits upon;
Heaven's choice, a low, inglorious, rightful drone.
But who by force a sceptre does obtain,
Shows he can govern that, which he could gain.
Right comes of course, whate'er he was before;
Murder and usurpation are no more.
   Indamora. By your own laws you such dominion make,
As every stronger power has right to take:
And parricide will so deform your name,
That dispossessing you will give a claim.
Who next usurps, will a just prince appear,
So much your ruin will his reign endear.
   Morat. I without guilt would mount the royal seat:
But yet 'tis necessary to be great.
   Indamora. All greatness is in virtue understood:
'Tis only necessary to be good.
Tell me, what is't at which great spirits aim,
What most yourself desire?
   Morat. Renown and fame,
And power, as uncontrolled as is my will.
   Indamora. How you confound desires of good and ill!
For true renown is still with virtue joined;
But lust of power lets loose the unbridled mind.
Yours is a soul irregularly great,
Which, wanting temper, yet abounds with heat,
So strong, yet so unequal pulses beat;
A sun, which does, through vapours, dimly shine;
What pity 'tis, you are not all divine!
New moulded, thorough lightened, and a breast
So pure, to bear the last severest test;

Fit to command an empire you should gain
By virtue, and without a blush to reign.

Morat. You show me somewhat I ne'er learnt before;
But 'tis the distant prospect of a shore,
Doubtful in mists; which, like enchanted ground,
Flies from my sight, before 'tis fully found.

Indamora. Dare to be great, without a guilty crown;
View it, and lay the bright temptation down:
'Tis base to seize on all, because you may;
That's empire, that, which I can give away:
There's joy when to wild will you laws prescribe,
When you bid Fortune carry back her bribe:
A joy, which none but greatest minds can taste;
A fame, which will to endless ages last.

Morat. Renown, and fame, in vain, I courted long,
And still pursued them, though directed wrong,
In hazard, and in toils, I heard they lay;
Sailed farther than the coast, but missed my way:
Now you have given me virtue for my guide;
And, with true honour, ballasted my pride.
Unjust dominion I no more pursue;
I quit all other claims, but those to you.

Indamora. Oh, be not just by halves! pay all you owe;
Think there's a debt to Melesinda too.
To leave no blemish on your after-life,
Reward the virtue of a suffering wife.

Morat. To love, once past, I cannot backward move;
Call yesterday again, and I may love.
'Twas not for nothing I the crown resigned;
I still must own a mercenary mind;
I, in this venture, double gains pursue,
And laid out all my stock, to purchase you.

To them ASAPH KHAN.

Now, what success, does Aureng-Zebe yet live?

Asaph Khan. Fortune has given you all that she can
        give.
Your brother—

Morat. Hold; thou showest an impious joy,
And think'st I still take pleasure to destroy:
Know, I am changed, and would not have him slain.

Asaph Khan. 'Tis past; and you desire his life in vain.
He, prodigal of soul, rushed on the stroke

Of lifted weapons, and did wounds provoke:
In scorn of night, he would not be concealed;
His soldiers, where he fought, his name revealed.
In thickest crowds, still Aureng-Zebe did sound;
The vaulted roofs did Aureng-Zebe rebound;
Till late, and in his fall, the name was drowned.

    Indamora. Wither that hand which brought him to his
      fate,
And blasted be the tongue which did relate!

    Asaph Khan. His body——

    Morat. Cease to enhance her misery:
Pity the queen, and show respect to me.
'Tis every painter's art to hide from sight,
And cast in shades, what, seen, would not delight.
Your grief in me such sympathy has bred,—[*To her.*
I mourn, and wish I could recall the dead.
Love softens me; and blows up fires, which pass
Through my tough heart, and melt the stubborn mass.

    Indamora. Break, heart; or choke, with sobs, my hated
      breath!
Do thy own work: admit no foreign death.
Alas! why do I make this useless moan?
I'm dead already, for my soul is gone.

To them MIR BABA.

    Mir Baba. What tongue the terror of this night can tell,
Within, without, and round the citadel!
A new-formed faction does your power oppose;
The fight's confused, and all who meet are foes:
A second clamour, from the town, we hear;
And the far noise so loud, it drowns the near.
Abbas, who seemed our friend, is either fled,
Or, what we fear, our enemies does head:
Your frighted soldiers scarce their ground maintain.

    Morat. I thank their fury; we shall fight again:
They rouse my rage; I'm eager to subdue:
'Tis fatal to withhold my eyes from you.
                [*Exit with the two* Omrahs.

Enter MELESINDA.

    Melesinda. Can misery no place of safety know?
The noise pursues me wheresoe'er I go,
As fate sought only me, and, where I fled,

Aimed all its darts at my devoted head.
And let it; I am now past care of life;
The last of women, an abandoned wife.

    Indamora. Whether design or chance has brought you here,
I stand obliged to fortune, or to fear:
Weak women should, in danger, herd like deer.
But say, from whence this new combustion springs?
Are there yet more Morats? more fighting kings?

    Melesinda. Him from his mother's love your eyes divide,
And now her arms the cruel strife decide.

    Indamora. What strange misfortunes my next life attend!
Death will be kind, and all my sorrows end.
If Nourmahal prevail, I know my fate.

    Melesinda. I pity, as my own, your hard estate:
But what can my weak charity afford?
I have no longer interest in my lord:
Nor in his mother, he: she owns her hate
Aloud, and would herself usurp the state.

    Indamora. I'm stupefied with sorrow, past relief
Of tears; parched up, and withered with my grief.

    Melesinda. Dry mourning will decays more deadly bring,
As a north wind burns a too forward spring.
Give sorrow vent, and let the sluices go.

    Indamora. My tears are all congealed, and will not flow.

    Melesinda. Have comfort; yield not to the blows of fate.

    Indamora. Comfort, like cordials after death, comes late.
Name not so vain a word; my hopes are fled:
Think you Morat were kind, and think him dead.

    Melesinda. I can no more—
Can no more arguments, for comfort, find:
Your boding words have quite o'erwhelmed my mind.

                [*Clattering of weapons within.*

    Indamora. The noise increases, as the billows roar,
When rolling from afar they threat the shore.
She comes; and feeble nature now, I find,
Shrinks back in danger, and forsakes my mind.
I wish to die, yet dare not death endure;
Detest the medicine, yet desire the cure.
I would have death; but mild, and at command:
I dare not trust him in another's hand.

In Nourmahal's, he would not mine appear;
But armed with terror, and disguised with fear.

Melesinda. Beyond this place you can have no retreat:
Stay here, and I the danger will repeat.
I fear not death, because my life I hate.
And envious death will shun the unfortunate.

Indamora. You must not venture.

Melesinda. Let me: I may do
Myself a kindness, in obliging you.
In your loved name, I'll seek my angry lord;
And beg your safety from his conquering sword:
So his protection all your fears will ease,
And I shall see him once, and not displease.   [*Exit.*

Indamora. O wretched queen! what power thy life can
   save?
A stranger, and unfriended, and a slave!

Enter NOURMAHAL, ZAYDA, *and* ABBAS, *with* Soldiers.

Alas, she's here!   [INDAMOR *retires.*

Nourmahal. Heartless they fought, and quitted soon
   their ground,
While ours with easy victory were crowned.
To you, Abbas, my life and empire too,
And, what's yet dearer, my revenge I owe.

Abbas. The vain Morat, by his own rashness wrought,
Too soon discovered his ambitious thought;
Believed me his, because I spoke him fair,
And pitched his head into the ready snare.
Hence 'twas I did his troops at first admit;
But such, whose numbers could no fears beget:
By them the emperor's party first I slew,
Then turned my arms the victors to subdue.

Nourmahal. Now let the headstrong boy my will control!
Virtue's no slave of man; no sex confines the soul:
I, for myself, the imperial seat will gain,
And he shall wait my leisure for his reign.—
But Aureng-Zebe is nowhere to be found,
And now, perhaps, in death's cold arms he lies!
I fought, and conquered, yet have lost the prize.

Zayda. The chance of war determined well the strife,
That racked you, 'twixt the lover and the wife.
He's dead, whose love had sullied all your reign,
And made you empress of the world in vain.

Nourmahal. No; I my power and pleasure would divide:
The drudge had quenched my flames, and then had
    died.
I rage, to think without that bliss I live,
That I could wish what fortune would not give:
But, what love cannot, vengeance must supply;
She, who bereaved me of his heart, shall die.
    Zayda. I'll search: far distant hence she cannot be.
                                   [Goes in.
    Nourmahal. This wondrous master-piece I fain would
    see;
This fatal Helen, who can wars inspire,
Make kings her slaves, and set the world on fire.
My husband locked his jewel from my view;
Or durst not set the false one by the true.

Re-enter ZAYDA, *leading* INDAMORA.

    Zayda. Your frighted captive, ere she dies, receive;
Her soul's just going else, without your leave.
    Nourmahal. A fairer creature did my eyes ne'er see!
Sure she was formed by Heaven, in spite to me!
Some angel copied, while I slept, each grace,
And moulded every feature from my face.
Such majesty does from her forehead rise,
Her cheeks such blushes cast, such rays her eyes,
Nor I, nor envy, can a blemish find.—
The palace is, without, too well designed:
Conduct me in, for I will view thy mind.   *[To her.*
Speak, if thou hast a soul, that I may see,
If Heaven can make, throughout, another me.
    Indamora. My tears and miseries must plead my cause;
                                   [Kneeling.
My words, the terror of your presence awes:
Mortals, in sight of angels, mute become;
The nobler nature strikes the inferior dumb.
    Nourmahal. The palm is, by the foe's confession, mine;
But I disdain what basely you resign.
Heaven did, by me, the outward model build;
Its inward work, the soul, with rubbish filled.
Yet, oh! the imperfect piece moves more delight;
'Tis gilded o'er with youth, to catch the sight.
The gods have poorly robbed my virgin bloom,

And what I am, by what I was, o'ercome.
Traitress! restore my beauty and my charms,
Nor steal my conquest with my proper arms.

 Indamora. What have I done thus to inflame your hate?
I am not guilty, but unfortunate.

 Nourmahal. Not guilty, when thy looks my power be-
  tray,
Seduce mankind, my subject, from my sway,
Take all my hearts and all my eyes away?
My husband first; but that I could forgive;
He only moved, and talked, but did not live.
My Aureng-Zebe!—for I dare own the name,
The glorious sin, and the more glorious flame,—
Him from my beauty have thy eyes misled,
And starved the joys of my expected bed.

 Indamora. His love so sought, he's happy that he's
  dead.
O had I courage but to meet my fate,
That short dark passage to a future state,
That melancholy riddle of a breath!

 Nourmahal. That something, or that nothing, after
  death!
Take this, and teach thyself.   [*Giving a dagger.*

 Indamora. Alas!

 Nourmahal. Why dost thou shake?
Dishonour not the vengeance I designed:
A queen, and own a base plebeian mind!
Let it drink deep in thy most vital part;
Strike home, and do me reason[7] in thy heart.

 Indamora. I dare not.

 Nourmahal. Do't, while I stand by and see,
At my full gust, without the drudgery.
I love a foe, who dares my stroke prevent,
Who gives me the full scene of my content;
Shows me the flying soul's convulsive strife,
And all the anguish of departing life.
Disdain my mercy, and my rage defy;
Curse me with thy last breath, and make me see
A spirit, worthy to have rivalled me.

 Indamora. Oh, I desire to die, but dare not yet!
Give me some respite, I'll discharge the debt.

[7] *I.e.,* "pledge my health."

Without my Aureng-Zebe I would not live.

   Nourmahal. Thine, traitress! thine! that word has
     winged thy fate,
And put me past the tedious forms of hate:
I'll kill thee with such eagerness and haste,
As fiends, let loose, would lay all nature waste.

             *[*INDAMORA *runs back: As* NOURMAHAL *is*
             running to her, clashing of swords is heard
             within.

   Soldier. Yield, you're o'erpowered: Resistance is in
     vain.   *[Within.*

   Morat. Then death's my choice: Submission I disdain.
                                    [Within.

   Nourmahal. Retire, ye slaves! Ah, whither does he run
                               [At the door.
On pointed swords? Disarm, but save my son.

   Enter MORAT, *staggering, and upheld by* Soldiers.

   Morat. She lives! and I shall see her once again!
I have not thrown away my life in vain.

             [Catches hold of INDAMORA's *gown, and falls by*
             her: She sits.
I can no more; yet even in death I find
My fainting body biassed by my mind:
I fall toward you; still my contending soul
Points to your breast, and trembles to its pole.

   To them MELESINDA, *hastily casting herself on the other*
                side of MORAT.

   Melesinda. Ah woe, woe, woe! the worst of woes I
     find!
Live still; oh, live! live e'en to be unkind!—
With half-shut eyes he seeks the doubtful day;
But, ah! he bends his sight another way.
He faints! and in that sigh his soul is gone;
Yet Heaven's unmoved, yet Heaven looks careless on.

   Nourmahal. Where are those powers which monarchs
     should defend?
Or do they vain authority pretend
O'er human fates, and their weak empire show,
Which cannot guard their images below?
If, as their image, he was not divine,
They ought to have respected him as mine.

I'll waken them with my revenge; and she,
Their Indamora, shall my victim be,
And helpless Heaven shall mourn in vain, like me.

> [*As she is going to stab* INDAMORA, MORAT
> *raises himself, and holds her hand.*

Morat. Ah, what are we,
Who dare maintain with Heaven this wretched strife,
Puffed with the pride of Heaven's own gift, frail life?
That blast which my ambitious spirit swelled,
See by how weak a tenure it was held!
I only stay to save the innocent;
Oh, envy not my soul its last content!

Indamora. No, let me die; I'm doubly summoned now;
First by my Aureng-Zebe, and since by you.
My soul grows hardy, and can death endure;
Your convoy makes the dangerous way secure.

Melesinda. Let me at least a funeral marriage crave,
Nor grudge my cold embraces in the grave.
I have too just a title in the strife;
By me, unhappy me, he lost his life:
I called him hither, 'twas my fatal breath,
And I the screech-owl that proclaimed his death.

> [*Shout within.*

Abbas. What new alarms are these? I'll haste and see.

> [*Exit.*

Nourmahal. Look up and live; an empire shall be
thine.

Morat. That I contemned, even when I thought it
mine.—
Oh, I must yield to my hard destinies,   [*To* INDAMORA.
And must for ever cease to see your eyes!

Melesinda. Ah, turn your sight to me, my dearest lord!
Can you not one, one parting look afford?
Even so unkind in death?—but 'tis in vain;
I lose my breath, and to the winds complain.
Yet 'tis as much in vain your cruel scorn;
Still I can love, without this last return.
Nor fate, nor you, can my vowed faith control;
Dying, I follow your disdainful soul:
A ghost, I'll haunt your ghost; and, where you go,
With mournful murmurs fill the plains below.

Morat. Be happy, Melesinda; cease to grieve,
And for a more deserving husband live;—

Can you forgive me?

Melesinda. Can I! O my heart!
Have I heard one kind word before I part?
I can, I can forgive: Is that a task
To love like mine? Are you so good to ask?
One kiss—oh, 'tis too great a blessing this—[*Kisses him.*
I would not live to violate the bliss.

Re-enter ABBAS.

Abbas. Some envious devil has ruined us yet more:
The fort's revolted to the Emperor;
The gates are opened, the portcullis drawn,
And deluges of armies from the town
Come pouring in: I heard the mighty flaw,[8]
When first it broke; the crowding ensigns saw,
Which choked the passage; and, what least I feared,
The waving arms of Aureng-Zebe appeared,
Displayed with your Morat's:
In either's flag the golden serpents bear
Erected crests alike, like volumes rear,
And mingle friendly hissings in the air.
Their troops are joined, and our destruction nigh.

Nourmahal. 'Tis vain to fight, and I disdain to fly.
I'll mock the triumphs which our foes intend,
And, spite of fortune, make a glorious end.
In poisonous draughts my liberty I'll find,
And from the nauseous world set free my mind. [*Exit.*

At the other end of the Stage enter AURENG-ZEBE,
DIANET, and Attendants. AURENG-ZEBE turns back
and speaks entering.

Aureng-Zebe. The lives of all, who cease from combat, spare;
My brother's be your most peculiar care:
Our impious use no longer shall obtain;
Brothers no more by brothers shall be slain.—
[*Seeing* INDAMORA *and* MORAT.
Ha! do I dream? Is this my hoped success?
I grow a statue, stiff and motionless.
Look, Dianet; for I dare not trust these eyes;
They dance in mists, and dazzle with surprise.

Dianet. Sir, 'tis Morat; dying he seems, or dead;

8 "Gust," "squall."

And Indamora's hand—
    Aureng-Zebe. Supports his head.   [*Sighing.*
Thou shalt not break yet, heart, nor shall she know
My inward torments by my outward show:
To let her see my weakness were too base;
Dissembled quiet sit upon my face:
My sorrow to my eyes no passage find,
But, let it inward sink, and drown my mind;
Falsehood shall want its triumph: I begin
To stagger, but I'll prop myself within.
The specious tower no ruin shall disclose,
Till down at once the mighty fabric goes.
    Morat. In sign that I die yours, reward my love,
                        [*To* INDAMORA.
And seal my passport to the blest above.
                        [*Kissing her hand.*
    Indamora. Oh, stay; or take me with you when you go;
There's nothing now worth living for below.
    Morat. I leave you not; for my expanded mind
Grows up to heaven, while it to you is joined:
Not quitting, but enlarged! A blazing fire,
Fed from the brand.   [*Dies.*
    Melesinda. Ah me! he's gone! I die!   [*Swoons.*
    Indamora. O dismal day!
Fate, thou hast ravished my last hope away!
      [*She turns, and sees* AURENG-ZEBE *standing by
      her, and starts.*
O Heaven! my Aureng-Zebe——What strange surprise!
Or does my willing mind delude my eyes,
And shows the figure always present there?
Or liv'st thou? Am I blest, and see thee here?
    Aureng-Zebe. My brother's body see conveyed with
    care,   [*Turning from her, to her* Attendants.
Where we may royal sepulture prepare.
With speed to Melesinda bring relief:
Recall her spirits, and moderate her grief——
               [*Half turning to* INDAMORA.
I go, to take for ever from your view,
Both the loved object, and the hated too.
      [*Going away after the bodies, which are
      carried off.*
    Indamora. Hear me! yet think not that I beg your
    stay;   [*Laying hold of him*

I will be heard, and, after, take your way
Go; but your late repentance shall be vain:
                    [*He struggles still; she lets him go.*
I'll never, never see your face again.   [*Turning away.*
  Aureng-Zebe. Madam, I know whatever you can say:
You might be pleased not to command my stay.
All things are yet disordered in the fort;
I must crave leave your audience may be short.
  Indamora. You need not fear I shall detain you long:
Yet you may tell me your pretended wrong.
  Aureng-Zebe. Is that the business? then my stay is
    vain.
  Indamora. How are you injured?
  Aureng-Zebe. When did I complain?
  Indamora. Leave off your forced respect,
And show your rage in its most furious form:
I'm armed with innocence to brave the storm.
You heard, perhaps, your brother's last desire,
And, after, saw him in my arms expire;
Saw me, with tears, so great a loss bemoan;
Heard me complaining my last hopes were gone.
  Aureng-Zebe. "Oh, stay, or take me with you when you
    go,
There's nothing now worth living for below."
Unhappy sex! whose beauty is your snare:
Exposed to trials; made too frail to bear.
I grow a fool, and show my rage again:
'Tis nature's fault; and why should I complain?
  Indamora. Will you yet hear me?
  Aureng-Zebe. Yes, till you relate
What powerful motives did your change create.
You thought me dead, and prudently did weigh;
Tears were but vain, and brought but youth's decay.
Then, in Morat, your hopes a crown designed;
And all the woman worked within your mind.—
I rave again, and to my rage return,
To be again subjected to your scorn.
  Indamora. I wait till this long storm be over-blown.
  Aureng-Zebe. I'm conscious of my folly: I have done.—
I cannot rail; but silently I'll grieve,
How did I trust! and how did you deceive!
O Arimant, would I had died for thee!
I dearly buy thy generosity.

Indamora. Alas! is he then dead?

Aureng-Zebe. Unknown to me,
He took my arms; and, while I forced my way
Through troops of foes, which did our passage stay,
My buckler o'er my aged father cast,
Still fighting, still defending as I past,
The noble Arimant usurped my name;
Fought, and took from me, while he gave me, fame.
"To Aureng-Zebe," he made his soldiers cry,
And, seeing not, where he heard danger nigh,
Shot, like a star, through the benighted sky,
A short, but mighty aid: At length he fell.
My own adventures 'twere lost time to tell;
Or how my army, entering in the night,
Surprised our foes; the dark disordered fight,
How my appearance, and my father shown,
Made peace; and all the rightful monarch own.
I've summed it briefly, since it did relate
The unwelcome safety of the man you hate.

Indamora. As briefly will I clear my innocence:
Your altered brother died in my defence.
Those tears you saw, that tenderness I showed,
Were just effects of grief and gratitude.
He died my convert.

Aureng-Zebe. But your lover too;
I heard his words, and did your actions view;
You seemed to mourn another lover dead:
My sighs you gave him, and my tears you shed.
But, worst of all,
Your gratitude for his defence was shown:
It proved you valued life, when I was gone.

Indamora. Not that I valued life, but feared to die:
Think that my weakness, not inconstancy.

Aureng-Zebe. Fear showed you doubted of your own
    intent:
And she, who doubts, becomes less innocent.
Tell me not you could fear;
Fear's a large promiser; who subject live
To that base passion, know not what they give.
No circumstance of grief you did deny:
And what could she give more, who durst not die?

Indamora. My love, my faith.

Aureng-Zebe. Both so adulterate grown,

When mixed with fear, they never could be known.
I wish no ill might her I love befall;
But she ne'er loved, who durst not venture all.
Her life and fame should my concernment be;
But she should only be afraid of me.
   Indamora. My heart was yours; but, oh! you left it
     here,
Abandoned to those tyrants, hope and fear;
If they forced from me one kind look, or word,
Could you not that, not that small part afford?
   Aureng-Zebe. If you had loved, you nothing yours could
     call;
Giving the least of mine, you gave him all.
True love's a miser: so tenacious grown,
He weighs to the least grain of what's his own;
More delicate than honour's nicest sense,
Neither to give nor take the least offence,
With, or without you, I can have no rest:
What shall I do? y' are lodged within my breast:
Your image never will be thence displaced;
But there it lies, stabbed, mangled, and defaced.
   Indamora. Yet to restore the quiet of your heart,
There's one way left.
   Aureng-Zebe Oh, name it.
   Indamora. 'Tis to part.
Since perfect bliss with me you cannot prove,
I scorn to bless by halves the man I love.
   Aureng-Zebe. Now you distract me more: Shall then
     the day,
Which views my triumph, see our loves decay?
Must I new bars to my own joy create?
Refuse myself what I had forced from fate?
What though I am not loved?
Reason's nice taste does our delights destroy;
Brutes are more blest, who grossly feed on joy.
   Indamora. Such endless jealousies your love pursue,
I can no more be fully blest than you.
I therefore go, to free us both from pain:
I prized your person, but your crown disdain.
Nay, even my own——
I give it you; for since I cannot call
Your heart my subject, I'll not reign at all.   [*Exit*

Aureng-Zebe. Go; Though thou leav'st me tortured on
    the rack,
'Twixt shame and pride, I cannot call thee back.——
She's guiltless, and I should submit; but oh!
When she exacts it, can I stoop so low?
Yes, for she's guiltless; but she's haughty too.
Great souls long struggle ere they own a crime;
She's gone; and leaves me no repenting-time.
I'll call her now; sure, if she loves she'll stay;
Linger, at least, or not go far away.
                    [*Looks to the door, and returns.*
For ever lost! and I repent too late.
My foolish pride would set my whole estate,
Till, at one throw, I lost all back to fate.

    To him the Emperor, *drawing in* INDAMORA:
                Attendants.

Emperor. It must not be, that he, by whom we live,
Should no advantage of his gift receive.
Should he be wholly wretched?—he alone,
In this blest day, a day so much his own?
                        [*To* INDAMORA.
I have not quitted yet a victor's right;
I'll make you happy in your own despite.
I love you still; and if I struggle hard
To give, it shows the worth of the reward.
    Indamora. Suppose he has o'ercome; must I find place
Among his conquered foes, and sue for grace?
Be pardoned, and confess I loved not well?
What though none live my innocence to tell,
I know it: Truth may own a generous pride:
I clear myself, and care for none beside.
    Aureng-Zebe. O Indamora, you would break my heart!
Could you resolve, on any terms, to part?
I thought your love eternal: Was it tied
So loosely, that a quarrel could divide?
I grant that my suspicions were unjust;
But would you leave me, for a small distrust?
Forgive those foolish words——   [*Kneeling to her.*
They were the froth my raging folly moved,
When it boiled up: I knew not then I loved,
Yet then loved most.

Indamora [*to* AURENG-ZEBE]. You would but half be
    blest!   [*Giving her hand, smiling.*
Aureng-Zebe. Oh, do but try
My eager love: I'll give myself the lie.
The very hope is a full happiness,
Yet scantly measures what I shall possess.
Fancy itself, even in enjoyment, is
But a dumb judge, and cannot tell its bliss.
    Emperor. Her eyes a secret yielding do confess,
And promise to partake your happiness.
May all the joys I did myself pursue,
Be raised by her, and multiplied on you!

A procession of Priests, Slaves *following, and last*
    MELESINDA *in white.*

Indamora. Alas! what means this pomp?
Aureng-Zebe. 'Tis the procession of a funeral vow,
Which cruel laws to Indian wives allow,
When fatally their virtue they approve;
Cheerful in flames, and martyrs of their love.
    Indamora. O my foreboding heart! the event I fear:
And see! sad Melesinda does appear.
    Melesinda. You wrong my love; what grief do I betray?
This is the triumph of my nuptial day,
My better nuptials; which, in spite of fate,
For ever joined me to my dear Morat.
Now I am pleased; my jealousies are o'er:
He's mine: and I can lose him now no more.
    Emperor. Let no false show of fame your reason blind.
    Indamora. You have no right to die; he was not kind.
    Melesinda. Had he been kind, I could no love have
    shown:
Each vulgar virtue would as much have done.
My love was such, it needed no return;
But could, though he supplied no fuel, burn.
Rich in itself, like elemental fire,
Whose pureness does no aliment require.
In vain you would bereave me of my lord;
For I will die:—Die is too base a word,
I'll seek his breast, and, kindling by his side,
Adorned with flames, I'll mount a glorious bride. [*Exit.*

Enter NOURMAHAL, *distracted, with* ZAYDA.

Zayda. She's lost, she's lost! but why do I complain
For her, who generously did life disdain?
Poisoned, she raves——
The envenomed body does the soul attack;
The envenomed soul works its own poison back.

Nourmahal. I burn, I more than burn; I am all fire.
See how my mouth and nostrils flame expire!
I'll not come near myself——
Now I'm a burning lake, it rolls and flows;
I'll rush, and pour it all upon my foes.
Pull, pull, that reverend piece of timber near:
Throw't on—'tis dry—'twill burn—
Ha, ha! how my old husband crackles there!
Keep him down, keep him down; turn him about:
I know him,—he'll but whiz, and straight go out.
Fan me, you winds: What, not one breath of air?
I'll burn them all, and yet have flames to spare.
Quench me: Pour on whole rivers. 'Tis in vain:
Morat stands there to drive them back again:
With those huge bellows in his hands, he blows
New fire into my head: My brain-pan glows.
See! see! there's Aureng-Zebe too takes his part;
But he blows all his fire into my heart.

Aureng-Zebe. Alas! what fury's this?

Nourmahal. That's he, that's he!
                    [*Staring upon him, and catching at him.*
I know the dear man's voice:
And this my rival, this the cursed she.
They kiss; into each other's arms they run:
Close, close, close! must I see, and must have none?
Thou art not hers: Give me that eager kiss.
Ungrateful! have I lost Morat for this?
Will you?—before my face?—poor helpless I
See all, and have my hell before I die!   [*Sinks down.*

Emperor. With thy last breath thou hast thy crimes
      confest;
Farewell; and take, what thou ne'er gav'st me, rest.
But you, my son, receive it better here:
                    [*Giving him* INDAMORA'S *hand.*
The just rewards of love and honour wear.

Receive the mistress you so long have served;
Receive the crown your loyalty preserved.
Take you the reins, while I from cares remove,
And sleep within the chariot which I drove.   [*Exeunt.*

EPILOGUE

A PRETTY task! and so I told the fool,
Who needs would undertake to please by rule.
He thought, that if his characters were good,
The scenes entire, and free from noise and blood;
The action great, yet circumscribed by time,
The words not forced, but sliding into rhyme,
The passions raised, and calm by just degrees,
As tides are swelled, and then retire to seas;
He thought, in hitting these, his business done,
Though he, perhaps, has failed in every one.
But, after all, a poet must confess,
His art's like physic, but a happy guess.
Your pleasure on your fancy must depend;
The lady's pleased, just as she likes her friend.
No song! no dance! no show! he fears you'll say:
You loved all naked beauties but a play.
He much mistakes your methods to delight;
And, like the French, abhors our target-fight:
But those damned dogs can ne'er be in the right.
True English hate your Monsieur's paltry arts,
For you are all silk-weavers in your hearts.
Bold Britons, at a brave Bear-Garden fray,
Are roused: and, clattering sticks, cry,—Play, play, play!
Meantime, your filthy foreigner will stare,
And mutters to himself,—*Ha! gent barbare!*
And, gad, 'tis well he mutters; well for him;
Our butchers else would tear him limb from limb.
'Tis true, the time may come, your sons may be
Infected with this French civility:
But this, in after ages will be done:
Our poet writes a hundred years too soon.
This age comes on too slow, or he too fast:
And early springs are subject to a blast!
Who would excel, when few can make a test
Betwixt indifferent writing and the best?
For favours, cheap and common, who would strive
Which, like abandoned prostitutes, you give?
Yet, scattered here and there, I some behold,
Who can discern the tinsel from the gold:
To these he writes; and, if by them allowed,
'Tis their prerogative to rule the crowd,
For he more fears, like a presuming man,
Their votes who cannot judge, than theirs who can.

355

DRAMABOOKS

Hill and Wang aims to establish DRAMABOOKS as a permanent library of the great classics of the theatre of all countries, in an attractive, low-priced format.

Published

Published

CRITICISM

D1 *Shakespeare and the Elizabethans* by Henri Fluchère. Foreword by
  T. S. Eliot

D2 *On Dramatic Method* by Harley Granville-Barker

D3 *George Bernard Shaw* by G. K. Chesterton

D4 *The Paradox of Acting* by Denis Diderot and *Masks or Faces?* by
  William Archer. Introduction by Lee Strasberg

D5 *The Scenic Art* by Henry James. Edited with an Introduction and
  Notes by Allan Wade

D6 *Preface to Hamlet* by Harley Granville-Barker

D7 *Hazlitt on Theatre* edited by William Archer and Robert Lowe.
  Introduction by William Archer

D8 *The Fervent Years* by Harold Clurman

D9 *The Quintessence of Ibsenism* by Bernard Shaw

D10 *Papers on Playmaking* edited by Brander Matthews

Ready in January 1958

D11 *Papers on Acting* edited by Brander Matthews

D12 *The Theatre* by Stark Young